Changing Countryside

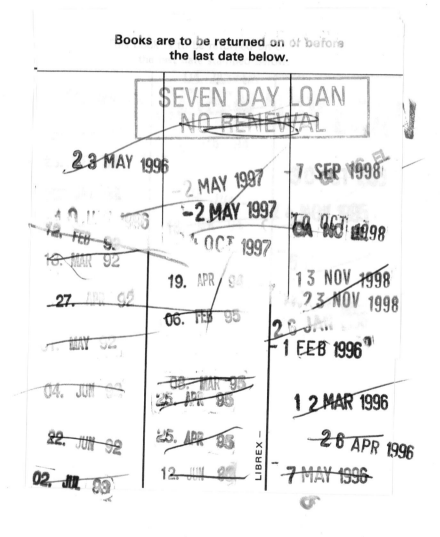

Books are to be returned on or before the last date below.

SEVEN DAY LOAN
NO RENEWAL

23 MAY 1996

-2 MAY 1997   - 7 SEP 1998

-2 MAY 1997

OCT 1997

19. APR 9   13 NOV 1998

06. FEB 95   23 NOV 1998

-1 FEB 1996

1 2 MAR 1996

25. APR 95   26 APR 1996

LIBREX —

7 MAY 1996

Selection and editorial material copyright
© 1985 The Open University
Copublished by Croom Helm Ltd, Provident House, Burrell Row,
Beckenham, Kent BR3 1AT
Croom Helm Australia Pty Ltd, First Floor, 139 King Street,
Sydney, NSW 2001, Australia
Croom Helm, 51 Washington Street, Dover, New Hampshire 03820, USA
and The Open University, Walton Hall, Milton Keynes, MK7 6AA

British Library Cataloguing in Publication Data
The Changing countryside.
   1. Country Life—Great Britain
   2. Natural history—Great Britain
   I. Blunden, John II. Curry, Nigel
   941'.009'734   S522.G7

ISBN 0-7099-3297-9

Typeset by Leaper & Gard, Bristol
Printed and bound in Great Britain

The Changing Countryside

The Open University in association with the Countryside Commission

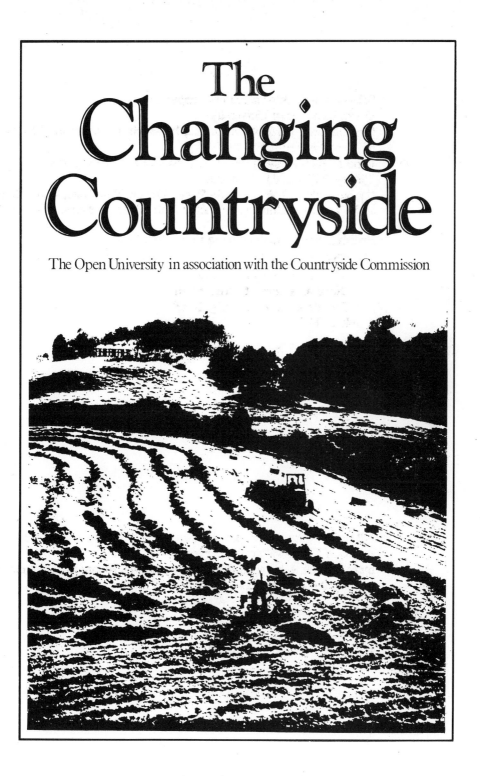

CROOM HELM

London · Sydney · Dover, New Hampshire

This book has been edited at the
Open University by John Blunden and
Nigel Curry on behalf of
The Changing Countryside Course Team:

John Blunden (Chairman)
Nigel Curry
Rees Pryce
Graham Turner (BBC)
Andrew Wood (Course Coordinator)

Contents

List of Colour Plates

1. Wildlife Habitats and Intensive Farming
2. The Cover of a Metroland Brochure
3. The Hertfordshire Structure Plan, 1968
4. Medieval Manuscript
5. Rydal Water, Lake District
6. Ploughed Moorland on Exmoor
7. The Summit of Snowdon, Gwynedd
8. New Quay, Dyfed
9. Work in Progress on a Bridge near Barrow House, Derwentwater
10. A Limestone Quarry in the Mendip Hills AONB
11. Coalbrookdale Iron Works on the Banks of the Severn
12. Development Commission Factory Development
13. Craft Homes in Northumberland
14. The Agricultural Land Classification

List of Figures

Acknowledgements

The inspiration for this book, its companion volume and the Open University course of which they are part, goes back to a series of discussions held in the late 1970s with the Countryside Commission, and it is with that organisation that we gladly begin our list of acknowledgements. We are grateful not only for the sustained and amiable dialogue that has been continued over a period of some five years with that body, but also its invaluable contribution to the financing of the overall project and upon which its ultimate fruition has so largely depended.

Whilst we were initially trying out ideas and attempting to give the subject matter an appropriate shape, we were considerably assisted in our efforts by the advice of a wide range of organisations and groups in England and Wales with an interest in rural affairs. Though most were ultimately consulted, we remain especially grateful to those who so kindly attended our consultative conference held at Walton Hall to initiate the project back in November 1981. Although the list of organisations who commented on our proposals is too long to mention in full here, it ranged from those representing important groups of users of the countryside, such as the NFU, the CLA and the Ramblers Association and ran right through to conservation groups such as the CPRE and state agencies such as the Nature Conservancy Council. The Council for Environmental Education, however, remains one group that deserves particular mention for its subsequent assistance with material prepared for registered students of 'The Changing Countryside' course.

In terms of individuals, we must single out first of all the contribution of Mary Powell who, as a former member of the Course Team, helped in the early days to grapple with the difficulties of handling the complex of interactive factors that make the countryside what it is. Hers was to be an invaluable contribution to the structure of both books and the course as a whole. Later, as the texts in question came to be written, our external assessor, Emeritus Professor Gerald Wibberley, formerly holder of the Ernest Cook chair in countryside planning held jointly at Wye College and University College in the University of London, proved a resourceful, scrupulous and tireless commentator on all that we did and has finally given his approval to *The Changing Countryside* in its book form and as an Open University course. We are also grateful to our other assessor Professor Colin Spedding of the Centre for Agricultural Strategy at the University of Reading for his comments on our efforts.

We express our thanks for the secretarial assistance given to us by Linda Charnley at the Open University and the cheerful way in which she 'word processed' our not insubstantial manuscript in a very short space of time. Our thanks also go to the thirteen people representing a variety of rural interest groups and organisations for test reading early drafts of the course materials and to Mary Geffen of the Institute of Educational Technology at the Open University. She helped us not only organise the testing programme but was instrumental in ensuring that our texts were ultimately tailored to the needs of our readers. Finally, we wish to acknowledge the patient assistance given by a number of people in our pursuit of appropriate illustrations and, in particular, the work done by Dr Jonathon Brown at the Institute of Agricultural History and Museum of English Rural Life, University of Reading. Nevertheless, deeply as we appreciate all the efforts made on our behalf by others, we must end by fully acknowledging the fact that it is the Open University Course Team that alone bears the responsibility for all that follows.

A Continuing Education Course from the Open University

Components of the Course

This book *The Changing Countryside* has been published for the Open University as the main element of a short course being offered under the auspices of its Continuing Education division and as part of its Personal and Cultural Education programme. The book is complete in itself however, and for readers who will be concerned about the ways in which rural England and Wales are changing, the reasons for change and the ultimate directions in which this may lead, its editors believe that it provides a relevant, informative and stimulating experience. For those who want to know more about the background legislation and significant documents pertaining to the country-side as well as something of the organisations and other bodies which have an interest in it, there is also the companion text *The Countryside Handbook* again published by Croom Helm for the Open University. This supplementary volume is in fact an invaluable compendium of background information about the countryside for anyone with an interest in such matters and, therefore, it also stands in its own right as a contribution to a better understanding of rural affairs.

As an accompaniment to these books, BBC2 is showing a series of nine television programmes with the same title as the main text. The first pro-gramme will be shown in March 1985, the rest following in subsequent weeks. The series will be repeated in the autumn, then twice a year for the next two years with one presentation in spring 1988. Viewers will find the series offers an extremely stimulating additional dimension to the textual experience for it emphasises the visual impact on the specific rural areas of the many social and economic forces both past and present that are examined in this book.

For those who would like, for professional or indeed personal reasons, an 'in depth' treatment of the subject matter contained in the books and the tele-vision programmes the Open University offers enrolment on 'The Changing Countryside' course itself (PD 770). This will provide opportunities for students to discuss issues raised in the main text at a day school and with their own individual tutor and undertake an assessed project in the form of a short dissertation under his or her guidance.

What Registration for the Course Offers

In addition to the two texts and the television programmes the course includes:

— a Study Guide to explain how all the parts of the course are related, including a study period timetable to help you work through the various elements
— allocation to a personal tutor who will give you detailed guidance and help in the preparation of a short project
— the opportunity to discuss issues raised in the main text at a whole-day seminar
— suggestions on how to use the course material to prepare and carry out the project work

— assessment and grading of the completed dissertation

To enrol for it you will be required only to pay a registration fee covering tuition and course materials which are additional to the main text and companion volume which you may have already purchased. However, if you are reading this from a book you have borrowed or only have one of the two texts, either can be obtained from the Open University.

For further information concerning the course, and television ·broadcasts together with an application form write to:

Associate Student Central Office
The Open University
PO Box 76
MILTON KEYNES   MK7 6AA

For copies of the main text and/or its companion volume, write to:

Learning Materials Services Office
Centre for Continuing Education
The Open University
PO Box 188
Walton Hall
MILTON KEYNES MK7 6DH

1
Introducing the Changing Countryside

Change and The Countryside

As the title suggests, this book is about change in the countryside. Because it now appears to be happening more quickly, more dramatically and with greater consequences for the people of England and Wales than ever before it is important to understand the nature of this change and the reasons for it.

Anyone who has lived for the last 20 years or so in an intimate relationship with a particular part of the countryside of England or Wales will be aware of changes that have occurred possibly in economic and social spheres, but certainly in the visual appearance of the landscape. In some areas, perhaps in the remote uplands, landscape changes will have been subtle and less widespread — a marshy piece of rough pasture drained, fenced, ploughed and re-seeded; a brook culverted; a stone wall removed; a road created where once lay only a rough stone track. But in the lowland countryside of much of South and Central England many may have witnessed more dramatic and widespread changes. Richard Mabey, the naturalist, has written of a tract of land that he has known from a childhood of a quarter of a century ago. It was, he says:

> A compact medieval relic, a square mile of ancient woods, hedges and pastures flanking the sides of a shallow river valley. The stream was a winterbourne, a 'woe water' supposed to flow in full spate only in times of war or trouble.

This Chiltern valley could have altered in his late teens as a result of the building of a motorway through it, but as it happens, this did not materialise. However, the landscape has none the less altered since then in a way which he describes as almost as drastic as if it had been covered by tarmac. Writing in the early 1980s, he says that:

> Not far short of half the hedges have been grubbed out. A thirty acre primrose copse was cleared for wheat. The 'woe water', ironically, vanished underground and the hollow oaks and ashes that lined it (which once had three species of owl nesting in them) were felled one by one. One spring I found the sheep pastures where I used to pick mushrooms covered with unfamiliar white granules and within a few years not only had the mushrooms vanished but the cowslips as well.

The 1980s landscape is indeed a sharp contrast to the rural scene that that valley had presented only 25 years earlier, at a time when George Orwell was able to write of a countryside in which were to be found: 'deep meadows smothered in flowers where the great shining horses browse and meditate, the slow-moving streams bordered by willows, the green bosoms of the elms, all sleeping the deep, deep sleep of England'.

This is a description, albeit a poetic one, of a landscape that suggests a

Figure 1.1: Agricultural Landscapes. (a) The traditional, medieval pattern, with a rich mix of small fields, old hedges, lanes and copses. (b) The modern, with wild and uncultivated habitats now confined to narrow marginal strips, chiefly in wet valleys and on steep slopes.

Source: Open University.

(a)

(b)

quality of changelessness as if over the centuries it had stood apart from the social and economic factors that had shaped the urban world. The reality is rather different, however — a difference reflected in Figure 1.1. If a period of rapid rural transformation can be identified, particularly since the 1970s, which has occurred largely as a result of changes in agricultural practice, so it is equally possible to identify a process of evolution that began long ago. It started with the clearings made in the great forests that clothed much of England and Wales by the first farmers. These peoples of a culture we now know as Neolithic needed to do this to grow crops and graze livestock. Indeed, the 6,000 years that have elapsed since then have been described as a 'centuries-long conversation between man and nature' in which the landscape has been continually evolving.

But just as in recent years the dialogue has become more earnest resulting in a period of rapid change, so in the past it is possible to identify similar situations from time to time. Perhaps of most significance were the changes wrought by the Agricultural Revolution of the late eighteenth and early nineteenth centuries. At this time new methods of stock rearing in particular necessitated the abandonment of the open pastures where the grazing of cattle had been communally undertaken, to a closed landscape of fields contained by newly planted hedges and freshly built stone walls. This transition is indicated in Figure 1.2. The landscape also contained a new pattern of roads. The impact of such change was witnessed by the great rural poet, John Clare, who lived through the statutory enclosure of his native Northamptonshire village of Helpston. There he saw and wrote about the fencing and ploughing of the common fens and pastures of Emmonsales Heath and the breakup of a pattern of life that had evolved after the establishment of the manorial system 800 years before. For him it was an experience every bit as traumatic as that which has caused Mabey and other writers of today to set down their feelings about rural change. Out of it came his powerful poem *Remembrances*. In one typical stanza he identifies the culprit of these changes for the worse — 'the axe of spoiler and self-interest':

And crossberry way and old round oaks narrow lane
With its hollow trees like pulpits I shall never see again.
Inclosure like a Buonaparte let not a thing remain,
It levelled every bush and tree and levelled every hill
And hung the moles for traitors —
    though the brook is running still
It runs a naked stream and chill.

Figure 1.2: The 'Ridge and Furrow' of Medieval Farming. This remains visible near Southam in Warwickshire in spite of subsequent enclosure.

Source: Aerofilms.

Later, even after this revolutionary change in the countryside had long been accomplished, Flora Thompson, in remembering her childhood in the 1880s in *Lark Rise to Candleford*, was able to contrast what seemed the time-less quality of the countryside as it appeared to her with the reality of the enclosure movement.

The hamlet stood on a gentle rise in the flat, wheat growing north east corner of Oxfordshire ... All around from every quarter the stiff clayey soil of the arable fields crept up; bare, brown and windswept for eight months out of the twelve. Spring brought a flush of green wheat and there were violets under the hedges and pussy-willows out beside the brook at the bottom of the 'Hundred Acres', but only for a few weeks in later summer had the landscape real beauty. Then the ripened cornfields rippled up to the doorsteps of the cottages and the hamlet became an island in a sea of dark gold.
To a child it seemed that it must always have been so, but the ploughing and sowing and reaping were recent innovations. Old men could remember when the Rise, covered with juniper bushes, stood in the midst of a furzy heath in common land and which had come under the plough after the passing of the Enclosure Acts. Some of the ancients still occupied cottages on land which had been ceded to their fathers as 'squatters rights' and probably all the small plots upon which the houses stood had originally been so ceded.

But if change in the appearance of the rural landscape has largely reflected changing agricultural practice, at times quite dramatically, the social, eco-nomic and cultural life of the people of rural England and Wales has also altered over time. Indeed, intensive farming systems (a phenomenon to which Mabey refers) with ever greater demands on capital equipment have made their mark on the social fabric of the village in many parts of England and Wales. It is a situation well documented in the wealth of information collected by the Women's Institutes of England and Wales when in the mid-1960s they set about the preparation of their 'Domesday' portrait of country life. In Combe Martin, Somerset, the make-up of the Parish Council was indicative of the declining significance of the agricultural worker in village life.

The Parish Council has seven members. The Chairman is a native of the village, a parish councillor for twenty years, the past eight as Chairman. It has a fair cross section of the community; local residents of long standing, a nominee of the WI, a newcomer, others earning a living locally or working from the village. At present the farming community is not represented, although it was until the sixties. In contrast the Council now has three out of its seven members engaged in the building industry. This may be no more than a coincidence. On the other hand, considered in relation to statistics which may be produced by other villages, it may be indicative of the shift of emphasis in community life in villages within easy commuting distance of larger centres of population and, therefore, subjected to great pressure for building development.

This comment also emphasises another aspect of changing village life recorded again and again in the Women's Institute reports: the increasing impact of the commuter and his family. As well as physical manifestations of this impact, for example Figure 1.3, there are also social and cultural connota-tions. St Bees, Cumbria, is typical in this respect:

The new estate and subsequent housing development is looked upon with alarm by many St Bees people who fear that the place may lose its village

character and become merely a dormitory suburb. On the other hand, the people who are coming into the village are often young, intelligent people who have had their fill of urban life and suburbia and are prepared to forgo some of the advantages of town life — mainly cultural activities — so that their children may grow up in a healthy atmosphere.

However, the essential mobility of the commuter with ready access to private transport contrasts with the transport problems of others in the village. This situation has been experienced with increasing severity over the past two decades. In the mid-1960s comment on this matter appears in numerous reports, especially those from the North, Wales and Eastern England. North Kelsey, Lincolnshire, is representative of many:

> Transport for the elderly, those on small incomes and the young is deplorable. The railway has been closed to passenger traffic between Barnett and Market Rasen. As from 1st November the nearest stations are each approximately six miles. The bus services are too few and wrongly timed. The Parish Council, Caistor Rural District Council and the local MP have all protested but without any useful result.

From these observations about change in the countryside, it is not surprising that this book should address as its main concern not only the theme of change in the countryside, but how and why this change has taken place over time. Thus, for example, while current changes in the landscape may be explained in terms of agricultural practices as Mabey implied, the countryside as a whole is certainly not simply a product of such practices. To these must be added the outcome of a complex web of social, economic and cultural factors that have impinged upon it over 6,000 years. Similarly the future will be determined by some new set of influences again acting upon this collage of all that has gone before. What these changes may be can be the subject only of enlightened and informed conjecture. As later chapters emphasise, however,

Figure 1.3: The Village of Brill, Buckinghamshire. This shows (central picture) the fifteenth-century buildings lying at its heart. Immediately beyond to the west is the modern post-war housing estate, typical of many similar developments in villages in lowland England lying close to major towns.

Source: Aerofilms.

as well as social, economic and cultural influences over the countryside, a comprehensive framework of policies has evolved in response to a sophisticated and complex society. This has demanded controls on the free enterprise forces of the market-place at work within the countryside. Society has required the opportunity to steer and to manage change. Thus as well as economic and social policy measures promoting change, measures of constraint or control have been exercised. And where these have been used within a physical planning framework they have also had a significant effect on the landscape and on social structures. What these policy frameworks are, their adequacy and the nature of the ultimate ends they may or may not serve, also must be a matter of great significance to all who are concerned about the countryside. Their discussion, therefore, also must be a major objective of this book. Indeed its reading should allow the reader to indulge in informed argument about the directions future change in the countryside ought to take, and the ways in which such change ought to be encouraged, particularly through policy changes and the creative use of policy instruments.

Before this stage is reached the relative importance of a multiplicity of activities beyond agriculture must be clarified. This multiplicity includes, for example, the extraction of minerals, the production of timber, the gathering of water, the generation of power and its transmission, communications, recreation and leisure activities. All of these express themselves with increasing impact directly upon the landscape and indeed to the extent that they generate rural employment, on rural settlements. The location and size of settlements, too, reflect not only the dynamic nature of such forms of rural enterprise but also the relationship between villages and country towns on the one hand and the urban population on the other. An example of this may be seen in the increasing popularity of commuter, retirement and second homes. This multiplicity of rural land uses, and indeed rural dwellers, leads increasingly to diverse demands on the limited resources of which the countryside is constituted, particularly on the land itself. Indeed in one small area many of these

Figure 1.4: Fernworthy Reservoir, Chagford, Dartmoor National Park. An example of the way in which a limited area is now used for several different purposes. The artificial lake designed for water storage has now been opened up for sailing and fishing. The shore line nearest the camera has been developed as a picnic site by the South West Water Authority in association with the Forestry Commission who have also provided public access to the conifer plantation (bottom centre), via nature trails and forest walks.

Source: South West Water Authority.

18

different land uses may be present as may be seen in Figure 1.4.

In some cases a stretch of country may be called upon to perform more than one function. For example, a Forestry Commission plantation may have a recreational role, may also provide a moderating influence over water catchment, may assist the farmer in acting as a shelter belt for livestock, may create rural employment and may provide a unique environment for many species of flora and fauna, as well as acting as a source of timber. Thus, this book sets out to show not simply these competing functions within the countryside but rather establishes it as a complex interacting system where the furtherance of an activity has widespread repercussions elsewhere.

The mix of functions or the dominance of one over another in any particular tract of countryside commonly does not meet with a consensus of opinion concerning their compatibility (see Figure 1.5) in either visual, economic, social or political terms. Different groups with different interests, perceptions and aspirations may disagree markedly about the desirability of a particular mix of uses. Thus, at its simplest, the agribusinessman — farming to maximise the return on his investment — may view a rolling East Anglian prairie with regular, wire-fenced fields, each 100 acres or more, to be the very acme of perfection yielding the largest profit from an investment in machinery, labour, fertiliser and pesticides. To the naturalist this landscape, which has experienced the removal of hedges, banks, trees, ditches and ponds with all that this means for the destruction of wild life habitats, may be viewed with complete distaste. At an increasing level of sophistication and complexity the naturalist may be happy to eat the products of the agribusinessman whilst the latter, when on holiday, may best enjoy just those stretches of countryside least modified at the hand of man.

As this book attempts to illuminate the relationship between such interest groups and reflect the nature of the debate that frequently occurs between them, as well as critically evaluating the arguments they put forward, two things will become very evident. First, it is impossible to achieve successfully a management framework or any form of long-term plan for the countryside that universally satisfies — and second — the realisation that derives from any such attempts — there are no right answers but many alternative scenarios. In

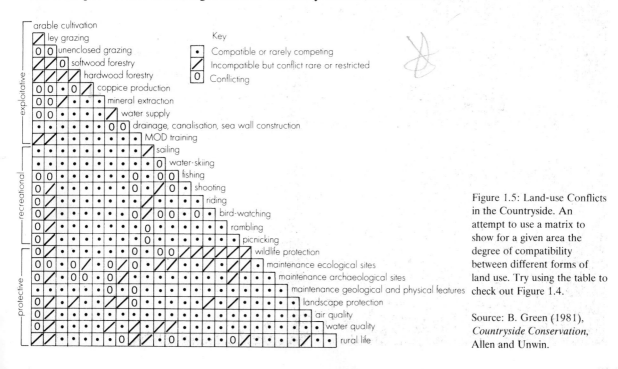

Figure 1.5: Land-use Conflicts in the Countryside. An attempt to use a matrix to show for a given area the degree of compatibility between different forms of land use. Try using the table to check out Figure 1.4.

Source: B. Green (1981), *Countryside Conservation*, Allen and Unwin.

the end this book is not, therefore, prescriptive in its prime purpose. Its ultimate objective is one of attempting to illuminate the complex interaction between the attitudes, perceptions and motivations of those who use, live in and have a role in shaping the future of the countryside.

Structuring 'The Changing Countryside'

In pursuing the objectives of this book attention was first given to what to avoid by way of structuring its material. Texts, for example, which attempt objective analysis and are often underpinned by a strong socio-political framework are of value as supporting material for the study of geography and planning. They are, however, best developed at length and used within the context of university courses — likewise the many other volumes that review agriculture, forestry, recreation and so on in turn, inside a resource-based approach. At the same time it was also necessary to avoid that whole range of books that are polemical in tone and lead the reader towards a particular point of view relating to the countryside.

CONTROVERSIAL

What *was* required was a means of making the reader aware that the changing countryside needs to be understood from the standpoint of differing interests and the way these interact with each other. This seemed to be an important foundation on which to rest any book that would ultimately encourage its readers to engage in a meaningful debate about rural change.

Thus the solution adopted here is to take slices through the complex interactive mix of social, economic and environmental factors that determine what the countryside is, giving each of these slices an 'issue'-based flavour. In choosing the 'issues' each of which provides a title for the following four chapters of this book, the intention is to offer adequate coverage of four major rural interests. Each 'issue' is expressed positively and demonstrates what society expects from its countryside from a specific standpoint. Moreover, the 'issue' chapters are designed to stimulate thought about the future, rather than simply be a contemplation of the past.

Although each 'issue' is given equal standing, the 'issues' themselves are not locked into the same standpoint or set of beliefs about rural change. Thus, 'Expanding Agricultural Productivity' is considered primarily from the standpoint of farming and food production, whereas 'Containing Settlements' is considered from a land use planning stance. 'Conserving the Wild' is viewed from the aspect of landscape and wildlife conservation while 'Sustaining Rural Communities' is considered from that of social and community welfare.

The declared standpoints used in each 'issue', however, do not totally preclude debate. Even though, for example, the agricultural 'issue' is based largely on the notion of the expansion of production, it must be and is challenged by legitimate questions about food surpluses, their impact on world trade and the resulting implications for Third World countries. The resource costs of high input systems involving the use of energy and fertilisers and the impact of agricultural policy on the environment are also given due consideration.

Similarly the containing settlements 'issue' must deal with doubts voiced about the value of continuing to resist urban expansion both to and in the countryside. Whilst it may be necessary to resist the proliferation of buildings across the countryside, rural people still need jobs. With regard to the wild, it may be asked on conservation grounds whether habitats and species at the margins of their range in England and Wales should be maintained when they are plentiful in other places. And finally, from a national social welfare point of view, why invest in rural communities when inner-city deprivation in such places as Liverpool or London may be so much worse?

These 'issue' chapters find common ground, however, in the chief all-pervading characteristic of this volume — that of considering each of them over time. Thus chapters two to five all look at the history of the 'issue' in question in a series of 'perspective' sections. The present is considered in each chapter in the respective 'early 1980s' sections and the likely shorter term future in the 'actions to steer change' sections. It is indeed the adoption of this chronology that provides the vital thrust for this study of the changing countryside.

Each of the 'issues' chapters also have other common characteristics. They are introduced by a number of short quotations or 'snapshots' to set the flavour of the chapter. At the end of the 'early 1980s' sections too, each chapter contains a 'grassroots' section where practitioners in their respective fields summarise their personal points of view on current issues. Finally the common format of these chapters lies in the 'who benefits, who loses?' conclusions to each chapter where the varying fortunes of people affected by change are summarised.

Beyond these four 'issues' chapters, the volume turns, in Chapter 6, to a consideration of more personal futures for the countryside. Here a number of writings of a disparate group of authors is presented to provide the reader with a diversity of notions about longer term change in the countryside. The final chapter draws together all of the ideas of change in the countryside and considers the policy process and politics as the frameworks within which change inevitably will take place.

By way of a conclusion, it remains only to say that what the editors believe is the best way to handle the complexities of the subject matter of this book is one for which they bear full responsibility. Although the comments of many people with an expertise in this field have been sought and they have been, in the main, supportive, the editors are aware of its deficiencies as well as its strengths. It has to be freely acknowledged, for example, that it has not been possible to do equal justice to all the major resource interests particularly forestry, minerals and recreation by the 'head on' treatment of them provided in many of the texts currently available about rural matters. However, on balance efforts have been made to produce a book which in an interesting way sheds light on what have been considered to be key factors shaping the countryside, whilst keeping the notion of their complex interactions to the fore.

Figure 1.6: 'He's never been the same since he started his Open University course on "The Changing Countryside".'

Source: Pamela Higgins.

2
Expanding Agricultural Productivity
SNAPSHOTS

I like to look at the winding side of a great down with two or three numerous flocks of sheep on it, belonging to different farms; and to see, lower down, the folds in the fields, ready to receive them for the night ... The sheep principally manure the land. This is to be done by folding; and, to fold, you must have a flock. Every farm has its portion of down, arable and meadow. ...
W. Cobbett (1830), Rural Rides, *Penguin Books, Harmondsworth (1967).*

Our countryside is like a multicoloured chequerboard. Its chief characteristic is its attractive patchwork appearance, with an infinite variety of small odd shaped fields of brown ploughland or green pasture, bounded by twisting hedges, narrow winding lanes, small woodlands and copses and isolated trees and hedgerow timber.
G.M. Young (ed.) (1943), Country and Town: A Summary of the Scott and Uthwatt Reports, *Penguin Books, Harmondsworth.*

Farm practice has, through generations of experience, been adapted to suit the natural environment, but there are, of course, other factors which influence the type of agriculture. Tradition, the character and outlook of the individual farmer, his capital resources, government policy and a number of external economic pressures bring about changes from time to time. Between 1935 and 1955, for example, many farmers turned to the production of liquid milk for sale, in an area long associated with store rearing and some fattening. Since 1955 a number of men have changed back to cattle rearing, in response to a favourable demand for beef and to changes in the regulations governing the production of milk.
W.M. Williams (1963), Ashworthy: A West Country Village, *Routledge & Kegan Paul, London.*

A new agricultural revolution is under way. If allowed to proceed unhindered, it will transform the face of England. Already a quarter of our hedgerows, 24 million hedgerow trees, thousands of acres of down and heathland, a third of our woods and hundred upon hundred of ponds, streams, marshes and flower rich meadows have disappeared. They have been systematically eliminated by farmers seeking to profit from a complex web of economic and technological change.
Marion Shoard (1980), The Theft of the Countryside, *Temple Smith, London.*

If British farming is so efficient, why does it need so much protection? Subsidies taken from public money make up something like two-thirds of farming's net income in Britain today. Yet even with subsidies running at almost £400 million per year, farm incomes are still well below those in other industries. Where is the efficiency here?
P. Cheshire and J. Bowers (1969), New Scientist.

The fact has got to be faced that farming is a backward industry by contrast with all other activities of the nation. It offers no opportunity to ability and ambition; it cannot retain its workers. The discoveries of science are too slowly applied; the experience of other industries and other countries is unheeded. C.S. Orwin (1942), Speed the Plough, *Penguin Books, Harmondsworth.*

The farm of Mr. Neilson, of Halewood, exhibits several points worthy of notice. A light tramway with waggons is made use of for taking the turnip crop off the ground in moist weather. The tramway is readily shifted, and the crop is thrown into the waggons, which are then each pushed along by a man, so that the entire crop may be removed from the ground, which receives no injury from the feet of horses. The tramway can be constructed for 1s 4d per yard, and might be very advantageously introduced on all heavy farms where it is found difficult to take off the turnip crop in moist weather. A gang of men are at present employed on a considerable field of Mr. Neilson's in taking off the turnip crop, which they draw from the ground, fill into the waggons, and convey outside the gate at the rate of 6s an acre, shifting the tramway at their own cost. At this work they earn 2s 3d a day.
Sir James Caird (1850), The Times..

'GROW AS MUCH AS YOU CAN': ADAS

Never mind the surpluses, just keep on producing as much as possible — that's the message to arable farmers from senior ADAS farm management adviser Bill Mitchell.

He told Lincs and Humberside farmers last week to forget about reducing crop inputs to help cut Common Market surpluses.

'Will the chap in Germany or France cut back if you do? The answer is no, so you get on and produce it,' he said.
Farming News, 20 January 1984.

Agricultural Perspectives: Under Free Trade

Since the Second World War the agriculture of England and Wales has been transformed by the application of science, widespread mechanisation and increases in the scale of the farm business. The volume of output has more than doubled, as have the yields of the major cereal crops, and the labour force has been halved, whilst the area in crops is little more than it was in 1950. These changes have been achieved against a background of considerable state intervention, not simply in guaranteeing prices and subsidising production inputs, but also in providing assistance in management techniques and a wide range of scientific advice. All this, however, is a comparatively recent phenomenon. Historically, agriculture has witnessed more variable fortunes. The first part of this chapter begins at the turn of the nineteenth century, just after the agricultural revolution, and considers how agriculture evolved to the start of the Second World War.

English and Welsh Farming in 1815

At the end of the Napoleonic Wars (1815) most of the population of England and Wales still lived in villages and in small towns and over one-third of the population depended upon farming for a living (see Figure 2.1). Farmers provided nearly all the food consumed in England although imports were necessary in years of poor harvest. Few farmers owned their land. Between 85 and 90 per cent of all farmers were tenants, and perhaps half of English agricultural land belonged to 2,000 to 3,000 families who in turn had great political power. Farms were much larger than those in Europe, but there were marked regional differences. About two-thirds of all farmers had less than 50 acres, that is, smaller than the most modest of London's open spaces, Green Park. In the west and north west of England and in Wales these predominated. In such areas few hired labour, farms being run by the farmer and his family. Most of their land was in grass and livestock was the main source of income. In the south and the east of England farms were larger, kept livestock, grew cereals and were worked by hired hands.

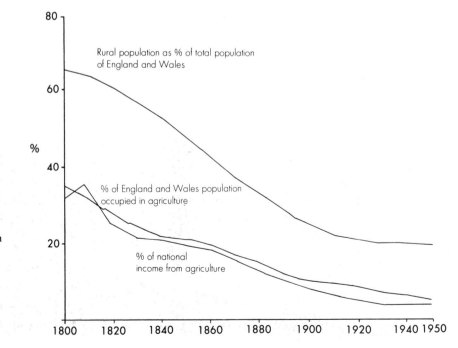

Figure 2.1: The Changing Importance of the Rural Sector in the Economy, 1800-1950. Note that 1815 represented the high point in the percentage of national income from agriculture, though by then the decline in the percentage of those employed in agriculture as against the industrial, manufacturing and service sectors had already begun.

Source: D. Grigg.

Here, there had been marked changes in farming after 1750, as a result of the agricultural revolution. The old open field rotation of winter grain, spring grain and fallow had been replaced by a rotation that included clover — which maintained the nitrogen content of the soil — and roots, which fed the cattle whose dung helped to raise crop yields. Iron ploughs drawn by horses, seed drills and horse hoes and the use of bone and urban waste as fertiliser had also helped to raise yields, while much new land had been brought into cultivation, particularly later in the eighteenth century. It was the wider adoption of these practices which was to help increase output in the next 60 years. However, in 1815 the picture of England and Wales at large was rather different. The agricultural revolution which began in the second half of the eighteenth century had hardly run its course and had so far had a limited impact on farming methods. In many places oxen still hauled heavy wooden ploughs although the horse was soon to replace them (see Figure 2.2). Land was still sown by a man broadcasting seed by hand although seed drills had been available since the 1730s. Crops were hoed by hand, and the harvest was cut by sickle, although in some places it had been replaced by the scythe. In the winter months corn was threshed with the flail, although a few threshing machines, powered by horse or water, were to be found in the north of England. Most farm tasks were done by hand. Steam power, characteristic of the Industrial Revolution, had made little impact on agriculture.

Thus the landscape must have looked very different in 1815 from today. Although the major onslaught on the woodland which had covered most of medieval England was over, there was much more woodland than now and much of the Fenland of East Anglia and the Sedgemoor levels of Somerset and the Lancashire mosses had still not been drained effectively. Although most arable land had been enclosed, upland areas were still held in common and commons remained in most parishes and even in many towns. In 1700 half the arable land in England was in open fields. Each farmer had numerous narrow strips scattered throughout the three or four great fields, which were without fences and hedges. However, by the 1820s these strips had been consolidated into compact fields and enclosed with walls or hedges, thus creating the 'patchwork quilt' pattern of farming that was to become a much valued visual amenity in the countryside of post-war England and Wales. New roads also had been built, invariably straight and often with wide, green verges.

Figure 2.2: Ploughing with Oxen. In the less advantaged arable areas the use of such animals persisted to the end of the nineteenth century.

Source: MERL (Museum of English Rural Life, Reading University).

Much of what is thought of as the traditional English farm landscape, therefore, appeared only in the period between 1700 and 1820.

An Age of Expansion: 1815 to the 1870s

The demand for livestock and grain grew throughout the first three-quarters of the nineteenth century. This was a result of a fivefold increase in the urban population and a growth in incomes, although financial inequality remained great and poverty widespread. The farmer was protected from foreign competition in grain until 1845 by Corn Laws that prevented imports until prices reached a given level. He was protected from the import of livestock and livestock products by the difficulty of moving milk, meat or butter any distance before the introduction of refrigeration in steamships in the 1870s. Thus whilst grain prices fell from their very high levels during the Napoleonic Wars, they were high enough to encourage an increase in output until the 1870s. From the 1850s livestock prices were more favourable than grain prices, and encouraged a continuing shift from grain to milk and meat production.

The period from 1815 to the 1870s was, then, one of expansion. More land was sown to crops. Fallow land finally disappeared, except on wet and heavy clay soils. New land was brought into cultivation, in the hills and moors, on chalk uplands, and by embanking coastal marshes. Most dramatically new land came about by the introduction of pumping into the Fenlands, converting seasonal pastures into the best arable land in England. By the 1860s there were possibly three or four million acres more land in crops than there were at the end of the eighteenth century. Wheat, barley and oats were still the leading crops, but there had been big increases in the area in fodder roots, temporary grasses grown in rotation and in potatoes, which had been of little importance in the field or the diet in 1800.

Yields of the grain crops also had increased. Although evidence from the period must be viewed with caution, for wheat an average of 20 bushels per acre in 1800 may well have increased by well over 30 per cent by the 1870s. This had been achieved by more careful ploughing and cultivation, using not only more labour per acre — the labour force in agriculture continued to increase until the 1850s and in some counties into the 1860s — but also through the spread of improved rotations including clover, rye grass and roots. The increased supply of farmyard manure from the greater number of cattle and sheep, and from the 1830s, the use of new manures also enhanced grain yields. Guano and Chilean nitrates were imported and from the 1840s superphosphates were manufactured in factories in England. But few farmers used the new chemical fertilisers before the 1860s.

The manufacture of tile pipes and the invention of the mole plough made the underdrainage of heavy clay soils easier and helped raise crop yields. The state provided cheap credit for underdrainage, one of the few instances of state support before the 1930s. The beginnings of the agricultural implements industry in the 1820s and 1830s increased the supply of implements such as ploughs, harrows and seed drills, and produced new implements such as clod-crushers and horse hoes. Whilst there was an abundant and cheap supply of labour there was little demand for labour-saving machinery. However the flail gave way to the threshing machine in the 1840s and 1850s, and the principal improvement in harvesting was the gradual substitution of the scythe for the sickle. But from the 1850s labour shortages at harvest time began to appear, and the American reaper and later the reaper-binder began to be adopted. These effectively did away with the labour intensive cutting of the crop by hand and the operation of tying the corn into stooks. Nevertheless, by 1870, three-quarters of England's grain crop was still cut by scythe or sickle (see Figure 2.3).

The period between 1850 and 1875 has been described as the golden age of English and Welsh farming. Still labour intensive, still dependent upon the

horse, with yields still depending on the supply of cattle dung, landlords and tenants prospered, and even farm workers, the poorest of all labourers, experienced some improvement in their standard of living, largely due to the decline in their numbers. Although corn was still the major crop, livestock products had been rapidly increasing in importance. They now accounted for more than half the value of output. This was so, not only in the pastoral west, but on the large mixed farms of southern and eastern England. Here, store cattle were brought from Ireland, Scotland and the west and fed on grain, roots and increasingly on concentrates made from imported maize and grain. But in spite of this great expansion of output from 1815, England and Wales could no longer feed themselves. Half the wheat consumed in the 1870s was imported, as was more than one-fifth of all food supplies. Demand had outrun home supply.

Figure 2.3: A Mowing Team at Wenham Grange, Suffolk, 1870. Although the introduction of the scythe was a major technological improvement, large numbers of men had still to be used to bring in the harvest using this implement.

Source: G. Winter (1966) *A Country Camera 1844-1914*, Country Life, Ltd., London.

Depression and Change, 1870-1939

In the 1870s depression came upon farming like a thunderclap from a clear sky. Indeed farmers initially attributed their distress to heavy rain, but it was soon apparent that the real cause was falling prices due to cheap imports. The fall in ocean freight rates and those of the railways inside the USA allowed farmers from the Midwest to undercut the home farmer in cereal crops. Later the invention of refrigeration, essential to the long distance transport of perishable produce, allowed the import of meat, butter and cheese from Argentina, Australia and New Zealand. Between 1875 and 1895 the price of wool and wheat halved, the sale price of cattle and sheep fell by between a quarter and one-third. Not surprisingly, the output of home agriculture showed little increase between the 1860s and the eve of the First World War. Rents fell, farm incomes stagnated and only the farm workers' standard of living rose, although their numbers continued to decline. But the impact of depression varied a great deal. It was worst among the corn producers of the east and the south of England, where there were few possible alternatives. Not only cereals, but fodder roots and sheep also declined in this region. In the west of England, however, where comparatively few farmers hired workers,

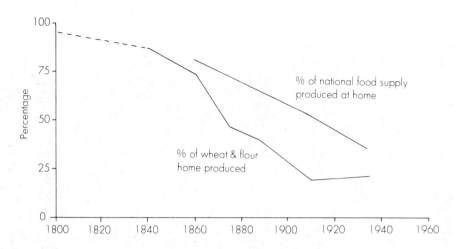

Figure 2.4: The Decline of Self-sufficiency.

Source: D. Grigg.

costs were more easily controlled, and furthermore fresh milk, protected from imports by its perishability, provided stable prices. At the same time the demand for milk in the towns was rising. Horticulture also prospered, not only in its traditional location on the edge of the towns, but in distant places with good soils or a mild climate such as the Fens and Cornwall. Home farming then continued its shift towards the production of livestock outputs acceler- ated by low cost grain that could now be fed to animals. The great increase in imports meant that by 1914 half the food supply of England and Wales was imported (see Figure 2.4).

The depression that began in the 1870s continued for the rest of the nine- teenth century and for part of the twentieth century. In terms of land use it was reflected in a continuous decline in the major cereals, wheat and barley, and in an increase in the area under both permanent and temporary grass. These changes were reversed temporarily late in the First World War, when food supplies were at risk and the government was compelled to guarantee grain prices. As a result much land was ploughed up for wheat. But these guarantees were abandoned in 1921 and the decline of cropland was resumed. Sheep, many of which were kept on lowland arable farms, also declined in number, but dairy cattle, pigs and poultry all increased as farming, especially in England, continued its long-term shift towards livestock production.

During the depression of the last quarter of the nineteenth century land- lords' incomes from rents declined dramatically, and farmers' incomes stag- nated. There was thus little incentive to improve farming methods or improve the land. Underdrainage ceased as incomes fell, and there was little increase in the use of fertilisers or lime. There were some advances in cereal production; the scythe had been largely replaced by the reaper-binder by 1910 (see Figure 2.5), the thresher was ubiquitous and the elevator was supplementing the pitchfork. Crop yields showed little increase after the 1860s. As the land in crops was declining, and the switch to livestock pro- duction was gradual the value of agricultural output increased very little. The value of output in 1910 was not much above that in the 1860s, and in 1935 not greatly above that of 1910.

The misfortunes of farming in England and Wales after the 1870s were due mainly to the imports of cheaper foodstuffs from North America and the southern hemisphere. The rest of Europe was also faced with this problem but it reacted in different ways. The Dutch and the Danes shifted further towards livestock production, improving quality and increasing specialisation. In France and Germany protection was the answer. In France the peasant was still thought of as the core of French life and political stability. In Germany

EVERYWHERE

the growing industrial population would have preferred cheaper food, but the political power of the Junkers, the landlords of Prussia, prevailed. In contrast in England and Wales the reform of Parliament in 1832 allowed manufacturing interests an increasing say in policy making and the rapid urbanisation of the country meant that landlord power had declined. There was little prospect of ending the policy of cheap food.

However, by the 1880s, the concentration of land into the hands of relatively few landlords remained much as before. It was only in the early twentieth century that the large estates began to be broken up. The proportion of English and Welsh farmland owned by its occupiers has since steadily risen, from about one-tenth before the First World War, to between 60 and 65 per cent in the 1980s.

The most significant changes in the farm landscape had taken place in the period of Parliamentary enclosure which had lasted from 1760 to 1815. From the 1830s, with reviving prosperity there was considerable investment in new farm buildings, and further construction of walls and hedges. New machinery did not lead to any demand for the removal of hedges; indeed in many parts of England the landlords' interest in shooting and hunting led to the planting and preservation of copses. Many farmers in limestone areas planted trees as windbreaks around their farm houses. There were even signs of a need to conserve other landscapes. In the 1870s Acts to prevent the further destruction of Epping Forest and other such areas were passed by Parliament (see the section 'Perspectives on Containment: Town and Country' of Chapter 3). But on the whole until the 1930s farmers made few radical changes in the landscape.

Figure 2.5: Harvesting with Horse Drawn Reaper Binder, Holbeach St John in the Lincolnshire Fens, 1900. Compare this with Figure 2.3. Far fewer farm workers are now required at harvest times following the replacement of the scythe.

Source: C.E. Mungay, *The Victorian Countryside*, RAP, London.

Signs of Change, Signs of Hope

Agriculture in England and Wales rallied in the late Edwardian period, and revived in the First World War, but prices fell again in the 1920s and 1930s, reaching their lowest point in 1932. But there were signs of hope. Early scientific and industrial advances were providing the means both of raising output and increasing efficiency. Plant breeding, beginning before 1914, was providing higher yielding, hardier and disease resistant varieties. Research on grassland and animal feeding was being applied by some farmers. Tractors, first used in the First World War, were slowly spreading in the corn areas (see Figure 2.6), and the milking machine, invented in 1895, was being adopted by

Figure 2.6: Ploughing with a Tractor, 1920. Compared with Figure 2.2 the manpower input to this task has fallen. Unlike working animals which require a considerable commitment of man-hours for their welfare, tractors require only routine maintenance which can be undertaken off the farm.

Source: MERL.

some dairy farmers, who were also replacing the Dairy Shorthorn cow with Friesian cattle. The heavy chemical industries were now producing cheaper and more convenient artificial fertilisers.

The English farmer was also receiving some help from the state. In 1925 a subsidy on home-grown sugar was introduced providing a valuable source of income for farmers in eastern England, while in 1932 the idea of a deficiency payment for wheat was adopted, ending nearly 90 years of free trade in food. Later there were subsidies on lime and basic slag. These measures reflected not simply the feeling that English agriculture should not be allowed to decline any further, but also the growing fear of war and the prospect of Britain again being cut off from overseas suppliers. This combination of scientific advance and government financial support was to come to full fruition only after 1945.

Agricultural Perspectives: A Comprehensive Support System

The new agriculture policies formulated after the Second World War provided the basis for a system of comprehensive support that still pertains in England and Wales today. Their evolution, however, took place in two distinct phases: the first phase when policies were created by England and Wales outside of Europe and a second phase when these countries accepted the policies which already had been formulated by the European Community.

England and Wales Alone

The principles of post-war agricultural policy were arrived at as a direct result of the experience of two events in the history of England and Wales. The first was the agricultural depression that preceded the Second World War and provided the first elements of an agricultural support system. The second was the war itself which because England and Wales could not rely on imports and had to feed themselves as best they could, transformed the status of the farming industry. The state, particularly in the period 1939-45, had acquired considerable managerial and purchasing powers over food production and in this artificial business environment the industry prospered to the extent that even the farmers' innate suspicions of government interference diminished a little. Against such success and with a determination to preserve the now apparent strategic role that agriculture could play in the future, the government determined to discover for itself the shape of post-war farming. To this end it set up a committee under Sir Leslie Scott, a Lord Justice of Appeal. When its report ultimately was published it advocated the protection of farming but its vision was pre-industrial, of a countryside of well-kept fields, craft industries and well-fed rustics. The only incursions of modern life were to be piped water and electricity to keep the workers in the countryside. Professor Dennison, in a minority report of the Scott Committee, and C.S. Orwin, director of the agricultural economics department at Oxford, challenged the economically irrational vision of Scott and sought a restructuring of agriculture in England and Wales to align it with a twentieth-century technology and business environment. What emerged in the post-war years was a combination of the reactionary sentiments of Scott and the progressive attitudes of Orwin. The 'special case' treatment was certainly given but the form of treatment allowed the industry to change with alarming speed in the direction advocated by Orwin and Dennison.

The years immediately following the Second World War were important in the wider field of planning. Although the 1947 Town and Country Planning Act laid many of the foundation stones of urban and rural planning, significantly the farming and forestry sectors were shielded from this new planning system, and were accorded their own separate legislation. As a consequence two entirely separate ministries acquired planning responsibilities in the countryside, creating a twin pronged and not always synchronised approach to rural problems.

The 1947 Agriculture Act was the legislative product of this new commitment towards the industry. Extolling the two principles of stability and efficiency it provided the basis for agricultural policy for over 20 years. There was almost complete consensus on policy needs: guaranteed prices would be paid in return for farmers submitting to a degree of state control. After the end of food rationing the return to the market-place was accompanied by the establishment of a deficiency payments system on most products. A deficiency payment is a sum of money given to the farmer for each unit of his product. It makes up the difference between a notional guaranteed price and the average price received by farmers for that product. Under this system of support cheap imports kept food prices low and the support was funded indirectly by general taxation and not directly from the consumer's purse, a situation that was to be reversed by entry into the EEC. Some products remained outside the deficiency payments system. Milk and eggs were still supported but by guaranteed prices from producer marketing boards.

The new Agriculture Act also gave farmers, through their union, the National Farmers' Union, the right to be involved in the annual policy and price review. Much has been written about this partnership and many would argue that the present health of the industry and emptiness of the countryside is a product of this cosy conspiratorial relationship. The late John MacKintosh, Professor of Politics at the University of Edinburgh, observed the privileged position of the Farmers' Union but noted perceptively that it was a relationship where government was perhaps the major beneficiary. The strength of the National Farmers' Union and indeed the Country Landowners Association in influencing policy must be recognized, but it lies less in institutionalised privilege and more in their formidable powers of lobbying and their high level of representation within parliament.

That other major user of rural land, forestry, went through a similar phase of wartime crisis and post-war reinvigoration as the farming industry. The war had exposed the nation's heavy reliance on timber imports. After the war three new Parliamentary Acts in six years created a more powerful Forestry

Commission to acquire new land for planting, to meet ambitious planting targets, to enter agreements for grant aiding private forest management (dedication schemes) which were also subject to tax concessions, and to control felling and re-planting. This resulted in a Forestry Commission seeking new land for trees, land that was of increasing interest to agriculturalists as a source of additional food production. There was no consensus as to how the allocation between farming and forestry should be carried out and much acrimony resulted.

In practice the implementation of the 1947 Agriculture Act falls into a number of distinct phases. The first period up to 1950 was a period when increases in the output of all products were sought. Farmers were encouraged to abandon their independence of spirit and suspicion of government by the fruits of the new policy and through the institutionalisation of their role in the annual price review. In the second period, up to mid-1950s the avenues of world trade began to move again. The government realised that domestic increases in production should come from increased efficiency and not from an open-ended state commitment. In the third period from the mid-1950s until the early 1960s the price reviews became increasingly acrimonious. As the farmers sought to maintain the buoyant state of the industry, the state sought to limit its liabilities. In 1957 government support for milk, eggs and potatoes was limited to a specified level of output and in the same year provisions were introduced which could be used to limit the support costs for other farm products.

The 1960s was a decade of uncertainty. There were two attempts to enter the European Community. The cost price squeeze began to pinch the farmers' prosperity, as inflation began to increase. The balance of payments situation was deteriorating. Import saving replaced strategic arguments as the basis for agricultural support and selective expansion of domestic agriculture was sought alongside a drive for greater efficiency. In other areas, however, the government sought to limit domestic output increases and control imports.

Though the 1947 Agriculture Act provided the basis for post-war agricultural policy there were other key elements. Efficiency could not be achieved overnight. Research and advisory services were needed to promote changes. Additional incentives were required to steer the direction of change. A safety net was needed to help the weak. There was also a need to take a wider perspective on rural problems.

The Agricultural Development and Advisory Service (ADAS) was born under a different name in 1946, a child of wartime circumstances. It subsequently grew into a leviathan among industrial advisory services. Its responsibilities range from running experimental farms and technical laboratories to giving technical, financial and socio-economic advice to farmers. Its role in changing the character of the farming of England and Wales should not be overlooked. The advisers were the sales representatives of the new scientific approach recommended by Orwin, steeped in agricultural fundamentalism but imbued with new ideas.

Figure 2.7: A Hill Farm in the Merioneth District of mid-Wales. This picture together with Figure 2.8 form an interesting contrast. The large single field in the latter is representative of the whole enterprise devoted to the production of cereals. The farm buildings tend to be overwhelmed by the scale of what is a heavily capital intensive monoculture operation capable of enjoying

Capital grants had been offered to hill farmers since 1946, under the Hill Farming Act but were extended to all farmers in 1957, under the Agricultural Act of that year. Their intention was clear; to encourage the intensification and capital re-equipment of farms. Whilst price guarantees were available to all, the capital grants had to be requested from, and then had to be approved by, the Ministry of Agriculture.

Minority groups of farmers were seen as vulnerable in the improved business environment of farming after 1947. The inevitable persistence of low incomes in the hills and uplands precipitated a number of support measures. These measures have persisted to the present day and so too have the problems. Small farmers rarely disturbed the advisory service, contributed little to the national agricultural output and received only the crumbs of the subsidy cake. From 1957 onwards schemes were introduced, ostensibly to offer small farmers a ladder to climb. But the uptake was low: indeed it has to be recognised that many small farmers had by then left the industry.

The final elements of policy in this period were the attempts to consider agriculture in the context of the wider rural economy, partly in the National Plan of 1965 but more in the Agriculture Act of 1967. Rural Development Boards were proposed, but only one was established in the North Pennines. In its short lifetime it was much criticised, although after its untimely death it was revered. In the 1970s the Strutt Committee and the Countryside Review Committee deliberated over rural affairs, but more recommendations were made than actions taken. Therefore, it is difficult to see the structural policy measures and the social policy measures in the hills as little more than palliatives. Certainly there was no concerted attempt to develop an integrated approach to the management of change in the countryside.

In retrospect it is possible to look back on the emergence of an agricultural policy more comprehensive than anything which had predated it in peacetime. It was policy that was flexible to an extent. Governments were able to adapt policies to meet exchequer needs and to encourage selective expansion. And the people of England and Wales remained the beneficiaries of cheap food policy. But if the public as a whole benefited equally the same cannot be said for all farmers. As the cereals barons prospered the livestock farmers, especially in the hills, fared less well (see Figures 2.7 and 2.8). Cheap food for all gave high incomes to some.

substantial support. In Figure 2.7 the farmstead dominates the picture in which the total system of stock rearing is apparent — the 'in-bye' land with its animal enclosures and the open hill grazing beyond. Such holdings depend on labour rather than capital investment. They not only have to cope with the unfavourable nature of the climate and terrain but by their organisation and size they are incapable of capitalising on support schemes. They exist on the margins of viability. The differences in the two types of enterprises in terms of income were further accentuated by the entry of England and Wales to the EEC.

Source: *Farmers Weekly.*

Figure 2.8: Cereal Production on a Large Scale — a Typical Downland Field in Southern England.

Source: *Farmers Weekly.*

England and Wales in Europe

In 1973 England and Wales joined an enlarged European Community. There were inevitable adjustments as free trade was swapped for protectionism. Section 39 of the Treaty of Rome provided for Europe what the 1947 Agriculture Act provided for England and Wales, in so far as it purported to be an attempt to increase producer efficiency, market stability and consumer equity. But if the legislation was remarkably similar in principle, it turned out to be remarkably different in practice. It is important to explore why these differences should have arisen.

In the years before England and Wales entered the EEC it had struggled with the problems of an agricultural industry that was burdened by the presence of many small and inefficient producers. Mansholt, the agricultural commissioner in the late 1960s, generated some radical proposals for modernisation, which emerged in the 1970s in much diluted form as structural policy. But the historical emphasis in the Community had been on protection. Although the entry of England and Wales to it might have occasioned policy change, the fact is that their cultural, social, economic and political experience created even further complexity for it and EEC policy was allowed to drift helplessly towards increasing price support to farmers.

The activities and the budgeting of the Common Agricultural Policy (CAP) fall into two discrete areas. The first area is of price policy which is funded by the *Guarantee Section* of the budget. This is the costliest part of the CAP which is in turn by far the most costly item in the total budget of the EEC, accounting for around 67 per cent of it. By raising farm prices the policy raises the cost of food and the consumer pays twice: once through his taxes and subsequently through a more costly basket of food. The second area of support is the *Guidance Section.* This deals with structural policy and a number of measures have been implemented to aid structural reform.

The key difference between the policy in England and Wales after the war and that of the EEC lies in the price support mechanisms. At home price support was dominated by deficiency payments, whereas in Europe a variety of arrangements operate to raise farm incomes and product prices to the consumer. The most common arrangement is one where a TARGET PRICE is

	Prices and production supported by:	Imports controlled by:	Special measures
Milk and milk products	Target prices and intervention prices backed up by buying up at intervention prices	Threshold prices backed up by Variable Import Levy	Various attempts to stimulate increased consumption especially of butter. Beginnings of attempts to control production by coresponsibility levy
Beef and veal	Guide prices backed by intervention at buying in price at given % of guide price	Customs duties Basic levies	Minor variations between UK and rest of EEC for price support. Special arrangements with some third world countries for imports
Sheepmeat	Basic guide prices backed by storage subsidy and intervention buying. Annual compensatory premia in first 4 years of scheme	Customs duties Quotas	Variations between UK and rest of EEC. Variable premia paid to sheepmeat producers
Pigmeat	Basic price backed by storage subsidy and possibility of intervention buying	Sluicegate prices and Basic Levies, etc.	
Cereals	Target prices and intervention prices backed up by buying up at intervention prices for 'quality' products	Variable Import Levy	Export levies charged if EEC price is below world price
Sugar	Target prices and intervention with the addition of production quotas	Variable Import Levy	Special arrangements for Third World country imports from certain countries
Oilseeds	Production subsidies to raise EEC production and prices		
Fruit and vegetables	Basic prices used as a guide. Producer organisations control marketing	Countervailing charges (effectively a variable import levy)	

Source: P.W. Brassley (1982) in Halley R.J. (ed.), *The Agricultural Notebook*, 17th edn.

Figure 2.9: Support Arrangements for Different Farm Products in the EEC, *c.* 1982. Although supported to different degrees, most agricultural products in the EEC are protected by some form of target or guide price and most food imports are restricted from coming into the EEC by import levies or quotas.

identified as a desirable market price for a product. If prices fall below a certain level beneath that TARGET PRICE to what is called the INTERVENTION PRICE agencies will buy up the product until the price rises above that level. Imports are controlled by levies and as a consequence of this and domestic price support, prevailing food prices for most products are normally above those prevailing in a 'free' market. The arrangements for different products vary, and are summarised in Figure 2.9. The result is that the degree of subsidy is also highly variable from product to product. Where products are in surplus in the EEC, 'lakes' of milk and wine, and 'mountains' of butter, beef and cereals have accumulated to be released back onto EEC markets at a later date or furtively disposed of by selling at below costs of production to third world countries and the USSR.

Since England and Wales entered the European Community, agricultural policy has been made more complex by political and economic manoeuvring relating to exchange rates. In the absence of a UK involvement in a European monetary union, and given floating exchange rates, agricultural prices have to be fixed at what are termed green rates. The greater the fluctuations in exchange rates between member countries and the more laggardly the adjustment of green rates, the greater the scope for discontent with the working of the system, and the greater the political manipulations.

The *Guidance Section* of the CAP covers the other elements of EEC agricultural policy. There is a wide range of measures including grants for food processing, schemes for structural reform and grants for farm modernisation programmes. Many of the policies under the *Guidance Section* replicated existing policies in England and Wales. The Mansholt proposals for structural reform were diluted for a number of reasons and appeared in directives in 1972 which set up the Farm and Horticultural Development Scheme (The Modernisation of Farms Directive); the farm structures and retirement grants designed to ease small farmers out of farming by lures of small payments and offers of grants for amalgamating holdings (The Cessation of Farming and the Reallocation of the Agricultural Area for Structural Improvement); and the provision of socio-economic advice to widen the conventional concerns of the advisory service (The Provision of Socio-economic Guidance for the Acquisition of Occupational Skills by Persons Engaged in Agriculture). The Less Favoured Areas Directive appeared in 1975 and has not been fully implemented in England and Wales. Compensatory allowances for sheep and store cattle largely replaced the old hill subsidies but the investment aid in areas such as tourism has not been put into practice in England and Wales. Whilst these guidance policies might be perceived by some as the social conscience of the CAP they, like the price support policies, have tended to direct support to where it was least needed, and have been exploited by those least in need of help.

By 1978 agricultural policy in England and Wales was fully adjusted to the European Community system. But the changes turned out to be by no means as great as a suspicious farming community had expected. Hallowed institutions like the Milk Marketing Board remained despite rumours of unfair competition. Farm capital grants were still offered by the Ministry of Agriculture. Increasingly national governments looked to their own farmers as the world-wide recession bit in the mid-1970s. In reality all that was common about agricultural policy was the common ditching of European altruism and the pursuit of national self-interest. As tempers soured so academics increasingly advised that agricultural policy should be more nationally determined. Price policy from the outset had had a truly European nature whereas in the field of structural policy and guidance individual member countries have had much great freedom to act. The Common Agricultural Policy thus remains a mishmash of national and European measures hanging uneasily together as the EEC moves inexorably towards insolvency.

The entry of England and Wales into Europe was the dominant but not the only element in home agricultural policy during the 1970s. Two White Papers were published advocating the expansion of agricultural output. At the same time as European surpluses were emerging, farmers in England and Wales were being exhorted to produce more of the products in surplus. It was, and still is, widely believed that the balance of payments situation can be enhanced by increases in agricultural production. These assertions though are made without really knowing whether the agricultural industry or some other sector of the home economy would be the best generator of export earnings. Thus, within the framework of a wider European policy, policy makers at home were devising their own appropriate national strategies, based on the assumption that agriculture could make a real contribution to balance of payments problems.

In the period after the Second World War when a more comprehensive system of agricultural support was being developed from within to suit the particular perceived needs in England and Wales, flaws in that policy were at least partially corrected. But since England and Wales have joined Europe the ability to adjust price policies appears to have been lost. The faults of the Common Agricultural Policy, despite some adjustments, remain in 1985. A policy with increasingly comprehensive intentions has had increasingly undesirable effects and a major challenge remains to sort it out.

All these policies that have so dramatically changed the state of the farming industry have also altered the appearance of the countryside. In general the farmed landscape is tidier and to many people's regret no longer reflects aspects of local custom and culture. Old farm buildings have become anachronisms as have many landscape features like hedgerows. The landscape has become more open and less variegated, subjugated to international policies rather than adapted to local or regional markets.

As for forestry, EEC entry saw no fundamental shift in policy. Indeed, it entered a period of stagnation in the early 1970s following the publication of a hotly contested Treasury cost-benefit study. In the late 1970s there was a resurgence of interest in forestry and the Centre for Agricultural Strategy argued strongly for additional afforestation. Virtually all of the planting since the Second World War has been coniferous afforesation in the uplands, generating landscapes that are abhorred by rural aesthetes and ramblers though they do offer widely used and well liked recreational facilities to the general public. In spite of these differences of opinion the existence of an expanding frontier of coniferous forest must be recognised as the principal landscape change of post-war years in many parts of the uplands.

Agricultural Perspectives: An Efficient Agriculture

The Vision Realised

The 1947 Agriculture Act provided the foundation stone for post-war agricultural prosperity. The 1950s saw the vision behind the Act realised. Inter-war agricultural commentators had thought that the agricultural industry was doomed, condemned by the inexorable laws of economics to an insignificant *RELENTLESS* role in the peacetime economy. But the war and the subsequent commitment to the industry effected a major transformation. While present-day economic historians have debated the number of agricultural revolutions in the eighteenth and nineteenth centuries, they have themselves lived through a revolution of greater significance to the industry and the countryside in general.

A cursory glance at the statistics reveals the extent of these changes. It is fortunate that the statistics of the industry are so full, although inevitably changes in the way data were collected constantly hinder any detailed long-term analysis.

The arable sector which had been in decline in the inter-war years experienced a remarkable revival. Grain yields which had been virtually static in the nineteenth century had edged up only slightly in the first half of the twentieth century. Thereafter they rose dramatically. Wheat yielded on average two tonnes per hectare in 1800, 2.25 tonnes per hectare in 1940 but 5.9 tonnes per hectare by 1980. In other arable crops like sugar beet, potatoes and turnips there was a similar upturn in yields though the increases were less dramatic. The stability engendered by the 1947 Agriculture Act allowed changes to occur. Plant breeding, better techniques of cultivation, enhanced disease control and improved weed control all contributed to this revolution in arable farming. Now machines carried out the fieldwork. The combine harvester a rarity in 1940, increased its numbers tenfold over the ensuing decade and a further fivefold over the 1950s.

The arable sector was not the only beneficiary of the changed policy climate. Cattle, sheep and pig numbers all increased significantly. Livestock ceased being rural ornaments and became more efficient converters of feed into meat and milk. Milk yields rose from 2,355 litres per cow in 1944-5 to 4,810 litres per cow in 1980-1. Improved breeding and feeding were major influences on this doubling of milk yields over 35 years.

There was more than a change in yields and output. A collective peacetime commitment to farming had emerged from the crisis of war and the depths of depression. Doubts still lingered but the farming community again felt wanted and not irrelevant.

The real significance of post-war policy was to cushion the farmer from the free operation of market forces. This was achieved primarily through the operation of the deficiency payments system mentioned earlier but was helped by the provision of capital grants and a number of other supports to the farming industry not least the fact that farmers are not required to pay rates upon their agriculture enterprise. A major achievement of post-war policy was that it allowed the real rises in income of wartime and the years immediately after 1947 to be maintained. The effects of the cost-price squeeze were much talked about but largely shrugged off for long periods of time (see Figure 2.10).

The extent of the advances made by the industry are reflected in the

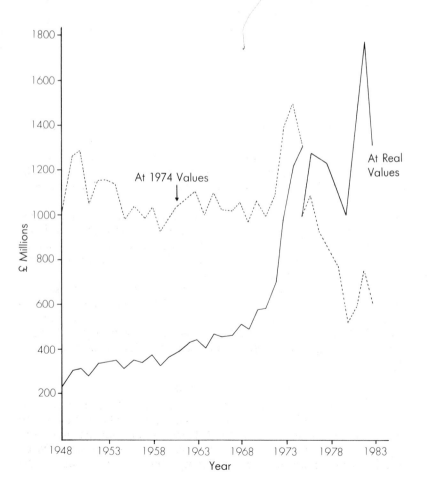

Figure 2.10: Aggregate Income of the UK Farming Industry. Note that the basis for calculating aggregate farm income was changed in the 1970s which explains the discontinuity in the graph lines.

Source: B. Slee.

38

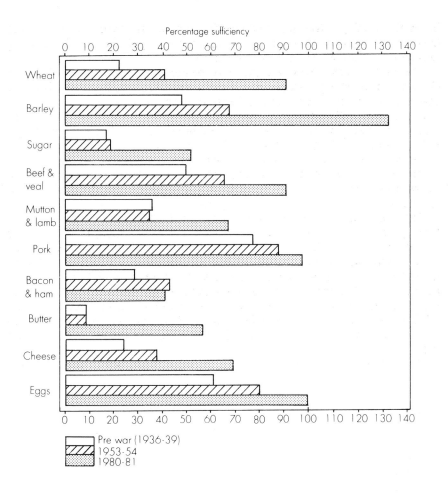

Percentage sufficiency

Pre war (1936-39)
1953-54
1980-81

Figure 2.11: The Degree of
UK Self-sufficiency in Various
Food Products, Pre-war
(1936-9) and Post-war
(1953-4 and 1980-1).

Source: B. Slee.

increasing level of food self-sufficiency attained in England and Wales in the post-war years (see Figure 2.11). But levels of self-sufficiency are only indirect indicators of efficiency and thus require careful interpretation. It is possible to increase self-sufficiency and reduce efficiency. Nevertheless the industry's response to the government's request to increase production cannot be ignored.

The structure of farming has changed radically under the influence of new policies and new technologies. Between 1950 and 1980 the number of holdings fell by over one-third, though the exact extent of the decline is clouded by changes in the way in which data were collected. Farm sizes increased allowing economies of size and scale to be realised.

On the remaining holdings the type of farming changed. Farmers streamlined their systems and specialised. Mixed farming became an anachronism to many. The new technology released the farmers from the shackles of pre-war farming (see Figure 2.12). The available evidence in the Ministry of Agriculture's analysis of farm classification indicates this significant process of specialisation.

The Vision Soured

The new found stability in home agriculture created a new type of farmer and new agricultural landscapes. In the early post-war years public sentiment and government policy had gone hand in hand. Here was an industry worthy of support. But doubts eventually began to pervade the minds of some. What had been rational under wartime food rationing which was continued in the

Figure 2.12: New Technology and the Dairy Farmer. The carousel milking machine (a rotary milking parlour) was introduced in the 1960s. The single operator allows each cow to join the carousel. It yields its milk during one rotation of the carousel and is then replaced by another cow.

Source: MERL.

years up to 1950, was less rational in 1960 and less rational still by 1980.

The deficiency payments system works most effectively for the taxpayer when the domestic producers' share of total national food supply is low, since the taxpayer is not called upon to support the price of imported foods. In such a situation it may be assumed that the level of support for most home-grown produce is not great since production remains under-stimulated. However, once substantial deficiency payments become available for a crop, this not only benefits the grower already producing, but encourages greater overall production at the taxpayer's expense. There is the real danger here of getting locked into a vicious spiral with increasing costs of support paralleled by increasing output which is in any case not wanted. With England and Wales alone there was scope for fine tuning, and the public still benefited from cheap food from world markets. Under the European system of support a significant additional burden is placed upon the consumer rather than the taxpayer. As the taxation system in England and Wales has been traditionally progressive in that the rich are taxed more harshly than the poor, a shift in the source of support from taxpayer to food consumer moves the burden of farm income support increasingly towards the poorer segments of the community. Consumer awareness of increasing policy costs and consumer criticism of policy has increased since EEC entry but ironically the consumer in England and Wales is in a weaker position than ever to change such policies. The immediate impact of these changes wrought by membership of the EEC was not great as the world was in the throes of a raw materials crisis in the mid-1970s which included agricultural products. But the mechanisms of the CAP inevitably arouse the awareness of the consumer about the cost of food whilst largely removing from national governments any freedom to control the total support costs. As is stressed in the section on the 1980s, however, the *total* cost of producing food remains largely indeterminate.

The decade after England and Wales entered Europe was one of consolidation for the environmental movement. The public was more interested in the countryside than ever before. Agricultural policy was subjected to intense public scrutiny and increasing criticism. These tensions were exacerbated by changes in rural society. Post-war policy had replaced men with machines. Ferguson and Fordson tractors replaced Hodge, the archetypal rustic farm worker. And Hodge's village was now occupied by urban refugees seeking a countryside image that was increasingly inconsistent with the changes they saw taking place about them.

The statistical evidence provides the proof of the dramatic changes that have occurred. The evidence on increases in production, self-sufficiency and labour productivity have boosted the confidence of the industry. But there is other statistical data regarding such matters as policy costs and European overproduction. The evidence this provides has sounded a warning note that is difficult to ignore.

The Efficiency of Farming

Agriculture in England and Wales frequently is regarded as highly productive and highly efficient. The industry is praised for increasing production and productivity and held up as a model for other industries by farmers and politicians. Economists have been more cautious, recognising that the measurement of productivity and efficiency is not easy. Terms like efficiency mean different things to different people. It is not pedantry to explore the various meanings attached to terms like efficiency. It is crucial if the layman is to disentangle the fact from the fiction.

But rather than confront the difficulties of assessing the efficiency of the industry, it is perhaps more useful to consider a single dairy cow. How is it possible to assess whether or not it produces milk efficiently? All of the following are possible measures:

litres of milk yielded;
litres of milk per kilo of concentrate feed;
gross margin[1] per cow (£);
gross margin per hectare under dairying (£);
litres of milk per unit of support energy;
cost of milk compared to a notional world price;
value of output relative to all inputs (land, labour, capital) at non-supported prices.

This complexity can be reduced by identifying four main approaches to the measurement of efficiency, each of which must be considered (see Figure 2.13).

The first group of efficiency measures is concerned with biological or technical efficiency. Milk yield per hectare might be considered on its own, but such a measure is partial. It ignores other inputs, such as the concentrate feeds, the nitrogen applied to the grass and the capital tied up in winter housing. Unless these and other changed inputs (like capital) are considered the ratio remains partial. But in order to consider bundles of inputs we must find a common denominator. Normally, this is the measuring rod of money.

Financial measures may be partial or complete. Partial financial statistics also can prove misleading. High gross margins might be associated, mistakenly, with high levels of efficiency. Attempts have been made to look at the overall financial efficiency of farming, culminating in work in the mid-1970s on size and efficiency in farming. For different types and sizes of farm the total value of output and, not without difficulty, the total cost of inputs was calculated. Average efficiency ratios thus derived showed in general that medium-sized farms were the most efficient but it was strictly a comparison within farming, and strictly a financial rather than an economic approach to measurement.

The first attempts to compare farming efficiency in England and Wales

1. A gross margin, whereby variable costs are deducted from the gross output, is a measure of the financial performance of an enterprise on a farm.

41

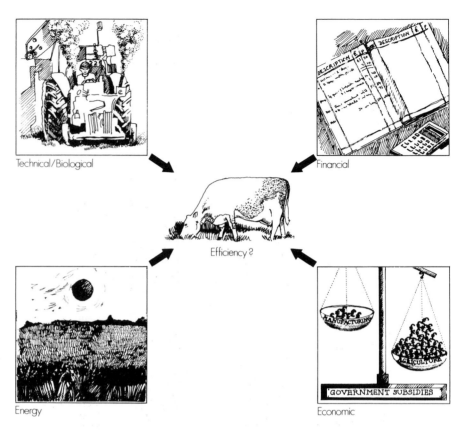

Technical/Biological

Financial

Efficiency ?

Energy

Economic

Figure 2.13: Four Approaches to Measuring Efficiency in Agriculture

Source: Pamela Higgins.

with that of European farmers was carried out by the Centre of Agricultural Strategy. They produced sufficient evidence to cast doubts on the assertion that farmers in England and Wales were the paragons of efficiency that many had assumed. Using various methods of calculation home farmers were consistently outperformed by those of Denmark. Subsequent studies of individual sectors of the farming industry, particularly milk production, point to a similar conclusion: that complacency about agricultural efficiency in England and Wales is misplaced.

The assessment of efficiency in different industries poses more difficulty. In terms of labour productivity the agricultural industry's record is unrivalled by other major industrial sectors over the last 30 years but this can be largely explained by the substitution of capital for labour. Capital investment largely has taken the form of the purchase of machinery which has enabled fewer and fewer hired hands to complete more expeditiously agricultural tasks which of themselves have been growing in technical complexity. Thus the often cited interpretation of agricultural statistics which simplisticly attributes gains in labour productivity to improvements in the workforce is seen to be wide of the mark. The ability of the industry to respond to additional injections of capital is subject to more debate. The most recent major study, by the Centre of Agricultural Strategy, has looked at the agricultural sector's efficiency using a number of criteria. Figure 2.14 points to the need to be extremely careful when interpreting evidence on efficiency. The high level of value added per £ cost of labour is borne out by the widely publicised figures of labour productivity. On the other hand, evidence of the low levels of efficiency of capital use in the industry is found in the less-well publicised data on capital productivity.

Economic measures of efficiency are more complex than financial measures but they are considered by most economic analysts desirable measures

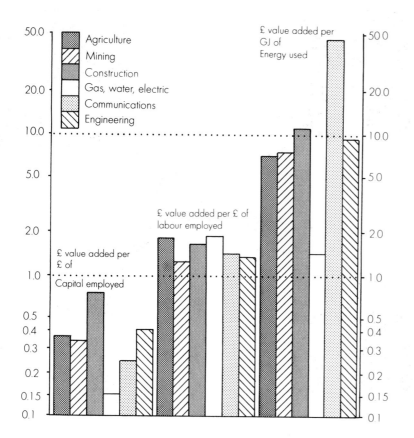

Figure 2.14: The Efficiency of Agriculture Compared to Other Industrial Sectors, 1972. This is a log graph which means that the vertical scale progressively contracts as the numbers increase. In so doing, the diagram can accommodate a much greater range of numbers than an ordinary arithmetic scale. Relatively more emphasis is given, therefore, to change at the bottom of the scale.

Source: B. Slee.

because they remove the distorting effects of grants, subsidies and import tariffs. To some of these analysts an efficient industry might be deemed to be one which combines various inputs in such a way as to maximise the benefits to society. Thus as far as agriculture in England and Wales is concerned increasing doubts about its economic efficiency have been expressed, it being acknowledged that high incomes are not necessarily indicators of high levels of efficiency. The economic analyst certainly needs to ask what the effects of the subsidies, grants, tax incentives, etc. would have been if they had been invested in other sectors of the economy. Can the UK dairy farmer really be economically efficient when the butter that farmer is producing costs the consumer vastly more than that which can be imported from New Zealand?

In the fuel crisis of the mid-1970s agricultural scientists became increasingly concerned with energy consumption, particularly in technologically advanced intensive production systems. The amount of non-renewable energy used in production (support energy) can be calculated and this forms an alternative surrogate of efficiency. An examination of the evidence shows, predictably, that crop production is more efficient than animal production. In the most efficient crop production systems in the world the energy produced is 50 times greater than the support energy used. In the least efficient animal production systems ten units of support energy are used for every one unit of energy produced. Technological advancement and intensive livestock farming are not support energy efficient (see Figure 2.15). Since 1947 demands on support energy have increased very substantially. On this criterion British agriculture has probably become less efficient and it is argued that, as non-renewable energy is used up, energy efficiency and economic efficiency will move closer together. High-input, high-output production systems may be appropriate when energy costs are low in financial terms. But as energy costs

Figure 2.15: Dairy Cows in a Controlled Environment. From the farmer's point of view shielding cows from the weather and providing a measured quantity of food maximises production. But what of the energy inputs demanded in servicing such a regime and that includes the fertilisers used to produce the food?

Source: MERL.

rise, as they are likely to as non-renewable sources are used up, so greater economy in non-renewable support energy use is likely to be associated with higher levels of economic efficiency.

Assessing the achievements of agricultural policy since the war is then bound to be difficult. Academics from different disciplines have debated the verdict at length. That the industry has been transformed by a technical and mangerial revolution is not in doubt. But how efficient is the industry? Is it the industry that the visionary of the 1940s would have wished for? One agricultural commentator has argued that 'All this talk of efficiency is a smoke-screen to protect the over-producers: there is nothing efficient in producing more than the market can absorb.'

The goals of policy must be returned to before making a final verdict. The post-war policy of support was largely motivated by strategic needs. But as the strategic *reserve* increased so the strategic *need* diminished. It is bad policy to pay high premiums for low risks.

There were other reasons for supporting farmers than those relating solely to strategic need. Both English and Welsh and European policies have sought to reward farmers fairly for their production, and to eliminate wide variations in their incomes. There is too, in both cases, an undercurrent of support for rural communities, but the notion of 'communities' metamorphosed into 'farmers', at the very time that the structure of rural society in England and Wales was being rapidly transformed by a major influx of urban 'refugees'. These new occupants of the countryside did not normally depend upon it for a living. It was a visual and physical playground which was being transformed, in their eyes, for the worse, by policies that had long since ceased to consider the countryside and looked only at agriculture.

If cheap food is to be the primary objective of policy the merits of a deficiency payments system are clear. The English and Welsh people were the beneficiaries of cheap food and paid lightly for supporting farmers' incomes through a progressive taxation system. But whatever lip service the CAP paid to consumers' welfare it is beyond doubt that the consumers' interests have been secondary to those of the producer for many years as the increasing upward trend in consumer costs clearly shows.

As for forestry, policy in England and Wales has followed a very different path of development to the agricultural sector. The Forestry Commission is a major land manager and has responded at least partially to the demands of those who accused it of desecrating the landscape with alien conifers, and not taking wider environmental issues into account. Thus wider notions of economic efficiency have guided policy for some time, though at times short term financial expediency may override long term economic interests. Whether these wider notions of efficiency will continue to act as a guide in an increasingly privately owned forest estate must be open to question. The issues relating to efficiency in the forest industry are complex. The forester who points out that the trees he plants will not be felled for 50 years must be sympathised with. Can such an industry be subjected to the normal tests of efficiency or must a forest industry always be, to an extent, an act of faith?

At a time when interventionism by government is increasingly questioned and frequently reduced, the agricultural sector remains a peculiar anomaly. Few people advocate a return to the hidden hand of the market with all its uncertainty and social costs. But is it impossible to devise policies which are sharper and cheaper, that give aid where it is needed and that treat the consumer fairly? In normal circumstances it might be naïve to expect a significant shift in policy. But the ramifications of the CAP within the farming community, within rural communities, on environment and on the landscape of rural England and Wales have created a major challenge to the *status quo*. The strength of agricultural interest groups has to date meant that the challenge has been withstood. However, the EEC budgetary crisis of the mid-1980s might just precipitate a move towards a more rational policy for agriculture within the countryside.

The Early 1980s

Landownership — The Forgotten Power in Agriculture

In its relationship with the countryside, farming in England and Wales since 1945 has been discussed so far primarily in terms of the development of agricultural policies and the concept of agricultural efficiency. In carrying the story forward into the early 1980s and describing in greater depth the recent attitudes towards further increases in productivity these dimensions must be kept very much in mind. There are, however, other factors that are important in the relationship between farming and the countryside that have so far not been embraced. Here questions of landownership and the character of agriculture as a business need to be considered. Although, in the early 1980s some 60 to 65 per cent of Great Britain's agricultural land is owned by those who farm it, the rest is worked under the landlord and tenant system in which the tenant is responsible for the farming working capital and enjoys the profits (or losses). The landlord, in exchange for a predetermined cash rent, lets his land and is responsible for the buildings, fences, etc. which make the land workable.

These two types of land tenure are important because different types of landowner have different motives for holding land — the one owning land as the basis for the all-important farming enterprise and the other regarding land primarily as a financial investment. As a result they are of differing taxation status; they have differing amounts of other non-land assets and they have differing views about important items such as investments in buildings and drainage, the removal of hedges, the preservation of woodland and other natural features, access by the public and so on. While landlords of rented land generally cannot control what crops their tenants grow, by their policy on rents they can influence the intensity with which their tenants farm.

Ownership is also important in influencing the rate of structural change. Most farmers appear to want to expand, even the larger ones, but their ability to do so can be frustrated by the lack of suitable land. The land market has a very low annual turnover (less than 2 per cent) and elderly farmers are reluctant to sell such an asset which, at least since the Second World War, has performed well as an investment. Indeed, because the long-term trend is for land values to rise faster than the rate of inflation, land confers on its owners, landlords or owner-occupiers, real capital gains. In the recent past a significant part of their total rewards for being in agriculture has been in this form. Finally, ownership determines who become farmers and who enjoys an income from the land in the form of farm profits or rents.

In the 1980s high land prices and a predominance of owner-occupation means that new farmers come largely from the families of established farmers. Where land is tenanted, the landlord has some choice of whom he takes as a tenant. But the very small number of farms currently being re-let each year, means that this method of entry for potential farmers has virtually disappeared. Unfortunately, in England and Wales there is little information about who owns land. Much detailed evidence is available on land held by public and semi-public bodies ranging from the Forestry Commission and the Crown to insurance companies and pension funds. But this should not obscure the fact that almost nothing is known about the 80 per cent which remains in private hands. This constitutes the most vital piece of missing information necessary to any assessment of how fast change in the countryside is likely to proceed and in what direction. And England and Wales remain among the few countries in the world without an open system of land registration.

Farming in the 1980s: The Mix of Business and Family

Farming in England and Wales is characterised by its wide variability in terms of sizes of farms and types of farming activity. There is little point in talking about an 'average' farm because this would be a very unusual and peculiar phenomenon. The industry has a wide range of farm sizes, with many small farms and relatively few large ones (Figure 2.16). This situation means that

Figure 2.16: The Distribution of Numbers of Agricultural Holdings and Area by Size of Holding in the UK, 1982.

Source: B. Hill.

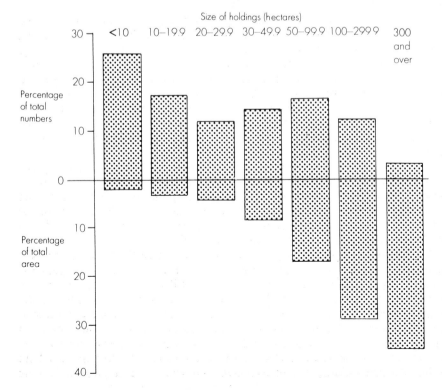

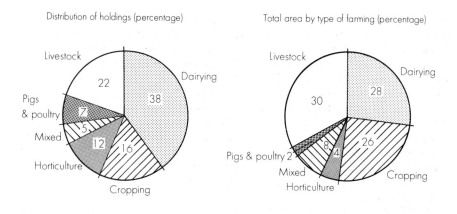

Distribution of holdings (percentage)

Total area by type of farming (percentage)

Figure 2.17: The Distribution of Holdings and Total Area by Type of Farming in England and Wales. Note that the holdings are full time as defined by an input of 250 standard man-days and over.

Source: B. Hill.

different approaches need to be taken in any discussion of the industry depending on whether the prime concern is with social aspects of farming or with levels of agricultural production. For example, if the need is to look at the problem of low incomes in farming, interest would have to centre on the numbers of farmers, particularly those large numbers at the small end of the farm size spectrum where low output per farm might be expected to lead to low incomes. However, if it is the small number of large farms to which special attention should be paid, concern would be with the level of agricultural production. These large farms are high output, high income businesses and occupy much of the total area of England and Wales with the top 3 per cent of farms accounting for one-third of the land area. They are also responsible for the lion's share of food production particularly in the case of certain commodities such as cereals, sugar-beet and poultry. The notion of a traditional British mixed farm with a wide range of livestock and crops is also far from the truth; only 5 per cent now fall into the Ministry's 'mixed' class (Figure 2.17). In the 1980s, the degree of specialisation is greater now than ever, with fewer, but larger, enterprises per farm.

Yet there are some common characteristics which are found throughout the range of farm sizes and types and which help explain the way farmers behave in the way they do. The first of these is that farms, even quite large ones, are by comparison with other industries small firms in terms of their labour force, output or working capital. Only their fixed capital may appear to be substantial by comparison, but this is because of high land values, a situation which makes owner-occupier farmers specially sensitive to capital taxation. Consequently, they normally use only simple business forms — sole proprietorships, partnerships and private companies — and are essentially family concerns.

Secondly, the overwhelming majority (at least 19 farms out of every 20) are owned by closely related family members. Frequently no distinction is drawn between the personal wealth of the farmer and the business assets he uses. In addition, some 60 per cent of the total labour force is made up of the farmer and his family members (Figure 2.18). Over two-thirds of farms employ no workers at all, apart from the farmer's spouse.

All this means that, unlike other small firms, motivations are not entirely commercial. There is an almost inextricable fusion between the personal affairs of the farmer and his family and those of his business. Farmers can be found who are investing in buildings or land not primarily because of the desire to increase profits but because they have a son who is likely to succeed them. Conversely, farmers can be found who are reducing their scales of activity because they are getting older and wish to take things more easily. Legislation which aimed to restrict the freedom of farmers to pass their land to the next generation could be expected to have a major impact on farming

Figure 2.18: The Family Farm. The Crook family have lived at Blue House Farm, Little Loudon, Suffolk since the main house was originally built in the sixteenth century. Howard Crook farms 200 acres and the whole family is involved.

Source: P. Isaac (1981), *The Farmyard Companion.*

practice. Any investigation of what motivates today's farmers must reveal a further common characteristic — a strong concern with the satisfaction derived from the farming process itself rather than just as a way of generating income. In other words, with farming as a way of life.

Similarly, investments in new buildings and machinery are heavily influenced by a desire to be technically up to date rather than by carefully assessed financial returns. Thus, while it cannot be denied that farmers are responsive to financial stimuli such as changes in relative prices between products, their behaviour cannot be understood properly unless the importance of non-pecuniary influences is recognised.

With a dominance of farm families providing the agricultural labour force in the 1980s, it is hardly surprising that the recruiting of farmers comes from existing farming families. The agriculture of the 1980s is characterised by a virtual 'closed shop'. The large amount of money now required to set up as an owner-occupier means that only the very wealthy or those with strong family links can enter this way, inheriting much or all of their capital. To enter from a non-farm background as an owner-occupier simply cannot be done using borrowed funds. The profits from farming are insufficient to repay interest charges on whole farm purchases. Even 20 years ago a farm worker might have found it possible to rent a farm, but in recent years entry as a tenant farmer has been much less easy than the proponents of the landlord and tenant systems have suggested. This path effectively has been blocked by the Agriculture (Miscellaneous Provisions) Act of 1976. This has given rights of succession to members of the family of tenant farmers subject to tests of eligibility.

Not all farms, even large ones, are a full-time activity for their occupiers. About one-quarter are run by farmers who have some other forms of earned income, and this usually means some other business or profession. Why these people choose to be part time in agriculture is complex. Some will have inherited the land while they had another occupation which they have not given up. Some will have been forced to seek an additional job because their farm was too small to give a good living. What is clear is that today's part-time farmers are usually not solely dependent on farming for their income or as their most important source of livelihood. Their motives and their farming responses are also unlikely to be identical with those of full-time farmers.

A similar point might also be made about farmers who own their land as opposed to tenants. Owner-occupiers who have held their land for a number of years, when it has risen in value faster than inflation or who have inherited it, are insulated from the changing fortunes of their farm by the large cushion of wealth which their land represents. They are less dependent than tenants on farm profits for their economic position, and might be expected to be willing to try new techniques of production, new crop or stock varieties or machines if they look economically attractive.

One remaining characteristic common to all farmers is that they have little power to influence the prices received for their products, notwithstanding the collective pressure that can be exerted by the National Farmers' Union (NFU). Unlike a car manufacturer or petrol company, which can fix its price (within limits and with an eye to the response of its competitors) the individual farmer is essentially a price-accepter rather than a price-setter. This is because each farm's output of milk or cereals is tiny in comparison with the agriculture's total production. However, technological advance — a new heavier yielding variety or a new machine — which enables him to produce more output, will enable him to increase the money from his sales proportionally. This has enormous implications for the expansion of agriculture and for the uptake of technological advances in farming. But technological advances frequently involve using more inputs. Higher yielding cereal varieties often require heavier applications of fertiliser for their potential to be realised. Equipment such as large tractors or rotary milking parlours (Figure 2.12) are only effective if their high work capacity is fully utilised. Farmers are, therefore, predisposed by their economic environment and technical development to expansion and enlargement, intensification and specialisation. And evidence on the way information travels in agriculture suggests that it is the larger farmer, probably younger and better educated, who will be most willing to take up these developments. But whilst the take-up of technological innovation in the farming industry is different from that among other small firms in the industrial sector because farmers are 'price takers' not 'price setters', the absence of a free market environment is also of great significance. An individual farmer can be confident that even though other farmers may reduce their costs through technological innovation and increase the overall supply of a commodity to the market, he will nevertheless be able to sell his own increased output (should he innovate) because of the assured market which a price support system provides. The whole relationship between technological innovation and commodity supply and demand and its implications for the farmer in an environment of price support compared with that of the free market situation is explored in Figure 2.19. The free market example is particularly instructive as far as the non-innovating farmer is concerned. With prices running at a lower level following the adoption by many of the technological advances, those farmers who had not adopted the new technique would probably find themselves faced with a stark choice; either adopt it in order to stay in production even though product prices are falling or cease production of that particular commodity altogether.

The Pattern of Farming Land Use in the 1980s

The use which agriculture makes of the countryside of England and Wales is not, in most cases, the result of deliberate and co-ordinated planning. Rather it is the result of a myriad set of business decisions taken by individual farmers. In turn, they are responding within the constraints imposed by the soil types, climate, location, other technical limitations and personal prefer-

Figure 2.19: The Economics of Technological Innovation in Agriculture.

1. Supply:
A new technological innovation results in greater output. As a result the supply curve S₁ becomes S₂.

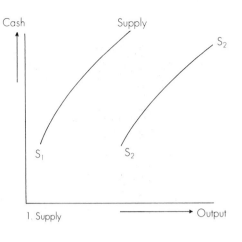

2. Demand:
The demand for foodstuffs in England and Wales is well satisfied. Therefore, if output of an agricultural product rises, consumers will not be ready to purchase much extra and so prices fall. The demand curve D/D is steep as a result.

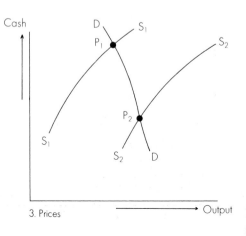

3. Prices:
Supply and demand fix prices if there is no intervention. Supply S₁ leads to Price 1 (P)₁; Supply S₂ leads to Price 2 (P)₂.

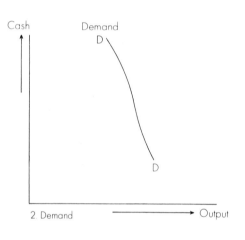

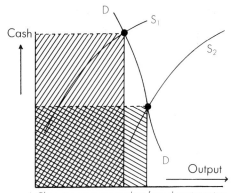

4. Changing revenues resulting from changing prices

Revenue 1

Revenue 2

4. Revenue:
The rectangles below price (that is, price times output) give the amount of revenue. If Revenue 2 is less than Revenue 1, as well it may be, then the new innovation has resulted in less for all farmers. But those farmers who have improved their methods of production have a larger output to sell and can still do well. They may be better off. Non-innovating farmers are worse off since they get a lower price for the former, lower output.
The situation is different with price intervention.

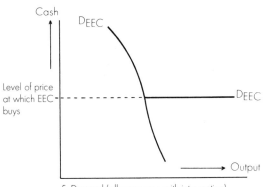

5. Demand (all consumers with intervention)

5. Demand (for all consumers when there is intervention):
At a certain point, which is different for different products and can vary between target and intervention prices, the EEC becomes, in effect, a consumer and buys an infinite amount of the agricultural product, so changing the shape of the demand curve, that is, D_{EEC}.

6. Revenue (from the supported price):
The increased supply S_2 that has resulted from the new innovation does not encounter consumer resistance as it would in a free market. Price is stable for all farmers — those who have adopted the innovation and those who have not. But the innovators earn more in so far as they are able to produce more.
The revenue earned on supply curve S_2 (shaded rectangle) would not have been earned under the former demand situation. Even supply at S_3 will be purchased. There is no reason why supply should not — in theory — go on increasing.

Source: Open University.

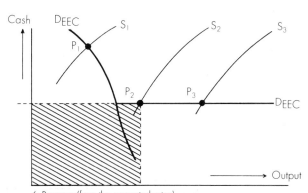

6. Revenue (from the supported price)

Figure 2.20: Land Use by UK
Agriculture. EEC membership
has had its most marked
impact on the crop area under
wheat. In the period
1971/3-1981/2 this increased
by 40 per cent. But perhaps
the most apparent in visual
terms has been the growing of
oil seed rape. Not only is the
bright yellow crop
unmistakable, but before 1973
the cultivation of it was
negligible.

Source: *Annual Review of
Agriculture*, 1983, HMSO,
London.

ences and objectives to signals coming to them predominantly in the form of prices of farm products and costs of inputs. With few exceptions, farmers are free to use their land as they wish. They could try to grow tulips or pineapples if this were their considered choice. Even in those areas which have been designated as being of particular environmental interest (such as National Parks, Areas of Outstanding Natural Beauty, National Nature Reserves and Sites of Special Scientific Interest) which together constitute less than one-fifth of the total area of England and Wales, there is little effective physical or planning control over farming. Owners of land are also normally free to improve its agricultural productivity. New buildings, improved drainage, better fences and hedge removal all can be carried out with few restrictions, and in instances with grant aid. The farmer's freedom to erect concrete, steel and asbestos structures which can have a major visual impact on the country-side is considerable although, depending on the site and location of the build-ing, not absolute. By contrast most non-agricultural developments of a much smaller scale require planning permission.

The present pattern of farming land use (Figure 2.20) is thus a reflection of farmers' response to past economic conditions, and changes in the appearance of the countryside largely can be explained in terms of rational business behaviour as the economic, technical and policy environment of farming

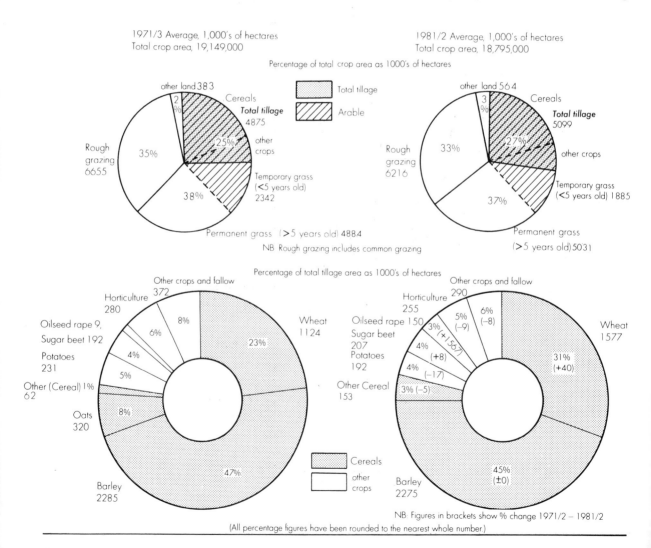

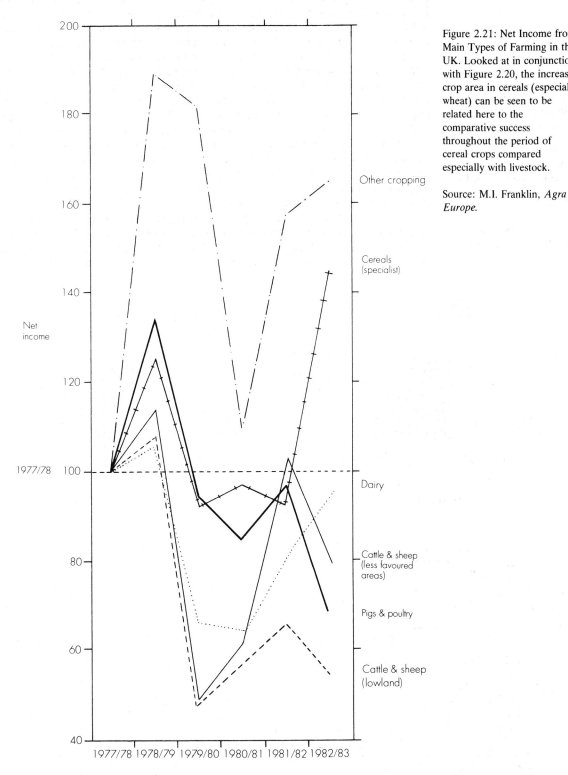

Figure 2.21: Net Income from Main Types of Farming in the UK. Looked at in conjunction with Figure 2.20, the increased crop area in cereals (especially wheat) can be seen to be related here to the comparative success throughout the period of cereal crops compared especially with livestock.

Source: M.I. Franklin, *Agra Europe.*

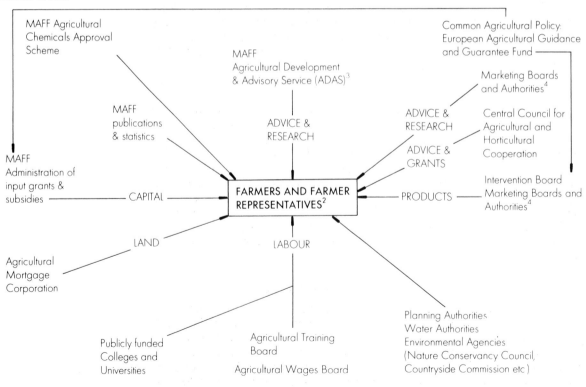

Figure 2.22: Public Institutions of Special Relevance to Agriculture in England and Wales.[1]

Notes:
1. Parallel organisations normally exist in Scotland and Northern Ireland.
2. The farmers' unions (the largest being the National Farmers Union of England and Wales), Country Landowners Association, Tenant Farmers Association, and Small Farmers Association.
3. Divided into Agriculture Service (advisors and experimental husbandry centres), Agricultural Science Service, Land and Water Service, and State Veterinary Service.
4. Marketing boards for wool, hops, milk and potatoes, plus the Apple and Pear Development Council, British Sugar Corporation Ltd, Eggs Authority, Home Grown Cereals Authority, and Meat and Livestock Commission.

Source: B. Hill.

alters. For example, the expansion in cereals acreage which has occurred since England and Wales entered the EEC is closely linked to the higher prices of these crops and the enhanced profitability of specialist cereal cropping farms compared with other enterprise types (Figure 2.21). If changes in the rural environment are occurring in the early 1980s which increasingly are causing concern, it is invariably the signals being given to farmers that help to explain these changes although it is important also to know about the decision-making process at the farm level if the degree of farmer response is to be understood.

At a personal level farmers have a reputation for being proud of their independence and show antagonism towards any attempt by civil servants or others in authority to meddle in agricultural affairs. Any proposal, for example, to control the spread of arable crops to pasture land by forms of planning permission is interpreted as a major infringement of a farmer's rights to do what he wants with his land. Indeed, land use planning is one area of control from which he has been comparatively free. But, paradoxically, at the industry level, agriculture is one of the least free sectors of the economy. As has been indicated previously in this chapter, farming is surrounded by a screen of agricultural policies which, while permitting changes which benefit most farmers, is highly resistant to influences which would result in a diminution of the fortunes of farming as a whole, even if considerable benefits could be demonstrated at the national level such as lower food prices for consumers and fewer surpluses. And to work and monitor these policies there is a formidable array of public institutions covering all stages of production, almost without exception working for the farmers' interest and with a bias towards the expansion of agriculture (see Figure 2.22).

Institutions and Policy in the 1980s

Of the institutions, special mention must be made of the Ministry of Agriculture, Fisheries and Food (MAFF). Despite the tripartite nature of its title, in practice the 'Agriculture' element would seem to be dominant. Not only does farming have a government department largely to itself, but through its Minister it has direct access to Cabinet decision-making. The Minister is identified with the interests of the industry, and the office holder is usually a farmer. Public statements by him and his junior ministers make it abundantly clear that agricultural expansion is, on the whole, welcomed. This is particularly so if expansion arises through increased productivity and if there are imports which can be displaced. Increasing the degree of self-sufficiency is a specific policy objective, despite there being Community surpluses in most temperate products. The functions of MAFF are too many to list in detail, but they extend beyond the implementation of CAP national policy measures to the provision of the free advisory service and the execution and commissioning of research, including censuses and surveys to monitor the industry — a sort of 'National Health and Social Security Service' to the farming industry. Thus, those organisations representing farmers directly, such as the NFU, reasonably could be expected to be in favour of producing more, and therefore the whole machinery of the agricultural industry has been biased towards expansion.

In the early 1980s, farmers continue to benefit from both the price and structural support mechanisms of CAP. In addition, the standard and range of technical advice continues to grow. In addition to the Agricultural Development and Advisory Service (ADAS) there is back up of experimental husbandry farms and research bodies. These include the National Institute for Research in Dairying, the National Institute of Agricultural Botany and the National Institute of Agricultural Engineering. The farmer also benefits from a wide range of government-supported boards and authorities, such as the Milk Marketing Board, the Potato Marketing Board and the British Wool Marketing Board. As well as arranging the orderly marketing of produce, they act frequently as arms of government in implementation of policy measures, such as the dairy regime of the CAP. Furthermore, in those parts of the UK designated officially as Less Favoured Areas farmers receive direct payments in the form of annual grants per animal under Hill Livestock Compensatory Allowances.

Comparing the original aims of agricultural policy contained in Article 39 of the Treaty of Rome with this list of measures employed, shows that there is one major omission. Lying behind many of the measures is a concern over low incomes in farming. Yet the most obvious way of supporting those sectors of the industry where incomes are unacceptably low — by some form of direct income support — is studiously avoided. Instead, the system of product price support is used which benefits most those farmers with high outputs and high incomes. Only in certain regions — hill areas — is any form of direct payment used and even here it is disguised by being termed a Compensatory Payment and based on a per animal basis, rather than the direct need of the farmer and his family.

The Consequences of Support Policies

These elements, and indeed omissions, of agricultural policy in the 1980s have significant consequences compared with what could be expected if no such policy existed. The level of farm production is higher than it would otherwise be because business decisions are taken on the basis of enhanced product prices and subsidised inputs. This implies that England and Wales are more self-sufficient in food, substituting high-cost home produced food for less expensive imported materials. A greater proportion of national resources

Figure 2.23: Modern Combine Harvesters at Work. These combines working together represent the ultimate in the substitution of machinery for labour. The contrast with Figure 2.3 is striking indeed.

Source: MERL.

(especially capital) is retained in agriculture and is thus not available to other sectors of the economy. Because product prices are supported, the most obvious spur to greater efficiency, that is, competition between farms driving down prices with the least efficient being pushed out, has its edge removed.

Distortion occurs both in the pattern of output and of inputs. Some products receive greater amounts of price support than others, giving disproportionate encouragement to expansion. For example, the price of beef is raised above world market prices by a greater extent than is pigmeat, and wheat more than barley. On the input side, capital items receive subsidies and tax concessions whereas hired labour does not. The result is that the balance between labour and capital pushes towards the substitution of machinery and buildings for labour (Figure 2.23).

Perhaps the most insidious impact of the present support system on today's agriculture is through land values. Land prices are jacked up so that the owners of land (primarily owner-occupier farmers but also landlords of tenanted farms) have seen their assets rise in value faster than inflation. Much of this capital gain can be attributed to price support. Rewards in the form of capital gain are attractive in that they are generally taxed at a lower rate than current farm profits. Therefore, farmers attempt to switch income to capital gain by buying land as an investment. They finance such transactions by borrowing, the cost of which can be treated as a deductible expense for income tax calculation. For England and Wales there is evidence that a one per cent rise in product prices is eventually associated with a 10 per cent rise in land prices.

As a result of price support and rising land values, a greater number of farms remains in existence, particularly small ones, than would otherwise be expected. While government schemes have existed until recently to attack the fundamental problem of a surplus of farmers, the incentives to leave have not been sufficient compared with the benefits of remaining (especially for farmers who own their land) provided by the cushioning effect of price support policy.

Social Welfare, Surpluses and the Third World

These results of policy imply a distorted pattern of production and an inefficient (in all meanings of the word) use of resources at the level of the farming industry. But there are related problems which go much deeper. An agricultural support system which raises food prices to consumers may lower the amount they eat, but the burden is not equally shared. Higher prices affect the poorer members of society disproportionately severely, since poorer people spend more of their incomes on food than do the better off. This goes against the general socio-economic policy of assisting the lower earners.

There are also problems of disposing of surplus production, problems which did not normally arise for England and Wales under their former (pre-EEC) system of support but which stem from the CAP practice of intervention buying. The present system results in a transfer of welfare from consumers and taxpayers to farmers who, at least in England and Wales, are generally both wealthier and of higher income than would otherwise be the case, though it is the smaller percentage of the larger lowland farmers that are particularly favoured. If in order to keep prices up, the Community buys and stores farm products, these surpluses have to be disposed of. Simply letting butter mountains or frozen beef rot is not a politically acceptable method. The use of cereals for animal rather than human consumption and wine as a basis for vinegar is less objectionable. Selling at preferential rates to educational establishments or old-age pensioners has limited application. Such sales tend to undermine the market price that the major regime is intended to protect. Giving it away to the inhabitants of poor countries can, unless carefully controlled, disrupt their own agricultures, making matters worse once the gift is exhausted, and such gifts carry the political implication of the dependence of a Third World country upon developed countries.

Substantial quantities, therefore, must be disposed of on the world market with the aid of subsidies. Apart from the political problems of the sort which selling cheap EEC butter to the Russians has run into, criticism has come from those who see the surplus food as 'dumped' on the world market and responsible for pushing word prices down. Lower world prices are to the detriment of exporting countries, especially the Third World food exporters. Subsidised exports of EEC food can disrupt established patterns of trade, with the reaction of the USA being particularly sensitive in this respect. However, the potential damage to Third World exports is not quite so simple, as some poorer countries are substantial food importers and could benefit from lower prices.

After considering the likely effects of agricultural policy on the efficiency of resource allocation, including the size of the industry and its mix of capital to labour, the effect on food prices and problems of dealing with the surpluses produced, the next logical step in assessing the agriculture of the 1980s would be to put figures to these various items. Unfortunately this is largely impossible, mainly because there is no way of knowing precisely what the size or composition of agriculture in the absence of support would be, or what food prices would be. The direct costs of the CAP are known, and one estimate suggests that consumers pay 15 per cent more than they might under a system whereby food could be purchased at world prices. However, the costs in terms of what is forgone by having additional resources tied up in agriculture, the impact on the countryside, the effect on the standards of living of the country and so on, can be only the subject of conjecture.

Agriculture in a Sea of Conflicts

Although the shape of agriculture in England and Wales, and hence the appearance of the countryside and the contribution of farming to rural society, is heavily influenced by the whole range of policies so far discussed, it would be wrong to give the impression that these had been created with agreed and well-conceived objectives. A major feature of the policy environment in which farmers operate in the 1980s is that there is no consistent, thoroughly designed policy, but a mass of measures usually introduced to solve particular problems and only imperfectly integrated with each other. The most glaring example of this though now a matter of recent history, was the co-existence for a time of two schemes for dairy farms. One gave payments to farmers who ceased milk production as a way of reducing the milk surplus. The other gave grants to farmers who wished to re-equip with new buildings which would allow them to expand their herd sizes. Even within a carefully thought out approach some conflicts are likely. For example, high cereal prices, while benefiting arable farmers would harm livestock producers who use cereals as animal feed, unless suitable steps were also taken to raise livestock prices. However, the likelihood of conflicts is greatly amplified by an *ad hoc* approach.

In addition to those policies which could be considered primarily agricultural, farming is affected by measures aimed at the general economy or other sectors of it. For example, monetary policy and interest rates, housing policy, taxation of capital and income, and environmental protection — all these have their impact. Frequently such policies are of great significance to farmers and are not infrequently at variance with agricultural policies.

Perhaps of most current public concern are the contradictory signals sent to farmers by MAFF and another arm of government concerned primarily with the countryside — the Nature Conservancy Council. Not infrequently Sites of Special Scientific Interest designated as such by the Council because they provide a habitat for rare species of flora and fauna, or are of geological or archaeological interest, have been destroyed by agricultural changes. Arguably, these would not have occurred without the grants for 'improvements' available from MAFF and the prices for farm products inflated by support policies. Until recently the Council has relied largely on education and the persuasion of farmers to protect these sites, not strong weapons against the financial incentives of agricultural policy encouraging higher levels of production. Where the Council has negotiated a voluntary management agreement with farmers, under the 1981 Wildlife and Countryside Act, to prevent a detrimental agricultural 'improvement' taking place (Figure 22.4) it has been required to offer compensation. But the size of the annual compensation payments has, of course, been a reflection of the supported price for farm products. This is because the compensation payment relates to the *value* of the forgone production of an 'improved' piece of land, measured at support prices. Further agricultural support necessitates more compensation. Frequently land purchase would appear to have been the only option open. But the Council has only a tiny budget and with land prices reflecting support policies, it has been all but impossible to pursue this course of action effectively.

The result of all this is that farming finds itself in the midst of a sea of conflicts of interest. Examples within the policies of the early 1980s include that between the farmer and the consumer over food prices. High support product prices for farmers conflict with the stated government aim of reasonable food prices for consumers. Greater self-sufficiency in food caused by inflated product prices can reduce trade, particularly harming those countries whose economies may rely on selling their agricultural produce. The inability of West Indian countries to sell cane sugar to the EEC because of the Community's own production of sugar-beet is a case in point. High prices, by encouraging intensive farming and expansion of certain enterprises, for example, cereals, are also contrary to the environmental objectives of retaining pasture land, hedges, easier public access and so on.

On the input side, capital grants for investment in drainage can conflict directly with environmental policies to preserve some areas undrained, while

the advisory and research services generally are directed towards expanding output. There is a difficulty here, however, in disposing of the surplus production that is already occurring.

Figure 2.24: Land Drainage in Progress. Frequently schemes of this kind can improve fields agriculturally without inflicting serious environmental damage. However, in the wetlands of the Somerset Levels and the Halvergate Marshes of Norfolk, the Nature Conservancy Council maintain that such schemes are destroying unique wildlife habitats.

Source: MERL.

There is conflict, too, between fiscal and agricultural policy. Capital taxation tends to break up large concentrations of wealth whereas, at least among small farms, the advice (and economic pressure) is to enlarge farms. Farmers are keenly concerned to arrange their affairs to avoid capital taxation, and frequently they use legal devices of baroque complexity to do so. There are also conflicts of a social nature. Greater security for existing farming families in the form of tax concessions for owner-occupiers or protection for tenants, for example, means that potential new entrants are kept out and farming becomes increasingly a 'closed' industry.

British agriculture is thus the product of a particular balance of conflicts and signals. As will be seen later, it is by no means accepted that this present balance is in the national interest and steps are being taken to effect change.

Grassroots

An NFU Official Talks About Farming in the 1980s

It is my opinion that within the last five years or so, when the conflict between the commercial demands on farming and environmental demands from the general public have come to greater prominence, we have not seen anything particularly radical happening in farming. It is the heightened awareness of what actually has been happening for 25 or 30 years that has made these current issues. Economies of scale have been taking place on farms for some 35 to 40 years so I would tend to say that if you are looking at 1985, nothing very different is happening now or has happened for the last four or five years. But we are in a climate of opinion that has completely changed and, of course, we are seeing attitudes being taken on farms which reflect that. Farmers basically have one of two attitudes to the environment: there is the 'macho' approach, the aggressive 'I'll do anything I want' type of reaction, and the attitude, which I find more acceptable, of farmers trying to develop conservation on their farms. Certainly this latter attitude may derive from the fact that farmers realise politically that they have got to be seen to be undertaking conservation measures if they are to retain the privileges and funding structures which they enjoy at the moment.

I think in any business one has to put first and foremost one's capacity to come out at the end of the year above the level of one's production costs. I would be quite wrong to give the impression that farmers are preoccupied with environmental matters. Now it seems to me that you do not have to look very far into farm management, and I mean husbandry matters, to realise that some environmental matters are tied in with good husbandry and there are many farmers and growers that I know who regard environmental care which they exercise on their farms as being of direct financial benefit to them. If you have to pay the sort of rates you have to for proprietary fertilisers at the moment and you could spread farmyard manure on your land, which is, after all, the traditional and, I suppose, environmentally acceptable way of fertilising land, then you will do it. That is a very simplistic example but I think a valid one.

I think there are many farmers who share the view of the farmer I was talking to recently who said that his father would turn in his grave if he saw the state of his gateposts and fences. I can see what he meant. Now actually that farm to you or I would look perfectly good. Maybe the hedging and ditching was not as immaculate as it would have been 40 years ago or the tiles were not back on the barn with the same degree of promptitude. I wonder if in the future that drive towards a traditional visual appearance of the countryside, which basically means farmland, may not eventually prompt farmers to employ more labour, possibly at the expense of investments in machinery?

I was talking to a farmer last night who was seriously wondering whether some of the investments he had made in machinery, and we are talking about very large investments, should not have been spent on employing more labour because we have seen over the years a steady run-down in employed labour. While we all like the concept of a family farm, unless you have an enormous number of sons and daughters the family farm cannot hold true in the sense of having no employed labour at all. Beyond a certain point in terms of acreage I would like to speculate that you may see a revision of people's attitudes towards employed labour.

I think if farmers lift their heads from the circumstances of their own farms and think about the industry in general terms, the first thing they always say to me is that they are deeply concerned over the imbalance between the livestock and the arable sectors. Now I happen to like reading R.S. Surtees who wrote in the 1840s and 1850s about this relationship and its impact on hunting. One can see from his writing obviously that that sort of situation has applied on other occasions over the last 200 years. One has seen these imbalances and presumably one will get back to where we see a better balance. Many of the problems like stubble burning are caused by a disproportionate weight of cereals being grown compared with what we were used to in the past. The imbalance is caused by the imbalance in the support mechanism, and what is quite interesting in this area is where one has seen the arable acreage increase considerably in recent years, in what has been traditionally sheep country. We have a sheepmeat regime which gives a good return to flock owners. But at the same time when people settle down and look at the books it is obvious that the profitability of cereals still means that land which not only traditionally but also under quite close commercial systems, has been in sheep production is now turned over to arable acreage. This has been brought about only by one thing — the greater return you get for cereals through the price support element of agricultural policy.

A West Country Farmer Talks About Farming in the 1980s

Farmers do get quite a lot of support from the EEC, but it is not totally straightforward. I mean, to sell your crops to intervention, for example, you need to have crops of a certain standard and minimum quantity. You have to offer 100 tons of barley I think, so the big farmer benefits most, you see. And it is this agribusinessman rather than what I call the farmer who gives farming and the CAP a bad name. They spend a lot of money to make a lot of money and don't really care about the countryside.

We could solve the European policy problem, by reducing subsidies on grain, beef and milk by 25 per cent. This would not hurt the small farmer quite so much because he is not laying out so much. Proper farmers would survive anyway, because they know what it is like to be poor.

They are bringing back the subsidy on single suckle herds to try and move people out of milk. But beef simply is not viable anyway because the cost of inputs is so high. It is inefficient in food value too, of course. We are stupid eating beef. We should eat beans. It is bloody daft and wrong. It is really cruel too. I think everyone who eats beef should go and watch the cows being killed first. I know a bloke who goes on about cruelty to dogs, while he chews a mouthful of steak!

The new milk quotas are a bit unfair, though, because they clobber the small farmer again. They will have a bad effect on the environment, too, because they will mean smaller herds, and farmers will have to turn their pasture into arable. You see, they will have fewer cows needing the pasture and they will have to grow their crops to keep their feed prices low. All this means more land being ploughed up, not less.

I think planning control over agriculture is not on really. I mean, who is going to administrate it? What is it they want to control exactly, anyway? Do you really think planners know enough about agriculture to make good decisions? You see, it is back to these agribusinessmen again. You would not need controls if it was not for them. The real farmers, which is most of us really, cannot afford to go around digging hedges out. It is labour intensive for a start.

Hedge removal grants are the same as all grants. It is only the rich ones who can afford to put the money up to get them in the first place. You need time to sit down and read up on them. Most farmers do not have the time, because they are out working all the time.

It is this new lot who sit in their offices with their computers working it all out that cause the problems. They only think about making quick money. It is a bit like the property boom of the early 1970s, and a lot of them came unstuck.

Of course, you could always get a grant for pulling out hedges, but you can now get one for putting them back in. So I suppose the new boys will make more money putting hedges back in, when the bottom drops out of the corn subsidies. The big bloke always wins.

These big landowners and farmers have also pushed the small farmer out with exorbitant rents. There are a lot of institutions and other Europeans buying land because it is cheap here, especially land in East Anglia. This is not doing traditional farming any good.

But I cannot really see how anyone is going to enter the farming industry as an owner-occupier, for one simple reason — if you could afford to, you would not have to!

In terms of the landlord-tenant thing, though, there is a trend now for landlords talking more to tenants. Round here, one landlord has actually reduced his rents this year, because he thinks they are too high. You see I think landlords know what is going on in farming. It is probably the Country Landowners' Association. They know more about what is going on than the National Farmers' Union.

The worst culprits on rents are the county councils. The rents on their holdings are higher than anyone else's around here, by some 25 per cent. They are astronomical. Talk about counties being supposed to start people off in farming — they are finishing them! Of course, starting in farming is made worse by the fact you can only really start in milk because of the initial outlay. Of course, the Common Market is clobbering milk the hardest. That keeps people out of farming.

I do not really think, in Europe, the Farmers' Union is very strong. The NFU is always going on about what it has done in the past, about how it created the Milk Marketing Board. But that was 40 years ago, wasn't it? They have not done much since, because they do not use their access to government very well. Still, most of the government are farmers anyway, particularly in the Lords. What is it? Tories go into politics because they are farmers; and the Labour do it the other way round? It all ends up the same.

You see the EEC policy is wrong for Britain, because we are so different from the rest of Europe; more capital, less labour, larger farms; totally different. It is the French that will dictate EEC policy because so many of their population are in farming, and it is a vote winning issue over there.

Actions to Steer Change

A Challenge to Basic Beliefs

In the early 1980s a mounting body of criticism has emerged which challenges the basic assumptions about farming in England and Wales and long-held public attitudes towards it. For much of the post-war period agricultural policy has been founded on certain beliefs about reality. Some of these may have been so obviously true at the time that the policy was designed that there was little point in questioning them. But the danger of continuing acceptance of these beliefs is that they become so embedded in the system of support that the reason for their very existence is lost sight of. Since the basic framework of policy was set by the 1947 Agriculture Act, agriculture has changed greatly and the economic and technical environment in which it now exists is very different from conditions of post-war recovery. In some ways entry to the CAP in 1973 was a step backwards in that by joining a Community whose farming industries were predominantly small-scale and associated with major social problems, the assumptions were once more buried. Although a number of serious academic criticisms of policy appeared in the 1970s, it is only in this decade that well publicised challenges have been made (most notably in books by Shoard, Body, Bowers and Cheshire) which have forced policy makers to acknowledge the existence of many such assumptions although they are as yet far from making any major revisions in the direction of policy.

The basic and rarely challenged belief that underpins existing policy is that, firstly, there is a farm income problem which requires remedies. This can be the result of instability of income from year to year caused primarily by weather; or low incomes resulting in poverty among some sizes or types of farm; or low standards of living and poor returns in farming compared with those earned in other industries. The second common belief is that it is desirable to increase the degree of self-sufficiency in home food supply by encouraging expansion of domestic farming. The reasons put forward for this are the increased security of supply it is believed to bring, and the benefits which accrue. Since joining the EEC there is also some budgetary advantage from importing less from non-Community members. The third belief is that the development of agriculture and the general economy is best served by technical advances which result in more capital being invested in farming in the form of machinery, buildings and drainage. Lastly, it is tacitly assumed, at least among agriculturalists, that farming is the most important user of the countryside, so that changes in land use resulting from price policies (such as the growth in cereals area on land of only moderate suitability) should not be restricted. Where conflicts of interest occur, in the case of land drainage between farmers and conservationists, the agricultural interest is naturally the more important on the grounds of food supply and people's livelihoods.

Almost all these assumptions are now under attack. Only the desirability of imparting a degree of stability to farm incomes remains unchallenged, although even this is viewed more in terms of product price stability than income stabilisation. Polemicists such as Body or Shoard merely serve to focus arguments which are generally in circulation, even though in the eyes of some observers, they may weaken their case by overstatement. However, the critics have asked what are the grounds for thinking that incomes are unacceptably low in agriculture, especially since the strength of the evidence seems to suggest that some of the larger lowland farmers are among the wealthiest members of society? If there are pockets of genuine poverty, is a separate body of institutions really justified or should farmers be encouraged to use the welfare mechanisms open to society in general? Where rural poverty exists, it is much more likely to be among hired farm workers, 11 per cent of whom were on Family Income Supplement in 1983, and people outside of agriculture altogether whose incomes are not indirectly affected by the prosperity of agricultural support.

A Revision of the Support Mechanism

The 1980s have also seen the emergence of another well-defined group of critics who wish to affect change. Their attack has been made on a rather more specific front — that of the methods used to support agriculture in England and Wales. Although the mechanisms by which farm incomes are supported has been seen for a long time to be inappropriate, dissatisfaction is now plainly apparent. The major mechanism, product price support, obviously distributes its benefits in proportion to the volume of output, so it is the large output/large area farmer who benefits most even though he is the least likely to qualify in terms of poverty. Similar arguments apply to the subsidisation of inputs such as capital. Large farmers are in a better position to take advantage of such schemes and the taxation system encourages them to invest with their businesses. The present system largely misses those in need but helps those who are already well-off.

As well as being inappropriate as a means of attacking low agricultural incomes, product price support has the additional disadvantage of stimulating output with its attendant detrimental impacts on the environment. In many cases this results in surplus production which has had to be stored, destroyed, sold outside the protected area or given away. In the absence of price support it would soon become apparent that the value of this additional output in terms of how much consumers would be willing to pay for it is very low. The most obvious way to prevent excess production is to allow its price to fall. Yet this simple remedy is effectively blocked by the fact that product prices are used as the method of supporting farm incomes. A change in the present system would involve a more discriminatory approach to incomes, probably with some form of direct income supplement to needy farmers. Such proposals are, not unnaturally, fiercely opposed by the farmers' lobby since the better-off farmers would suffer and it is this group who are vocal in pressure groups such as the NFU. The cost of agricultural policy would be more evident to taxpayers, and embarrassing to farmers. The level of agricultural production might well decline, but almost certainly land values would fall. While farmers are keen to deny the relevance of rising land prices, they are even more eager to predict the catastrophes to be expected from such a fall, a prediction which would seem unlikely in the light of the strong equity position of most farmers.

There is one major reason why action to steer agricultural support away from product prices and towards direct income support can have only a slow effect. It is because agricultural policy in England and Wales must be integrated in major matters with those in the rest of the EEC. Not only is there the problem of many more small farmers, especially in France, Italy and Germany, which would impose a sizeable administrative burden, but unlike England and Wales where virtually all farmers keep accounts, this is not the case in other Community countries (and especially those with the most severe small farm problems). Accounting would seem to be a prerequisite for any more direct approach to the income problem. Thus, although, the present agricultural support system may be regarded at home as unsatisfactory, reform can be only partial until either the CAP becomes more fragmented and nationalised, or until structural change (with the reduction of small farm numbers) and the spread of accountancy practice takes place throughout the EEC. Financial crises in the budget of the European Community, as experienced in 1983 and 1984, may accelerate the acceptance of a more direct approach to farm income problems.

If major reform is likely to be slow, there are still a number of changes which are occurring or which are likely to occur in England and Wales that could have a significant impact for change in the countryside. Principal among these are the development of part-time farming, legislation on land tenure and direct efforts to control the pattern of farming in certain areas of special environmental interest.

Encouragement of Part-time Farming

Part-time farming is a world-wide phenomenon and in those developed countries where data are available it appears to be growing. In England and Wales the limited evidence available suggests that here too it is on the increase. At present probably about one-quarter of farm households in the UK have another source of earned income. The official attitude towards part-time farmers has been until recently to ignore them. In terms of agricultural output they have been assumed insignificant and certain grant schemes have sought to exclude them. However, from a variety of viewpoints their role has become increasingly recognised, and an element of official encouragement has now been added to those pressures which, independently, are causing them to become more numerous. By having another source of livelihood the family is less dependent on the farm.

In practice most part-time farmers do not rely solely on the farm for their main source of income which may involve on-farm activity such as letting accommodation to tourists, but more commonly some other outside business venture or profession. The suggestion is that part-time farming enables more small farms to stay in existence, with the benefits of retaining people in the countryside who are still connected with farming. Since the main interest of the part-time farmer may lie in the direction of living on a farm rather than farming for profit, environmental changes such as field enlargement and hedge removal may be reduced. However, at a time when entry to farming is difficult, the problem may be eased if the would-be entrant is prepared to be part time and thus may take advantage of holdings which would not be viable if they provided the only means of support.

Because the drive to intensify land use may be abated on small part-time farms there is even the suggestion that a move towards more part-time farming may help relieve the problem of agricultural surpluses, although because of their generally small size this impact on total supply is likely to be only small. Part-time farming is thus more important to the social aspects of the rural community and appearance of the countryside than to food supply. The MAFF now offers the services of its advisers to such farmers and they can help in this respect. But growth of part-time farming is likely to be affected more by external factors, principally the buoyancy of the rest of the economy. Rather than being viewed as a transitional state for people leaving or entering agriculture, part-time farming increasingly is being accepted as a stable combination of activities, and as an important component of farming in England and Wales.

Land Mobility and Entry to Farming

The most specific action being taken to steer change in the early 1980s is, however, of modest dimensions compared with those so far discussed. It attempts merely to improve the mobility of land between farmers or would-be farmers by removing the ossifying effects of existing legislation on land tenure. The 1948 Agricultural Holdings Act gave lifelong security of occupation to tenants and established a rent arbitration formula (later modified) which had the effect of keeping rents low and maintaining a premium for land with vacant possession. These conditions encouraged landlords to sell, especially to sitting tenants, and reduced the number of farms available for re-letting. It made entry to farming for persons of limited wealth less easy and diminished the ease with which farm size could be adjusted to allow for technological change or to match the individual farmer's evolving needs. Owner-occupiers, who might have wished to reduce their scale of activity as old age approached, were similarly discouraged from letting off part of their land since they could not regain possession from the tenant.

This situation deteriorated in 1976 when the Agriculture (Miscellaneous Provisions) Act allowed members of a tenant farmer's family to claim a new tenancy on his or her death, subject to tests of eligibility and suitability. In effect this meant that a landlord could lose possession of his land for three generations. This legislation further reduced the farms available for re-letting. Those which did become vacant (because the tenant had no eligible and suitable successor) tended to be sold by the landlord, farmed directly by him or in partnerships or in other legal arrangements which circumvented the constraints of the legislation.

The optimal degree of security of tenure required on the one hand to encourage efficient farming, and on the other to give the turnover of farms necessary for an adequate supply of land coming newly available for renting by able tenants, is a matter of conjecture. It is evident, however, that as a result of the 1976 legislation, the number of new lettings made annually has shrunk and even more the area of tenanted land has continued to decline. Paradoxically, some of the new partnership-type arrangements involving landlords may enable a few talented people without much capital to enter farming more easily than as traditional tenants.

However, the main action to steer change in this area and contained in a Bill which came before Parliament in 1984 proposes principally to remove the succession rights for new tenants, though the position of current tenants is not altered. A revised rent arbitration formula is also proposed. To improve land mobility and increase the area available for renting, there is also the suggestion of permitting fixed-term (as opposed to life-long) tenancies. While fixed-term leases (say 10 years or 20 years) for new letting would seem to provide an adequate degree of security for tenant farmers, any attempt to impose these on existing tenancies would naturally be opposed by the farming lobby. Both the succession and fixed-term lease measures would thus take very long to have much effect on land mobility. Both receive support on the grounds of equity in that they make entry by able persons from non-farming backgrounds easier. This, however, seems unlikely to be so in practice since the financial barrier to those without substantial funds would still be too high and most benefit would seem to accrue to existing farmers who wished to enlarge or contract their areas.

More Effective Control of the Environment

The impact of agriculture on the environment provides a further dimension to the calls for a reform of agricultural policy in the 1980s. Whilst new tenure legislation is of direct relevance to a small number of people actively concerned with farming and of no immediate concern of the rest of society, the protection of the visual and ecological characteristics of the countryside, particularly in high quality environmental areas such as National Parks and Sites of Special Scientific Interest may affect few farmers but is of benefit to the whole of society. The environmental lobbyists have become increasingly dissatisfied at the ability of existing measures to protect such areas against the expansion of agricultural output by intensive methods promoted by agricultural policy. Such encouragement appears to some to be particularly anti-social where products are already in surplus and overproduction is being disposed of at further cost. Once again legislation has been passed to counter changes in the countryside occurring at least in part as a result of the general productionist stance of agricultural policy.

The 1981 Wildlife and Countryside Act has created what appears to be improved protection for Sites of Special Scientific Interest (as designated by the Nature Conservancy Council). The system of compensation to farmers for leaving sites unimproved (for example, not draining valued wetland habitats) is supposed to be made more effective by the availability of monies put aside for this purpose. But one major danger would appear to be that the sum is inadequate, coming as it does from the NCC rather from the Ministry of Agriculture. As a result either compensation payments will have to be suspended or the number of agreements reached on Sites will have to be reduced, or both. A similar compensatory system applies in the National Parks for forgoing farming improvements which would elsewhere normally receive grant aid (for example, the ploughing of moorland). However, the concentration of conservation on a relatively small proportion of the total land area has produced what some consider to be a most unsatisfactory situation for the vast majority of the 'unprotected' countryside. This is particularly true in the lowlands where economic incentives are most likely to affect changes and which are the most accessible to large populations. Rather than allow a greater polarisation into 'protected' and 'unprotected' areas, there is a growing body of opinion which wishes to extend a continuous conservation ethic to the use of all agricultural land (see Colour Plate 1).

Indeed, in the 1980s, conservationists are joining with other critics to increase the 'politicisation' of agriculture's impact on the environment. Three main alternative strategies are proposed for agriculture in this respect. Many conservationists support the removal of or reduction in both structural and price support measures for agriculture on the assumption that this would restore a less intensive system of farming which would be more in accord with environmental goals. Others are keen to promote persuasion and demonstration to enhance a conservation awareness among farmers. To this end, the Countryside Commission has been running a Demonstration Farms Project for a number of years and a majority of counties in England and Wales have their own Farming and Wildlife Advisory Groups. A third group of conservationists would favour direct planning controls over agriculture which would cover both buildings and the area under cultivation.

However, it is by no means evident that these changes would guarantee the desired outcome, a point that is considered more fully in Chapter 4. Perhaps a complete rethinking of the objectives of rural (rather than just agricultural) policy is what is required which may involve more, not less, public expenditure, but distributed in a very different way. This point is taken up again in the final chapter of this book.

Who Benefits, Who Loses?

The development of agricultural policy and farming systems in England and Wales has provided substantial benefits to a number of people and organisations but has placed a considerable burden on others.

The food consumer before entry into the EEC, for example, enjoyed 'cheap' food subsidised directly by exchequer (deficiency) payments to the farmer. This system was progressive to the extent that exchequer revenues themselves were generated to a large extent through a progressive income tax: the rich paid more proportionally for cheap food than the poor. On joining the EEC the consumer has lost out. Not only does the burden of inflated farm prices now fall directly on the consumer, but, since poorer families spend a larger proportion of their total incomes on food than the wealthy, the burden falls relatively more on them. The system is now regressive. Further, this transition from cheap to 'expensive' food caused a sufficient rise in food prices on accession to the EEC to provide one of the main 'fuels' to the price inflation of the mid-1970s.

As some compensation for this consumer burden, it can be legitimately claimed that the Common Agricultural Policy does ensure relatively stable levels of food output at reasonably stable, albeit inflated, prices.

Within the farming community itself, farm policy has had differential effects. Agricultural workers' jobs have been lost wholesale in the face of massive capital substitution for labour aided by capital grants for farm structural improvement. The farm workers remaining, though, can lay some claim to enhanced wages as a result, not least from their own higher productivity. However, their wages still lag a long way behind those of manufacturing industry. Farmers, too, have encountered varying impacts. The large cereal products of the lowlands have become wealthy in the face of preferential price support for their output. Differential levels of subsidy for agricultural products have also led to increasing degrees of specialisation and monoculture, all of which have been encouraged by ADAS, perhaps the most comprehensive — and to the farmer, cheapest — industrial advice service in the world.

The upland livestock farmer on the other hand has had less of a beneficial experience. Price support measures have not favoured his enterprises relatively and as a more remote traditional farmer, he has tended to make less use of structural support opportunities and advisory services. Support measures such as the Farm Modernisation and Less Favoured Areas Directives, though, have allowed him to stay in business, where otherwise he might have been forced out by economic circumstances.

In landownership terms, both the owner-occupier and the absentee landlord have had a bonanza, particularly in lowland England and Wales. Inevitably, the huge levels of support going into agricultural production have inflated agricultural land prices. This has been accentuated by two further factors: grant aid for land purchase in farm amalgamation schemes and tax 'roll over' provisions for farmers selling and then repurchasing agricultural land. Thus, land for the existing farm landowner not only has an inflated price but is in a sense, subsidised. This serves to concentrate the ownership of agricultural land, and thus virtually eliminates the possibility of a non-inherited career as an owner-occupier.

If, on balance, farmers have done well out of post-war policy for agriculture, the wider rural community has not. Farm policy — apart from the brief existence of the North Pennines Rural Development Board under the 1967 Agriculture Act — has paid very little heed indeed to the non-agricultural rural population. The increasing affluence of farmers has developed side by side in many parts of England and Wales, with increasing rural deprivation — low incomes, few job opportunities, poor housing and so on. Farm policy has generated dual standards of affluence in many rural areas.

The agricultural support industries, on the other hand, have fared better than this. The thrust of post-war policy towards capital substitution has ensured a secure future for machinery, fertiliser and pesticide producers (and indeed the machinery maintenance sector). Large food processing industries too, particularly in dairy products, have enjoyed financial input into the conversion of milk into butter, cheeses and dried milk. More recently, the endemic food surpluses generated by CAP have provided a stable base for the food storage industry. But all this has taken place in a European economy in which, through public policy, the agricultural sector is characterised by over-capitalisation at the same time as the manufacturing sector is undercapitalised.

At a wider level, countries both within the EEC and outside have felt the influence of CAP. Within Europe, the absence of European monetary union has meant that countries with strong currencies have fared better in the annual fixing of commodity prices than those with weaker currencies. This still pertains, despite the moderating influences of the European Unit of Account and the 'green pound'. At an extreme, all countries within the EEC must live with the possibility of European 'bankruptcy' in the absence of any substantial agricultural policy reform. Undoubtedly, the CAP does improve the balance of payments of each member state but, it may be postulated, at too great a cost.

Outside the EEC, agricultural exporting countries suffer in two main ways unless they have a special arrangement with the Community. Firstly, CAP import restrictions at prices below the target price deprive them of competing in the European food market, and cause a substitution of European produce for that of those countries. Secondly, through export refunds, the EEC can subsidise the 'dumping' of European food surpluses on other countries at artificially low prices. This has the effect of precipitating unfair international trade and, except in years of European shortage, depressing world prices.

Since most industrial economies have similar types of agricultural protection, it is the poorer third world countries whose economies are more dependent on agriculture, that suffer most from this type of protectionism. To say the least, the detrimental nature of these effects does not engender political harmony at an international level.

From the point of view of other sectional interests agricultural policy also places a burden on the recreationist who in many parts of the country has suffered a loss of access to agricultural land and often experiences a loss of visual amenity as a result of agricultural landscape change. The conservationist, too, is witnessing a deterioration in the physical landscape — loss of hedgerows, hedgerow trees, moorland and wetland and so on as well as a reduction in species diversity of both fauna and flora — as a result of agricultural capitalisation particularly in lowland Britain.

Figure 2.25: 'You heard these rumours about a new process for making fertiliser out of EEC directives?'

Source: *Punch.*

3
Containing Settlements
SNAPSHOTS

To do nothing but revile those who spoil the country with their nauseous little buildings, or merely to laugh darkly at their pathetic failure to achieve an imagined rusticity, is beautifully easy. But it is unjust, cynical and lazy — as though you were to curse a stricken family because in flying from the burning home it trespassed over your lawns and flower-beds.

What we must try to do is both to put out the fire — that is to make town life not merely tolerable but attractive — and also to show how one may in very truth genuinely escape to and live in real country without offence and without thereby trampling underfoot and annihilating the very things that are so justly desired and so valiantly sought.

Let us mitigate the shameful necessity for this diffusion of living and, having brought the thing within manageable bounds, let us so arrange things, so revise our laws and by-laws and public opinion, that the homes of the people are no longer disfiguring eruptions on the face of the land, but a welcome and becoming adornment as they were in the days when England was beautiful because of them.
Clough Williams-Ellis (1928), England and the Octopus, Portmeirion, Penrhyndeudraeth.

Particular pieces of unfortunate development get publicity but no one hears of the unsatisfactory projects for development which are being day to day successfully prevented by planning authorities or transformed under their influence and made more attractive.
Walter Elliot (July 1938) Minister of Health, in correspondence with a Member of Parliament, Public Record Office, HLG52, 544).

The Town and Country Planning Act rightly includes the statutory powers to deal with both cases of broad divisions of the land under one instrument. But there should be no attempt at a fusion or confusion between the two: town should be town, and country country; urban and rural can never be interchangeable adjectives. If this polarity is grasped there should be no danger.
Patrick Abercrombie (1943), Town and Country Planning, Oxford University Press.

I am convinced that for the well-being of our people, and for the preservation of the countryside, we have a clear duty to do all we can to prevent the further unrestricted sprawl of the great cities.
Duncan Sandys (26 April 1955), Parliamentary Statement of Intention to introduce Green Belt circular.

There should be clear distinction between town and country. Towns should be towns, with people living in terraces or in blocks of flats. Green Belts should be maintained to contain urban development. I would deplore any tendency on the part of the present Government to provide land for housing by nibbling away Green Belts.
Lord Molson (4 November 1963). Proceedings 'The Countryside in 1970, Conservation Working Party'

The landscape of our city fringes, whether Green Belt, Grey Belt or no belt at all, is depressingly similar everywhere — an incoherent limbo which is our particular twentieth century contribution to the scenery of the world. It is a landscape of mutual destruction by two incompatible environments, and the sickness infects them both: cities invade the countryside with eyesores, while to travellers from city centres the opening landscape reveals nasty ugliness.
Nan Fairbrother (1972), New Lives, New Landscapes, Penguin Books, Harmondsworth.

In its objectives and methods the orientation of the physical planning system has been overwhelmingly urban in emphasis. In theory as well as in practice rural planning has been preoccupied with the question of where and where not to build. In the circumstances of the 1940s there was ample justification for this view: the planners approach, like the national outlook was inevitably conditioned by the pre- and immediately post-war experience. The role of planners in the countryside has thus been one of protection against urban developments, but in this their efforts have undoubtedly been successful. The expansion of agriculture after 1947 on land safeguarded from urban uses, allowed British farmers to increase their contribution to the total home food market to above fifty per cent. The countryside of today would certainly be less extensive, less beautiful and probably less accessible if building development had been less rigidly controlled.
Joan Davidson and Gerald Wibberley (1977), Planning and the Rural Environment, *Pergamon Press, Oxford.*

British land use planning is a system of response to change, a system of guidance and regulation of a predominantly private development market; and, above all, it is a political system. . . . The policies which are made between competing alternatives for development are the product of a variety of largely unregulated influences and pressures, some of them powerful, others weak.
Planning law sets the battle lines for the resolution of conflict over land use between the interests of private property and the prevailing 'public' or 'community' interest. It is neither a static nor a neutral system of rules and the balance which it sets between private and public interest, and between the different institutions representing the public interest, is constantly changing.
M. Grant (1982), Urban Planning Law, *Sweet and Maxwell, London.*

Ministers show no signs of withdrawing their threats against the Green Belts. A draft circular last summer proposed opening more of these vital, if not always lovely, landscapes to building. The Environment Secretary has sought to reassure us with a speech containing that notorious Whitehall weasel-word 'balance'. The Council for the Protection of Rural England rightly took the issue to a meeting at the Conservative Party conference at Blackpool. Will their constituents permit Conservative MPs for the Green Belts to abet destruction of British planning's most prized triumph?
Christopher Hall (1984), The Countryman, *Burford, Oxfordshire.*

Perspectives on Containment: Town and Country

So far the countryside has been considered from the standpoint of the farmer and how he can maximise output from the countryside. At the same time the effects that such efforts have had upon the landscape and social fabric have been considered. Whether the countryside is considered in this way, primarily as an agricultural resource, or in terms of one of its many other functions, it may be of some importance to maintain that stock of land that makes up the countryside in such a way that it is not threatened by urban development. This question of containing settlements provides the basis for this chapter. In establishing an overall perspective in this context, it is unnecessary, as in the previous chapter, to go back to the beginning of the nineteenth century. A further 50 years had elapsed before it was possible to talk of England and Wales as both a truly industrialised and an urbanised society. The need to control urban growth was not given serious attention until that time.

Some Historical Relationships

Throughout history, urban centres have exercised an influence over the countryside, out of all proportion to their geographical extent and population. They have provided a market for foodstuffs and raw materials, and supplied their rural population with imported and manufactured goods. Towns have attracted rural migrants, and acted as a focus for social, cultural and religious activities and as centres of innovation. The relationship, however, has always been a dynamic one — closely reflecting what was happening within the towns and the countryside. Shifts in economic activity and general well-being have affected the intricate hierarchy of urban centres and the degree to which rural settlement might be nucleated or dispersed, expanding or contracting.

Writers in the early nineteenth century were increasingly conscious of the effects of urbanisation. In 1843, an author of numerous religious tracts, Robert Vaughan, produced a book with the title 'The Age of Great Cities'. On the premise that 'the world has never been so covered with cities ... and society generally has never been so leavened with the spirit natural to cities', he assessed the effects of city life on popular intelligence, morals and religion.

Commentators directed most attention to London, 'the Metropolis of England, at once the Seat of Government and the greatest Emporium in the known world'. One in ten Englishmen lived in London by the nineteenth century. By its sheer size, London suggested a new kind of society but, as Raymond Williams had emphasised, it also reflected the social reality of the nation as a whole. It was the most astonishing creation of agrarian and mercantilist capitalism. Also by the nineteenth century, a quite different sort of town was beginning to emerge, namely, the industrial town of the north of England, based on a small range of manufacturing activities. Bradford grew by 65 per cent between 1821 and 1841, and Manchester, Leeds and Sheffield by over 40 per cent (London expanded by only 20 per cent). It was not simply a matter of numbers. These northern cities were much more obviously under the physical, economic and social dominance of the workplace — the mills and engines.

Urban Expansion: 1851 to 1914

The period 1851 to 1914 has often been cited as the time of most obvious change in the town/countryside relationship. The population of England and Wales doubled, living standards almost doubled, industrial output quadrupled, and the number of people living in towns trebled. England and Wales became an increasingly industrialised and urban society. Over half the towns with populations of over 50,000 were situated on or near coalfields. The impact of these national trends on individual families and communities could vary widely. As J.B. Priestley later wrote, Bradford had

the good fortune to be on the edge of some of the most enchanting country in England. A sharp walk of less than an hour from more than one tram terminus will bring you to the moors, wild virgin highland, and every mill and warehouse will be out of sight and the whole city forgotten (see Figure 3.1).

The significance of these tramps across the moorland was enormous and in his *English Journey*, Priestley recalled:

however small and dark your office or warehouse was, somewhere inside your head the high moors were glowing, the curlews were crying, and there blew a wind as salty as if it came straight from the middle of the Atlantic. That is why we did not care very much if our city had no charm, for it was simply a place to go and work in, until it was time to set out for Wharfedale or Wensleydale again.

A conscious effort was required in order to preserve the open spaces around many towns. At a time when the commons around London were assuming great importance for recreation, they were also threatened by enclosure for building development or more intensive forms of farming (see Figure 3.2).

A Commons Preservation Society was formed in the 1860s. As a voluntary body, it lacked both the locus and resources to embark on such campaigns as that needed to save Epping Forest from further physical enclosure. The corporation of London had both, and the founder and chairman of the Society, Lord Eversley, persuaded the corporation to bring a suit, challenging the legality of the enclosures made. Judgement was given in favour of the corporation, and, in 1878, the corporation was empowered to buy out the lords of the manor. It became responsible for controlling and managing the area in perpetuity for public recreation and enjoyment. The actions of the corporation highlighted the mixed motives that often lay behind interventions in the use and management of land. Not only was the preservation of Epping Forest a popular act in itself, but it helped to demonstrate the importance of the corporation at a time of mounting demands for its abolition in favour of a single form of municipal government in London.

Discussions over the future government of London and towns generally reflected both their increasing size, and the far-reaching changes in the way they functioned. An obvious manifestation of change was the installation of

Figure 3.1: A Northern Woollen Town Viewed from the Nearby Countryside, 1890. Huddersfield, like most of these northern industrial towns, was characterised by its easy access to the surrounding moors and fells.

Source: Huddersfield Public Library.

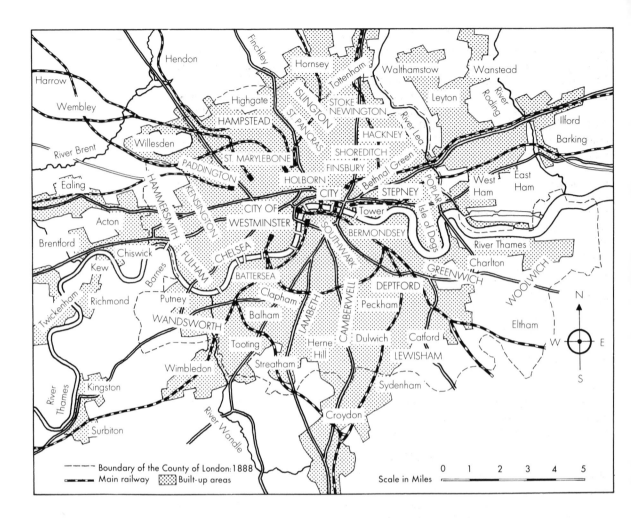

Figure 3.2: London in 1888. The urbanised area had already overrun the county of London boundary at this time. Formerly separate villages such as Highgate and Hampstead were now part of the metropolitan area, though Harrow, Wembley and Hendon st ll maintained their independent existence.

Source: C. Hibbert (1969), *London; the Biography of a City*, Longmans, London.

an explicitly urban system of sanitation. Whereas previously, towns were made up of private plots, each with its well and privy, now an integrated system of water-supply and waste-disposal was available. Networks of small diameter, mass-produced piping brought fresh water increasingly long distances to the urban consumer, and another network acted as a self-cleansing system of sewage removal for the entire urban community. Such innovations enhanced the sense of urban corporateness, and had both direct and indirect repercussions for town and country. As towns became healthier, their population was sustained by natural increase, as well as by immigration. Towns became more densely populated, expanding outwards into the neighbouring countryside. Among the less direct effects of this were the construction of reservoirs and acquisition of rural land for sewage works. By 1900, one of the drainage boards in Birmingham required an additional acre of land per week to keep pace with the city's sewage outfall.

If the construction of urban water and sewage systems epitomises the dynamism of the Victorian years, the increased role of horse transport indicates how such terms as 'urban revolution' may be too simplistic in describing what was really happening to the towns and countryside. In a period of bustle, smoke and modernity, horses had never been so important in the economy. Without them, the railways could not have functioned. At the large urban termini, stabling occupied as much land as locomotive sheds. The amount of horse-drawn traffic did not decline until the early years of the present century.

Between the Wars

By the inter-war years, almost half the population of England lived in the built-up areas of London, south-east Lancashire, Merseyside, the west Midlands, west Yorkshire, and Tyneside. Of these, over half lived in the London area. Over four million houses were built in the inter-war period, representing about a third of the total number when war broke out again in 1939. Whilst such statistics could be gleaned from the decennial population census and the annual reports of government departments, most people, whether in town or country, continued to rely for their knowledge of the other upon firsthand impressions and anecdotal evidence. Friends and relations, the newspaper accounts and advertisements, the film newsreel, and the occasional outings, had an important part to play in conveying a sense of what was happening in both the towns and the countryside. But many of the factors that promoted these changes in population distribution and land use were themselves responsible for enabling people to see these changes at first hand. The mass-produced, cheaper bicycles of the late 1890s made town and country people alike more mobile as the Edwardian Mr Polly discovered when he 'cast a strategical eye' over Chertsey or Weybridge in the novel by H.G. Wells. Of perhaps even greater significance was the extension of rural bus services, and the increasing availability of the motor cycle and motor car, during the inter-war years. Not only was it easier to live further from the place of work, but new horizons were opened up for the sightseer and holiday maker. No longer was the tripper to the Lincolnshire coast confined to Skegness, Mablethorpe or Cleethorpes — the full length of the Sandhills was opened up, as was demonstrated by the appearance of car-parks, and of weekend and holiday 'homes'. Whether attracted or repelled by what they saw taking place in the changing relationship between town and country, the generation of the inter-war years were better informed than any previously.

Contradictory Trends

Not all visitors to the town or the countryside were content to return to their respective homes. In the view of some observers, the daily bus service pushed many villages still further 'to the edge of destruction by draining off the young people'. The young especially demanded the labour-saving gadgets about the home, the greater variety of food and clothing, and access to the cinema, which they associated with town life. Conversely, some of the more enterprising urban families sought a home in the countryside. A planning text of 1941 commented on how some had 'gone to live in the depths of Essex, where they could indulge their primitive inclinations and find freedom from urban restraint'. Whether such commentaries were exaggerated or not, a paradoxical situation was arising in the first half of the twentieth century, whereby increasing numbers of townspeople sought a home in the countryside, whilst many rural families were leaving in search of a better life in the towns and cities.

One response to these contradictory trends was to create conditions whereby an urban way of life could be enjoyed in what many perceived to be a rural setting. From the early 1900s onwards, books and papers began to appear on how this might be achieved. Although living standards were about as high as anywhere in the world, very little thought had been given to the 'dreariness and sheer ugliness' of urban life. In a seminal work of 1909, the architect and surveyor, Raymond Unwin, wrote of how 'the amenities of life' had been neglected. Endless brick terraces looking out on dreary streets and squalid backyards, were 'not really homes for people'. There had to be 'the unifying touch of art which would give completeness and increase their value tenfold; there is needed just that imaginative treatment which would transform the whole'. The obvious attributes of the countryside, grass and tree-foliage, and winding lanes and variety of housing styles, were an important part of that treatment.

Drawing on his experience in Birmingham, and more generally in Britain and Germany, a businessman and councillor, J.S. Nettlefold, gave further publicity to the concept of town planning by defining its main objective as enabling 'all classes of the community to live and work in decent surroundings so that they may be fit for their work and able to enjoy life in a rational manner'. The aim was to empty the slums into the countryside where there was plenty of room for good, cheap houses and for allotments, playgrounds and playing fields. The individual housebuilder and the community at large stood to benefit from the greater cost-effectiveness of planning. Five years previously, in 1909, local authorities had been given discretionary powers, under the Housing, Town Planning and Country Act, to introduce planning schemes for regulating the layout and design of surburban housing. Once a scheme was devised by the authority, and approved by the Minister, it had the legal force of the Act itself.

The need to make explicit provision for suburban growth became even more pressing after the First World War. Not only was there greater personal mobility, but the increase in service and tertiary employment meant a rise in incomes and job security. In the words of one housing historian, here were families, 'keenly anxious to demonstrate their arrival by the adoption of a life style which separated them from the respectable poverty from which many had risen'. Taking advantage of low cost house mortgages and the bus service, the commuter train or motor car (see Colour Plate 2), their aim was to move to a new suburb. No matter where it came in the hierarchy of snobbery, each suburb 'shared the same characteristic of one-family houses in gardens and in an environment more or less removed from the dirt, noise and congestion of the city'.

Metroland and Beyond

By the outbreak of the Second World War, suburbs made up a large proportion of the entire built-up environment in Britain; they accommodated half the population. The peak in the loss of rural land to urban use occurred in the 1930s, when some 25,000 hectares a year were built over (see Figure 3.3). Around London, the suburbs extended up to 15 miles from the City centre.

Figure 3.3: Inter-war Suburban Sprawl on the Edge of London. By the 1930s the separate villages referred to in Figure 3.2 had been overwhelmed by development. Even the larger separate entities of Kingston and Surbiton were engulfed by expansion of the capital.

Source: Radio Times Picture Library.

Nowhere was safe from building development. The most affluent moved beyond the 'half-way house' of the suburban estate and into the countryside itself. Although their houses were well designed and set in spacious grounds, they neither intruded upon the skyline or marred the open vista. In a paper of 1930, a leading planning consultant, Professor Patrick Abercrombie, wrote of the challenge of accommodating more and more people in the countryside, without its becoming 'de-countrified'. A new approach to landscape perception was needed. Whereas planners had thought in terms of a single building or street, now they had to plan in terms of 'a complete landscape'. If the task was tackled in a 'thoroughly scientific manner', it might be possible to save and enhance the countryside.

It was no longer enough to design and construct suburbs to the highest standards possible. Conscious thought had to be given to the *location* of suburbs and all other forms of building development, wherever they occurred. Under the Town *and Country* Planning Act of 1932, the discretionary powers granted to local authorities were widened to include, in practice, 'all land that could be usefully planned'. With hindsight, it was an Act of enormous significance. Statutory planning passed into a new dimension, becoming more universal in its application and more demanding in its resources. Although there was insufficient time and finance to enable the Act to have much direct impact on building development in the 1930s, the Act provided valuable insights into how urban expansion might be contained.

Perspectives on Containment: Campaigns for Separation

Urban Constraints and the Garden City

It would have been surprising if the loss of countryside to urban development had not provoked some kind of response. From as early as 1580 proclamations had been made against new buildings in London. In so far as they had any impact, they accentuated overcrowding. The experience of Nottingham in the early nineteenth century indicated what could happen when physical constraints were imposed without any concurrent attempt to control population growth. A report to the Health of Towns Commission in 1845 described how 'nowhere else shall we find so large a mass of inhabitants ... so clustered upon each other; court within court, yard within yard, and lane within lane, in a manner to defy description'. By the time the city was able to expand across the neighbouring fields, three times as many people lived in the old confines as was recommended by the health standards of the late 1840s.

The literature of the eighteenth and nineteenth centuries contains many expressions of concern lest the countryside should be taken over by urbanising forces. Historians have concentrated most of their attention on the writer, Ebenezer Howard. As the title of his book of 1898 implies, *Tomorrow: a Peaceful Path to Real Reform*, Howard was primarily concerned with social progress rather than with physical forms. But even when his book was re-issued in 1902 with a more tangible title, *Garden Cities of Tomorrow*, his prescriptions struck most contemporaries as futile and impracticable.

Howard's aim was to revitalise urban life on the one hand, and the intellectual and social improvement of rural life on the other. To achieve this, the attributes of town and country had to be preserved in a new kind of partnership, which he called the *Garden City*. This was far from being a loose, indefinite sprawl of individual houses. Rather, it was to be a compact, rigorously-confined urban grouping. The physical spread of the built-up area would be prevented by a permanent belt of open land, used for farming. Industrial development would be encouraged as a means of providing employment for the greater part of the population. Once the projected population had been

Figure 3.4: Welwyn Garden
City Master Plan. Devised by
Louis De Soissons in 1924.

Source: C. Burke (1971),
Towns in the Making, Edward
Arnold.

reached, and the existing land and social facilities occupied, new communities
would be founded elsewhere. The municipality would administer both the
built-up and rural areas, and each would function as part of a larger grouping
of cities. As working models of the larger concept, Letchworth Garden City
was founded in 1903 and Welwyn Garden City in 1920 (see Figures 3.4 and
3.5).

Despite a vigorous propagandist lobby, and the obvious interest aroused in
the Garden City movement, it was a concept more talked about than realised,
although it was to influence the development of new towns after 1945.
Howard certainly did nothing to adapt his concept to the existing pattern of
local government. The extant structure of local government, with its boroughs
and urban and rural districts tended to preserve individual autonomy and
boundaries and to exclude the co-ordination Garden Cities needed. On

paper, at least, they already provided ample scope for preserving the identity of town and country.

Some of these authorities displayed resourcefulness in tackling the consequences of population and land-use change. In his maiden speech as a Member of Parliament, Aneurin Bevan described in 1929 how local authorities were a political laboratory, where experiments were being carried out every day. Confronted by social and economic change, each could apply to Parliament for Local Acts or Provisional Orders, which might help it to adapt to new circumstances. When found to be relevant to other authorities such powers were often, in fact, taken up and generalised in national legislation. Given these attributes, and the fact that the authorities were often responsible for providing water, gas, local public transport and other essential services, there seemed little point in abandoning them for another, untried type of authority.

Figure 3.5: Housing in Welwyn Garden City. Although the city was designed to be a closely packed, rigorously defined unit, individual housing developments were constructed to give a feeling of spaciousness.

Source: MERL.

Pressure Groups and Planners

But what part did the various pressure groups and professional planners have in encouraging central and local government to enact legislation which, among other things, extended the scope for separating town from countryside? An important landmark was the founding of the National Trust for Places of Historic Interest or Natural Beauty in 1894. By its name and objectives, it extended the fusion of historic interest and beauty that had characterised the study of Fine Art. This was perhaps not surprising. Three of the four vice-presidents of the National Trust were members of the Royal Academy. Under a Private Act of 1907, the Trust secured the right to declare inalienable its lands and buildings, taken into permanent protection 'for the benefit of the Nation'. The fact that the properties could not be sold, taken away or otherwise disposed of, without the express consent of Parliament, encouraged further bequests to be made.

A further landmark in arousing public awareness of what was happening in the countryside was reached in 1926, when a Council for the Preservation (now Protection) of Rural England (CPRE) was formed (with an equivalent body for Wales (CPRW) in 1927) comprising 22 member societies, and a large number of affiliated local bodies. The CPRE sought to protect rural amenity and to promote further opportunities for outdoor recreation. The North Riding of Yorkshire may be cited as an example of where the local branch of the CPRE actively collaborated with, and gave valued support to, the local planning authorities as they took their first faltering steps in statutory planning.

Both the local authorities and voluntary bodies made considerable use of the few professional planners available. Acting as consultants, these planners advised on the scope for land-use planning under existing legislation, and they drafted reports describing the existing pattern of land use and setting out prescriptions for the future. Most plans envisaged a range of land-use zones. In addition to a built-up zone, and one where no development would be permitted, a zone was designated where any future residential or industrial development should be concentrated. The fact that nothing very tangible came of most of these plans did not entirely detract from their longer-term value. What was needed in the 1920s and 1930s was a goal — something to strive for. Although there was no hope of the perfection of that goal being attained, the fact that councillors and officials, and members of the voluntary bodies, became aware of what the models represented, marked at least the beginnings of a new and important approach to practical planning on a local and regional scale.

Ribbon Development and Attempts to Contain It

Although the participation of the voluntary bodies and the planning expert was essential to the making of planning proposals it did not make either their initiation or execution inevitable. Nowhere was this more abundantly clear than on the fringes of towns and cities — along the roads leading to and from the countryside. It was on these roadside plots that statutory planning was most needed and where it was weakest. For the speculative builder and house occupants, the frontages along these main roads made highly desirable building plots. They offered immediate access to a made-up road, the basic utilities and often a bus service, and a view across the countryside at the rear. There was no shortage of this type of land available. Whilst the acute agricultural depression of the 1920s and 1930s may have persuaded some farmers to sell, even the most prosperous farmers found the prices offered by the builder irresistible. The urban sprawl in the Home Counties took place on some of the finest land for farming and market-gardening in the country.

It was the community at large which suffered from what came to be known as *ribbon development* (Figure 3.6). Not only did the vehicles parked outside or entering the frontages increase traffic congestion on what were often the most modern and expensive roads to be built, but any view of the countryside from the roads was blotted out. Abercrombie likened ribbon development to a cancer, 'a growth of apparently healthy cells but proceeding without check or relation to the whole body'. An obvious way of halting ribbon development was to introduce planning schemes which banned all development unless the consent of the local planning authority had been obtained. The procedure was, however, cumbersome, and most authorities were deterred by the fact that anyone adversely affected by the controls imposed by the planning authorities could claim compensation for the losses sustained. Land development values were particularly high along such roads, and few local authorities had sufficiently high rateable income to meet the claims for compensation that were expected to arise. Under considerable public pressure, an attempt was made to remove the impasse in 1935, by means of an *ad hoc* Restriction of Ribbon Development Act. It was more than usually a work of expediency and compromise. The Government accepted that the design and efficiency of the classified road network was a national responsibility, and agreed to the central Exchequer meeting the cost of compensation, where it would 'remove the highway danger'. This would be achieved by prohibiting building development within 200 yards of the road. In the Government's view, any further restrictions could be justified only on the grounds of preserving the amenity of the

countryside, the Government continuing to insist that this was a local issue and should therefore be decided upon and financed by the local authorities. Critics argued that the Act did nothing to prevent ribbon development behind service roads and long drives. As in the case of the Town and Country Act, the compensation issue prevented the new Act from achieving in many parts of the country 'what one would infer from its title'.

It was particularly hard to achieve effective planning where more than one authority was involved. Even where a group of authorities formed a joint committee to co-operate in drawing up a regional scheme, there was no assurance that each would implement the essential feature of zoning land use. Despite the passing of planning resolutions, 'the same rickety estate planning' and 'promiscuity of land use' continued. Despairing of the slowness and animosity aroused by planning schemes, some authorities resorted to purchasing land for regulated development, or for open-space purposes. This provided not only immediate and certain control over the land, but it often proved only a little more expensive to buy the land than to meet claims for compensation for loss of development value at a later date.

The government's insistence on the notion that the amenity of the countryside was a local issue and should be decided upon and financed locally, largely accounted for the fact that another form of ribbon development — that of the coastline of England and Wales — was largely ignored in the inter-war period. This was in spite of a report from the CPRE in 1936 that had spelled out its iniquities in no uncertain terms.

Although the National Trust had succeeded in acquiring some coastal properties especially in the south west of England and Wales, the problems created by indiscriminate building developments were a particular feature of the south east with Peacehaven on the chalk cliffs of East Sussex the most notorious example. If the problem was not to be taken seriously at national level until the latter part of the Second World War, mainly as a result of the efforts of J.A. Steers who had undertaken his own review of the situation, the

Figure 3.6: Ribbon Development Along the Great West Road. Housing developments like these west of London occurred along the A4. This traversed the river terraces of the Thames valley, some of the best horticultural land in England.

Source: Aerofilms.

Figure 3.7: Box Hill, Surrey, Part of London's Green Belt. Established on the North Downs, this area of chalk upland now contains a field studies centre. The Green Belt in which it is situated acts as a check on urban growth.

Source: National Trust.

wider protection of the countryside was thus only occasionally promoted at local level by land purchase in the 1930s. Surrey County Council, for example, had such a scheme for acquiring open space for scenic and recreational purposes with contributions towards the cost from the urban and district councils, and, latterly from the London County Council. From 1935 onwards, the London County Council helped local authorities to purchase land accessible to the inhabitants of London. The explicit aim was to establish a reserve of open space and recreation areas, in the form of a green belt or girdle around London (see Figure 3.7). The implicit intention was to restrict or control metropolitan growth. By the outbreak of war, some 25,000 acres had been secured from development.

Industry in the Countryside

The financial implications of planning were even more formidable when it came to regulating the location and nature of industry. The increasing role of road transport and electric power meant that many industries could now be located away from existing urban or industrial centres and could be described as 'footloose'. As in the case of house building, the best solution lay in grouped development, by means of which roads and public services could be provided on sound and economic lines, without sacrificing wide stretches of countryside. Experience (in the inter-war years) at Welwyn Garden City and elsewhere demonstrated the difficulties of achieving a 'balanced' community, where as much attention was given to the planning of industry as to housing and other activities and services. Without compulsory powers *and* large sums of money, little could be done to attract industry to the 'right' locations, and to deter it from others. The difficulties proved so great that many planning schemes focused on the relatively simple task of site-planning of housing schemes, rather than on the much harder goal of ensuring that 'the new dwellings should be located within reasonable range of present or prospective places of employment'. Such a limited response gave statutory planning a sense of unreality and irrelevance — a stigma which it never entirely succeeded in shaking off.

London and other major centres continued to sprawl, and the already distressed areas continued to be depressed. There was no shortage of suggestions as to how the quality of planning might be improved for the benefit of town and country alike. The deficiency of planning was often attributed to 'our inability to visualise the future'. If schemes were to excite public interest, and to secure the resources and political will to implement them, there had to be much more in the way of thought and imagination. A more comprehensive and positive approach was needed. Instead of waiting for some kind of regional and national plan to evolve out of the mosaic of local schemes, the concept of a Ministry of Planning was advocated. Created for 'the sole purpose of the territorial planning of national life', it would lay down a national plan, within which local and regional planning would operate. Because the new Ministry would have an immediate, active and continued involvement in planning, it would be much better placed to tackle the fundamental problem of land values and compensation, and the distribution of population and industry.

Towards a 'National Plan'

It would be misleading to suggest that there was wide support for the idea of a centrally-formulated national plan in the 1930s. On the contrary, it was strongly contended that the country could not afford to weaken the sense of local responsibility for planning. The idea of an omnipotent Ministry of Planning reflected a tendency 'to look upon development as something mechanical, as something of which the parts can be moved about at will as though society were made up of a number of bricks'. Society was organic. The location of industry, homes and much else was determined largely 'by forces within the body social', and the character of these forces would have to be fully understood before planning on so grand a scale was attempted. Without this understanding, any attempt at detailed national planning would be too much a leap in the dark.

Much was subsequently made of three official reports that appeared in the early part of the Second World War. The first, that of the Royal Commission on the Distribution of the Industrial Population (the Barlow report), was actually finished before the war broke out. Government departments dismissed the report as having 'thrown back' the very problem the Royal Commission had been appointed to investigate, namely how far industry could be directed to those parts of the country where the social benefits could be greatest. The two other reports dealt with land use in rural areas (the Scott report), and the process of compensating or taxing people as the result of the development process (the Uthwatt report). Neither had much impact. As Chapter 2 has made clear the Scott report was regarded by government departments as being too sentimental in its outlook, and too diffuse in its recommendations. The proposals made in the Uthwatt report were too contentious for a Coalition Government to implement in the midst of a world war.

It was not until the fourth autumn of war, and a major upheaval in public attitudes towards the role of central government that any great notice was taken of the three reports and their calls for stronger central direction in land-use planning. A Minister of Town and Country Planning was appointed in 1943, charged with the task of securing 'consistency and continuity in the framing and execution of a national policy with respect to the use and development of land'. Numerous references to the trio of reports were made during the last months of the wartime Coalition Government and throughout the post-war Labour Government. They conferred a legitimacy on policies that might otherwise have been castigated as being left wing and socialist.

As forewarned, it was comparatively easy to set up a new Ministry of Town and Country Planning; it was much harder to decide on the machinery by which its ambitious objectives might be fulfilled. It was by no means obvious where the limits of ministerial power should be drawn in relation to the local authorities. The advantages of making the county councils the primary planning authorities in local government were far from clear. How could the 'bugbear' of compensation be removed without resorting to outright land nationalisation? The extremely complicated formula adopted by the Town and Country Planning Act of 1947, which included the nationalisation of land-development values, proved so contentious and cumbersome that amending legislation soon followed.

Given the uncertain progress of the inter-war years, and the constraints imposed even in the heady days of post-war reconstruction, the scope of the Town and Country Planning Act of 1947 was remarkable. It went far beyond the rehabilitation of war-damaged areas. It created the foundations of a system of urban and rural land-use controls that survived for over three decades. Nevertheless, it has to be remembered that 1947 saw the passage of two Acts of immense significance. Together with the long lasting and fundamental Town and Country Planning Act, there also came onto the Statute book the equally significant Agriculture Act in which government permanently promised to support prices and markets for the main farm products. Thus, in essence in 1947 two different systems of planning were enshrined in their separate legislation. One was for towns, cities and villages and major permanent changes in land use; the other was the system of price signals, grants and subsidies that decided the pattern of land-uses over the remaining 80 per cent of the land surface of England and Wales.

Perspectives on Containment: Post-war Control

Principles of the 1947 System

The new land use planning system was conceived in a climate of urgency and optimism. The need to rebuild bomb-damaged cities was a high priority. However, the incoming Government of 1945 particularly accepted the need to restrain the physical spread of large cities, to decentralise population to new and expanded towns, and to protect agricultural land. Other elements of the post-war pattern were to be policies for the 'proper distribution' of industry, the creation of National Parks, and the comprehensive agricultural support system.

The 1947 Town and Country Planning Act comprised perhaps three important elements in a system designed to make decisions on the use of land in the public interest. The first was the *nationalisation* of the right of landowners to develop their own land as they saw fit. Compensation was to be paid on a once for all basis for the loss of such development rights from a £300 million fund set up for the purpose. Second, local authorities, who were charged with operating the system, were obliged to prepare *development plans* looking 20 years ahead (see Figure 3.8). These would show the manner in which land in their areas was to be used; which areas were to be developed for housing and schools, and which were to be kept for agriculture or open space. The third element was a set of rules determining when owners proposing development would *need to apply for planning permission* to the local authority. The system would operate by local authority council committees making decisions on proposals, guided by the advice of their planners, and having regard to the provisions of the plans they had drawn up. The Act gave wide discretion at local level. A local authority could permit development contravening its plan if individual circumstance merited it. A number of checks and balances were incorporated from the outset. Landowners, for example, had a right to have their objections heard before development plans were finalised. Persons refused planning permission at local level could appeal to the Minister and have the facts of the case reassessed by an Inspector.

The system of development plans and development control was comprehensive in coverage. Commentators at the time saw development plans as the new 'Domesday Books' of England and Wales! The system was also centralised. It was the duty of the new Minister of Housing and Local Government, superseding the Minister of Town Planning, under the Act to secure consistency in the operation of planning in the 'national interest'. Apart from using formal and informal means of negotiation with authorities, this was to be done by issuing circulars. These gave instruction on how various policies should be interpreted at local level. For example, three Circulars issued between 1946 and 1952 urged the need to avoid taking productive agricultural land for development where less productive land could reasonably be made available. In addition Ministry planners vetted all development plans and frequently proposed significant changes before approval. Planning applications of national significance could be 'called in' and determined by the Minister. Approval of the National Exhibition Centre in the Birmingham Green Belt in 1971 is an example of a decision made by this latter procedure.

Although land use plans were comprehensive in coverage, controls were limited in scope, particularly in rural areas. Many changes associated with later agricultural development, such as the construction of intensive animal rearing houses, barns and large silos were not subject to control unless over 465 sq. m in floor area or where for example they were located close to a trunk road. Also proposals to change the appearance of the countryside landscape, and for afforestation, were outside the definition of development. Responsibility for the distribution of industry was given to the Board of Trade, and under the 1949 National Parks and Access to the Countryside Act, the Government made provisions to encourage access to the countryside for leisure the responsibility of a separate agency, the National Parks Commission (see Chapter 4). Developments on land owned by the Crown, the Ministry of Defence, and other Government Departments were not subject to the normal permission requirements.

The Ministry of Housing and Local Government, a new and weak Department, was not given the powers to intervene in order to co-ordinate the specific land development demands of other Ministries. This was thus left in the charge of a system of interest mediation at local level with the cumbersome tool of the approval of five-yearly-reviewed development plans as a main means of doing this. With 145 local authorities involved, this proved a contentious task. Each authority has its own political and land development aims not necessarily in accord with the central Government policy of the day. Various pressure groups, increasingly well-organised over the years, have seen scope for influencing this relatively loose pattern of central guidance and local initiative.

The attitudes of Governments to the dilemmas of providing for urban growth, yet retaining valued agricultural and other natural resources, have also varied. The system was not, therefore, a set of rules rigidly applied. In practice it provided a context for making decisions which weighed the national interest against local interests, and for deciding between conflicting local interests.

But what *policies* were pursued? The most important can be summarised thus:

Urban containment, the idea being that there were overriding disadvantages to allowing the unchecked spread of large cities. Low density, widely spread cities would lead to high congestion and journey-to-work costs, and to higher costs in providing necessary roads, sewers and other services. Peripheral suburbs would, if constructed, form a barrier between the mass of people living in the city centres and the open countryside, stifling the needs of urban people for fresh air and green fields. Complementary to this was the idea of:

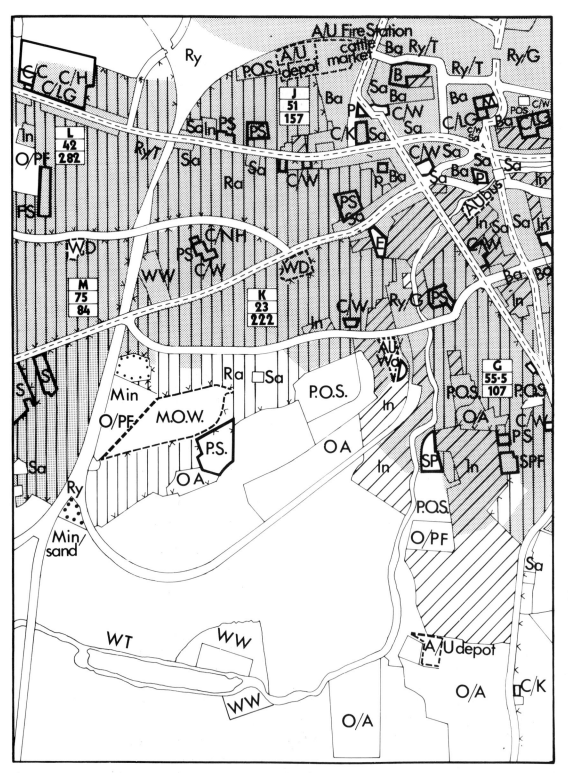

Figure 3.8: Part of the Development Plan for Reading, 1957. This shows planned development over a 20-year period according to major types of land use. This section of the overall plan running south from the town centre may be set in its context by reference to Figure 3.10.

Source: Reading Borough Council.

NOTATION

In Areas primarily for Industrial Use

Ba Areas primarily for Principal Business Use (i.e. offices and wholesale warehouses)

Sa Areas primarily for Shopping Use

Sa Shopping Centres, approximate location

C/ Areas primarily for groups of buildings for civic, cultural or other special uses marked:—

C/H   for Hospitals
C/C   for Health Centres & Clinics
C/NH for Nursing Homes
C/W for Places of Worship
C/G   for Government Buildings
C/K   for Cinemas
C/CC for Community Centres
C/LG for Local Government Buildings
C/A   for Other Places of Assembly

Ra Areas primarily for Residential Use

ᴧᴧᴧ Boundaries of Residential Units
The Cartogram superimposed shows

    Index Number
    Gross Population Density in Persons per acre
    Approximate area in acres

Principal Traffic Routes

⁼R⁼ NOTE. Road bands only accentuate road lines and their width does not relate to the future width of any road

B Stations for Public Service Vehicles

P Principal Car Parks

Ry Land for Railway purposes

Ry/T Railway Passenger & Goods Stations
Ry/G marked T & G respectively

WT Waterways whether docks, harbours or Inland Waterways of Traffic Importance

Wa Other land covered by water

✳ ✳ Principal Traffic Roads ⎤ for which Street
✳⁼✳ Other Roads ⎟ Authorisation
                          ⎦ Maps are approved

WW Waterworks

S/D Sewage Disposal Works

▒ Existing built-up area

SS for Secondary Schools

PS for Primary Schools

S for Other Schools and Residential Colleges

E for Non Residential Colleges & other education land

SPF for School Playing Fields

▱ Approximate location of School & School playing fields with appropriate letters

POS Areas held or to be held for Public Open Space

O/ Areas for Open Space not open to the General Public marked

O/SA for Statutory Allotments
O/A   for Other Allotments
O/C   for Cemetery
O/GC for Golf Course
O/NG for Nursery Gardens
O/O   for Orchards
O/PF for Private Playing Fields

⌐⌐ Large areas for Service Departments marked

AM   for Air Ministry
WD   for War Department
MOW for Ministry of Works
MOS   for Ministry of Supply

AU/ Local Authority & Statutory Undertakers marked

AU/Wa for Water Department Depot
AU/Bus for Bus Depot
AU/Dept for Highways Depot
AU/Cattle Market
AU/Fire Station
AU/Gas for Gas Works
AU/Elec for Electricity Power Station
AU/TC for Thames Conservancy

Min/ Areas which are intended for the working of minerals other than coal

M Ancient Monuments

Wd/P Woodlands subject to a tree Preservation Order

ByLPA Boundary of Local Planning Authority's Area

the protection of agricultural land, in a situation where food rationing was still in force, and where memories of wartime food shortages and the Battle of the Atlantic were strong. It was seen to be in the national interest to retain as large a stock as possible of good agricultural land to form a basis for policies designed to move towards self-sufficiency in food production (see Chapter 2).

These first two ideas were brought together in:

the notion of green belts around cities. These would create a clear visual division between town and country, the sense of order thus created combining forcefully with economic and social argument. It would also provide the 'townsman's countryside', the new recreation lungs for the congested cities. Beyond the green belts, policies stressed:

the creation of self-contained and balanced communities. These could be new towns, or expansions of existing smaller centres. Self-contained towns with a balance of local jobs and people would lead to reduction in travel time and cost, would also reap economies of scale in the provision of services and would provide potentially ready access to open countryside.

In villages development not associated with primary needs (agriculture, forestry and rural-based industries) *would be discouraged.* Rural settlements might accept some carefully sited 'infill' development between existing houses and even some limited 'rounding off' on their edges. But policies specifying village boundaries or what were termed village envelopes would curtail their general spread. However, some authorities took the view that key villages might be specially earmarked for development since economies of scale in the provision of rural services might also be achieved at this level in the settlement hierarchy. This would require careful attention being given to their choice in relation to the overall settlement pattern but its effects could also be beneficial in terms of the wider protection of the environment against development pressures.

In the remainder of the countryside *scattered residental development was to be firmly discouraged,* and normally only housing essential to rural activities such as farming and forestry would be permitted. Scattered development would harm 'amenity' (the appearance of the countryside) and would be extremely costly to service.

These ideas were most effectively combined by Patrick Abercrombie in his Greater London Plan of 1944 (see Figure 3.9). Abercrombie had been an influential figure in developing many of the ideas outlined above as the first Secretary of the (then) Council for the Preservation of Rural England, and as a member of the wartime Barlow Committee. The essence of his proposals was a physical rearrangement of the major land-users in the region. A clear visual break was to be made between town and country by means of a green belt or 'cordon sanitaire' around London. Complementary proposals suggested the 'overspilling' of one million people from the city to new and expanded towns beyond the belt. As a result of this thinning-out process solutions to the problems of the renewal of housing, and the rearrangement of poorly juxtaposed residential, industrial and commercial uses in the congested city, would be made possible.

. This set of physical prescriptions has been seen as utopian, the plan embodying a blueprint of an orderly environment at some future date. It appealed to some as preserving the threatened countryside from the threatening town. It was a system of ideas traceable from concerns about the health of over-densely packed urban populations. Health, amenity and convenience were its watch words.

Local authorities around the country adopted much of the Abercrombie prescription as a basis for their plans. In 1955 Duncan Sandys as Minister of Housing and Local Government extended the idea of green belts to areas out-

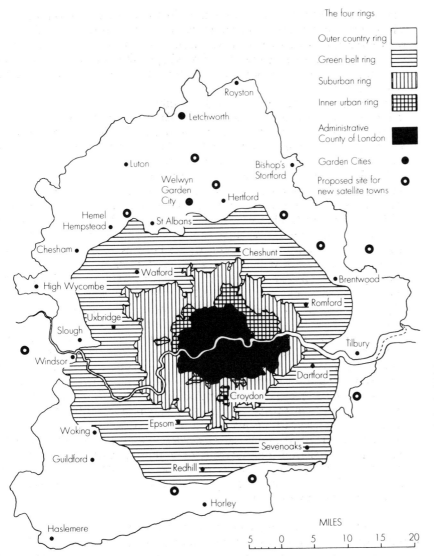

The four rings

Outer country ring

Green belt ring

Suburban ring

Inner urban ring

Administrative
County of London

● Garden Cities

◎ Proposed site for
new satellite towns

Royston
● Letchworth
● Luton
Bishop's
Stortford
Welwyn
Garden
City ●
● Hertford
Hemel
Hempstead ●
● St Albans
● Chesham
Cheshunt ■
● Watford
● High Wycombe
● Brentwood
Uxbridge
Romford ●
● Slough
Tilbury
Windsor ●
Dartford ●
Croydon ■
Epsom ■
Woking ●
Sevenoaks ■
● Guildford
Redhill ▼
● Horley
Haslemere ●

MILES
5   0   5   10   15   20

Figure 3.9: The Greater
London Plan, 1944. Devised by
Professor Sir Patrick
Abercrombie, the plan
attempted to show how
population growth might be
handled within a framework
which contained the expansion
of London and protected
agricultural land.

Source: H. Evans (1972) *New
Towns: the British Experience*,
Charles Knight, London.

side London, and by 1960 some 12,000 kilometres of countryside (9 per cent
of England and Wales) was covered by the policy. Green belts were not seen
primarily as a recreation policy but as a means of checking the spread of
selected built-up areas, and avoiding the coalescence of settlements. Inside
green belts, the Ministers' 1955 Circular suggested that only developments
associated with agricultural and forestry production, low intensity recreation
activities, and 'other uses appropriate to a rural area' would normally be
allowed. Farmers were to be the normal custodians of the land.

The development plans allocated housing land at densities of 15 to 20
buildings per hectare to produce compact urban settlements. Beyond the
edges of built-up areas pockets of 'white land' were shown between the land
allocated for development and the new green belt boundaries. This was land
where it was intended that existing, largely agricultural, uses would remain
undisturbed. The land was a reserve for possible urban use beyond the 20
year time period of the plans.

The Growth Era

The Abercrombie solution was based on no growth in population. Rapid rises in the post-war birth rate and a tide of voluntary out-migration from cities, placed severe pressure on containment policies. By the time the first development plans were approved the Ministry of Housing was suggesting a need for land for two to two-and-a-half million more people. Pressures were made more acute by the need to rehouse persons displaced from the major urban housing renewal programmes which, by this time, had gained high momentum. The administrative map of England and Wales consisted of large County Boroughs seeking to expand their boundaries into the surrounding countryside to accommodate peripheral development. Ranged against them, in political and planning terms, were rural county authorities who were unwilling to accept planning overspill to new towns, or other developments. Having given municipal authorities wide powers to determine the use of land locally, central government then found it difficult to intervene to adjust the balance in a situation of growth. The history of land-use planning in the 1955 to 1970 period is, therefore, one of continued attempts by governments of both political persuasions to wrest more land for development from reluctant rural authorities.

In the early 1950s the compensation and betterment clauses of the 1947 Act were repealed by a Conservative Government convinced that such provisions were hindering the flow of land for development. A succession of circulars suggested that land allocated in plans should be developed at densities higher than 15 to 20 dwellings per hectare. In 1962 progress on the confirmation of green belts was halted and a number remained unconfirmed in approved development plans until the early 1980s. In 1963 alarmed by the rising price of land, Keith Joseph instructed local authorities to release small areas of green belt which would ease housing demands with least damage to agricultural interests. Later attempts included the preparation of regional plans more able to address the problems at a scale related to the patterns of dispersal that were occurring. These lacked teeth, local authorities tending only to adopt those policies which suited their own needs. In 1965 the Labour Government set up the Land Commission, one of whose major tasks was to identify land not already in development plans — in countryside pressure areas — for early release for development. At its demise in 1970 the Commission was preparing to take a range of test-case greenfield sites to appeal to break through local authority policies.

The system set up as a result of the 1947 Act was designed to programme and guide the location of a largely public sector housing programme. Industry was to be encouraged to relocate to new and expanded towns, but was to be discouraged in smaller country towns and villages. In practice the majority of housing was built by private builders in a situation where large profits could be gained by obtaining farmland at agricultural value with a view to persuading local authorities to grant planning permission. Thus development plans became known as the 'speculators' charter' and much of the white land they contained was the subject of bitter dispute. These focused around whether the need for housing outweighed the damage to amenity, rural appearance and food production that would result from development.

Rapid increases in car ownership and improved rail communication led to the enlargement of city regions. An office worker in central London could live in a country town 50 miles away and travel to work daily across the intervening countryside. Thus wide areas of rural country became functionally connected to the cities in ways that went beyond their traditional role as local centres for the provision of certain goods and services and as market places for the sale of agricultural produce from these hinterlands. Because the supply of development land was severely controlled the system contributed to the creation of rapid inflation in land prices. The wealthier and younger sections of the population were those able to exercise a choice for rural-based living. Within the cities, hemmed in by green belts, lower income groups were accommodated in council housing. Thus what Peter Hall has termed a 'civilised form of apartheid' had been created. This accompanied a growing separation of homes and workplaces as people moved into the country, with office and clerical jobs remaining in the cities.

Land use controls reduced dramatically the amount of land converted from agricultural to urban use. Compact and contained forms of urban development were attained. An annual inter-war loss of agricultural land to urban uses of 25,000 hectares a year had been reduced to a post-war one of around 15,000 hectares, despite far higher rates of population growth. Annual fluctuations appear related to the health of the national economy and the reactions of central government to insistent cries of a shortage of land for building. For example, the impending enactment of the Land Commission Bill in 1965 may have helped raise the figure to 20,000 hectares in that year, from which it slumped to 14,000 in 1966. Robin Best, in a comprehensive study of the land loss debate, concluded that it is not true that urban growth engulfs greater amounts of agricultural land each year. With 78 per cent of the land area of the United Kingdom in agricultural use we have a higher proportion of farmland than any other EEC country. Between 1951 and 1971 the total of land in England and Wales devoted to urban uses grew from 9 per cent to 11 per cent. Estimates suggest that this figure might reach 14 per cent by the end of the century (see Figure 3.10). Rapid rises in agricultural productivity of over 2 per cent per annum have easily outweighed the relatively small losses of agricultural land. The nation has gradually moved towards higher proportions of food from its own resources.

One side-effect of containment and high land prices has been an increase in densities in new private housing estates. Gone are the allotment-sized plots associated with the Addison Act's 'homes fit for heroes' of the 1919 to 1921 era. Improved housing layouts, the 35-foot back garden, and the smaller rooms in modern houses still retain family privacy but they allow developers to maximise profits on the limited areas of land available.

The Urban Fringe and Recreation Demands

Although new urban development was compact in form, this was not the whole story. Much of the most productive farmland is found adjacent to urban areas. Yet this 'urban fringe zone' had become a location for an assortment of activities that service the town and its hinterland but could not afford space within it. These include hospitals, prisons, airfields, sewage works, gravel pits, waste tips and reservoirs (see Figure 3.11). Such uses have fragmented the original pattern of farm holdings near towns. Farmers have, as a result, adjusted the way they operate their enterprises and many have reduced the amount they invest in maintenance. The possibility of development has led to 'farming to quit' and a consequent rundown in the appearance of the landscape. In some areas urban residents have bought land to use on a hobby basis. Extensive areas are grazed by horses catering for the equestrian demands of suburban schoolgirls! Various writers have deplored the creation of a 'no-man's-land', visually incoherent and economically inefficient. Nan Fairbrother, in her powerful polemic written in 1970 saw it one way:

> The landscape of our city fringes, whether Green Belt, Grey Belt or no belt at all, is depressingly familiar everywhere — an incoherent limbo which is our particular twentieth century contribution to the scenery of the world. It is a landscape of mutual destruction by two incompatible environments, and the sickness infests them both: cities invade the countryside with eyesores, while to travellers from city centres the opening landscape reveals most ugliness.

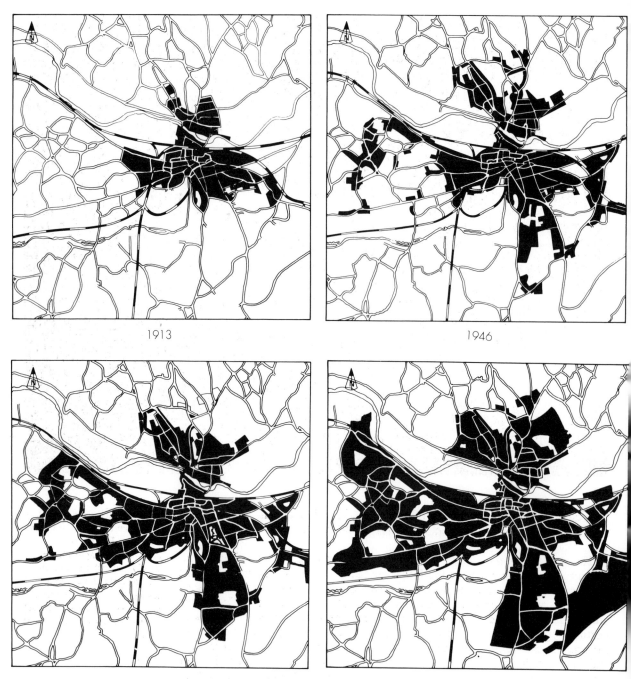

1913

1946

1960

1983

Figure 3.10: Stages in the Urban Development of Reading. This Figure is illustrative of the degree of land taken from agriculture by an expanding town over time. The solid black areas show urban usage.

Source: Reading Borough Council.

On the other hand the National Farmers Union see their members as 'bewildered proprietors of a battleground' of conflicting interests. One of their spokesmen had put it this way:

... the farmer and the farmland of the fringe are under pressure; physical pressure on the land and psychological pressure on the farmer ... Direct conflict with people ... is most acute on land closest to the urban areas ... Trespass and dumping come high on the list ... Many of the problems

cause actual financial loss, but often it is the fear of problems which causes a change in the farming system or causes the farmer to sell up and leave.

The green belts and urban-rural fringes around towns have provided a convenient location for many of the less acceptable land uses. The gaps between towns are often criss-crossed with motorways and the super-grid 400 kW electricity pylons. Large areas of sand and gravel workings, a use permissible within green belts, have been approved largely due to the unacceptable cost of transporting aggregates to cities from alternative sites in the deeper countryside. Private and public playing fields have been taken from development in cities and new provisions have been made in the accessible countryside. But the land-use planning system does not always cope well with these 'externalities'. No system exists fully to compensate the farmer for his holding being fragmented into separate parcels. Restoration of mineral land to agricultural use had occurred, and with the encouragement of the Ministry of Agriculture, and the Sand and Gravel Association, demonstration restoration schemes have been mounted to inform improved practices in the future. It has to be recognised, however, that many such efforts involve rehabilitating the landscape to uses such as water-parks rather than as agricultural land.

The 1950s and 1960s are typified for most people by an explosive rise in demands for countryside recreation and relaxation. Fuelled (literally) by a growth in car ownership of nine million between 1950 and 1970, a wave of recreation seekers sought to drive around and use the countryside. Michael

Figure 3.11: Rickmansworth — the Urban Fringe in the 1970s. Although difficult to encompass a range of fringe uses in one picture, this aerial view typically shows a large sewage works and worked out gravel pits (now in amenity use) in what is otherwise agricultural land.

Source: Aerofilms.

Dower predicted in 1964 that a 'fourth wave' would cross the face of Britain. Industrialisation, railway construction and the sprawl of car-based suburbs would be followed by a wave of 'gambolling humanity' brought to rural environments by motor car. The problem was seen as one of accommodating mass demands with least harm to existing rural interests. The prognosis was so startling, a 19 million growth in population by the year 2000 and a 26 million growth in cars on the road by 1980, that Government was strengthened in its view of widening the remit of the National Parks Commission to the whole countryside. The Countryside Commission, established in 1968, was charged with keeping under review and proposing policies for the preservation and enhancement of natural beauty, and of encouraging the provision of areas and facilities for informal recreation. In the locations of most severe pressure near towns early provisions were to take the form of Country Parks and Picnic Sites. Purpose-designed reception areas, largely reserved for recreation use by car-borne visitors were to be provided by local authorities and the private sector with grants from the Commission.

Entering the 'No Growth' Era

During the 1970s land-use planning attempted to accommodate all interests—whether for agricultural land protection, house-building and employment-generating development, or leisure and conservation. However, this was being done at a time which saw stagnation in the economy, a deceleration in the growth of population, and changed attitudes to the location of land using activities. Such are the changes that a consensus about dispersal of population, and containment of development, can no longer be taken for granted.

The reorganisation of local government which was implemented in 1974 created over 450 new planning authorities in a two-tier system of counties and districts. These authorities operate a new development plan system. This comprises *structure plans* at county level outlining the general principles for land use, and *local plans*, most often prepared by districts, giving site specific details. In order to provide flexibility, local plans can deal with relatively small areas for immediate development (action area plans), specific topics such as minerals or green belt (subject plans) or they can deal comprehensively with larger areas (district plans). These are then approved by county councils to reduce the need for Government scrutiny of detail.

One reason for reforming local government, and adjusting boundaries, was to reduce the debilitating urban-rural conflicts that had typified the earlier period. Theoretically 40 or 50 economic blocks centred on large urban areas might have been chosen as administrative units. But this model was not followed and did not always accord with the scale of new urban and countryside problems. The journey-to-work area of Manchester, for example, spreads well into Cheshire yet there are no realistic provisions to co-ordinate development across the two areas. Similarly the boundary of the West Midlands Metropolitan County was drawn so that Birmingham can move only towards the solution of its problems by involvement with Warwickshire and Staffordshire. With no effective *regional* planning, conflict has remained. This conflict now is compounded by disagreement between counties and their constituent districts concerning appropriate rates and locations of urban development.

At the same time the content of planning policies has broadened although the tools available to implement them have changed little. The structure plans have addressed a far wider agenda of issues than their predecessors, and the balance of concern has altered. Concern about absolute decline in employment and populations within inner cities led to a focus on *urban regeneration*. The scale of removal of private sector investment from the inner city led, by 1980, to some 7 per cent of the main urban areas in England and Wales being made up of vacant land. At the same time pressures for suburban residential development in attractive locations have continued. The need to protect agricultural land is still asserted as strongly as ever by the Ministry of Agriculture and the visible manifestation of conflicting policies in the countryside have, if anything, increased.

Planning authorities have attempted, as did their predecessors, to provide a framework for the simultaneous resolution of these problems. A firm attitude to the containment of urban settlements at County level would, it was hoped, retain agricultural land and divert development back into the cities where land was available. Thus green belts have been expanded with a further practical aim added to those at their inception. Instead of deflecting development to towns beyond their outer boundaries green belts would encourage economic uses back into city areas. Certainly this has been the justification for green belts recently approved around Liverpool, and the North East Lancashire and

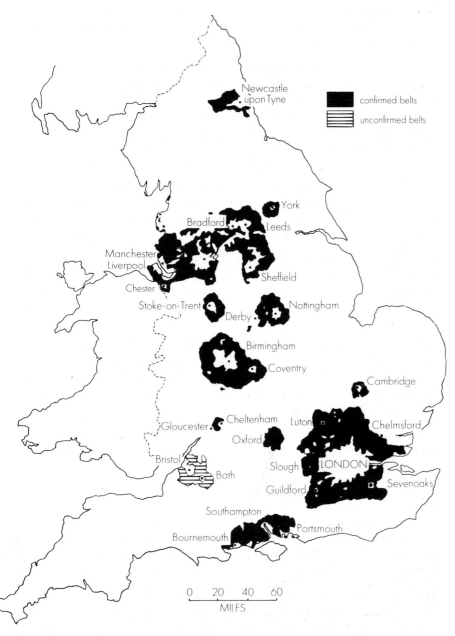

Figure 3.12: Green Belts in England, 1984.

Source: House of Commons Environment Committee, HMSO (1984).

Potteries towns. Many urban authorities who previously opposed green belts are now in favour of them (see Figure 3.12).

In the immediate countryside surrounding towns, authorities have moved towards systems of land-use priority to lessen conflicts. The aim has been to buffer farmland from urban intrusion by creating recreation areas where town meets country. Recreation provision has been encouraged on degraded and otherwise derelict land to avoid the use of working farmland for the purpose. Indeed some counties have gone so far as to establish agricultural priority areas. Here few intensive recreation facilities are allowed, such as large intensively used Country Parks, golf courses or commercial sports activities. These are to be distinguished from 'recreation priority areas' which, although farming remains the major *land using* activity, more intensive recreation provisions are also acceptable. Hertfordshire, for example, has this basic division (see Colour Plate 3). Other counties distinguish areas where considerations of landscape quality have a major effect on the scale and appearance of any necessary new development. At the same time rural development policies have sought to balance the maintenance of the quality and appearance of the environment with some provision for locally-arising needs for housing and jobs, though it is evident that the policy of selecting key settlements for development as a means to this end has not been an unqualified success. Recent studies would indicate that although key settlement policies are theoretically sound they have been poorly implemented in practice; not least because they were either improperly thought out in the first instance or the level of co-ordination needed among the relevant agencies (education, housing, water and electricity) was not achieved. But in spite of this, structure plans still exhibit a keen adherence to such policies and the broad themes of policies as a whole continue to stress the need for economy in the use of land, and the conservation of natural resources.

The Early 1980s

Population Change and Countryside Pressures

The 1970s saw an increase of half a million in the population of England and Wales compared with the 2.8 millions of the previous decade. As in the 1961-71 period there were losses in the largest urban areas, and gains in the least urbanised ones. The 1981 census, therefore, appeared to show a pattern of *dispersed decentralisation* with rural counties such as Suffolk, Norfolk, Hereford and Worcester, and Somerset having populations more than 10 per cent higher than a decade earlier (See Figure 3.13).

This cannot be described, however, as a flight to the countryside. The largest numerical gains have been in the planned dispersal areas of the previous decade; Milton Keynes, Washington New Town, Runcorn and Redditch. But towns such as Royston (Hertfordshire), Droitwich (Worcestershire), St Neots (Cambridgeshire) and Ashby de la Zouch in Leicestershire seem to typify the type of small town (10,000-20,000 population) and parts of the country attracting more spontaneous growth over the 1971-81 period. In Norfolk, one of the fastest growing counties, apart from the town expansion schemes at King's Lynn and Thetford the smaller centres of Cromer, Downham Market and North Walsham have grown faster than in the previous decade. The overall movement of people into the county, led by a growth in local jobs in the early 1970s, has tailed off with the economic recession of the early 1980s. Retirement migration has now become significant in increasing the population as the more traditional south coast retirement areas have filled up.

Manufacturing jobs in England and Wales have declined by a quarter over the last decade. There has been an urban to rural shift in the balance of those

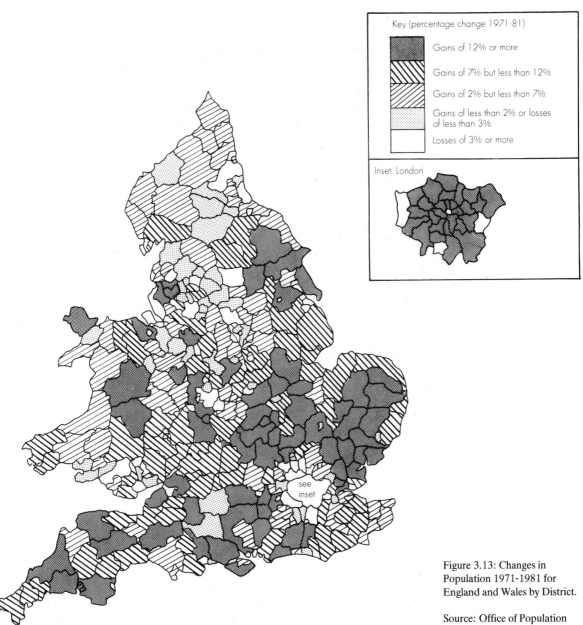

see
inset

Figure 3.13: Changes in
Population 1971-1981 for
England and Wales by District.

Source: Office of Population
Censuses and Surveys.

remaining. Office and clerical jobs have also been moving out of cities. London lost 40 per cent of its manufacturing jobs between 1960 and 1978, and the remaining cities lost a quarter of theirs. Since 1978 some 25 per cent more jobs have been lost in areas like Greater Manchester and 15 per cent have been lost even in attractive rural counties such as Hertfordshire. At the other end of the spectrum, manufacturing employment in rural areas rose by nearly 40 per cent during the same period — although the absolute numbers involved are quite small. The reason appears to be *not* that firms are changing location, though some are. More it seems that existing firms in the smaller country towns and other rural locations are successfully increasing their output and employment. Although large and small firms are closing at similar rates in urban and rural areas, *new jobs* are far more likely to be created in the small town rural environments. This is partly due to the extra expansion space available, physical expansion being a necessity where capital investment is replacing labour, the most common form of rationalisation. Local authority rates are also lower in countryside areas and attractive environments appeal to all grades of staff.

Looking closely within regions more detail can be ascertained. In the South East, for example, the green belt zone took the most pressure in the 1951-71 period for housing. Population increases were greatest in and around a ring of towns some 10 to 15 miles from the outer edge of Greater London. In the 1971-81 period the population of parts of the green belt zone has decreased. The children of those who moved out in the 1950s and 1960s have tended to move further afield for housing, particularly to the west of London.

The Public Sector Response

The land-use planning system is best equipped to adjudicate betwen demands made in situations where there is *pressure* for development. It moulds the initiative of the private developer creating compact forms of new development, on the whole well integrated with existing settlements. For example, in Staffordshire over the period 1971-8 only 25 per cent of the total land taken for housing and industry was from land in agricultural use. With ever greater difficulties in marketing completed houses and factories, development pressures have become more localised. The types of environments still in demand have clashed increasingly with containment and countryside policies. Development pressures are greatest where accessibility and a good environment can be combined.

The construction of the M25 motorway, a yet-to-be-completed circular route around London, almost entirely within the green belt, is a good example of this combination. Accessibility will prove high to and from Heathrow yet lower rates will be payable here on commercial premises than their equivalent in the City. Nearby are attractive country towns for residential use with a wide range of educational opportunities for children. Costly and wasteful commuting to London can be avoided by staff recruited from the vicinity which already contains a pool of skilled labour. It is not difficult to see why such possibilities, guaranteeing secure rental growth for the pension and insurance funds who will probably finance the development, are attractive.

Invested in the inner city such monies may not yield the same return. The financial imperative is matched by the irrelevance of city location to many new forms of employment (see Figure 3.14). Firms whose business is information technology and those in other professional services may well prefer green field campus developments with lush green surroundings and plenty of room to grow.

The 1960s were typified by a negative approach to industry among planners. Industry was to be tucked out of view near city centres or on new estates and it was certainly to be kept out of the countryside and away from rural environments. With unemployment trebling in the two years following 1979 local authorities now want to attract new employment to their areas. In the north of England where problems are more severe, there is intense competition to locate any employment in a variety of greenfield locations freed for the purpose. But there is virtually no *new* development to be had. What is developing is a fiercely competitive situation where authorities make available greenfield sites, preferably not too far from motorways, to attract firms who come mainly from the inner-city authority next door. This is hastening a restructuring of land-use patterns. Decline can lead to dispersal and a breakdown of concern for containment as well.

With pressures to develop new sites relatively low, the agricultural land budget looks more healthy. By the early 1980s average annual land take for

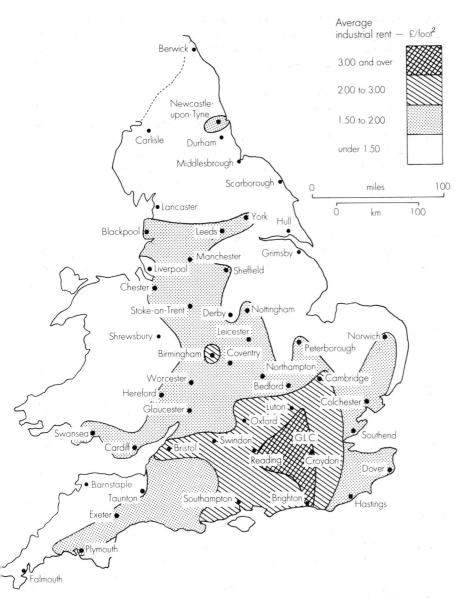

Figure 3.14: Industrial Rents in England and Wales. The best returns appear to be along the M4 corridor and in the general area bounded by Bristol, Cambridge, Brighton and Southampton/Bournemouth. It includes areas which are regarded as largely rural but have a high degree of accessibility. City areas now appear to be much less relevant.

Source: Town and Country Planning, May 1981.

urban purposes had declined to 8,000 hectares, just over half of that of ten years earlier. There remain, however, conflicting views over the success of land-use planning in protecting agriculture. In addition to the work of Robin Best, noted earlier, a research team at Reading University concluded in 1976 that, given even high estimates of population growth, no problem regarding the provision of home-grown foods would arise in the foreseeable future. On the other hand, Alice Coleman has in trenchant terms put forward the view that around 20 per cent of all farms in lowland Britain were significantly compromised by the effects of urban proximity. The urban fringe or 'zone of transition', as she rather inelegantly termed it, was expanding in size at an unacceptable rate. Britain would be covered in concrete in under 300 years. Some authors have suggested an embargo on the taking of agricultural land.

As if to mediate between these two sets of views, the Agricultural Committee of the National Economic Development Council, although aware that agricultural land loss was falling, stated in 1977 that while fully recognising other interests the emphasis in policy priorities in favour of agriculture should be strengthened. They had doubts about the ability of the industry to sustain future growth in farm productivity. Also they feared that because of financial stringency local authorities would be attracted to land which was less costly to develop and which may mean a greater proportion of high quality land being taken. Indeed, their report underlines the way in which the remarkable growth in agricultural productivity and self-sufficiency between 1970 and 1980 has weakened the real strength of the case for strict controls on the transfer of agricultural land to other uses. But the Advisory Committee on Agriculture of the Ministry of Agriculture has remained aware of the need for caution over the loss of land to other uses and in 1979 suggested that the Department of the Environment should 'call in' planning applications at the Ministry's behest where there was an unresolved objection by the Ministry to the taking of agricultural land for development. The taking of *any* further land should be made conditional on it being demonstrated to the Department of the Environment that there was no suitable under-used or derelict land elsewhere in the related urban areas.

Housebuilders, on the other hand, have accused the land use planning system of denying people the right to own their own homes. They would like to see government state the total number of houses to be built each year and allocate each county a specified share. They consider at least 250,000 are required per annum and that inner-city sites should not be taken into the calculation, but regarded as a bonus. The green belt has been developed into an all embracing anti-development tool, they contend, and they suggest that the 'haves' of the shire counties by constant parochial objections, are stultifying even reasonable proposals for the small-scale spread of towns. As a result twelve new villages in greenfield locations are being proposed in the South East. These will house between 15,000 and 20,000 people and will be financed entirely by the private developers on a commercial basis. As Tom Baron, secretary of the Volume Housebuilders Association puts it:

> To keep expanding existing settlements, you're going to get political outcry because the 'haves' are going to object to the green fields going. It is better to have one big row and solve it by dropping it in an area surrounded by cows, because moo's don't vote.

Nevertheless, in drawing the new green belts, the local authorities appear to have provided realistic amounts of land for new housing. A *balance* has been struck between new greenfield sites and re-using urban land. However, in revising upwards the greenfield allocations in many plans the DoE are expressing the primacy of the housebuilding interest over that of agricultural land retention. The question as to how much housing land we need has recently been addressed in a report by the Housing Research Foundation. No numerical answer was forthcoming although the figure is believed to be in the range of 200,000 to 225,000 acres per year.

Thus although economic stagnation has slowed down migration and employment relocations, it has changed the types of demands for new land. Housebuilders want a higher proportion of greenfields, and industrial and commercial developers are attracted to open land near motorways, and major airports such as Heathrow (London), Ringway (Manchester) and Elmdon (Birmingham). Local authorities that put in place policies of urban regeneration and peripheral containment in the mid-1970s are now adjusting the balance. In the West Midlands it is argued that some loosening of containment will *benefit* urban regeneration by helping to stem economic decline. The proposal to allocate 150 hectares for high technology firms near the National Exhibition Centre in the West Midlands Green Belt is a manifestation of this (see Figure 3.15). It is mirrored by greenfield provisions near Ringway Airport in Manchester and at Washington Airport near Sunderland in the North East.

Figure 3.15: The National
Exhibition Centre in the West
Midlands Green Belt.

Source: NEC.

A realisation that land-use policies only reflect societal and political priorities has led to more insistent lobbying by the various pressure groups. Most now employ professional lobbyists to put their views forcibly at all levels. The agricultural case is now most effectively put by the Land Use Department of the National Farmers Union. It has been assiduous in appearing at public inquiries related to structure and local plans and has increased in size and effectiveness during the decade. The House Builders Federation now has a regional network of land and planning officers whose job is to assist in the process of making available the more attractive areas for building. Neither group existed until the late 1970s, whilst the Volume Housebuilders' Study Group set up in 1978 has already gained the ear of Ministers. The Council for the Protection of Rural England works nationally, and through its many county branches, to put the countryside and conservation case. It lobbies nationally, but its strength in numbers is at the local level. Local branches are frequently found countering House Builders' Federation arguments at inquiries over specific developmental proposals.

The other change from the 1950s and 1960s is the burgeoning number of local civic, amenity and environmental groups. There are many hundreds of individual village and town conservation groups who are active in seeking to protect local environments. They may be affiliated to umbrella groups, for example the Surrey Amenity Council, the London Green Belt Council, the Wirral Green Belt Society in Merseyside, or the Green Belt Defenders in Nottinghamshire. These groups frequently have members who are also on committees of District and County Councils. Protection of one's local environment from new development is thus a strong, and fully articulated, desire in England and Wales in the 1980s.

All these groups see the process of arriving at land-use policies in development plans as of major importance. Central and local government have found it difficult to tread an acceptable path between their various claims. Clear concepts or 'blueprints', of the 1947 development plan type assumed to benefit all and to be applied in the general interests of the community, are unlikely to survive the present combative climate. More flexibility is being written into plans. There is no doubt that a more lenient attitude now obtains to the expansion of *existing* sources of employment in green belts. Also the pressure to turn attractive country houses in large grounds into offices, or research and development suites, is also gradually being accommodated as it is realised that reduced public funds are available for otherwise conserving such buildings.

Recreation Provision and Countryside Management

The shortcomings of a mainly regulatory system of land-use planning were appreciated at an early stage by the Countryside Commission. Two types of response, it was felt, were required. Recreation provision and environmental improvement could occur only through positively designed and implemented expenditure programmes by public authorities. The reduction of conflict between users of the urban-rural fringe countryside required the introduction of some third party mediation — a form of countryside management.

The 1970s saw increased recreation demands despite a stagnant economy. Real disposable income grew by 40 per cent over the decade, and there were four million more cars on the road in 1980 than in 1970. Although the average working week declined little, 15 per cent of male manual workers had four or more weeks of paid annual leave by 1980 contrasting with less than 10 per cent in 1970. Surveys showed that many sought a day out in the country, most often a drive to a natural looking area where children could play and a picnic could be taken in relative peace and quiet. Rather fewer were looking for places to walk, hike or ramble, but here the coast and cliff scenery proved popular. A large number of stately homes, attractive gardens and wildlife parks opened in the decade. The Countryside Commission's household survey of England and Wales in 1977 showed that one in eight of those making a trip to the countryside visited such attractions. This was the period of purpose-designed new provision. Between 1970 and 1980 some 156 Country Parks, and 188 picnic sites, largely put in place by local authorities, were grant-aided and approved by the Countryside Commission. A total of 2,500 kilometres of new long distance footpath routes were created and a national system of way-marking was brought into use. Meanwhile the National Trust was well on the way to purchasing one-fifth of the coast of England and Wales under the Enterprise Neptune campaign.

However, from the middle years of the decade, and into the 1980s a number of factors have combined to lay emphasis upon the improved management of existing provision. Firstly, increased concern with the issues of urban-rural fringe led to the view that positive management for recreation could solve a number of problems simultaneously. As Joan Davidson stated at the time:

> ... the (urban-rural fringe) location seems to be an ideal one for developing a variety of opportunities including facilities for day recreation and for sporting and educational activities. The fringe is near to the obvious centres of demand in urban areas, even though access may be poor, particularly for those without cars. Recreation developments can help solve some of the resource problems of the fringe, providing the *raison d'être* for those areas of farmland or waste ground which face an uncertain future ... In Britain the recreation potential of the fringe locale, the opportunity it offers for blending urban and rural environments and leisure pursuits in a unique way, has not been exploited.

Secondly, local politicians and land-use planners realised that under-used countryside land near towns was most likely to be taken for urban development. Government entreaties to free land from the green belts for housing in 1963 and 1972 had suggested that untidy, unkempt and unsightly land should be contemplated first for development, as it contributed little to the appearance of the belts. Thus positive moves to enhance urban fringe environments would form a useful *complement* to urban containment policies. Those living in such areas, and in nearby cities, were increasingly keen to assist in practical tasks either as voluntary wardens at sites or as conservation volunteers carrying out simple but necessary tasks such as fencing and the repairing of stiles and gates.

These various factors have been combined in the concept of countryside management. It is based on the proposition that the aims and conduct of individual managers of rural land can be modified to accommodate the wishes of other users and the public at large by agreement with owners and occupiers. Starting from a position outside the conventional land use planning system, a number of experimental schemes have been mounted to demonstrate the possibilities of reconciling urban and rural, recreation and farming interests in sample areas. In essence they constitute four main activities.

First of all, *agriculture*. Here the emphasis has been on the reduction of the conflicts associated with farming in the urban fringe and the encouragement of restoration of under-used land to farming or other acceptable uses.

Secondly, *countryside recreation*. Attempts have been made to improve existing facilities and to identify further needs for a wide range of recreation activities. The co-ordination of the efforts of volunteers and voluntary organisations has also been a priority.

Thirdly, *wildlife and landscape*. Through advice and direct action attempts have been made to improve conditions in areas given over to woodland and to farming.

Finally, *education and advice*. Here information gained in these experimental schemes, by the work described, has been passed on to the interested bodies particularly sponsoring local authorities, educational establishments and local community groups.

The experiments have involved employment of an independent *project officer*, concerned with getting things done. For example, in the clearance and surfacing of footpaths or in the negotiation of new routes for these. Or help would be given to small scale tree planting, to small scale woodland management, or in the provision of facilities for small picnic areas among woodland. It was realised early on that the officer would be most effective if seen as *neutral*, and thus able to build bridges between owners and land managers and the remote machinery of government. Reg Hookway has listed the desirable attributes of such a person.

He needs to know about the countryside and, in most areas, about farming. He needs imagination and practical ability; he must be reliable and absolutely trustworthy, because of delegated responsibility to spend small sums of money; he needs to be able to respond to the ideas of others, and have a high level of commitment to achieve practical results. He needs an ability to listen and communicate his specialist knowledge to local people on grants, and application procedures, in order to develop and implement management solutions in close association with farmers and other landowners. Finally, he should be able to organise and inspire voluntary effort.

Such management schemes now number over 30 around the country testifying to the success of the method in resolving localised small scale conflicts of interest. There are projects in the Tyneside, Greater Manchester, West Midlands and London green belts. Some counties, for example, Hertfordshire, have five countryside management projects covering most of their green belt area (see Figure 3.16). Landscape renewal projects exist adjacent to the Potteries and in South Staffordshire. After an initial period devoted to the resolution of immediate conflicts the projects move towards a permanent presence and the preparation of management plans to secure planned object-

Figure 3.16: A Hertfordshire Countryside Management Project. Surfacing work is carried out on the Riverside Way in the Green Belt Management Area.

Source: Herts County Council.

ives. A management plan for the south Hertfordshire/Barnet area immediately north of London has recently been prepared. Management can work to a framework provided by local subject plans as in river valleys such as the Tame, Mersey and Medlock in Greater Manchester.

Grassroots

The Honorary Secretary of the Surrey Amenity Council Considers Increasing Pressure on the County's Countryside

As the M25 nears completion providing improved accessibility, and new development applications for industry, other activities are likely to present a serious challenge to the Green Belt. It is essential to resist these processes — once an exception is made you are in deep trouble. The towns in Surrey, as in Hertfordshire, are very close together. There is a little bit of a lung for people to enjoy and this is protected by Green Belt policies. Once these are eroded, there is a danger that settlements in Surrey will coalesce.

The Amenity Council is opposed to speculative housing development. Much private housing is simply to provide a profit for developers. We must guard against this. However, we are in favour of provision of the right sort of accommodation — sheltered housing and small units for young people and families. Surveys have shown that the young would like to stay in Surrey but are driven out by housing problems. I would support the conversion of large older houses into smaller units and the building of small dwellings in villages.

A different sort of pressure appears to be occurring from Government actions. The trouble now is that the Secretary of State seems to have taken more powers to himself. He is overriding the normal procedures of public inquiries and thereby his own approved structure plans. The 1983 draft Circulars on Green Belts and Land for Housing are a case in point. The Amenity Council took full part in the national campaign, masterminded by the CPRE. There were fears that more land for housing would be allowed, eroding the Green Belt as approved in the Surrey Structure Plan. Meetings were organised in London to co-ordinate action. Local societies lobbied Members of Parliament, wrote to newspapers, and encouraged members to write and object. The Circulars were subsequently withdrawn and reissued in an amended form.

An Oxfordshire District Planner Talks About Development Issues in the Green Belt in the 1980s

The City of Oxford has considerable propensity for growth and remains economically buoyant despite the recession. This has caused a number of problems in the preparation of the Oxford Fringe Local Plan which is a district plan and aims to control the growth of Oxford and to define the inner boundary of the Oxford Green Belt.

The Green Belt should have a considerable degree of permanence. Therefore the development issues need to be thrashed out. Oxford City wanted more development than that proposed in the Structure Plan. Three rural Districts and the county opposed this. When the Structure Plan went through its public participation stage (the Examination in Public) the city lost the argument but gained some ground. The Secretary of State for the Environment, who has to approve the Plan, decided that its housing provision for Central Oxfordshire should be met in full (rather than the reduced provision accepted elsewhere) and that local plans to implement this provision should be produced quickly.

The District set about meeting this level of provision. Joint working parties of members and officers went through endless meetings discussing various sites. At one stage it appeared that it was not possible to find enough land to meet the Structure Plan target. There were two options to make good the short fall; either to release a large site, on the southern edge of the City, known as Greater Leys, or to find more small sites on the edge of the City.

Both options involved development in the Interim Green Belt. (This is the Oxford Green Belt identified in the Structure Plan which has not yet been formally endorsed by the Secretary of State in terms of its specific boundaries. These are being sorted out in the Fringe Local Plan.) Because the City owned much of the land at Greater Leys and could, if it so desired, meet the needs of the City, the first option was chosen. It would also be easy to enlarge the area to cater for the period 1991-6, making it possible for the local council to recover infrastructure costs.

Largely because of this possibility of future expansion, the county refused to certify the Local Plan as being in conformity with the Structure Plan on the grounds that too much development was being proposed. Although the Local Plan has now been sent to the Secretary there have been a number of serious objections to the housing, industrial land and Green Belt proposals. In addition the Department of the Environment is trying to get the County at least partly to certify the Plan which is holding things up even more. We are caught in an awkward position. If we now proceed with the statutory process there is likely to be a long and expensive Local Public Inquiry into the Fringe Local Plan, to be followed by an Examination in Public into the review of the Structure Plan. All the arguments will be rehearsed twice over and the Fringe Local Plan will be four years old before it is finally approved. We are now considering using the existing draft plan as council policy rather than carrying on with the Statutory procedure at this stage.

The problem about the Green Belt more generally is that it is widely misunderstood. It is really a planning device you use to stop things happening and to implement a strategy. It does not have any recognisable characteristics of its own. The green belt legislation is now so old that the presumptions contained within it, that certain forms of development are appropriate, no longer apply. Take the case of recreation buildings — some of these are no different to urban buildings. There is not a lot of difference between a brick built factory and a brick built squash court attached to a recreational complex. The same applies to many modern agricultural buildings but it would not be possible to prevent such developments throughout the Oxford Green Belt where the usual exceptions to restraint would not apply. A case in point is a narrow gap between settlements where there is already a garden centre and two farms which could erect large agricultural buildings. You would only need to add a golf course and there would be very little Green Belt left. This proposition was discussed at an officers' working party where there were opposing views. Some Districts adopted the proposal and some did not.

We need a new Green Belt statement which would define more clearly the types of development which are appropriate in Green Belts. An example might be that playing fields are appropriate provided the associated buildings are kept to a minimum. The scale of some modern agricultural buildings is inappropriate in Green Belts and should be controlled. We also need clarification in relation to large institutions in open grounds. Whilst an isolation hospital might need to be sited away from urban areas, I can see no reason why conference centres should not be located in towns rather than the Green Belt.

A Hertfordshire Property and Building Consultant Discusses the Relationship Between Industry and the Planning System

Individual firms seeking sites lay down tight criteria. Their requirements vary according to operational needs. Unless a firm is seeking to open up new territory, it will generally seek a site as near as possible to its existing base. The residential preference of the Managing Director is often a major factor. He or she will decide where they want to live and then justify the decision on other grounds. A good local labour supply is also important. Prestige firms may wish to locate near an airport to ensure good access for executives. The degree of priority accorded to road access (for example, access to the motorway network) will depend on the nature of the firm. A pharmaceuticals company may not worry too much about these factors if its raw materials are not bulky.

Tenure is important. For most companies a freehold site is of primary concern. The freehold provides collateral when times are hard. Conversely leasehold property, particularly when there are frequent rent reviews, can be a positive disadvantage. This requirement rules out many new town and development area locations. Whilst Corby will release freehold sites, Milton Keynes and Northampton will not. The only effective method of getting industry into areas of high unemployment is by offering freehold sites.

Industrialists may go to areas such as Norfolk or Somerset either because their wish to develop in more central locations is frustrated, or in search of cheap freehold sites. The Local Planning Authorities there are willing to make sites available. Often such firms succeed after initial difficulties. If such an area then becomes successful, the planning authority may be driven to apply restraint and the vicious circle starts again.

Individual industrialists are not catered for by the system of allocating land in development plans. Such land is often bought up by developers and does not necessarily come onto the market for its original purpose. Applications for major industrial development now tend to be fought on appeal and the present appeal system is time-consuming. More often than not, industrial land coming onto the market belongs to the local authority or another public body. It is much more difficult to take a farmer's field. Public bodies tend to profit out of development far more than is good for them.

Statutory plans are too inflexible. These are often prepared for a ten-year period and they are unable to adjust to rapid change in the economic climate. Also, there is too much public participation. The result is often that a line is drawn around an area saying 'we will have no more development here.'

I am unhappy at the role played by many planners. They don't think enough about industry. It is all very well to have their vision of perfection, but they must look at job opportunities in a real situation. Take for example the Green Belt. I believe in Green Belt policy, but people do have to live in the Green Belt, and that means employment. Green Belts and the green areas between villages and towns should be absolutely sacrosanct, but development must go somewhere and the old concept of 'white land' was fine. We should return to it.

Actions to Steer Change

Land-use Planning

The return of a Conservative government in 1979 brought with it a new emphasis on removing what were seen as the unnecessary obstacles to development. Land-use planners were told by Tom King when he introduced a new wide-ranging Circular on development control: 'I regard this Circular as a most important advance in the evolution of the British planning system. Hitherto there has been too much emphasis on restraint and restriction. From now on we intend to ensure that positive attitudes prevail.' Beneath the rhetoric, however, do the detailed changes reflect a fundamental redirection of policy?

The land use planning system, the Government maintains, 'balances the protection of the natural and built-environment with the pressures of economic and social change'. Developments should be approved unless there is a clear-cut reason for refusal. The clear-cut reasons sound familiar — the presence of land of good agricultural or landscape quality, Green Belts and Areas of Outstanding Natural Beauty. Indeed successive Secretaries of State have gone out of their way to assure critics that the Government's commitment to conservation has not weakened.

However, the detailed changes suggest that land-use planning is being fashioned to facilitate housing and industrial development. In doing this it is taking into account, but perhaps not according such great weight as before to good agricultural land, landscape and green belt considerations. At the same time it is clear that many local authorities, faced with declining employment have found or made available a limited number of attractive greenfield sites particularly for industrial and commercial development (see Figure 3.17). However, there are great differences in such attitudes across England and Wales. In Merseyside, for example, large industrial developments will be allowed in the green belt if their proponents can convince the authorities that there are no suitable urban sites. Cheshire County Council is investigating the feasibility of developing Council-owned land in the green belt for industry. Even in the South East, however, new industrial activity cannot simply be fostered by allocating greenfield sites. The pension funds will build the buildings but occupiers for the large amount of new space on offer are difficult to find. The problem for industry, commerce and retailing is that as peripheral and greenfield sites become more available the incentive to locate on more expensive redevelopment sites in towns evaporates. Take shopping as an example. Out of town superstores located near motorways are at the highest points of accessibility for motorists and for delivery vans and lorries. The main supermarket chains argue that such purpose-built stores can retail groceries at 10 to 15 per cent lower cost than if the same goods are sold in a town centre. For a car-borne shopper there is the convenience of easy parking and a wide variety of goods under one roof. It is not difficult to see why over 200 such stores have received planning approval since the mid-1970s and why the M25 corridor is a crucial target location for firms like Asda, Woolco, Sainsbury and Carrefour (see Figure 3.18).

In the case of housing, local authorities now have to identify a five-year

Figure 3.17: Aztec West Office and Industrial Accommodation. An advertisement from the *Estate Times*, Sept. 1983, promoting greenfield sites adjacent to the M4 near Bristol.

Source: *Estate Times*, 16 September 1983.

supply of land 'in areas where potential house buyers are prepared to live and suitable for the wide range of housing types which the market now demands'. House Builders' Federation representatives can negotiate to adjust a land supply assessment if they consider, for example, that it does not contain sufficient sites in the 'upper' and 'middle' market categories. In 1983, in response to entreaties by the housebuilders the Government had suggested that the land supply required to be identified in plans should be raised to seven years supply. Land in the ownership of unwilling vendors will no longer form part of such calculations. In seeking to steer change local authorities have pursued a number of tactics (for steering change is a game of tactics and counter-tactics). Where development restraint is desired by local politicians, the aim

Figure 3.18: The Carrefour Superstore Just Outside Swindon.

Source: Carrefour Ltd.

has been to rely on urban sites first, infill sites second, and only to allocate peripheral sites as a last resort. Fortuitously there are now coming onto the market large amounts of surplus institutional land in urban areas. These include school sites with their large playing fields, hospitals often on large sites and a considerable amount of railway land occupied by surplus sidings. In counties like Buckinghamshire, Berkshire, Hertfordshire and Surrey these are providing a valuable alternative to the taking of agricultural land. In Slough, for example, a town surrounded by the green belt near Heathrow, there are estimated to be some 150 hectares of such land. As this type of land is often in the control of local authorities it can be released through agreements made with builders so that those in local need of a house may get the first opportunity to purchase. This neatly assuages local feelings that residents will be priced out of the housing market by incomers. In addition around 25 to 30 per cent of new dwellings commonly arise by infilling or redevelopment. This may involve demolition and building in the grounds of large Victorian properties at densities in tune with the 1980s. Where development does occur on farmland it is almost invariably in contained additions to existing development avoiding, as far as reasonable sewerage and other costs will allow, the better agricultural land. There is now a provision in the 1980 Planning Act which strengthens the power of MAFF in respect of local plans. Where development is proposed on good quality agricultural land in a local plan, and where MAFF object, if this objection is not accommodated the Department of the Environment may 'call in' the plan and decide the issue. In its first three years of existence this power has yet to be formally used.

The Government are clearly determined to see that local authorities keep to the totals of population to be accommodated in countryside pressure areas. Authorities must now list land in public ownership in registers with a view to its disposal. Reserve powers exist to compel authorities to dispose of developable urban land. Government is now suggesting that authorities make one-off departures from previously agreed plans if unforeseen problems of developing allocated land arise. (This 'departure' procedure has existed since 1947 and is an example of the amount of discretion built into the land use planning system.) In addition, the Government adds, new rural settlements may need to be planned if peripheral growth is considered unacceptable. The likelihood is that land which was previously used for industry increasingly will be recycled for residential use in green-belt towns.

The ability of the land use planning system to bend investment trends depends on the relative strength of the authorities' policies and the power of the economic arguments facing developers. For this reason, in a depression, employment generating proposals will have enhanced appeal to local politicians seeking to provide jobs. They will sacrifice their green fields for manufacturing jobs. The signs are, although there is no firm evidence, that the same attitudes are beginning to apply to out-of-town superstores. If a typical large store creates 200 or more jobs, the consequent attrition of small traders in the town centre is less startling and newsworthy. It could be, then, that medium sized country towns surrounded by a green belt or similar form of restraint policy are turning inside out. Employment opportunities may appear on the green fields around the edge, rather than round the town centre. And new housing may be found near the centre on the vacated industrial land.

The Urban-rural Fringe and Recreation

Until recently countryside recreation facilities were planned on the basis that growth in participation would continue. This may, however, now have a reached a plateau. The effects of having over three million unemployed are depressing such demands. The 1980 National Survey of the Countryside Commission showed only 81 million visits to the countryside per average summer month, compared with 101 million some three years earlier. Day trips from home had declined by 5 per cent but day trips taken whilst on holiday had declined (because of a reduction in short second holidays) by a third. As the real value of money available for expenditure on recreation by local authorities had declined, emphasis has switched to the more effective management of existing facilities. One major initiative that has appealed to hard-pressed authorities has been that of managing Country Parks according to firmer market principles. At Rufford Park in Nottinghamshire, for example, a scheme devised by Coopers and Lybrand Associates is being put into operation. A careful cost analysis of alternative projects within the park, including a craft centre and interpretation centre, led to the selection of a desired mix of attractions. These have then been priced and marketed according to consistent principles. The result should be more visitors, hopefully gaining a more rewarding recreation experience from their visits, the whole costing less to the Nottinghamshire ratepayers than the former arrangements. These principles are being applied more widely across the country.

Another development which may gain momentum in the 1980s is the idea of countryside interpretation. It is an invaluable way of informing the townspeople about the workings of the countryside and of imparting the conservation message. An interpreter is someone who devises a theme selected from perhaps the social history, landscape or economy of a countryside area, and uses it as a peg for an explanation of processes occurring within the natural environment. Various media may be used such as self-guided trails, listening posts and fixed message repeaters or displays of working machinery and the undertaking of practical conservation tasks. Many of the techniques used were developed in the USA. If tastefully deployed they undoubtedly satisfy a thirst for knowledge about the countryside. However, it will remain true that self-discovery rather than guided discovery is more appropriate at many countryside recreation venues.

For many years large scale recreation provision in the countryside near towns has often been dependent on other expenditure programmes. In the

North the presence of 80, then 100 per cent derelict land grants gave an impetus to environmental improvement. The most common after-use has been for leisure. As a result recreation budgets have added the tree planting, waymarking and other visitor facilities at this later stage. The Rother Valley Regional Park on the edge of Sheffield is one such example, reclaimed from colliery pit heaps and, on the edge of Newcastle-on-Tyne, Bladon Burn is a similar but smaller scale example of this sequence of events.

In Greater Manchester environmental improvement in the main river valleys has been under way as a developed expenditure programme for 15 years (see Figure 3.19). Derelict land clearance was the spur financially, but local involvement through such bodies as the North West Civic Trust kept it to the fore politically. After local government reorganisation a highly effective scheme of County-District co-operation was worked out. The improvement and subsequent management of informal recreation in combination with other countryside uses, of five major river valleys, has proceeded using finance largely from the county. On-site work and maintenance labour has come from the contributing district authorities. For each Valley statutory local plans have been prepared which assist in resolving potential conflict, providing a framework for piecemeal schemes including private investment, and giving guidance to statutory bodies with interests in the areas. Progress has been made on reconstructing a landscape framework for each Valley, on improving access, and on provision of informal recreation. Each area has a Joint Management Committee made up of elected county and district members, served by local authority officers. Day-to-day management is the responsibility of a warden who directs the work of a small team. In this way consistent policies are operated across district boundaries dividing up the Valleys, and it is hoped that a consistent identity will be built up in each area as a result. This work is a model of its kind and a positive demonstration of how different levels of local government can work together.

Despite much publicity concerning the problems of the countryside near towns, governments have not accepted the need for new measures to give special assistance to landowners and public authorities in such areas. Suggestions that a system of annual expenditure programmes be instituted, supported by a special allocation from central funds, fell on stony ground. The idea that farmers be given 'Less Favoured Area' status, as in the uplands, was also not taken up. No enhanced powers for land acquisition for recreation, landscape or farm reamalgamation have been thought appropriate. The government view has been that the requisite powers exist to improve the urban-rural fringe *if they can be effectively deployed* in one area at one time.

Evaluation of the countryside management projects suggests that they can be successful in solving small-scale conflict. If pursued consistently in the long term they have the potential to become an indispensable part of the countryside scene near towns. Where they have had more difficulty is in tackling the larger-scale environmental and land-use problems of the type found in the Manchester River Valleys. One lesson of the early experiments was that some way of increasing and concentrating the total monies that were being spent in improving such environments was required.

The Countryside Commission conceived the idea of promoting an experiment in environmental improvement, recreation provision and farmland improvement on a larger scale. This would include funding from the major agencies investing in the urban fringe countryside. In 1980 Operation Groundwork, covering the countryside around St Helens, was launched basing its work on a natural resource information bank built up by Merseyside County Council. In 1982 a regional programme — Groundwork North West — was also set up, and five schemes covering Wigan, Macclesfield, Rochdale/Oldham, Rossendale and Saltford/Trafford are currently under way.

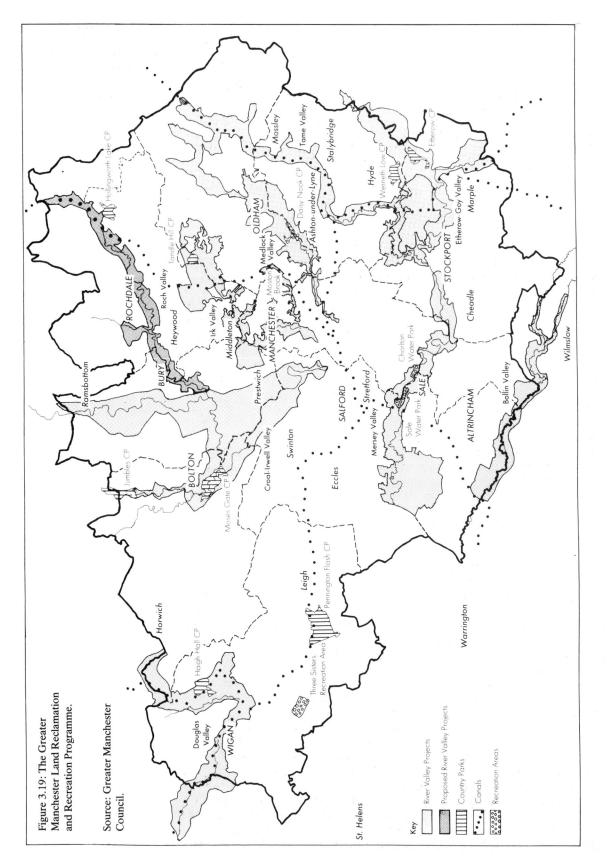

Figure 3.19: The Greater
Manchester Land Reclamation
and Recreation Programme.

Source: Greater Manchester
Council.

Key

| River Valley Projects |
| Proposed River Valley Projects |
| Country Parks |
| Canals |
| Recreation Areas |

Figure 3.20: 'Let's enjoy it
while we can — this is where
they're going to build a new
leisure centre.'

Source: *Punch.*

Groundwork projects aim to reach out into the local community to involve a wide range of organisations and individuals. The intention is to co-ordinate effort to clear dereliction, find productive uses for waste land, bring country-side closer to the homes of townspeople, and create conditions that allow farming and forestry to prosper. Each project is co-ordinated by a charitable trust set up as a focus for commitment, and financial and manpower resources. In this way it is hoped that the various interests will fuse together in practice spurred by a common wish to improve the environment.

Initially the regional scheme has an earmarked £3 million for derelict land clearance in 1983/4, and a further £1 million will be spent by the Countryside Commission to provide initial running costs for the Trusts and grants for small scale works. An important element of the schemes is the involvement of the private sector, including industry and commerce. The MAFF and Nature Conservancy Council have committed staff to the projects. The aim of these Trusts is to act as mobilisers of voluntary, local authority and commercial interest, and they aim to be financially self-sufficient after three years. Although it is too early to assess the success of these ventures it is clearly the aim of the Countryside Commission to spread such projects to the urban-rural fringes of all our major conurbations. Certainly the use of the environmental trust as a means of containing settlements in an environmentally sensitive way seems destined to grow.

Who Benefits, Who Loses?

From the very first attempts to control the transfer of agricultural land to urbanised uses through to the Planning Act of 1947 and beyond, it would seem that it ought to have been possible broadly to categorise the prime bene-ficiaries of, and the losers from, such policies. However, the situation has always been a more subtle one than first impressions might suggest when only the chief 'actors' are considered. Especially in the immediately post-Second-World-War climate, the consumers of food (which means everyone) pre-sumably gained from the preservation of farmland as part of a strategy to control the expansion of settlements. Every bit of food that could be produced at home was needed to feed the population, at the same time easing the balance-of-payments problem. The extent to which such considerations remain at all valid now that England and Wales are part of the EEC would depend upon how far it might be argued that there is good cause to continue to support a prosperous indigenous agriculture industry, coincident with the maintenance of a healthy and prosperous rural community. Here the argu-ments put forward by those who make a case for the conservation of agricul-tural land have not been helped by greatly increased agricultural efficiency as measured through output per person employed in that industry. At the same time it might be argued that maximising the amount of land in agriculture would imply an increased strength for the farming lobby which in turn could better put the case for the maintenance of its own interests.

However, the individual farmer under planning control has certainly lost his ability to decide for himself how his land may be used outside of agriculture. It is not for him, if an opportunity arises, to decide to sell up to a property development company in the expectation of receiving building land prices, though it must be added that the incentives to do this have diminished with the spectacular rise in agricultural land prices through the 1970s. Agricultural land with planning permission for such development, however, will still allow the farmer to make significant financial gains. Only at the urban fringe may prices be high enough without planning permission to act as the carrot for the sale of agricultural land, with the pressures resulting from crop damage due to trespass and other forms of urban vandalism performing the role of the stick. Of the other 'actors' the most obvious ones who stand to lose out in the context of very restrictive controls over development are the property developers themselves. Though greater personal mobility and higher incomes have increased the demand for housing away from the centres of the cities and into the suburbs or beyond into the smaller towns and villages, a level of demand for new housing development at what might be prime sites is simply unlikely to be met because of planning controls. This is not to say the private individual or his family will not succeed in their desire to live in a rural situation — merely that constraints are at work. But people may find, for example, that limitations to the number of houses at their dreamed-of sea-side locations, brought about by restrictions on such developments, means that most property is beyond their financial reach. Such restrictions on development are principally advantageous to those already in possession of property at such locations. Others, already located in houses on prime sites next to open spaces on the urban fringe or in a position quickly to reach desirable rural locations, will be similarly privileged.

These more specific gains may be countered by other more general losses brought about by planning controls on development. Town dwellers, for example, may find that the increased demand brought about in a situation of controlled land availability results in their having to live at higher densities than they would like. Those who do succeed in leaving for the countryside find that restrictions on development opportunities for new housing may force upon them longer journeys as part of their daily commuting to their work in the towns.

For the indigenous rural dweller, possibly the farm worker, the price of houses or cottages, already in limited supply, is forced up to levels he cannot afford, by both incoming urban workers, and development restrictions. Indeed it has to be remembered that the income of the agricultural worker is well below the national average and this is a situation accounted for partly by planning controls themselves. In keeping industry out of rural locations, competition for labour has essentially been reduced thus allowing agricultural and other rural wages to remain at a low level.

Turning finally to the more general impact of the containing of settlements through planning control, if the desirability of drawing a clear division between what should be urban and what should be rural is accepted, then such policies might be recorded as a major success. Of course, some would argue that had such policies permitted greater control over the agriculturalist's use of the countryside the success might have been even greater. Whilst the cynical might take note of the huge expansion in local government created by the development of planning as a profession and its proliferation since 1947, others might register with satisfaction that the nurturing of the countryside as essentially a rural rather than a sub-urban experience has enhanced its recreational desirability to the town dweller (the vast majority of the population).

The use of the countryside for such purposes has spawned a whole industry geared to looking after their needs from innkeepers to national park wardens, hoteliers and the once-proud owners of country seats. Countryside pursuits are clearly no longer the sole prerogative of the wealthy guest at the manor down from London for a weekend among the pheasants.

If that strong division between town and country now begins to become less clear cut, it will be as a result of a new whiff of political grapeshot from the guns of the current Conservative administration, combined with a degree of hard economic realism which recognises the desires of new technologically-based industries for greenfield sites and of the general public for cheap out-of-town shopping. But there is no doubt that the more peripheral impact of such changes will be resisted strongly by the ever increasing effectiveness of conservation and amenity groups.

4
Conserving the Wild
SNAPSHOTS

Take not too much of the land, weare not out all the fatness, but leave in it some heart.
Pliny the Elder, AD 23-79. Cited in Richard Merrill (ed.)(1976), Radical Agriculture.

Nature knows nothing of what we call landscape for Nature's scenery is the natural habitat, while our landscape is the habitat manipulated by man for his own uses. Landscape therefore is not a static background which we inhabit, but the interaction of a society and the habitat it lives in, and if either man or the habitat changes then so inevitably must the resulting landscape.
William Marshall (1796), Planting and Rural Ornament.

In the eighteenth century, energy was turned into the more feasible channel of landscape gardening under the influence of the picturesque. The new school accepted the natural irregularity of the country and aimed at emphasising it. Mr Christopher Hussey in his book The Picturesque has drawn attention to the influence upon English country planning which the great painters Claude and Poussin exercised with their calm grand manner; and the Dutchmen, Ruysdael and Hobbema, with their delight in the rough and apparently artless but really skilfully composed scenes. Kent, the architect, and Capability Brown, the gardener, were the protagonists of this new method, and like all reformers they swept away much that was beautiful in the formal flower gardens surrounding the houses and many

a stately straight avenue. But though their theories were often absurd, their parks were superb, as may be seen at Blenheim, Chatsworth and Fountains Abbey; and every country squire became an amateur in planting and in the study of the picturesque. It is still by no means realised — if it can ever be definitely known — how much of England was consciously laid out during this time, far beyond the boundary of the home park.
Repton, a later practitioner, who restored the formal house garden, aptly described the object of landscape art, 'to improve the scenery of a country and to display its native beauties with advantage'. The regularising and angular hand of man has thus been softened into heightening an effect here, opening a prospect there, or planting out an unseemly object.
P. Abercrombie (1933), Town and Country Planning.

From 1920 onwards, country people and lovers of the countryside gradually became aware that throughout wide areas the tranquillity of the countryside was being destroyed, traditional landscapes were disappearing, ancient buildings were being removed and that in many places natural fauna and flora were suffering drastic modifications and often destruction. The problem of preserving access to the countryside which had been the preoccupation of nineteenth-century footpaths and commons preservationists had become a problem of preserving the countryside itself.
H.E. Bracey (1959), English Rural Life.

. . . visitors from Worcester, coming through Malvern Wells, used to see the unspoilt northern hills with an indescribable pleasure. They now see it hideously disfigured by three gigantic scoops, reaching so nearly to the top of the ridge that they bring home with a shock the appalling conviction that before very long the scoops will go right through, leaving between them a couple of enormous jagged teeth of hill, which will presumably be blasted away in their turn, changing the Malvern Hills into the Malvern Flats.
G.B. Shaw (1929), Letter to The Times. Cited in Sheail (1975), Nature in Trust.

The landscape of England and Wales is a striking example of the interdependence between the satisfaction of man's material wants and the creation of beauty. The pattern and the beauty of the countryside as we know them today are largely the work of man during the past few centuries. Its present appearance is not by any means entirely the work of nature and it is not enduring, for nature is dynamic, never static. If land were left uncultivated, if downs and mountains were not grazed by cattle or sheep, the countryside would gradually but inevitably return to its former natural condition of forest in the valleys and on the lower slopes, and a scrub of brambles, thorn bushes and bracken on the higher levels — unless, of course, many thousands of men instead of many thousands of animals were employed to keep nature in check by cutting bracken, uprooting

bushes, and keeping down scrub and undergrowth. Experience has shown how quickly land can revert to an unkempt, wild and ragged condition, even where it is only neglected and not wholly abandoned. The beauty and pattern of the countryside are the direct result of the cultivation of the soil and there is no antagonism between use and beauty.
Scott Report (1944), Committee on Land Utilisation in Rural Areas.

When I am reporting on the merits of a proposed nature reserve, after describing the scientific importance of its flora and fauna, I often find it hard to resist bringing in the scenic beauty of the landscape or the attractiveness of the vegetation, though my allusions to these tend to take on an almost apologetic tone. It is as if I were trying to say 'and, of course, the place really is beautiful as well, though perhaps I ought not to mention the fact!'
Sir Arthur Tansley (1953), First Chairman of the Nature Conservancy Council.

Other threats to natural beauty and open-air recreation included the training grounds of the defence departments, overhead electricity transmission systems, the multiplication of masts for telecommunication, quarrying operations, and water catchment and storage. Water engineers naturally looked upon reservoirs with the eye of favour. Lloyd George's remark was recalled when at a public inquiry learned counsel for the Warrington water undertaking claimed that 'the

valley would look better under water'. 'So would Warrington,' Lloyd George commented, 'but we do not propose on that account to submerge it.'
Lord Molson (1963) Countryside in the 1970s Conference Proceedings.

A tree's a tree. How many more (redwoods) do you want to look at? If you've seen one, you've seen them all.
Attributed to Ronald Reagan when a candidate for the Governor of California (Quoted in Krieger, M.H. (1973), 'What's Wrong with Plastic Trees?' Science, 179, 446-55).

We are now in danger of losing a substantial proportion of all our wildlife. If current trends continue many species of plants and animals will become extinct in Britain before the end of this century . . . SSSIs occupy less than 6% of the land of Britain: even their complete protection is not enough. What we really need is a national policy for rural land use which takes full account of the requirements for wildlife.
D. Goode (1981), 'The Threat to Wildlife', New Scientist. Cited in McEwen, M. and McEwen, A. (1982), National Parks: Conservation or Cosmetics, George Allen & Unwin.

Meanwhile the Government is busy assuring votes among farmers and landowners. The first millionaire created by the compensation provisions of the Wildlife and Countryside Act 1981 is likely to be Mr. Phillip Merricks with whom the Nature Conservancy Council is trying to negotiate a management agreement. According to an NCC internal paper,

which I have seen, it is expected to cost the NCC about £100,000 a year to prevent him draining 1,143 acres of grazing marsh on the Isle of Sheppey, north Kent. Half the north Kent marshes, an internationally important haunt of wildfowl and waders, has disappeared in the last fifty years. But it will take less than ten for Mr. Merricks to make his million.

Paying farmers to do nothing is an odd policy for a government devoted to the work ethic and it makes all the more curious the shenanigans of the Sedgemoor farmers who burned NCC officials in effigy as a protest against their land being designated a Site of Special Scientific Interest. Under such a designation the worst that could happen to them is that they would be paid handsomely not to drain it. No wonder that Environment Secretary, Tom King, hurried to cool their heated passions.
Christopher Hall, The Countryman, Summer 1983.

'It is an uncanny experience' wrote the Cambridge woodland ecologist, Oliver Rockham, 'to trace an identifiable wood or hedge through five or seven centuries and then going to the spot to be just in time for the dying embers of the bonfires in which it has been destroyed.'
Charles Pye-Smith and Chris Rose (1984), Crisis and Conservation, Penguin.

Perspectives on Conservation: Natural Values

So far, this volume has undertaken an analysis of two particular aspects of change in the countryside: agriculture and urban containment. A third important element of change, considered in this chapter, is conservation. Conserving the countryside of England and Wales is, however, a little more elusive a concept. What, for example, is meant by conservation? Why should the countryside be conserved? What should be conserved within the countryside?

These notions are embraced within this chapter. In so doing, this first section breaks the mould of specifically analysing the deeper historical antecedents of countryside conservation. Although these historical origins are assessed from pre-biblical times, they are done so within a broader discussion of the meanings of conservation up to the present day. The development of more specific conservation policies is then taken up from the late nineteenth century in the following section.

The need to have a clearer understanding of what countryside conservation means derives from the fact that people perceive the countryside in very different ways. To some it is a factory where food and fibre must be produced under far less controllable conditions than those experienced by most other industries. At the opposite extreme it is to others primarily a source of spiritual inspiration and renewal, of freedom and pleasure in wildlife and beautiful views. People like farmers and foresters who appreciate the countryside in a functional way see change as a desirable, indeed inevitable, result of man's essential mastery over nature. To them there is merit in whatever kind of landscape results, provided gross misuse is avoided and the land remains 'in good heart'. This kind of attitude is summed up in a statement by Jerry Wiggin which he made in 1981 as Parliamentary Secretary to the Ministry of Agriculture, Fisheries and Food:

> ... there is no such thing as the natural beauty of the countryside. The countryside as we see it today has been made by the efforts of countless generations of landowners and farmers since this land was first inhabited, and the landowners and farmers of today are just as conscious of the beauty of the countryside around them as were their forefathers. It is totally untrue therefore — and I reject utterly the accusation — that farmers and landowners are damaging the countryside. Of course they are not. The countryside is a living, ever-changing entity and I know of no greater conservationists than those people who live in it and who eke a living from their work within it.

For many of those to whom the countryside is essentially an aesthetic experience, their ideal is often one of 'wilderness' where there has been no human impact whatsoever. Ranged between these two polarities there is a whole series of positions which see both utilitarian and aesthetic benefits as being maximised at some intermediate, harmonious level of exploitation by man. Those who think this way are usually prepared to accept the inevitability of change in the countryside, but wish to control it in order to maintain those qualities thought to be most desirable.

There are differences of extent as well as quality in the way different people perceive the countryside. People do not only sense merit in quite different attributes of the countryside, but perceive the environment at different levels. Some see much more detail than others. Thus the bird watcher becomes very concerned when a single species such as the sparrow-hawk is lost from an area because of pesticides. Other countryside users may not notice, may not even be aware of the existence of such a species. But they would notice the loss of a copse where the sparrow-hawk nests and hedgerows where it hunts. Such changes might not bother the average farmer, but he certainly would be concerned at changes such as soil erosion. It is important to appreciate these different perceptions of the countryside since they are a source of much confusion and conflict in land-use planning and management today. It is possible for one group of people to believe, quite genuinely, that disastrous damage is occurring in the countryside, whilst another equally genuinely believes virtually no change is taking place at all.

It is within this spectrum of contemporary attitudes that conserving the countryside must be understood, but all these viewpoints can be traced back to the beginning of recorded history. In Western cultures utilitarian attitudes towards nature have always predominated. This is commonly attributed to the Judaeo-Christian teachings of the Bible which can be readily interpreted as giving man complete authority to exploit the natural world for his own ends. Two quotations from Genesis (1:28, 9:2) illustrate this point:

> And God blessed them, and God said unto them, be fruitful and multiply, and replenish the earth, and subdue it . . .

and

> And the fear of you and the dread of you shall be upon every beast of the earth, and upon every fowl of the air, upon all that moveth upon the earth, and upon the fishes of the sea; into your hand are they delivered.

It is true that there is also support in the scriptures for the very opposite view, namely that it is incumbent upon man to look after the environment (Genesis 2:15):

> And the Lord God took the man, and put him into the garden of Eden to dress it and to keep it.

Yet, there is no doubt that this idea of stewardship has always been subordinate to that of exploitation. The well known biblical verses, Luke 3:5 and Isaiah 40:4, popularised in Handel's *Messiah* might easily have been written as a creed for the modern industrial developer, highway or water engineer or farmer:

> Every valley shall be filled, and every mountain and hill shall be brought low; and the crooked shall be made straight, and the rough ways shall be made smooth.

These words, however, are equally descriptive of man's impact on the Chinese or Japanese landscapes, largely the products of cultures which have adhered to ideologies that have always thought that man is part of nature and must conform to her laws. Pre-literate peoples, such as the Red Indians of North America, commonly had a profound reverence for nature and seem, even today, to live more in harmony with their environment. This is well expressed in a statement by Chief Seaith in a letter written in 1855 replying to the American President's offer to buy his tribe's land:

> How can you buy or sell the sky — the warmth of the land? The idea is strange to us. We do not own the freshness of the air or the sparkling of the water. How can you buy them from us? We will decide in our time. Every part of this earth is sacred to my people. Every shining pine needle, every sandy shore, every mist in the dark wood, every clearing and humming insect is holy in the memory and experience of my people.
>
> We know that the white man does not understand our ways. One portion of the land is the same to him as the next, for he is a stranger who comes in

the night and takes from the land whatever he needs. The earth is not his brother, but his enemy, and when he has conquered it, he moves on. He leaves his father's grave behind and does not care. He kidnaps the earth from his children. He does not care.

This delight in nature and a longing for a tamer time when man lived in harmony with it has none the less always been an undercurrent flowing counter to the prevailing exploitative utilitarian attitudes. From the Song of Solomon in the Bible to the present day, wild plants and animals have been dominant in the imagery of poetry, painting and music. Sir Julian Huxley in his preface to Rachel Carson's book, *Silent Spring*, which drew attention to the effects of pesticides on the environment, said that after reading it his brother, Aldous, had felt that 'we are losing half the subject matter of English poetry'. The Romantic tradition has always had a countervailing balance against utilitariansim.

Although the Saxon and Medieval Chronicles and illustrated manuscripts show that some people were clearly keen observers of nature (see Colour Plate 4), the general interest in plants and animals in those times and for most of our history was, however, largely confined to their usefulness to man, whether as food, medicine, fibre, beasts of burden or quarry to be hunted. Animals were widely credited as being without the perception of pain in the human sense and subjected to unbelievable cruelties. It was not until the early part of the nineteenth century that the developing modern science began to classify plants and animals according to their intrinsic properties and to demonstrate without dispute the close affinity of man with the higher animals, that attitudes began to change. Early natural historians, such as John Ray in the seventeenth century through their study of plants and animals, undermined the separateness and uniqueness of man which was at the heart of the predominantly utilitarian attitude to the rest of creation.

The eighteenth and early nineteenth centuries were a time of more rapid and fundamental change in the social structure and face of the British countryside than hitherto. They marked the culmination of the Agrarian and Industrial Revolutions with a fairly speedy transition from a largely subsistence based peasant agriculture to a much more commercial one and a huge movement of population to the towns in response to labour needs in the expanding manufacturing sector. The parliamentary enclosures imposed a new regularity and reduction in access to the countryside where previously both people and animals had been able to roam unconfined over vast extents of downland and heathland 'wastes'.

It was these changes which aroused regret at what was being lost and the desire to preserve as much as possible of what remained. These feelings are quite explicit in contemporary poetry. For example, Matthew Arnold's poem of 1860, *Thyrsis*:

I know these slopes; who knows them if not I! —
But many a dingle on the loved hill-side,
With thorns once studded, old, white-blossomed trees,
Where thick the cowslips grew, and far descried
High towered the spikes of purple orchides,
Hath since our day put by
The coronals of that forgotten time;
Down each green bank hath gone the ploughboy's team,
And only in the hidden brookside gleam
Primroses, orphans of the flowery prime.

It was Wordsworth who in 1810 first proposed the idea of a national park to protect the Lake District in his *A Guide to the Lakes*. At this time man's mastery over nature became more manifest and a more relaxed attitude to the remaining wild areas was possible. Previously, mountains, forests and marshes had been justly regarded as places of fear and dread. Wilderness literally means the place of untamed beasts and for much of history until medieval times, bear, boar and wolf had been a real threat to people and their stock. A mid-seventeenth-century poetical dictionary included in its epithets for a forest: 'dreadful', 'gloomy', 'wild', 'desert', 'uncouth', 'melancholy', 'unpeopled', 'beast haunted'. Yet in 1812 Byron in *Childe Harold's Pilgrimage* was extolling the 'pleasure' of the pathless woods and 'rapture' of the lonely shore. This duality has been present at least since biblical times where contemporary writers considered the wilderness to range from 'cursed ground' to 'a place of refuge and contemplation'.

When the environment was mainly wild, beauty was seen in order imposed by the hand of man. When the wastes had gone, to be replaced by a chequerboard countryside of enclosed fields, beauty came to be seen in wilderness. 'Hideous' mountains, pests and weeds were no longer seen as examples of divine wrath, but as evidence of God's awesome handiwork. Nowhere was this more marked than in garden design. This was the time when the formal geometrical garden (see Figure 4.1) gave way to the landscape designs of Kent, Brown and Repton which mirrored wild nature (see Figure 4.2). It was because of these changing values of what was to be conserved that there was little significant objection to the influence of man, and particularly of agriculture on the countryside until late in the nineteenth century.

The conservation movement in Britain, when it did develop, to a large extent grew out of this concern to protect what was left of unenclosed wild countryside for *amenity* reasons, particularly those areas near towns which could be readily enjoyed by the now largely urban population. The first British conservation organisation was the Commons, Open Spaces and Foot-

Figure 4.1: A Formal Garden of the Seventeenth Century at Hampton Court.

Source: John Kipps, *Britannia Illustrated*, 1709-16.

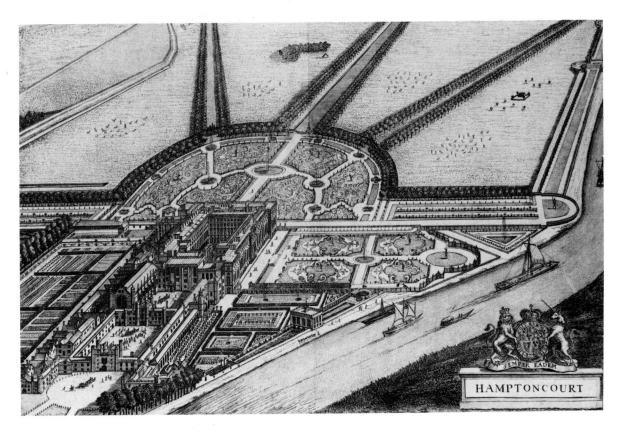

HAMPTONCOURT

121

Figure 4.2: The Grounds of Knowsley Hall. Laid out by Capability Brown, it exemplifies the period ideal of a romantic parkland around a country house.

Source: Mansell Collection.

paths Preservation Society formed in 1865. The National Trust for Places of Historic Interest or Natural Beauty grew from it, being founded in 1895 to perform the vital function of holding and managing land for cultural and amenity objectives. Leading figures in the Romantic movement such as Ruskin, Hunt and Morris were prominent in its early activities.

The biologist Thomas Huxley, Darwin's champion in the great debate on evolution, was at the Trust's first meeting. He represented the other main driving force in the British conservation movement — the increasingly influential natural scientists. Their demonstration of the intrinsic interest and sensibilities of animals was accompanied by a growing compassion for animals and concern for their welfare. This led to the formation of the Society for the Prevention of Cruelty to Animals in 1824 and Society for Protection of Birds in 1889. The study of plants and animals in relation to their environment began to crystallise into the new discipline of ecology towards the end of the nineteenth century. The potential value of natural or near-natural areas, with minimal human intervention, as 'outdoor laboratories' for research in this new subject was soon evident. The provision of nature reserves to serve the *scientific* function has thus been a second main objective of the conservation movement.

A third element in the development of the modern conservation movement is the *utilitarian*. Those people who exploit resources have always appreciated that some kind of rationing is necessary if any living resource is not to be overexploited so that it becomes commercially or even biologically extinct. There are injunctions to this effect in the Bible (the laws of Moses, Deuteronomy 22:6):

> When you come across a bird's nest by the road, in a tree or on the ground with fledglings or eggs in it, and the mother bird on the nest, do not take mother and young. Let the mother bird go free, and take only the young; then you will prosper and live long.

Game laws providing close seasons, or limiting the number of birds caught to enable the quarry species to restore its population are recorded throughout history. This resource-rationing and concepts such as exploitation to maximise sustained yield were much more influential in the development of conservation in the United States of America than in this country. There settlers from Europe changed the whole face of the land within 200 to 300 years of arrival and many resources, such as the buffalo, were rapidly overexploited to near extinction. This emphasised the need for resource conservation much more dramatically than in Europe where the exploitation of natural resources had been a much more gradual process.

Thus, concern for wildlife and the countryside has developed from a number of rather disparate ethical, aesthetic, scientific and utilitarian interests which initially came together in the rather uneasy coalition of the modern conservation movement. The values which are mainly promoted by the conservation movement today, for example, in the World Conservation Strategy, are essentially man-centred and utilitarian. The principal objective is resource conservation based on the common-sense principle that all kinds of exploitation, development and land-use should be regulated to ensure the continuing supply of resources. Environmental protection, to keep the conditions in which we live within the rather narrow limits which we can tolerate, is the other main objective. Both are clearly vital to our survival.

The third main conservation objective — the preservation of amenities (notably wildlife, landscape and access for people to appreciate them) — is not so exclusively utilitarian, nor so obviously vital to our survival. Many feel that animals and plants themselves have a right to survival, even if they have no apparent use to mankind. This kind of conservation often receives a much lower priority. But quite possibly it is just as vital to us as humans. The overall objectives of the first two kinds of conservation are to maintain man's physical well-being. There is evidence that sensory deprivation places people under mental stress. The variety and unusualness of the countryside are in contrast to the monotony and uniformity of much urban existence and many believe therefore that the countryside is thus of considerable therapeutic value.

The different ways in which people perceive the countryside and react to change depend very much on which ideas of conservation they identify with and how such an idea relates to the other concepts of conservation. It is clear from the writings of committed conservationists that most have been, and still are, fundamentally motivated by aesthetic and ethical feelings, sensing an identity with nature that is essentially transcendental (see Colour Plate 5). Few have had the courage, or ability, to express these almost mystical feelings in a convincing everyday manner that would persuade hard-headed politicians or businessmen to forgo utilitarian benefits. Nor are the materialists any the more convinced by the works of those poets, painters and musicians who have so beautifully captured these sensations. Ironically the artefact itself is usually much more highly valued than the miracle of existence which inspired it. More cogent scientific arguments have thus been used and these in turn have led to the promotion of conservation in the same utilitarian currency of those conducting the developments which threaten those things cherished by conservationists.

To many conservationists this has dangerously diluted the fundamental essence of the conservation concept to the point where 'preservation' becomes almost a dirty word, and those advocating it classed as backward-looking and reactionary. 'For above all, the word (conservation) should signify a dynamic process, one which incorporates, indeed depends on, change ...'

More insidiously, they feel, it leads to the notion that resource conservation in the sense of controlled exploitation automatically can guarantee the environmental and amenity objectives of conservation. This may often be so, but is by no means always the case. The seductive idea 'that the land of Britain should be both useful and beautiful and that the two aims are in no sense incompatible' is regrettably far from being so, as early writers clearly recognised. Were it so, current conflicts between agriculture and conservation could not be as deep rooted as they seem to be.

It is a heartening feature of the conservation movement in the last decade that these very real differences in values have been widely accepted and addressed by an increasing diversity of people, and that conservationists have been more ready to admit their real motivations. A proportion of this may be attributed to the increased role of the wild and natural as a subject for television. The 'wilderness' movement in the United States and other countries including the United Kingdom, is showing that this may open up a much wider and more sympathetic constituency of public support than has the policy of promoting conservation as controlled materialism or as rather unintelligible science. Values change as society changes. We may be currently, as a result of the electronics revolution, at the beginning of changes in society as radical and rapid as those at the time of the Industrial Revoluton. Opportunities for leisure and pleasure may greatly increase and natural values assume much greater cultural significance than ever before.

Perspectives on Conservation: Designating for Conservation

The Emerging Concept of Designation

From a discussion, in its historical context, of strands in the countryside conservation movement, and the breadth of objectives that conservation can embrace, it is now important to trace the evolution of conservation policy. It has already been noted that the amenity and scientific strands of the conservation movement brought into being movements such as the National Trust (1895) and the Society for the Protection of Birds (1889). Indeed, during this time several pressure groups were formed; each had its own particular set of aims and ways of working, but they shared a common desire to extend public control over the private use and development of land.

In the long term, legislation and 'education' were seen as the only certain ways of fostering more environmentally-caring attitudes. Immediate threats to the heritage had to be met with direct action. Voluntary bodies had meagre resources, so it was inevitable that they would concentrate their protective efforts on highly-valued landscapes. It is from this initial focus that the concepts of Nature Reserves and National Parks developed.

Wildlife was threatened in several ways. Birds were indiscriminately trapped and killed; egg-collectors and specimen-hunters were endangering populations of rare species. Agricultural developments — particularly drainage — were destroying many rich botanical sites and their living ecologies. At the same time, naturalists were extending their interest in wildlife from the classification of individual species to the examination of interrelationships between species. The increasing popularity of an 'ecological approach' was shown by the founding of the British Ecological Society in 1913.

There was thus a need to acquire sites well endowed with rare or specialised species and to establish them as Nature Reserves. Here wildlife would have sanctuary from marauders and developmental threats, and an elite of scientists would have opportunities to describe the workings of plant and animal communities. The Reserves would have no recreational role: the prevailing view among conservationists was that while relatively few people were capable of appreciating nature, most others were intent on damage. Public access, therefore, was to be strongly discouraged.

The National Trust was the first body to establish Nature Reserves, and by 1910 it had 13 sites. Some naturalists were not impressed: their geographical spread was uneven and their selection apparently random. From this concern came the formation of the Society for the Promotion of Nature Reserves (SPNR) in 1912. It sought to help the Trust by surveying areas worthy of protection and seeking benefactors willing to sponsor acquisition.

In carrying out this work the SPNR relied almost entirely on the personal contacts of its patrons. There was no desire to excite general public interest in Reserves. The SPNR, therefore, remained a small elitist organisation. When the National Trust's commitment to Reserves faltered, the SPNR had insufficient manpower and drive to acquire sites itself or to persuade others to act. Throughout the 1930s, little was done to advance the cause of Nature Reserves. In contrast, the national parks lobby sought maximum publicity at all times, and was successful in creating a populist cause.

Concern over development threats to the countryside intensified greatly after the First World War. Major developments affecting rural areas included quarries, reservoirs, road improvements and extensions to the main transmission lines of the national electricity industry. Sporadic housing and industrial development was encouraged by the depressed state of agriculture; farmers were willing to sell even their best land for development, a point discussed in the first section of Chapter 3. A new threat to rural landscapes came from the Forestry Commission — created in 1919 and charged with the task of securing a strategic reserve of timber. Afforestation with conifers, not found naturally in England and Wales, sometimes on an extensive scale, led to fierce arguments — especially in the Lake District — over the preservation of landscape, wildlife and access opportunities. Throughout the countryside, better public transport and increasing private ownership of cars greatly improved accessibility for day, weekend and holiday trips. Advertising, holiday chalets and petrol stations were prominent associated disfigurements in many popular rural and coastal sites.

The piecemeal acquisition of threatened sites by the National Trust was no solution: government action was urgently needed to control development throughout the countryside, and to ensure that highly-valued landscapes were adequately protected. A strong and concerted campaign for these causes was mounted by the Councils for the Preservation of Rural England and Wales (CPRE and CPRW), established in the mid-1920s. The concept of the National Parks soon became a major part of their strategy. The idea as an administrative concept originated in America and Africa, where extensive, uninhabited, publicly-owned wildernesses had been designated as reserves for wildlife, places for recreation and monuments to society's stewardship of natural resources. Certainly in Britain, however, Wordsworth had proposed the notion as early as 1810. British conditions were different, but the Councils believed that to apply this protective concept to inhabited, privately-owned yet relatively wild and attractive landscapes would be a bold, imaginative and practical experiment.

Government recognition of the National Parks case first came in 1929 with the appointment of the Addison Committee. The Committee's Report supported the concept, but the government decided that the economic situation precluded action. At the same time, a further obstacle to the case for National Parks emerged: the Town and Country Planning Act of 1932. The Act reflected government experiments with planning legislation since the First World War and consolidated existing provisions. It introduced a system whereby all development proposals would be scrutinised and approved, modified or rejected on the basis of development plans prepared by local authorities. Where there was a special need to safeguard or enhance landscapes or amenities, the Act encouraged local authorities, voluntary bodies and individuals to co-operate. The government argued that these provisions obviated the need for special National Park measures.

The CPRE and CPRW firmly rejected these views, and publicised their case more vigorously. In 1934, the support of the large and vociferous access lobby was secured in the formation of a Standing Committee on National Parks (SCNP). A detailed critique of the planning legislation was published and widely circulated. It argued that the preservation of outstanding landscapes and promotion of access to them were national responsibilities demanding central funding. A central body should be appointed to designate National Parks and to exercise planning powers, carry out enhancement works and facilitate public access and recreation. Sustained lobbying and prominent media coverage provoked intense government discussion. Further action seemed inevitable — but was temporarily forestalled by the advent of the Second World War.

War-time Concern and Legislative Action

Early in the War, the government decided to prepare a national plan as a basis for post-war reconstruction. This provided an important boost to the National Parks and Nature Reserves causes. In 1942, joint delegations from the SCNP and SPNR met government ministers and persuaded them of the need to include National Parks and Nature Reserves in the post-war scheme. There followed a highly active period. A civil servant, John Dower, was engaged to report on the practical problems and needs of potential National Park areas, and a Nature Reserves Investigation Committee (NRIC) was established. By 1945, a vast amount of information, argument and comment had accumulated — but the government was still reluctant to act hastily. Accordingly, a National Parks Committee (Hobhouse Committee) and a Wild Life Conservation Special Committee (Huxley Committee) were appointed. They reported in July 1947.

The Hobhouse report was highly idealistic in its proposals and aims for National Parks. It believed that a National Parks Commission (NPC) should designate twelve areas, covering some 9,500 sq. kilometres, and that four main principles should dominate policy and action. These were: preservation of landscape beauty; provision of access and facilities for open-air enjoyment; protection of wildlife, buildings and places of architectural and historic interest; and the effective maintenance of existing farming use.

. It was agreed that three measures would be needed to achieve these national park principles: planning controls of development by local authorities; sensitive land management by private landowners; and acquisition and/or management of land by the NPC and local authorities. The first priority was to control development. Certain types of development should be excluded from National Parks or tolerated 'only under proved national necessity'. This included water supply, mineral extraction, military and forestry development. Local authorities, supported by the Commission, would need to establish and enforce strictly protective planning strategies.

With the bulk of the land in private ownership, the co-operation of landowners, in particular their acceptance and support of conservation and recreation as secondary uses of their land, was vital. The Hobhouse Committee of 1947 saw no serious conflict between these different forms of land management. Indeed, it argued that a progressive agriculture would improve the landscape by bringing into productive use the neglected features of the depression years of the 1930s. Derelict pastures and woods, unkempt hedges and dilapidated buildings had been common and much deplored elements in pre-war landscapes.

The Hobhouse Committee did not believe, however, that responsiblity for management should devolve entirely upon landowners. The National Parks Commission and local authorities would need to promote and carry out positive works such as woodland management, eyesore removal, footpath and camping-site provision. To achieve their aims it might be occasionally necessary to acquire land — for hostels or car-parks, or perhaps for preservation against over-zealous agricultural reclamation. But the active purchase of land was seen very much as a last-resort measure.

The Huxley report of 1947 was framed on a much less ambitious scale. Partly this was because the perceived land needs of Nature Reserves were

Figure 4.3: Ebbor Gorge, a National Nature Reserve on the Mendip Hills, Somerset. One of 181 'outdoor laboratories' set aside for the scientific study of a particular habitat.

Source: P. Wakeley/NCC.

nowhere near as ambitious as those of National Parks. More importantly, the report was serving the direct interests of a very much narrower section of the community. Partly through fears of possible damage to habitats from uncontrolled public access, the lobby had distanced itself from the National Parks movement, and thus had relatively little popular support. Although the landscape beauty and recreational potential of Nature Reserves were mentioned in the report, the Huxley Committee's recommendations were determined primarily by the needs of ecologists. Whereas Hobhouse placed an *amenity* approach to conservation to the fore, Huxley's approach was essentially *scientific* (see Figure 4.3).

This distinctive background was reflected in the different emphasis placed on the measures needed to implement a nature conservation strategy. Acquisition, rather than strict planning policies, was the main element. The Huxley Committee's first aim was to bring important habitats under protective management and to facilitate their use for scientific study. This absolute control of land use and management could be secured only by acquiring land and placing it under the control of a Biological Service. The committee wanted 73 National Nature Reserves (NNRs) covering 28,000 hectares to be established in this way.

This relatively small 'core' of protected land would need to be supplemented by further areas if effective nature conservation was to be achieved throughout England and Wales. The Huxley Committee, like the Hobhouse Committee, of the same year, believed that sympathetic management by private landowners would largely secure this aim. But it did not see the impact of agricultural developments being quite so simple; reclamation of heathland, downland and woodland during the war, though accepted as strategically necessary, had been much regretted by naturalists. The overall threat was not enough, however, to merit the introduction of controls over agriculture.

Town and country planning played only a minor part in the Huxley Committee's strategy. Sites of Special Scientific Interest (SSSIs), areas of special interest by reason of their fauna, flora or geological or physiographic features, were to be notified to local authorities, who would then consult the Biological Service on any development proposals. Their designation would not hold up plans for development; it would merely ensure that scientific interests were considered before development proposals were approved, and might allow modifications to be made to protect particularly interesting areas 'without detriment to the undertaking contemplated'. The schedule of SSSIs was also to provide a basis for the establishment of Local Nature Reserves (LNRs) by local authorities. These were to be sites of local interest, generally publicly-owned and safeguarded for public education and enjoyment.

While quite different rationales lay behind the Committees' concepts of National Parks and Nature Reserves, their proposals for Conservation Areas were remarkably similar in their purpose. Both Committees felt there was a need for some form of designation to safeguard additional extensive areas outside their proposed National Parks and NNRs. Each Committee drew up a separate list of possible areas, but on comparing these they found considerable agreement. Therefore it was decided jointly to propose the designation of 52 Conservation Areas covering 16,400 sq. kilometres. Their purposes would be to maintain and enhance landscape beauty, scientific interest and recreation opportunities. This Conservation Area status was the only one in which both the Hobhouse and Huxley Reports explicitly recognised the essential interdependence of both recreation and conservation aims.

The Hobhouse and Huxley Committees' proposals had markedly different experiences in the legislative processes which led to the National Parks and Access to the Countryside Act 1949. For the Hobhouse Committee, the major problem was the appropriate balance between central and local control. The Committee wanted a combination of strong central direction and effective local planning. This combination was not achieved. In 1947, a new Town and Country Planning Act had given local authorities unprecedented planning powers. It was now politically impossible to transfer some of these responsibilities to a new, central and non-elected body. The NPC could not, therefore, be given executive status; it was empowered only to designate and to advise local authorities on planning and management matters.

No such problems beset the Huxley Committee's proposals. Nature conservation was propounded as a scientific matter, requiring only minor involvement on the part of planners. There were few conflicts. Further, there was strong support in government for the establishment of new scientific research bodies at that time. Accordingly, the 'Biological Service' was established as the Nature Conservancy (NC) in 1949. The Conservancy, compared to the NPC, emerged relatively unscatheed and far stronger. It had both executive and advisory powers, and could own and manage land, set up a regional structure and carry out research.

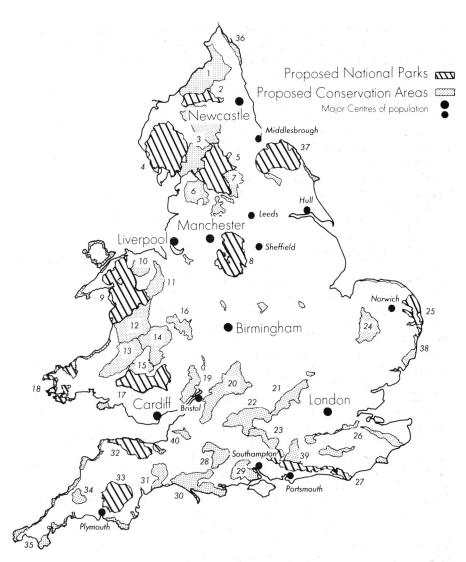

Figure 4.4: Proposed
Designation of National Parks
and Conservation Areas, 1947.

Source: *Hobhouse Report*
(1947) Cmd 7121, HMSO.

Proposed National Parks
Proposed Conservation Areas
Major Centres of population

1. Cheviot and Rothbury Forests and Kilder Moors	21. Chilterns
2. Hadrians Wall	22. Marlborough and Berkshire Downs
3. North Pennines	23. Hampshire Downs
4. Lake District	24. Breckland
5. Yorkshire Dales	25. Broads
6. Forest of Bowland	26. North Downs
7. Nidderdale Moors	27. South Downs
8. Peak District	28. Cranborne Chase
9. North Wales	29. New Forest
10. Denbigh Moors	30. Dorset Downs, Heath and Coast
11. Clwydian Range & Berwyn	31. Blackdown Hills and Sidmouth
12. Plynlimmon	32. Exmoor
13. Elenith Mountains	33. Dartmoor
14. Eden and Radnor Forests	34. Bodmin Moor
15. Epyn	35. Cornish Coast
16. Shropshire Hills	36. Northumberland Coast
17. Black Mountains	37. North York Moors
18. Pembrokeshire Coast	38. Suffolk Coast and heaths
19. Wye Valley	39. Hindhead
20. Cotswolds	40. Mendips

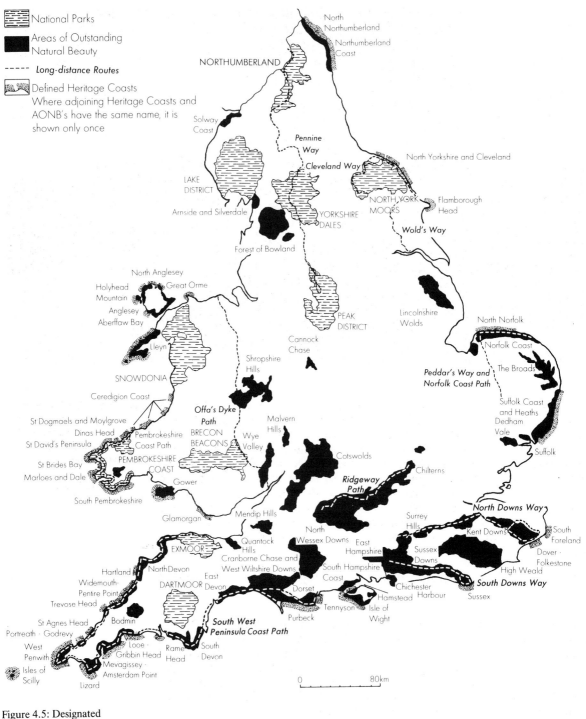

Figure 4.5: Designated
National Parks and AONBs,
Defined Heritage Coasts and
Long Distance Footpaths,
1982.

Source: Countryside
Commission, *Annual Report*,
1983.

The outcome for the designations reflected the different range of powers held by the two conservation bodies. National Parks became essentially a local authority responsibility. The proposals for NNRs, LNRs and SSSIs were little changed. Perhaps more significant was the replacement of the Conservation Area concept by that of the Area of Outstanding Natural Beauty (AONB). These areas were to be designated simply for conservation purposes (see Figures 4.4 and 4.5). By its creation of two quite different agencies, and abandonment of the concept of Conservation Areas which went some way towards uniting their distinct purposes, parliament had engineered a split which was to have important implications for the success of countryside conservation in later years.

Figure 4.6: Fyiingdales Early Warning System. An example of an intrusive development in a National Park (North Yorkshire Moors).

Source: United States Air Force, MARC, Lincolnshire.

Perspectives on Conservation: The Discovery of Conflict

Post-war Disillusion

The newly-established bodies moved quickly on their designation programmes. Four National Parks were established by 1951, and the present number of ten by 1957. The first Area of Outstanding Natural Beauty was designated in 1956; a decade later there were 21. The Nature Conservancy had established 82 National Nature Reserves covering some 24,000 hectares in England and Wales by 1966. More than 1,400 Sites of Special Scientific Interest had also been notified to local authorities.

It was not always easy to secure these designations. Arguments over administration held up many National Park proposals, in particular where designation involved two or more counties and local authorities could not agree on unified approaches. Once designation had been achieved, serious difficulties in securing agreement over the objectives of such a designation arose through a combination of unprecedented recreation and development pressures and a serious shortage of financial manpower and resources.

Major developments provided an early challenge to the commitment of local planning authorities and government to the objectives of designation, once they had been agreed. In the designated areas, the NPC strongly resisted developments which it felt were inappropriate and damaging and should be directed elsewhere. These included the Trawsfynydd nuclear power station and its associated pylons and power lines in Snowdonia, the Fylingdales early warning station in the North Yorkshire Moors (see Figure 4.6) and the oil terminal and associated industrial development at Milford Haven in Pembrokeshire. The Commission secured some delay in these projects, but its arguments did not, in the end, convince the minister who approved the proposals. Permission for such developments proceeded very much on a piecemeal basis.

More widespread though localised impacts resulted from developments in the extractive industries. A post-war boom in building, improvements to major roads and the beginning of motorway construction led to a high demand for aggregates of all kinds. Industrial development stimulated demand for coal, ironstone, limestone and china clay. Advances in technology permitted the introduction of capital-intensive methods which could exploit relatively low-grade resources on a far greater scale than previously. Local impacts on scenery and wildlife were often dramatic. Proposals for new quarries or for extensions to existing works, both within and outside designated areas, were keenly contested at planning inquiries by amenity groups, the NPC and the Nature Conservancy. It was often very difficult to resolve the conflict between the local interest in employment and income and the national interest in landscape and wildlife conservation.

Reservoir and water extraction proposals were also a major cause for concern. Particularly well-publicised was the proposed reservoir at Cow Green in Upper Teesdale (see Figure 4.7). The local water board proposed to flood some 310 hectares of a unique habitat, part of which was an NNR and the remainder an SSSI. The Nature Conservancy vigorously opposed the scheme, arguing that the complex of unusual plant communities and soil containing many rare plants were irreplaceable and that important scientific research

Figure 4.7: The Site of Cow Green Reservoir. This section of the upper Tees river, formerly an SSSI and an NNR was dammed and flooded to provide water for Teesside.

Source: Countryside Commission.

(a)

(b)

Figure 4.8: The Development
and Consequences of Land
Drainage Systems. With such
high levels of grant aid for
drainage, even farmers with
conservation interests have
found it difficult to resist the
straightening and deepening of
water courses. Contrast the loss
of visual appeal and of habitats
in (b) compared with (a).

Source: M. Shoard (1980), *The
Theft of the Countryside*,
Temple Smith, London.

would be frustrated. The case eventually went to Parliament, where it was decided in 1967 that the urgent need for water outweighed the wildlife loss.

Throughout the countryside, the government's desire to revitalise agriculture and to sustain forestry led to further strong conflicts over land management and land use. Highly visible changes which were now occurring included hedge removal, conversion of chalk grassland, heathland and meadows to arable production, the loss of moorland through afforestation and the extensive planting of coniferous trees in broadleaved woods. The extent of post-war impacts on flora was documented in the first *Atlas of British Flora*, published in 1962. This revealed numerous local extinctions and drastic declines in the geographical range of many species.

Agricultural improvements were encouraged and sustained through Ministry of Agriculture grant-aid. Before 1968, the desirability of agricultural improvements was judged solely on technical criteria; amenity considerations and environmental impacts were not considered. From the habitat losses taking place it became clear that with incentives so heavily weighted towards development, the good will of farmers and landowners was inadequate to safeguard conservation interests (see Figure 4.8).

Forestry developments were promoted by the Forestry Commission through its own extensive planting programme and grant-aid support for landowners and private forestry companies. The limited range of species used, the blanketing effect of modern plantations, the straight lines and sharp boundaries of new plantings and the stark impacts of clear-felling were all heavily criticised.

These developments had particularly important implications for the work of the Nature Conservancy. It found that many of the sites proposed as NNRs during the war had to be dropped from the designation programme because their scientific value had declined through changes in agricultural or forestry management. Further, a large number and diversity of habitat types, formerly widespread, now had to be included in the designation programme because so few undisturbed examples remained. With such extensive losses, SSSIs were becoming much more important to conservation than the Huxley Committee had ever envisaged; yet they were as susceptible to subsidised destruction as any other areas. The need to protect sites through acquisition thus became increasingly urgent. Here shortage of funds hampered the Conservancy's work, and it was forced to seek less secure protection through leases or agreements with landowners. In 1966, only 20 per cent of the total area of NNRs was owned by the NC. Having established NNRs, there was often little money left for management works, and no staff to implement them.

In the mid-1960s it was widely felt that providing for leisure and recreation needs was one of the greatest challenges facing planners. Several factors — including rising levels of car ownership, a decline in the length of the average working week, an increase in the incidence of paid holidays and the growth of formal education over the age of 15 — had stimulated a dramatic post-war rise in the number of day and holiday visits to the countryside and coast. The early small-scale and sparse experimental attempts to cope with this demand were soon quite overwhelmed. Local authorities did not have the expertise, finance or staff to plan appropriate recreational provisions or to manage the associated problems of congestion, erosion, litter and vandalism. Popular 'honey-pots' experienced particularly disruptive over-use and development (see Colour Plates 7 and 8). There was a need for more robust sites, specifically dedicated to recreation, to which demand could be redirected from the National Parks and other vulnerable areas.

These three main post-war impacts on the countryside: development pressures, the environmental impact of agriculture and forestry, and recreation activity, combined to create a disillusion among many who had applauded the ethos of the Hobhouse and Huxley reports. At the same time, however, a popular interest in the protection of the countryside was proceeding at an unprecedented rate. Romantic, amenity and scientific approaches to conservation were coming increasingly under public scrutiny, amid talk of the post-industrial age. Growing environmental consciousness was thus reflected in stronger support for voluntary bodies and increased media attention to their activities. These included: alerting statutory bodies and the public to development threats; presenting vigorous defences of conservation interests at planning inquiries; acquiring ownership of threatened sites, and maintaining constant pressure on government to strengthen statutory powers and to provide more resources for conservation. Increasingly, voluntary bodies were becoming watch dogs on countryside change and complements to the NPC and Nature Conservancy — helping to close the gap between the reality of heavily-constrained conservation action and the principles behind the 1949 Act.

An important opportunity for voluntary bodies to share their criticisms of the prevailing situation was provided by the 'Countryside in 1970' conferences held in 1963 and 1965. The failure of planning to prevent major developments, the challenge of recreation management, the burgeoning threats to wildlife and the need for more resources for effective conservation were strong themes at these conferences. It became clear that the statutory provisions and resource needs to deal with these major issues could not be provided satisfactorily by minor amendments to legislation which was now 20 years old. The government response was to introduce and pass the Countryside Act 1968.

The Management Era

The Countryside Act 1968 introduced two new elements in countryside policy. The first of these reflected government awareness that conservation and recreation problems existed outside statutory designated areas, and that a stronger, more active advisory body was needed to deal with them. A Countryside Commission, with a remit extending throughout England and Wales, was established to replace the National Parks Commission. The new body could now become much more actively involved in planning and management matters outside the National Parks and AONBs. The second provision with national implications was a clause which shifted the overall balance of policy towards conservation. The Act required all ministers and public bodies, in discharging their duties, to 'have regard to the desirability of conserving the natural beauty and amenity of the countryside'. Thus, for example, in deciding whether to grant-aid land reclamation, the Ministry of Agriculture now had to take account of amenity as well as purely technical, agricultural, considerations. This was the furthest that the Act went in establishing a new, stronger, position for conservation in relation to other policy aims. The remainder of the provisions fell very much within the framework of the 1949 National Parks and Access to Countryside Act, albeit with a new emphasis.

The role of land purchase by the public sector in achieving policy aims was strengthened with the introduction of the Country Park concept. This applied the theory behind the establishment of National Nature Reserves to securing recreational objectives. Local authorities were empowered to purchase land and to manage it — with Countryside Commission grant-aid — principally for recreation purposes. Country Parks were to be established mainly close to towns and cities. It was hoped that they would help to reduce recreational pressures on the National Parks and high quality amenity areas. At the same time, they would relieve visitor pressures on popular beauty-spots by providing alternative, readily-accessible recreation opportunities.

To some extent this provision reflected something of a lack of confidence in the ability and desire of landowners and farmers to manage land in ways which could support recreation and conservation objectives. Yet the Act did not opt for a policy of total segregation of competing land-uses. One section provided for the Nature Conservancy to pay agreed compensation to land-owners for continuing management practices which fostered the scientific interest of SSSIs. These designations were seen as a means of protecting those numerous small areas that could be relatively easily safeguarded if their value and interest were known. Management advice was mainly given by qualified natural scientists from the Conservancy's regional offices. Another required landowners in National Parks to notify their intention to plough moorland, so that local authorities could negotiate agreements to protect the areas. The Countryside Commission was given powers to grant-aid tree-planting and other environmental improvements, the aim being to encourage voluntary bodies to build on their emerging role as essential complements to the statutory conservation agencies.

The decade following the Countryside Act saw a marked strengthening of the environmental lobby and a change in its focus of concern. Proposals for major developments such as quarries, motorways, airports and power stations were still strongly resisted at the local scale. But of growing national concern were the increasingly ubiquitous changes brought about by developments in agriculture and forestry.

While concern in the 1960s had mainly centred on the loss of particular landscape features, it was the comprehensive changes in the rural scenery and wildlife which attracted attention in the 1970s. The actions of individual farmers and landowners were bringing about the bulk of these changes — securing conservation and recreation aims on private land presented the main problem. Within a voluntary framework, landowners had to be dissuaded from carrying out developments inimical to these aims, and encouraged to sustain the wildlife interest, scenic beauty and recreational opportunities of their land.

The solution propounded by the Countryside Commission was 'countryside management' — a refined form of proposals made originally in the Dower, Hobhouse and Huxley reports of the late 1940s. The Commission took advantage of its new research and experiment powers to establish projects which would test the management approach. The first of a number of these was set up in the Lake District in 1969 with Commission and local authority funding. A project officer was appointed to promote small-scale improvements throughout the National Park. This involved maintenance works — hedging and repairing walls (see Colour Plate 9 and Figure 4.9), gates and stiles — and new developments such as amenity tree-planting and footpath signposting and waymarking. The success or failure of the project depended on the establishment of good rapport between the project officer and farmers through informal, personal contact. There were no formal ways of ensuring the project's success. No legal agreement of compulsion was involved. Farmers were encouraged to carry out the work themselves, and the costs of materials and labour were met by project funds. The Lake District experiment was successful largely because of the personality of the field officer, rather than the concept of management itself.

An event which also attracted great interest from voluntary bodies, farming and landowning organisations and indeed some farmers was the 'farming and wildlife' exercise held at Silsoe in 1969. Here farmers and conservationists came together to explore compromises which would allow improvements in farm productivity while minimising damage to scenery and wildlife. From this, a Farming and Wildlife Advisory Group (FWAG) was formed in 1969, under the auspices of the Royal Society for the Protection of Birds (RSPB), in order to foster contacts between farming and conservation interests. Several county branches were soon formed and during the 1970s their influence grew considerably.

Figure 4.9: Repairing a Walled Pathway at Watendlath in the Lake District.

Source: Countryside Commission.

The Countryside Commission was quick to apply the management approach to urban fringe areas and to the coast. The National Trust, worried by development threats and recreational demands, had been stepping up its programme of coastal acquisitions since the early 1960s, and had launched a national appeal — 'Enterprise Neptune' — for this purpose. A Trust survey, which concluded that planning policies were failing to protect attractive coastlines, prompted the Commission to carry out its own study. It advocated the introduction of a new, non-statutory designation — the Heritage Coast. This would focus local authority attention on the most vulnerable areas where special planning policies were needed. Plans would be drawn up to provide a framework for voluntary and local authority management action supported by Countryside Commission grant-aid. By the end of the 1970s, some 30 lengths of coast, extending to 1,200 kilometres had been defined as Heritage Coast, and several management projects were in operation.

This strengthened management approach initially promised to solve many management conflicts on private land. Both the Sandford Committee on National Park policies and the inter-departmental Countryside Review Committee, which examined countryside policies in the mid-1970s, expressed their support and confidence in the use of this voluntary, consensus and compromise solution. Some observers, however, questioned the extent to which there could be any common ground between interests seeking, on the one hand diverse wildlife habitats in varied landscapes, and on the other highly productive monoculture. They argued that, despite the 1968 Act, the trend was very much towards the latter in almost all aspects of land management.

A Nature Conservancy Council report on nature conservation and agricul-

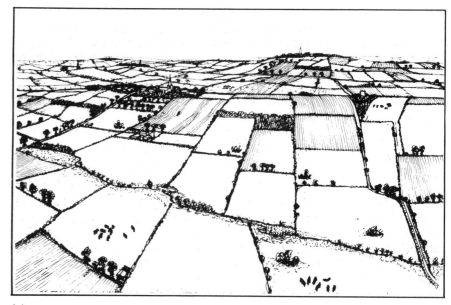

(a)

Figure 4.10: The Changing Lowland Countryside. Two examples from *New Agricultural Landscapes* show the same area first mainly under grass (a), and the concomitant loss of hedges and hedgerow trees in the change to arable farming (b).

Source: Countryside Commission.

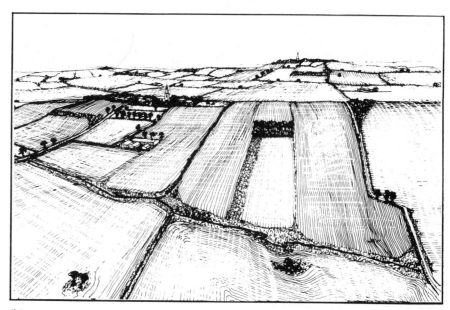

(b)

ture identified two main causes of species loss. Firstly, the agricultural area was being extended through the reclamation of woodland, heathland, moorland, bogs and grazing marshes. Secondly, intensification of agriculture on existing cropland, with increasing use of large-scale machinery, fertilisers, herbicides and pesticides, was leading to losses of arable weeds, herb-rich grassland, hedges, copses and ponds with drastic effects on their associated fauna. The Countryside Commission's study of change in lowland landscapes — *New Agricultural Landscapes* — came to similar conclusions, three years earlier (see Figures 4.10a and 4.10b).

The evidence of these two reports suggested a widespread reduction, since the war, in the diversity of scenery and wildlife throughout the countryside of England and Wales. The NCC felt that a stronger and more co-ordinated national conservation policy supported with vastly increased resources was needed to stem these trends. The Commission urged the further extension of countryside management initiatives. Both bodies also extended the debate over conserving the countryside to include historic and archaeological landscape conservation. This would be particularly important to national parks, where larger areas rather than specific sites would be brought into consideration. These remoter rural areas would provide good 'historical reservoirs' because of their relative lack of development.

The voluntary conservation movement, now showing increased cynicism at the value of policies which relied on landowners' co-operation and interest in conservation, sought stronger measures. There were calls for a more radical policy which attacked the causes of change — government agricultural and forestry policies — rather than attempting to ameliorate their effects through cosmetic management. Whatever the solution, it was clear that the 1968 framework was now inadequate in a number of respects. The debate entered the 1980s with viewpoints becoming increasingly polarised and calls for new legislation increasingly strident. The following section summarises these viewpoints and examines how the new legislation came into being. The increasing polarity of the debate led to conservation becoming a much more 'political' issue.

The Early 1980s

The Contemporary Conflict Between Agriculture and Conservation

Undoubtedly, the main threat to rural conservation in the early 1980s is seen, at least by conservationists, to come from agricultural intensification. This derives from the fact that the agriculture industry pushes towards higher and higher yields of single crops on land being continually re-used with all competition from other plants, fungi, insects and birds being removed as far as possible. Conservationists, on the other hand, want to place an emphasis on variety and numbers of fauna and flora, with lower crop yields, more mixed land-uses and lots of cover in the form of bushes, hedges and trees.

In a survey of members of the British Association of Nature Conservationists conducted on the eve of the 1983 general election, 55 per cent of respondents identified the reform of the agricultural support system as the most pressing task for the new government in the field of conservation. This is somewhat surprising, given that, prior to the 1970s, agriculture would probably not have appeared on any list, drawn up by conservationists, of the greatest threats to the countryside. In the 1930s, for example, afforestation, ribbon development and urban sprawl would have headed such a list (see Chapter 3). In the 1960s, it would have included reservoirs, power stations, military installations (see Figure 4.6) electricity pylons, caravan sites, the motor car and new road schemes.

What accounts for the current salience of agricultural development? There are three reasons: the diminution in other, external pressures on the countryside with economic recession; the recognition of the destructive potential of modern agricultural technology through its greatly enhanced power to modify the rural environment, and the limited achievements of various efforts to remedy the conflict between agriculture and conservation.

Turning to the first point, the decline in housebuilding, the curtailment of the new towns programme, the low level of industrial activity, government cancellation or postponement of major capital projects such as the third London airport and the Channel tunnel, the slow-down of public works such as reservoir construction and road building — have all served at least to delay major threats to the rural environment. Similarly, one of the major fears of the 1960s, that the countryside would be swamped by recreational motorists, has failed to materialise because the spectacular growth of car ownership and use, during the late 1960s and early 1970s has not continued. Agriculture is one of the few established industries, apart from the extraction of North Sea oil and gas, to have continued to grow steadily throughout the recession. This shows how entrenched is the open-ended policy (and, therefore financial) commitment to agricultural expansion.

Few people anticipated the rapid transformation in agricultural practices that occurred in the post-war period. Even so, agricultural development through capital substitution fostered by government and realised through the adoption of new technologies, the spread of mechanisation and the consolidation of holdings (discussed in Chapter 2) has transformed the rural environment. The sheer pace of development has destroyed any illusions that agriculture is intrinsically an unchanging or slowly evolving activity. Nowadays, many conservationists regard it as austere and capitalistic, no longer the embodiment of rural society and rustic virtue; and the image of the farmer as the conserver of the countryside has given way to the image of the agribusinessman. In the title of a recent highly publicised book by Marion Shoard, an ex-staff member of the Council for the Protection of Rural England, farmers are accused of 'The Theft of the Countryside'. This is a far cry from the Scott Committee's characterisation of them as 'unconscious landscape gardeners'.

Over a period of about 20 years from the mid-1950s to the mid-1970s elements of the conservation movement came to recognise, via a series of controversies, the various environmental implications of agricultural intensification. The appearance of industrialised farm buildings first aroused concern. Then the dramatic decline in the numbers of certain birds drew attention to the side-effects from some synthetic pesticides. Other issues followed, including the loss of hedgerows, moorland and heathland reclamation, the drainage of wetlands and the destruction of, or damage to, Sites of Special Scientific Interest (SSSIs). Initially, such controversies were viewed independently, with conservation groups seeking specific remedies through isolated campaigns. They gained more corporate force, however, with the publication of the Countryside Commission's and Nature Conservancy Council's two reports outlined in the previous section.

As a result of this failure of statutory planning, the totality of agricultural change and its sweeping impact on the rural environment have drawn attention to the limitations of existing, protective measures to moderate or deflect the tide of change. National Parks and Areas of Outstanding Natural Beauty cover 19 per cent of England and Wales; and Sites of Special Scientific Interest 4 per cent. The administration of these designated areas is in the hands of the local planning authorities and the Nature Conservancy Council but they lack any significant control over farming and forestry which occupy 90 per cent of the land so designated. Though, in principle, any development of land is subject to their control, the definition of development in the planning Acts specifically excludes 'the use of any land for the purposes of agriculture or forestry (including afforestation), and the use for any of those purposes of any building occupied together with the land so used'. This means that the measures intended to safeguard the countryside, ·introduced in the 1949 National Parks and Access to the Countryside Act, are quite impotent in relation to the forces now recognised as dominant in the creation or destruction of landscape and habitats.

The Countryside Commission pursued and refined its management approach, discussed earlier in this chapter, in various selected areas — in Heritage Coasts, in the uplands, on the urban fringe, and in the intensively farmed lowlands. In addition, National Park Management Plans, introduced by the 1972 Local Government Act, extended the approach, at least within the National Parks. The Plans provided a formal process for co-ordinating the management activities of public and private landowners and for liaison with relevant government bodies and interest groups. Implementation of these plans, as well as countryside projects elsewhere, has sometimes made use of management agreements, which are formal or informal agreements, whereby an owner or occupier of land undertakes to manage the land in a specified manner. This will require him to satisfy a particular public need, usually in return for some form of consideration.

Area management, management projects, management plans and management agreements together represent a set of refined tools for public authorities pursuing conservation policies. However, since the mid-1970s the limitations as well as the strengths of countryside management have steadily become more apparent. On the one hand, it has proved particularly effective in tackling tactical problems — such as small-scale landscape improvements (see Figure 4.11), the provision of minor recreational works, and easing of the friction between farmers and visitors. On the other hand, management policies have not been able to deal with fundamental conflicts between land users nor to hold out in the face of economic pressures or structural changes in the rural economy. Moreover, because more farmers and landowners are unwilling to relinquish their right to improve or develop land for any considerable length of time, management agreements tend to offer only short-term security for the public interest or public investment, and can prove very expensive. Indeed, countryside management has had relatively little demonstrable impact on agricultural practices or agricultural development, particularly since a lot of agricultural areas simply fall outside its influence.

Recognition of these shortcomings has fuelled demands for fundamental reforms. With the growing appreciation of the totality of agricultural change, the whole system of state support for the farming sector and particularly the support for cereals has come under attack as the root cause of agricultural capitalisation, rather than the activities of individual farmers. In addition, pressures have built up from conservation groups for general powers to regulate the environmental impact of agricultural and forestry development.

The farming lobby has, not unnaturally, resisted with almost total success such curbs. The Country Landowners' Association and the National Farmers' Union have responded to the charges of conservationists by presenting

Figure 4.11: Traditional Hedge Laying. An example of positive conservation and landscape improvement on a small scale.

Source: MERL.

141

farmers as stewards of the countryside. They have also stressed the need to retain the goodwill and voluntary co-operation of the farming community if practical remedies are to be found to conservation problems. While staunchly resisting any form of planning constraint to encroachment on a farmer's eligibility for government improvement grants, they have pressed for payments and tax incentives for farmers to pursue conservation objectives and, in particular, to compensate for any potential income forgone through farming so as to preserve the landscape and wildlife of an area.

Conservation and the Political Process: The Wildlife and Countryside Act 1981

The argument of controls versus voluntary co-operation came to a head over the issue of moorland reclamation on Exmoor. Attention had first been drawn to the ploughing up of open moorland there in the early 1960s (see Colour Plate 6). The Exmoor Society, a branch of the CPRE, had commissioned a study of the extent of change which suggested that the very fabric of the National Park was threatened, and an unsuccessful attempt was made to amend the 1968 Countryside Act during its passage through Parliament to give the National Park Authority powers to control moorland conversion in designated areas. Losses of moorland continued, such that by the mid-1970s one-fifth of the open land on Exmoor had been enclosed and improved since its designation as a National Park in 1954.

Eventually, pressure from the CPRE and the Countryside Commission led the Government to appoint Lord Porchester to enquire into the issue. It was largely to implement his recommendations that the Labour Government introduced its Countryside Bill in 1978, including powers to control moorland conversion in specific areas. The NFU and the CLA opposed the Bill. So did the Conservative Opposition which rejected any form of compulsion or regulation in favour of reliance on the voluntary co-operation of farmers, arguing that more generous compensation would lead to suitable voluntary agreements. The Bill was lost with the fall of the minority Labour Government.

Once in office, the Conservatives introduced their own Bill, which eventually became the Wildlife and Countryside Act 1981. Before examining its passage and contents, it is important to compare the strengths of the main protagonists in the debate over the Bill — the farming and landowning interests and the conservation lobby. Pressure groups seeking to influence legislation bring differing skills and competences to the process of negotiation and vary in their ease of access to the parts of the political system which are important at successive stages of the legislative process. It is crucial to appreciate, therefore, just how close and continuous is the relationship between the NFU, the CLA and relevant ministries, and the extent to which their involvement with numerous pieces of legislation provides recurrent opportunities to present a coherent philosophy to civil servants and politicians.

Conservation groups do not enjoy this intense and sustained involvement in policy making. They are not of central importance to the effective performance of government or the economy and consequently do not have the symbiotic relationship with senior civil servants which corporate interest groups enjoy. Failure to be closely involved with policy formulation at its pre-public stage often means an uphill campaign at later stages against courses of action to which officials and major interests are already committed.

Good media and parliamentary relations can only partially compensate for this, though on occasion a combination of parliamentary pressure and public censure has enabled conservation groups to take the offensive against recalcitrant government departments and win concessions. With the Wildlife and Countryside Bill, however, conservation groups confronted interests with extensive parliamentary contacts and, particularly in the case of the NFU, exceptional lobbying expertise. Of course, at the stage of implementing legislation, decisive advantage lies with those interests whose co-operation is vital to its successful administration and, if anything, the position of the farming and landowning community has been enhanced by the provisions of the Wildlife and Countryside Act. In contrast, conservation groups not directly involved in the process of implementation may find it difficult to sustain the pressure needed to ensure the full realisation of hard-won reforms.

The intention of putting forward a Wildlife and Countryside Bill was announced on 20 June 1979. But the previous month, within days of the Conservatives taking office, both the CLA and NFU had separate meetings with Agriculture and Environment Ministers to discuss their legislative proposals. Broad agreement on the proposed Bill was reached and from this point through to the enactment of the legislation of Government, the CLA and the NFU remained in essential accord on the philosophy of the Bill and their approach to its more contentious aspects. The Government's proposals were set out in six consultation papers which had been drafted by civil servants in the DoE's Rural Directorate and not by the government's statutory advisers, the Countryside Commission and the NCC. Indeed, their views were not formally sought until the public consultation stage — surely an indication of their political marginality.

The consultative papers embodied the view that control of farming operations was unnecessary and potentially counter-productive. Conservation objectives should be secured, it was argued, through the voluntary co-operation of farmers and landowners, encouraged, where necessary, by management agreements drafted and financed by conservation agencies. The only elements of compulsion proposed were reserve powers to be activated by Ministers. These were to require landowners or tenants to give twelve months notice of any intention to convert moor or heath to agricultural land in specified parts of National Parks, or to undertake operations which could be detrimental to the scientific interest of selected SSSIs. Ministers assured the NFU and CLA that there was no intention to use the reserve powers for National Parks and that only a few especially important SSSIs would be given the extra safeguard (a maximum of about 40 was suggested out of a total of some 3,500 SSSIs).

Environmental groups responded unfavourably but the impact of their response was blunted by the diversity of their prescriptions and the lack of an overall co-ordinated approach. The environmental lobby is large and diffuse and this militates against strong central co-ordination. Lord Melchett, the Labour Peer, convened a Wildlife Link Committee which sought to rectify this and co-ordinate the response of nature conservation groups. Legislative safeguards for wildlife habitats were central to their counter-proposals. All owners of SSSIs, they suggested, should be obliged to notify proposed changes of agricultural practice to give the NCC an opportunity to negotiate a management agreement and, where a reasonable agreement could not be reached, the Secretary of State should have powers to make an order preventing harmful change to the site.

Landscape and amenity interests — with the CPRE, the Council for National Parks and the Ramblers' Association taking the lead — also stressed the need for order-making powers to protect areas of landscape or wildlife interest and a new system of agricultural grants and subsidies to encourage farm enterprises which might contribute to conservation as well as food production. A package of proposals was agreed with the Countryside Commission but rejected by the Nature Conservancy Council on the grounds that it was too sweeping to be politically practicable. This meant that there was no strategic consensus on the Bill across the conservation lobby.

The Bill's passage attracted considerable public attention and generated a sustained debate in the media, most of which was very sympathetic to the conservationists' case. Much publicity was given to their evidence indicating widespread destruction of landscapes and habitats, such as an NCC survey which suggested that some 13 per cent of SSSIs suffered damage to their wildlife interest each year. In this atmosphere, a combination of filibuster by the Labour opposition and pressure on ministers from some Conservative MPs and peers won limited concessions from the Government. The most significant was a requirement that all owners and occupiers of SSSIs should be legally obliged to give the Nature Conservancy three months notice of their intention to carry out any potentially damaging operations, and that, in return, the NCC should notify them of the features to be protected, and of the agricultural operations to be avoided.

Amenity groups achieved much less satisfaction. The CPRE and the CNP brought forward the preliminary findings of the Birmingham University Moorland Study (see Figure 4.12) which indicated extensive and continuing losses of open moorland (rough pasture) to agricultural reclamation and afforestation — not just on Exmoor, but throughout England and Wales. Ministers, however, used their parliamentary majority to defeat amendments aimed at establishing reserve powers for moorland protection, but they did accept the need to monitor moorland change within National Parks.

Figure 4.12: Net Changes in the Area of Rough Pasture (Moorland) in Each of Six Upland Areas, 1950-80. (These results derive from the University of Birmingham Moorland Study.)

Note: Dates quoted for each area are median dates. Figures have been rounded to nearest 100 ha.

Source: Alan Woods.

Study area	Actual period	Total area (ha)	Rough pasture (moorland) area, 1950 (ha)	Rough pasture (moorland) area, 1980 (ha)	Net change in rough pasture area, 1950-80 (ha)	(%)
Mid-Wales Uplands	1948-83	130,800	100,900	72,400	−28,400	−28
North York Moors NP	1950-79	144,000	68,000	50,900	−17,100	−25
Northumberland NP	1952-76	106,000	83,600	71,500	−12,000	−14
Brecon Beacons NP	1948-75	135,400	74,100	65,800	− 8,300	−11
Snowdonia NP	1948-75	89,100	65,600	63,000	− 2,500	− 4
Dartmoor NP	1958-79	95,600	51,000	49,300	− 1,800	− 3
Total		700,800	443,200	373,000	−70,100	−16

The most contentious change to the Bill followed pressure from the agricultural lobby. This related to changes in the farm capital grant scheme introduced the previous year. In an effort to cut civil service staff, the government had removed the requirement that farmers should seek prior approval to carry out work for which they intended to claim a grant. As this also removed the possibility of any official persuasion or advice being brought to bear to safeguard natural features, the change in procedures elicited strong protests from conservation organisations. The Government had responded by requiring farmers wishing to carry out work in National Parks or SSSIs to consult respectively the National Park authorities or the NCC. Amendments to the Wildlife and Countryside Bill instigated by the Ministry of Agriculture, Fisheries and Food took these new procedures one step (albeit a big step) further. The new clauses required that where an agricultural grant was refused on conservation grounds, the objecting authority (whether the NCC or a National Park authority) would have to compensate the farmer. The change was staunchly resisted by the conservation lobby but welcomed by the CLA and the NFU as a means of providing the necessary financial safeguards and recompense for farmers affected by conservation objections.

Colour Plate 1. Wildlife Habitats and Intensive Farming

Michael Mulliner, winner of the Shropshire Farming and Wildlife Group's Conservation award for 1984
for the careful integration of a series of wildlife habitats with his 74 ha. intensive dairy farm.
Source: *Farmers' Weekly.*

Colour Plate 2. The Cover of a Metroland Brochure
One of the many advertising pictures used by the Metropolitan Railway to extol the virtues of the
environments through which the lines passed. It was the only London railway to exploit commercially
property development during the inter-war years through its own company, Metropolitan Railway
Country Estates Ltd.
Source: London Transport Museum.

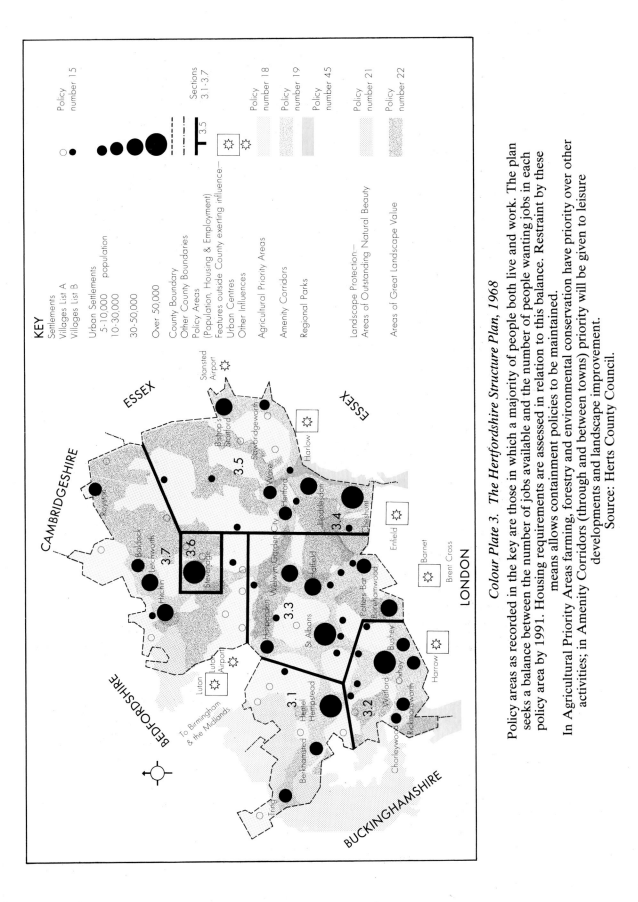

KEY

Settlements
Villages List A
Villages List B

Urban Settlements
5-10,000   population
10-30,000
30-50,000

Over 50,000

County Boundary
Other County Boundaries
Policy Areas
(Population, Housing & Employment)
Features outside County exerting influence—
Urban Centres
Other Influences

Agricultural Priority Areas

Amenity Corridors

Regional Parks

Landscape Protection—
Areas of Outstanding Natural Beauty

Areas of Great Landscape Value

Policy
number 15

Sections
3.1-3.7

Policy
number 18
Policy
number 19
Policy
number 45

Policy
number 21
Policy
number 22

Colour Plate 3.   The Hertfordshire Structure Plan, 1968

Policy areas as recorded in the key are those in which a majority of people both live and work. The plan
seeks a balance between the number of jobs available and the number of people wanting jobs in each
policy area by 1991. Housing requirements are assessed in relation to this balance. Restraint by these
means allows containment policies to be maintained.
In Agricultural Priority Areas farming, forestry and environmental conservation have priority over other
activities; in Amenity Corridors (through and between towns) priority will be given to leisure
developments and landscape improvement.
Source: Herts County Council.

Colour Plate 4. Medieval Manuscript
Many books of the time contained pictures of birds and animals as embellishments.
Source: RSPB.

Colour Plate 5. Rydal Water, Lake District

Is it scenes such as this that evoke an essential ethical and aesthetic commitment among conservationists?
Source: English Tourist Board.

Colour Plate 6. Ploughed Moorland on Exmoor

Land reclaimed in the 1970s adjacent to unreclaimed moorland and Bronze Age barrow.

Source: Ed Maltby.

Colour Plate 7. The Summit of Snowdon, Gwynedd
The mountain railway from Llanberis and the facilities provided by its terminal building make the summit popular with the tourist. But its ease of accessibility on foot via its six main footpaths increase its appeal still further. The result has been such severe erosion that a management programme sponsored by the Countryside Commission and the National Park Authority and aimed at restoring the paths was begun in the late 1970s. This work is expected to last beyond 1986.
Source: The Welsh Tourist Board.

Colour Plate 8. New Quay, Dyfed
One of the prettiest sea ports on Cardigan Bay, it has developed as a coastal 'honey-pot' for summer
visitors. It offers accommodation in the caravan parks and holiday cottages and refreshments
in the tea shops, chip shops and bars.
Source: The Welsh Tourist Board.

Colour Plate 9. Work in Progress on a Bridge near Barrow House, Derwentwater

Part of a new pathway across the lake shores.
Source: Countryside Commission.

Colour Plate 10. A Limestone Quarry in the Mendip Hills AONB

Workings of this kind in the area expanded rapidly in the 1970s to meet the fall in output of aggregates in the south-east of England. Current levels of production totalling around eight million tonnes are expected to expand by a factor of four in the next 25 years.
Source: West Air Photography, Weston-super-Mare.

Colour Plate 11. Coalbrookdale Iron Works on the Banks of the River Severn

The birthplace of cast iron manufacture located on a coalfield, close to sources of raw materials and a means of transport — by water.

Source: Ironbridge Gorge Museum Trust.

Colour Plate 12. Development Commission Factory Development
These units at Bakewell, Derbyshire, have been financed and designed through the Development
Commission.
Source: Development Commission.

Colour Plate 13. Craft Homes in Northumberland
A new type of development which combines the provision of workshop facilities with residential
accommodation.
Source: Development Commission.

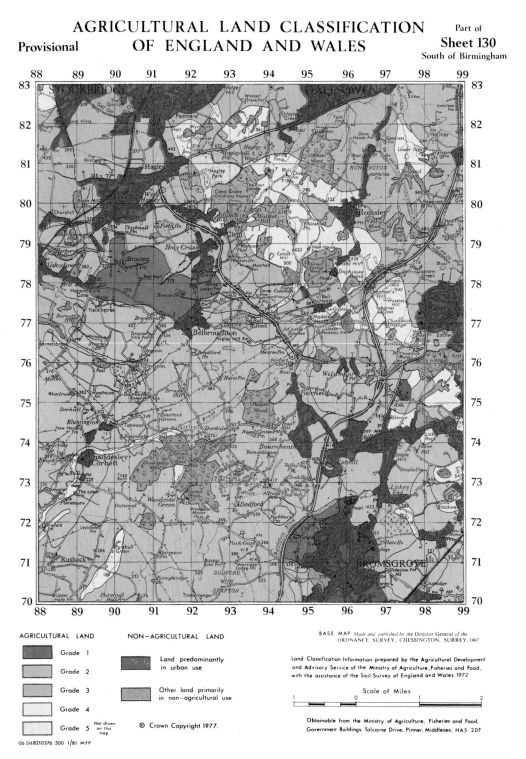

AGRICULTURAL LAND CLASSIFICATION
Provisional   OF ENGLAND AND WALES

Part of
Sheet 130
South of Birmingham

AGRICULTURAL LAND

Grade 1

Grade 2

Grade 3

Grade 4

Grade 5   Not shown on this map

06 Dd 8210376 500 1/81 MFP

NON-AGRICULTURAL LAND

Land predominantly in urban use

Other land primarily in non-agricultural use

© Crown Copyright 1977.

BASE MAP Made and published by the Director General of the
ORDNANCE SURVEY, CHESSINGTON, SURREY, 1967

Land Classification Information prepared by the Agricultural Development
and Advisory Service of the Ministry of Agriculture, Fisheries and Food,
with the assistance of the Soil Survey of England and Wales, 1972

Scale of Miles

Obtainable from the Ministry of Agriculture, Fisheries and Food,
Government Buildings, Tolcarne Drive, Pinner, Middlesex. HA5 2DT

Colour Plate 14. The Agricultural Land Classification

A land classification that has come under much criticism for being too broad and for overlooking the
economic value of land. Would a new comprehensive land classification assist in steering change in the
countryside?

Source: Ministry of Agriculture, Fisheries and Food.

The polarisation of the debate has made the position and future of the two conservation agencies particularly problematic. For some years both the Countryside Commission and the NCC have pursued policies based on the notion of a consensus between agriculture and conservation and the Act propels them further in this direction. As the Bill progressed through Parliament, this produced a growing rift between voluntary groups and the conservation agencies as the former grew frustrated at the Government's intransigence while the latter could do little to change the Government's intention.

Suspicions of the agencies among environmentalists have been heightened by the recent trend of political appointments to their governing councils and national advisory committees. Whereas traditionally these bodies have had, in their representatives, a mix of environmental and farming interests, a majority of the new appointments made by the Conservatives have farming, forestry or landowning interests, and most of them have served or currently serve in an official capacity with the NFU, the CLA or their Scottish or Welsh equivalents.

The main intention has been to press the two conservation agencies into line behind the implementation of the Act. A similar trend has occurred among the ministerial appointees to the National Park authorities.

Popular Support for Conservation

The debate surrounding the passage and implementation of the Act has stimulated public interest in conservation, and popular support for the conservation movement is higher than ever before. This is mirrored in Europe where membership of the Green Party in Germany and other ecology parties elsewhere has grown considerably in recent years. The combined membership of nature and rural conservation groups in England and Wales is about one million, and this figure does not include the 1,140,000 people who belong to the National Trust. This makes conservation a sizeable social movement. Even so, it is important to know whether the values it promotes command support beyond those who are active in voluntary groups, particularly as the membership of conservation groups is unrepresentative of the general public in terms of social composition.

The vast majority of members of conservation groups are middle class. The RSPB's membership is mainly lower middle class, attracting those employed particularly in technical and clerical occupations. Most other groups are strongly upper middle class, drawing the bulk of their support from those in professional and managerial occupations. The more radical groups do not deviate from this picture. Surveys of Friends of the Earth and the Conservation Society have shown them to be solidly middle class, with their memberships strongly concentrated in the personal service professions, such as medicine, teaching, social work, academia and the arts. The distinctive characteristics of radical environmentalists are that they tend to be younger (in their twenties and thirties, unlike the predominantly middle-aged membership of the more traditional groups) and highly educated — a majority of the members of Friends of the Earth and the Conservation Society have degrees.

Does the fact that membership of environmental groups is predominantly middle class mean that the environment is basically a middle-class concern? This need not be so. It could be that environmental groups are merely reflecting a general characteristic of voluntary organisations — that they tend to be formed and supported mainly by the middle class. The critical question is whether the values expressed by environmental groups are more widely shared. Here we can rely only on indirect evidence. There have been few systematic surveys of public opinion on environmental matters in Britain. These suggest, however, that the general public is very sympathetic to the environmental movement; and that this passive sympathy is socially much more broadly based than membership of environmental groups themselves.

Evidence of general concern for wildlife and the countryside also comes from mass culture. Wildlife programmes on television and radio have perennial appeal. Some nine million people regularly watch 'Wildlife on One'. Wildlife programmes also register the highest levels of audience satisfaction. Television has been responsible for establishing nature as a central feature of popular culture. Sentimental attachment to wildlife is exploited by advertisers in selling anything from cosmetics to confectionery. The fact that trips to the countryside are the most prevalent form of out-of-the-home recreation suggests that this attachment is not just sedentary or mawkish.

More specific evidence of attitudes towards conservation comes from a public opinion survey conducted in 1983. Some 53 per cent of the 1,991 respondents said they would support an increase in income tax of one penny in the pound to pay for measures to protect wildlife and the environment, and 26 per cent said they would oppose such a move. As many as 31 per cent claimed that within the last year or so they themselves had donated money to a charity concerned with conservation, and 4 per cent claimed to belong to a conservation organisation. The respondents were also asked which of a number of amenities made a valuable contribution to the overall quality of their life. Apart from 'streets safe to walk in', 'attractive countryside' was mentioned most (by 53 per cent of respondents) — and much more frequently than other amenities such as good public transport, parks, access to a car, libraries, sports facilities, leisure centres and theatres. Only 2 per cent of respondents said that attractive countryside did not make a valuable contribution to the quality of their life.

This all suggests very widespread support for the objectives of the conservation lobby. On the specific issue of the conflict between agriculture and conservation, however, opinions were more divided and ambivalent. When respondents were asked which out of 13 possible functions are the most important ones for farmers to fulfil, from a national standpoint, 'ensuring that activities are not harmful to the environment' was mentioned with the fourth highest frequency. The functions which achieved even greater support were, in descending order, 'providing high quality food', 'buying British machinery and raw materials' and 'increasing production each year'. Evidently, many people perceive no contradiction between increased agricultural output and a conserved environment, or at least they expect British farmers to encompass both functions.

When respondents were asked which functions farmers are particularly poor at, 'looking after wildlife' was mentioned with the third highest frequency, surpassed only by the negative evaluation of farmers' performance in remuneration of their employees and providing jobs. Even so, a critical view of farmers' contributions to conservation is still only a minority opinion, though held by a sizeable minority. This became apparent when respondents were asked their opinions as to whether, on balance, places for wildlife and attractive countryside are being needlessly damaged by farmers; or whether farmers are making new wildlife habitats and a different but just as attractive countryside. Some 49 per cent of respondents held the latter view — the traditional view of farming — but 36 per cent were of the opinion that there is needless destruction by farmers. It would seem that the popular image of farming is undergoing a fundamental change; and that a sizeable body of opinion (though still a minority of the populace) shares the concern expressed by conservationists about the impact of agriculture on the countryside, as well as the level of agricultural subsidies and the generation of food surpluses.

Other Pressures

Though conservationists are currently preoccupied with the consequences of structural and technical changes within the countryside's predominant industry, it is important not to overlook other, non-agricultural pressures on rural landscapes and habitats. Timber production and the provision of public water supplies also exploit natural resources and in the past have attracted much criticism for their lack of sensitivity to the rural environment, but the recent development of policy in these sectors presents an alternative approach to that of agricultural policy. Since the late 1960s, both the Forestry Commission and the Water Authorities have had wider responsibilities forced upon them and now they actively pursue measures for conserving the landscape and opening their land for recreation. This has been done in part as a response to their environmental critics but mainly because of government directives. It has also been an astute move by these industries to broaden the justification for their work, in the face of diminished growth projections for their primary product, and trenchant criticism of the social returns to public expenditure on, say, afforestation or reservoir schemes. Environmental objections have thus been turned on their head, and now amenity and conservation benefits are actively pursued in such schemes to help justify continued development and public expenditure. Perhaps there are pointers here to the way in which agricultural policy may be adapted.

The countryside is likely to face intensified pressures from urban development once the economy comes out of recession. Since the late 1970s a number of changes have been made in planning policy and procedures, to relax local planning controls and thereby create a more sympathetic climate for developers. The CPRE has warned that, 'Quite new economic and political pressures are building up for the extensive use of virgin countryside sites for industrial, commercial and housing developments'. Certainly, some of the locational trends for new private housing, for hypermarkets and warehouses and for footloose, high-technology industries would seem to favour greenfield sites and out-of-town locations, particularly in those parts of the countryside and the urban-fringe which are accessible to the motorway network.

Other pressures on the remote countryside will come from the extraction of minerals, particularly aggregates, as the availability of supplies from sites close to urban areas diminishes (see Colour Plate 10). But other energy-related developments, arising from open-cast coal mining, the nuclear power programme and the extraction of natural oil and gas, both on land and offshore may also be significant. A shift to alternative energy sources would not necessarily ease the burden. Any large-scale programme of exploiting wind power, for example, will need extensive arrays of wind generators in open, coastal or hillside locations — generators which would dwarf the traditional windmill. Similarly, the Severn barrage, if built, would have a considerable impact on the landscape and wetland habitats of the Severn estuary. Britain's economy in the late twentieth century is peculiarly dependent on the energy sector and, from the point of view of rural conservation, there are no easy options. The merits of each will have to be weighed carefully against its environmental impact.

Grassroots

A County Council Farm Conservation Adviser Talks About Conservation and Agriculture in the 1980s

My current job derives from a Countryside Commission experimental project — which I have been involved with since its inception in 1978 — designed to tackle problems of landscape decline specifically in six parishes within this area.

The project derived from the Countryside Commission's *New Agricultural Landscapes* study of 1974 which had demonstrated how changes in arable farming were comprehensively altering the lowland landscape. The Commission, though, was optimistic that with proper guidance modern agriculture could produce a new yet equally attractive countryside, and this was the philosophy behind the launch of a number of New Agricultural Landscape projects. The intention was to extend the approach of area management, developed by the Commission in parts of the uplands and the urban-fringes, to the intensively farmed, lowland countryside.

The aims of the five-year-long project were to encourage both the conservation of existing landscape features and wildlife habitats, and the establishment of new features of interest where the landscape was impoverished. Much of my work is with the local farmers, seeking to interest them in conservation and giving them advice, information and practical help on such matters as tree-planting, woodland management, the maintenance of hedgerows and green lanes, and pond clearing.

My present job is an extension of this earlier experimental work, and is one of a number of countryside advisory posts that the Countryside Commission partly funds in various counties. The essential elements of my role are really education and advice. I am continuing to build up and extend my contacts with farmers, and I work closely with our local Farming and Wildlife Advisory Group. Part of my work entails arranging training courses where farmers can see practical demonstrations of conservation management. My educational activities also take me to schools, colleges, amenity societies, Women's Institutes, young farmers' clubs — to promote wider appreciation of the need to conserve landscape and wildlife. My greatest challenge, though, lies in winning the respect and sympathy of the farming and landowning community.

Most farmers are willing to listen to what I have to say. Any advice, however, has to be practical and geared to their particular circumstances. So I must be sensitive to the problems and constraints that they face. I have to be a good listener, as well as an advocate of conservation measures on farms. The staunch individualism of many farmers and farmworkers, some of whom resent the intrusion of an outsider or the gratuitous advice of a young conservationist, can be one of the most difficult problems for me to overcome. Above all, any planting or maintenance work that I suggest to farmers must be neither costly nor interfere with the smooth running of the farm.

Some farmers are readily receptive and anxious to do what they can to maintain the natural interest and diversity of their farms. They do not need encouragement so much as technical information and specific recommendations as to what steps they might take. This may even extend to a complete farm conservation plan, involving a survey of existing habitats and landscape features; proposals for their management; identification of areas in need of improvement or replanting; and guidance on the phasing of tasks, sources of grant-aid and labour requirements.

The large majority, though not indifferent to conservation, do need a certain amount of prompting or persuasion to consider taking action. With time, however, many do respond to some of my suggestions. Face-to-face contact works but not always immediately. It is simply a case of dropping a thought into a conversation. Occasionally something results but it may be many months later. Offering practical assistance, calling in volunteers or job-creation labour for such tasks as ride clearance, digging out ponds, coppicing and tree-planting are all part of the job. Small grants have also proved a strong inducement to otherwise reluctant farmers.

A minority of farmers, however, about one in five, prove to be either indifferent or hostile to the claims of conservation. They can cause particular concern because any positive efforts made on surrounding farms can be offset by their depredations — whether it be the destruction of small woodlands, the erection of poorly designed and ill-sited outbuildings, ploughing up road-side verges, cutting hedges to the ground, or the creation of vast, featureless fields of 40 hectares or more. These farmers really are land bandits, businessmen, first and last — they do not see the land as a heritage and they have no feeling for its husbandry. However, I would not like to see planning controls imposed on agriculture: that would be too cumbersome — and counter-productive, because it would alienate the farmers who are sympathetic towards conservation.

Instead I would like to see greater efforts to encourage more responsible attitudes towards the husbanding of natural resources — a return to former notions of stewardship. Most of what conservationists are trying to achieve is no more than the forgotten common knowledge of past generations. I do come across farmers who still accept that their business is built on a heritage and that their responsibility is to hand that heritage on. In the main, however, I deplore the fact that a once independent and self-sufficient breed of men are now so manipulated by MAFF boffins and Eurocrats.

The present system of agricultural support is quite inimical to conservation. *HARMFUL* It demands of farmers that they squeeze more and more out of their land; it encourages a profligate use of machinery, chemicals, and fossil fuels; it forces *EXTRAVEGANT* up land values; and it displaces traditional farming methods and the small, independent-minded, family farmers. Around here, all the pressures are for farmers to grow more and more cereals. It is simply against their interests to retain land in other uses. Therefore, the small, marginal areas — the water meadows and the woodlands — that are so important to wildlife are rapidly disappearing, at a considerable cost to the taxpayer, in order to produce yet more cereals. Ultimately, however much goodwill there is towards conservation, it is overwhelmed by the pressures pushing in the opposite direction — the capital grants, the price supports, the inflated land values and the technical advice.

In the short term, I would like to see steps taken to redress this enormous imbalance of resources. That would entail greater technical support services for conservation and additional money for conservation grants. At present, the sort of advisory work that I do is carried out on a shoestring; just modest increases in the budget could achieve substantial improvements in its coverage and impact. In addition, farmers increasingly expect payment for carrying out conservation work on their own land.

It would seem out of the question, however, that local authorities or conservation bodies should ever try to match existing agricultural subsidies. I would think, for example, that to save all the grazing meadows which are likely to be ploughed up in the country over the next ten years, my council would have to pay £3 million annually and indefinitely in compensation under the guidelines of the Wildlife and Countryside Act.

In the medium term, therefore, I hope for a reform of agricultural subsidies. I would like to see price support for cereals removed. Farmers would continue to grow them, but it would take the pressure off the remaining, uncultivated land, especially if grants for draining marginal land were withheld. In general, I would favour the redirection of agricultural grants towards social and conservation objectives — for example, as help for small farmers to farm in a traditional manner. Greater official encouragement also should be given to organic husbandry and to alternative farming systems less reliant on chemical energy inputs. Equally, I would welcome a legal ceiling on the amount of land any individual might farm. This should curb the amalgamation of holdings and restrict the scope of those who acquire the land simply as a financial investment without any feeling for the rural heritage. There are many changes needed, particularly at national level and, as a countryside adviser, I can have little influence in such matters. The challenge is to achieve as much as possible, within existing constraints, until the situation changes and meanwhile to publicise both the good and the bad of modern farming and learn from them.

An Officer of a County Trust for Nature Conservation Talks About Conservation and the Voluntary Sector in the 1980s

With management agreements made under the 1981 Act the main problem we have is one of secrecy. Our local National Park has entered into a number of agreements. They have told us how many and even where they are, but the big unknown is what the *conditions* of the agreements are — what the farmer is still allowed to do. The general attitude seems to be that the Park does not want people to know what the agreements are. They certainly will not divulge the level of compensation payments. I think if conservation was really the purpose behind these agreements then things would be more open. This would also encourage more farmers to come forward and make agreements. Confidentiality surrounding these agreements is a great myth — a hangover from the ADAS grant-aid system which is all done in strict secrecy.

We are also concerned about how agreements are being monitored (in our local National Park). We are told that some monitoring of the conditions takes place, but since we do not know the conditions, this is hard to verify! Things seem a little too cosy for comfort.

Also, the National Park has used agreements on landscape rather than nature conservation grounds. The Park's interpretation of natural beauty under the 1949 Act seems to be landscape, but most people's understanding is landscape *and* nature-fauna and flora. All landscapes ultimately derive from vegetation types anyway. Some areas in the Park have a high ecological value, but because they are not visible from the road they have been considered less important.

I think the National Park could be doing more in seeking and negotiating management agreements particularly since they get 90 per cent of their funding from the Countryside Commission. There is a bit of rivalry between them and the Nature Conservancy Council, though — if there is any whiff of an SSSI being designated in the park, they will pull out and let NCC take over, presumably to save money.

The NCC also have an element of secrecy in negotiating agreements. We do not know how many agreements they have completed in our local wetland area. We are putting pressure on NCC for them to discuss and agree with us (and the Royal Society for the Protection of Birds) what should be areas for agreement and what should be agreed management actions. As a voluntary body it is very difficult for us to do our work looking out for habitat destruction if we do not know where agreements have been negotiated and what their conditions are. In general, the NCC seem much more committed to the management agreement process and there seems at present to be almost unlimited funding for it. They are now agreeing very high levels of compensation on the wetlands. If we are going to use this approach to managing conservation it should be explained more fully to farmers. Farmers should be willing to have SSSIs on their land, for the alternative income it brings. NCC should broadcast the advantages more and thereby avoid the problems of farmers destroying their sites so that they will not become SSSIs.

In the longer term though, we do not like compensation payments. We would much sooner see grants given for positive management. At present both in the National Park and on most SSSIs there is no *positive* conservation management — it is all negative. The NCC do seem to be quite interested in developing the notion of positive management, however. Such positive management is much better implemented through a system of grants, than through any form of planning control over agriculture, although there do need to be some reserve powers. Only in this way will you get positive conservation in SSSIs rather than just low-level agriculture.

I also think that at last the NFU is cottoning on to the fact that positive conservation will, in the longer term, provide a more stable source of income when the CAP is reformed. They are beginning to tell the farmers of the advantages of management agreements and there is much less antagonism from farmers than there used to be. There is now less ploughing up and draining done by farmers to avoid SSSIs and their restrictions than there was a couple of years ago.

In fact, it is the internal drainage boards that are now the biggest problem in terms of draining the wetlands. The committee members are made up of the politically more aggressive farmers and they are the ones, in the main, who would be going for drainage. Water Authority engineers, too, justify their existence by designing flood prevention and drainage schemes. It is only the NCC and the lack of public money that is preventing the majority of our wetland being drained.

The dairy quotas may increase the tendency to drain the wetland as farmers move out of cows and into arable production. But this would have to be done on borrowed money and farmers are increasingly worried about getting financially overstretched. As the CAP is reformed and quotas introduced, it is the farmers with the lowest overheads that suffer least, which is why having a management agreement on an SSSI is probably the best position for a farmer to be in, over the next 20 years.

In terms of the town and country planning system, there is a need for much greater responsibility over factors that damage the countryside as a whole. I believe that local authorities need to have greater expertise among staff, and awareness among members, on nature conservation and amenity issues. Very few of the operations that affect the countryside actually come under the current system of planning controls, but those that do are usually treated abysmally superficially. For example, mineral extraction, tipping, highway improvements, woodland and forestry proposals, etc. often pay scant regard to conservation interests. Similarly, local authorities have been very slow to use existing powers to benefit conservation, through for instance, the establishment of Local Nature Reserves as enabled under the 1949 Act, the establishment of management agreements, the acquisition of 'amenity' land, the use of Article 4 Directives to control damaging land-uses, etc. Further to this, I believe there is a need for new legislation to extend the powers of local authorities over certain damaging operations in the countryside, for example, hedgerow removal, and 'agricultural reclamation' by tipping into ponds or quarries, etc.

It is important though that sites of SSSI quality are dealt with solely by the NCC. We have recently had a County Council produce a local plan that designated wildlife conservation areas over areas also proposed as SSSIs, yet the council's areas are half that of the NCC's; a local authority has no role in this aspect, and should be protecting those areas that are of lower quality than SSSI but still of great county or local significance.

The voluntary sector as a whole, and I would include pressure groups in this, has grown very rapidly during the 1970s and 1980s. However, at present there is a perceivable gap between the 'radical' bodies like Greenpeace and the more 'established' groups like ourselves. Basically pressure groups are becoming so popular and forming so quickly that they could fragment the conservation movement. This is because some of the traditional conservation bodies have become too introverted and do not put sufficient energy into 'campaigning'.

It is difficult to know why conservation groups are growing so quickly but a lot of it has to do with the education of the 1960s and 1970s. We studied ecology, for example. I think also people are becoming more sensitive to the destruction of natural habitats everywhere, as this accelerates over time. The media, too have had a terrific influence.

I think, finally, the main note of caution I would sound about countryside conservation in the 1980s is that we must beware of the danger of equating conservation with cosmetics. The Farming and Wildlife Advisory Groups have been disastrous in this respect. They encourage farmers to believe that all they have to do for conservation is to plant trees and dig out ponds. It perpetuates the belief that farmers are doing the right thing, whereas they are often continuing to destroy important habitats. But at the same time, a committed voluntary sector is often accused of interfering with the seemingly God-given rights of landowners. Owning the land, though, does not give the right to despoil the nation's natural heritage.

Actions to Steer Change

The Current Status of Conservation Values

It was noted, in the conclusion of the first section of this chapter, that conservation values are in a state of flux. In the 1960s and early 1970s the predominant theme in conservation was a utilitarian one which stressed the importance of the scientific management of rural resources to ensure their sustained utilisation. The critical need seemed to be for suitable techniques to integrate the various pressures and demands on the countryside. The traditional concern with the aesthetics of the rural landscape was a secondary theme but even this seemed destined to be redefined as yet another rural product ('amenity'), the demand for which was to be integrated into the wider managerial matrix. Thus, the utility of a Norman church and a major breeding ground for Brent geese were carefully ranked in the early 1970s by the Roskill Commission in its quest for the correct site for the Third London Airport. Ardent technicians sought to determine the human carrying capacity of the New Forest; others attempted to place a monetary value on a trip to the countryside; and others still, using complex computer procedures, sought to refine an objective measurement of landscape attraction, stripped of all personal and subjective bias. Much of this type of work went under the title of cost-benefit analysis. In this context, values had to be relative; flexibility and pragmatism were the order of the day, in the face of what seemed to be ubiquitous change. The CPRE in an effort to modernise its appeal changed the P in its title from 'Preservation' to 'Protection'. Preservation had come to seem old-fashioned, even reactionary, and certainly very different from the 'wise use of resources' notion of conservation.

The management approach was steadily challenged during the 1970s by the growth of political conflict over conservation — clearly some demands on the countryside were not reconcilable. It was also overshadowed by a gathering sense of an enveloping environmental crisis. With a number of pundits such as the Club of Rome predicting imminent ecological collapse, environmental groups, the foremost being Friends of the Earth, sprang up to question the direction that society was taking. These new affiliations were much more radical and international in their outlook and more explicitly political than the established conservation and preservation groups. They view individual environmental problems as interrelated, identifying the profligate use of earth's non-renewable resources as the most serious problem and economic and population growth as the fundamental cause of crisis.

Previously people had been alarmed at the prospect that human profligacy and industrial power might eliminate the natural world. Now it seems that these forces even threaten human survival. Anxiety over this prospect has endowed the traditional concerns of conservationists with new significance as an integral part of the task of conserving the human habitat and husbanding the world's natural resources. The penalties of neglect are not only a loss of natural interest and beauty, but also a hazard to man's future. This has given conservation a strong, moral imperative. Indeed, a new philosophy and a new set of justifications for nature, landscape, archaeological and historic conservation are emerging, emphasising their roles as essential components of a balanced relationship between man and environment.

The Implementation of the Wildlife and Countryside Act, 1981

Official actions and legislation have not kept pace with this change in values which has led to growing disillusionment. The implementation of the Wildlife and Countryside Act, in particular, has been attended by considerable controversy. A number of its provisions, especially the requirement for owners of SSSIs to give notice of potentially damaging operations and the preparation and annual update of moorland maps by National Park authorities ensures continuing public prominence for disputes between agriculture and conservation (see Figure 4.13). Similarly, provision for consultation before the new SSSI designations has meant more publicity for the process of designation itself, including reports of damaging operations being carried out during the three month consultation period.

The greatest controversy surrounding the Act, however, has centred on the amount of money available for its implementation and the related issue of how the conservation agencies are to discharge their new powers and duties. The recurring fear is that financial stringencies may deter them from pressing their objections to MAFF-supported schemes of agricultural intensification. A related concern was that the Nature Conservancy Council's wariness of antagonising local farmers was leading to considerable delay and even reluctance in the designation of new SSSIs, particularly in areas where agricultural or forestry development was in prospect. First, the Friends of the Earth, and then the Royal Society for the Protection of Birds, threatened the NCC with legal action if it failed to fulfil its statutory duty of designating land which met its scientific criteria.

Rather than bridging divisions and stifling debate, the passage and implementation of the Act have polarised positions and sharpened the controversy. Few conservationists are prepared to accept it as the final word on the matter and a number of groups have begun to campaign for its reform, building on the political links they made during its passage. Various proposals of a more fundamental nature have been canvassed and they are reviewed below.

Although conservation issues in the countryside in the mid-1980s clearly embrace the broad spectrum of rural activity (such as water resource development and forestry), proposals for the reform of the 1981 Act centre on agriculture, and three alternative means of integrating conservation into agricultural policy and farm management have been suggested. One approach focuses on the agricultural support system; another on the structure of advice and conservation incentives to farmers; and yet another on means of regulating or controlling farmers' actions. None of these approaches is incompatible; indeed, an ideal package of reforms might contain elements of each.

Reforms for Conservation and Agriculture

In general terms, current support policies for agriculture, which are discussed in Chapter 2, oblige farmers to adopt ever more sophisticated technologies and to push up output relentlessly. This leads to an inevitable incompatibility of these policies with conservation. Reform of the agricultural support system has focused, therefore, on means of curbing the thrust towards expanding production and, in particular, of inducing a partial shift away from high intensity, arable farming and towards low intensity grassland farming. A number of these policy modifications are discussed in Chapter 2. The most fundamental means would be a substantial scaling down of the enormous burden of direct and indirect support for agriculture. A relative fall in agricultural prices, for example, would diminish farming prosperity and land values. This in turn should decrease the intensity of exploitation of land and lower capital investment in farming, with beneficial effects for the environment and other users of

Figure 4.13: The Agriculture and Conservation Debate in the National Press..

Source: Various newspaper cuttings.

the countryside. Within a reduced level of protection, a readjustment of price support to favour dairying and livestock rearing over tillage cropping would also be desirable in conservation terms, if not in terms of energy efficiency, as would the abolition of agricultural capital grants. Though, in general, grants play a much less important role than price support in promoting intensification, they do provide a significant incentive for bringing ecologically important marginal land into production.

However, there is some difficulty in anticipating the full response of farmers to a reduction in support. In the short term at least, many farmers might seek to expand production simply to maintain their income. In livestock farming this might mean further losses of permanent pasture and rough grazing, and an increase in improved pasture, temporary grass leys and the use of intensive housing units — all of which would represent a further impoverishment of the wildlife, landscape and amenity of the countryside. A related difficulty is that, whereas a reduction in support might well create a much more favourable economic climate for rural conservation, it would do nothing specific to ensure that particular features or areas of conservation interest would either not be destroyed or be actively cared for and managed. Thus a reduction in the levels of agricultural support will not be sufficient on its own to ensure good conservation practices within the countryside. It must, therefore be considered with more positive measures.

Among these more positive measures the second approach to reform focuses on the structure of advice and conservation incentives to farmers (see Figure 4.14). Management agreements under the 1981 Wildlife and Countryside Act embody the principle that forms of agricultural production that conserve the environment should be subsidised. Though many conservationists accept this principle, they reject the way it is applied in the Act. The main objections are as follows. First, the Act's obligatory provisions apply only to SSSIs and National Parks, implying a retreat from the notion of caring for the environment as a whole back to the discredited notion that the conservation of wildlife and landscapes can and should be confined to specifically designated areas. Second, the requirement that a farmer who if refused grant-aid from MAFF on conservation grounds must be compensated with a management agreement seems to give farmers a legal right to agricultural grants. The third and final iniquity is that this compensation has to be paid from the small budget of the conservation agencies, rather than by MAFF whose relentless promotion of agricultural output and new farming methods is creating the problem.

To take account of these objections would involve a major reform of MAFF. Its remit would have to be expanded to include rural conservation, and this new objective would be reflected in the grants and advice it gave to farmers. New types of grant to encourage amenity or ecological husbandry would have to be devised. The Agricultural Development and Advisory Service would also be recast to cope with the local realities of integrating conservation and agriculture, and would need additional sources of expertise in conservation management and land-use planning, In this context, an important role could be performed by the Farming and Wildlife Advisory Groups, which bring together farmers and conservationists in each county. The official conservation agencies would be the effective watchdogs of the new arrangements and would, therefore, need their roles to be strengthened in relation to MAFF.

The third and final approach to reform focuses on means of regulating or controlling farmers' actions. Planning controls, if introduced, must operate

Figure 4.14: Action on Conservation Advice at Croydon House Farm, Croydon, Cambridgeshire. Positive conservation advice has led to the replacement of a hedge previously removed to enlarge a field.

Source: *Farmers Weekly.*

effectively. In other words, they must be able to cope with the technicalities of modern agriculture without becoming an intolerable burden on the farming industry, but at the same time they must have a positive impact on farm development decisions, by discouraging, modifying or blocking developments which would clash with the public interest (see Figure 4.15). The main fears of the farming community, apart from the loss of freedom, are that planners would not be able to understand the finer points of agricultural practice and that farmers would be subjected to bureaucracy and delay. Delay could be particularly serious in view of the seasonality of farming. Any new powers, therefore, would require the commitment of sufficient skilled staff to operate them efficiently.

At present, the training of planners does not deal sufficiently with land management skills. But it is no defence of agriculture's exclusion from planning controls to assert that only farmers can comprehend farming decisions. It has long been accepted that planning authorities should make judgements affecting other industries of whose practices their officers have no intimate understanding. Moreover, a decision to improve a tract of open moorland or to drain a water meadow is not inherently more intractable than a decision to build, say, a hypermarket or a housing estate.

More formidable difficulties relate to the definition of development and its extension to incorporate significant farming changes, without increasing too many legal loopholes or a system of controls which could not be enforced. Agriculture is subject to inherently unpredictable environmental conditions and deals with living systems, one of whose properties is inexorable change. The areal scale of change and intensive overlapping of different interests on the same parcel of land bring a unique complexity to rural land-use issues. Any regulatory system would have to accommodate all these distinctive characteristics. Living systems need also to be managed. Yet, in themselves, controls can prevent only the construction, removal or material change of features; they cannot ensure that what is thereby not obliterated is managed in a sympathetic manner.

None of these caveats concerning the difficulties of regulating organic change through planning controls, applies to those agricultural operations which already fall within the definition of 'development' — namely, the construction of farm buildings above a certain size, roads and yards, and drainage works. Given the industrial character of most modern farm buildings and that many are ill-designed and ill-sited from any but an agricultural point of view, it could be considered an anomaly that these and other construction and engineering operations on farms do not need planning permission. They should pose no technical difficulty for the development control system and could be brought within its ambit simply by amending the General Development Order. These comments apply equally to afforestation schemes and building and engineering operations associated with forestry.

To apply development control procedures to other farming activities would be to use a quite inappropriate and insensitive sledgehammer, since what is generally sought is the preservation and management of some traditional features. If this is the goal, then the ethos for the preservation order is more pertinent. Already there are precedents, such as Tree Preservation Orders and Limestone Pavement Orders, which indicate how specific features and sites might be preserved on a wider basis. Farmers would be required to give notice to the local planning authority or one of the national conservation agencies if they intended to remove or alter a landscape feature. The authority would then have time to assess the importance of the feature and, if appropriate, seek to make a financial or other type of agreement for its conservation. In cases where an agreement was sought and the farmer refused, powers to impose a preservation order would be available as a last resort. The advantages of such a system compared with development control are that it would

Figure 4.15: The Visual Impact of Farm Buildings. Silos, like other farm structures, can be visually obtrusive if poorly sited. Yet provided they are not within 400 yards of a road they do not require planning permission.

Source: Countryside Commission.

be more flexible and selective and could be introduced in a piecemeal and responsive way; and management activities could be included without creating too many legal loopholes and problems of enforcement.

Both development control and agreement/order procedures would, however, place an additional administrative cost on the control of the countryside and trade-offs would have to sought between this and the degree of environmental control achieved, particularly in the context of the size of state support to agriculture.

Desirable Packages: Feasible Options

An ideal package of reforms might contain elements from each of these three approaches. Currently, the official emphasis is exclusively on conservation advice and incentives. The limitations of this approach, without reform of the agricultural support system, is that there are much more powerful and ubiquitous incentives pulling farmers in the opposite direction of intensification. Not only do they weaken the appeal of conservation incentives but they also make conservation *seem* expensive because compensatory payments are calculated taking into account all public subsidies. Thus, the full potential of conservation incentives could be realised only in the context of a reformed system of agricultural support which fully acknowledged conservation as a legitimate and integral objective of state assistance to the farming sector. If the economic pressures on farmers were so radically altered, it might be thought that this would invalidate the case for planning controls over agriculture. This is not so. On the contrary, planning controls tend to be more effective, the less they have to combat powerful economic pressures. Ideally, incentives and controls should be complementary and mutually reinforcing — the one maintaining a favourable climate; the other policing and mitigating farming changes, and providing a democratically-accountable safety net for valued sites and features.

What is desirable may not be politically feasible. Attempts to introduce any of these reform proposals would be staunchly opposed, at least initially, by the farming lobby. No government, therefore, would lightly embark on such a path. On the other hand, the conservation lobby has kept up the pressure on the issue and a flow of unfavourable publicity that no government would willingly endure for long.

Radical reform on this matter is unlikely from the Government at present: it is too deeply committed to the Wildlife and Countryside Act and it has too many farmers and landowners in its ranks. The Labour Party, in contrast, is pledged to make all agricultural aid subject to environmental criteria and to extend development control to farming.

In the short and medium terms, the prospects are more propitious for piecemeal changes that may favour conservation. Public expenditure pressures, for example, are likely to curb spending on agricultural intensification. Another possible change might be to bring all building works connected with agriculture and forestry under development control. Such incremental change may not be sufficient, however. With such a wide-ranging debate concerning the basic premises of policy in this field, a very fluid political situation pertains.

Who Benefits, Who Loses?

Conserving the countryside is inextricably linked with the activity that takes place in rural areas. Because agriculture has such a dominant impact in this respect, beneficiaries and losers from agricultural practices also will be affected by conservation measures. Sometimes agricultural beneficiaries will be losers in conservation terms, but this will not always be so. It will be useful, in reading this section, therefore, for comparisons to be drawn with the final sections of Chapter 2.

Farmers, particularly those who farm in National Parks or who have SSSIs on their land, both benefit and suffer from the consequences of current conservation policy. They benefit to the extent that if national park authorities or the Nature Conservancy Council wish to object to improvements that the farmer is intending to make (or at least claims to be), it is required that in the last resort, a management agreement be negotiated. This agreement requires that the farmer be compensated either with an annual payment over a period of years, or one discounted lump sum. These payments are based on the value of the production lost on the assumption that the improvement was made. In effect, then, farmers benefit under these circumstances from a compensation payment that is paid for them to do nothing. In cases, this has been as high as £100,000 per annum.

Farmers quite clearly lose from the opportunity to undertake improvements on their farms under these circumstances. But if this is negotiated through an agreement, can it really be counted as a loss? Farmers may also suffer from having their land compulsorily purchased, as an alternative to negotiating a management agreement. This rarely happens in practice, however. On balance farmers remain among the few who have any legal right to compensation for state intervention that might be considered to inhibit their industrial goals.

The fact that the 1981 Wildlife and Countryside Act pertains only to SSSIs and national parks is a loss to a more comprehensive conservation programme in England and Wales as a whole. Both within and outside these areas, farmers and indeed foresters enjoy further privileges within the envelope of conservation policy. These relate to exemptions from planning control for a majority of developments. Not only does this afford a degree of immunity from controls over the siting of buildings, but also in most areas, their design. The visual appearance of the farmed and afforested landscape also does not come under specific control even though criticisms abound concerning, for example, the monotony of coniferous monoculture and the losses of hedgerows and hedgerow trees.

Whether a net benefit would accrue from the imposition of more rigorous planning controls would hinge in the short term on whether planners are suitably qualified to make appropriate evaluations of the farmed and forested landscape. Even in the longer term, it has been argued that planning control simply represents the imposition of a further layer of bureaucracy on the countryside, at a further unnecessary cost.

The political process within which conservation policy has developed since the war also has created advantages and disadvantages for various people. It has been argued that the ineffectiveness of policy has led to conservation losses through developmental pressures, agricultural intensification and the recreation growth. The last of these has been counteracted to some extent by the recreation provisions in the 1968 Countryside Act, where recreation designations were required to have specific conservation objectives. Latterly, therefore, recreationists may be considered to have become beneficiaries of conservation policies.

Despite this, since Lord Sandford reviewed policy for National Parks in the mid-1970s, conservation has always been accorded a higher priority than recreation in the countryside (although Lord Sandford stipulated that this should be so only in national parks) where the two are considered to be in conflict.

The politicisation associated with the 1981 Wildlife and Countryside Act has further identified a number of beneficiaries and losers. Firstly, the whole process has served to popularise notions of countryside conservation. Interest in the countryside on the part of the general public has, in its growth, provided political leverage for the conservation movement. The process of the Act has also provided invaluable experience in political lobbying for a number of countryside pressure groups, although it must be considered that the agriculture industry inherently has one of the most effective accesses to government of any sector. Even with this politicisation, wildlife and landscape interests have remained subservient to productive ones in the countryside, in both an economic and political sense. This could be due to the large degree of fragmentation of the conservation lobby.

In terms of the outcomes of the Act, perhaps the major beneficiary has been the Ministry of Agriculture which was relieved, during the passage of the Bill, of the burden of compensation payments for management agreements. This burden fell to the relatively minor budget of the Department of the Environment. Within the National Parks, however, Exmoor does have the advantage of having to bear only 10 per cent of these costs directly (the remainder being paid by the DoE). All of the other parks must pay 25 per cent.

Conserving the landscape and wildlife of our countryside also offers a number of perhaps less tangible benefits to the wider population. Certainly the countryside remains a principal stimulus to an English and Welsh artistic tradition enjoyed both nationally and internationally. Through tourism and recreation the countryside provides therapeutic and psychological benefits that are also felt beyond England and Wales. These benefits have grown domestically this century with increases in mobility and leisure time being enjoyed across the wider population. It must be said, however, that these benefits accruing from recreation in the conserved countryside are felt chiefly by the urban (and generally middle-class) population. Such benefits often are achieved at the expense of rural dwellers themselves since conserving the countryside has been invariably at the expense of developing a well-structured rural industrial base.

The scientist is also well served by specific conservation measures such as the designation of both National and Local Nature Reserves. Such areas maintain 'reservoirs' for the study of habitats that might otherwise be lost. All of these artistic, therapeutic and scientific benefits are both historical and

Figure 4.16: 'Sorry Sir — this gent informs me the main ring has been declared an SSSI.'
Source: *Farmers Weekly.*

current, but they also provide benefits for the future. Although intangible, conserving the countryside for future generations provides a dominant stimulus for policy.

5
Sustaining Rural Communities
SNAPSHOTS

Those men plough for the lord for each virgate (about 30 acres) four acres for spring sowing. And besides this they shall find ploughs for the lord's use thrice in winter, thrice in spring, and once in summer . . . And those men work three days in each week. And also they render yearly from each virgate by custom 2s. 1½d. And all the men render 50 hens and 640 eggs.

An account of the services and dues to be rendered by a peasant to the lord of the manor of Kettering in return for the use of a virgate of his land. Cited in A.L. Poole, 'From Domesday Book to Magna Carta', Oxford History of England, vol. III, Oxford, and taken from the Black Book of Peterborough drawn up between 1125 and 1128 AD.

In Elizabeth's time a great deal of this (Central England) and more outside the area was open country: that is to say, it was cultivated by the villagers upon a common system of agriculture in great open fields in which they held open strips and patches. The fields ran endlessly to the eye over the gentle undulations of the landscape like the famous fields of Laxton in Nottinghamshire.
A.L. Rowse (1973), The England of Elizabeth, Cardinal.

The common was very extensive (in Maulden). I conversed with a farmer and several cottagers. One of them said enclosing would ruin England; it was worse than the wars. Why my friend (I said) what have you lost by it? (He replied) 'I kept four cows before the parish was enclosed and now I

don't keep so much as a goose; and you ask me what I lost by it! Bedfordshire Report (1830), General Report on Enclosures.

When a labourer becomes possessed of more land than he and his family can cultivate in the evenings . . . the farmer can no longer depend on him for constant work and the hay-making in harvest . . . must suffer to a degree which . . . would sometimes prove a national inconvenience.
    The village poor are designing rogues who, under various pretences, attempt to cheat the parish . . . and their whole abilities are exerted in the execution of deceit which may procure from the parish officers an allowance of money for idle and profligate purposes.
Two farmers commenting on aspects of village life.
Commercial and Agricultural Magazine (September and October 1800).

You have this time brought us under the heaviest burden and into the hardest yoke we ever knowed. It is too hard for us to bear. You have often times blinded us saying that the fault was all in the Place-men of Parliament but . . . they have nothing to do with the regulation of this parish.
    You do as you like, you rob the poor of the Commons right, plough the grass up that God send to grow, that a poor man may feed neither Cow, Pig, Horse or Ass . . . There is five or six of you have gotten all the whole of the land in this parish in you own hands and you would wish to be rich and starve all other part of the poor . . . We have counted up

that we have gotten about sixty of us to one of you; therefore should you govern, so many to one?
An anonymous Norfolk labourer's letter, dated 22 May 1816, to 'the Gentlemen of Ashill'. Quoted in E.P. Thompson (1968), The Making of the English Working Class, Penguin Books, Harmondsworth.

On the day I was eight years of age, I left school, and began to work fourteen hours a day in the fields with forty to fifty other children of whom, even at that early age, I was the oldest. We were followed all day long by an old man carrying a long whip in his hand which he did not forget to use . . . For four years, summer and winter I worked in these gangs — no holidays of any sort with the exception of very wet days and Sundays and at the end of that time it felt like Heaven to me when I was taken to the town of Leeds and put to work in the factory.
Quoted in R. Groves (1981), Sharpen the Sickle: the History of the Farm Workers' Union, Merlin Press, Devon.

April 23, 1890. Field-work, gathering stones, cowkeeping and farm work had reduced the school attendance to 35 out of 61. It is impossible, in my opinion, to teach either geography or grammar owing to the bad attendances caused by the farmers sending the children out to the fields. Many children are always ill with coughs and colds and stay at home half the year.
Ronald Blythe (1969), Akenfield, Penguin Books, Harmondsworth.

In 1921 the Ambrosia Milk Company established a milk processing factory at Lapford (Devon). From here the company was able to cover most of the inland farms of the area. There were many local objections to the proposed industry, but the factory offered some alternative occupations ... There are some ninety employees ... Two thirds are men and the others are girls ... The Factory has set new standards in local employment ... The men earn from £2 to £2 10s a week while the girls ... weekly wage is £1 7s 6d. The effect of these higher wages on the villages is easily seen. A girl will often take home more money than her father who has worked longer hours on the farm. Moreover foreigners (the skilled technicians) have come to live in the village. All of the employees take some of their earnings into the village and add to its economic wealth. New houses have been built in the village for the first time for many years ... Thus this small factory has contributed immediately to the social rehabilitation of the area.
F.G. Thomas (1939), **The Changing Village**, *Thomas Nelson and Sons Ltd, London.*

There is still a nucleus of the original population who live and work in the village. Many of them belong to local families such as Cooper, Lomas, Yates, Bownmer. But there is also an entirely new population who have come from all parts of the country, mainly younger people with young families who are rapidly being absorbed into the community ... Class distinctions which existed

before are fast disappearing and it seems that Duffield is becoming an example of the class-less society fostered by the Welfare State ...
Duffield, Derbyshire.

Employment in the village is difficult to find and young people leaving school find it hard to obtain the type of job they would like to do. Here in Bellingham, this is certainly one of the main reasons why the younger people, young marrieds especially, tend to leave the area and seek employment in the surrounding towns. For the child with talent there is little opportunity and many go away to college and to hospitals never to return.
Bellingham, Northumberland.

Since the last war Cornwall has been invaded by many folk of retiring age who find the climate of this district much kinder than the cold North, and if the mass exodus of young people continues, by the end of the century this last Celtic Outpost will have become an Eventide Home!
Grampound, Cornwall.
Three extracts from Women's Institute Scrapbooks quoted in Paul Jennings (1969), **The Living Village,** *Hodder and Stoughton.*

The special problems of rural areas stem primarily from the loss of the industrial and employment base, resulting in depopulation of the remoter rural areas, immigration of the retired or commuters, and an extremely poor infrastructure of local services. The poor are faced by inadequate services based on an unequal distribution of resources between areas, as well as an inability to gain access easily to those services

that do exist in their locality or in the nearest population settlement. Thus the rural dweller is burdened by the extra costs of gaining access to services, doing without them or consuming inadequate services. These costs bear disproportionately on the rural poor. There is a need for policy-makers and planners to consider the problem of rural deprivation and to propose special measures to ensure that the rural poor have an equal opportunity to participate in services that the urban dweller accepts as commonplace.
Alan Walker (1978), **Rural Poverty,** *Child Poverty Action Group, p.114.*

A rural strategy must be based on a rounded view of the role of the countryside and of the social and economic needs of country people — not on the damaging sectoral approach whereby different agencies each pursue their own independent policies. There must be sensitivity to the widely varying circumstances and needs of rural communities, and to the attitudes and views of rural people themselves. There must be hard thought about the choices which face the countryside of the future, in relation for example to settlement patterns, methods of transport, use of energy, patterns of employment. There must be willingness to innovate, to experiment, to encourage the capacity of rural communities to help themselves.
'A Rural Strategy', **Rural Voice** *(1981).*

Rural Community Perspectives: Medieval and Early Modern Economy and Society

A major objective for each of the 'issue' chapters has been to emphasise the temporal dimension of change in the countryside whilst acknowledging the specific factors or events that have been important at particular times. Central to an understanding of the importance of this process have been those sections of each 'issue' dealing with perspectives. But the approach to these has varied according to the needs of each chapter with historical considerations being taken only as far back as it is useful to the sustenance of the argument in the chapter. Thus, in the case of expanding agricultural production the discussion is taken from that point at which agriculture whose purpose was the support of the family and local community was transformed to one of food production geared towards a wider market. In containing settlements the discussion does not go beyond comparatively recent times. The chapter begins at the period when the expansion of urban areas was first perceived to be an important phenomenon consuming rural land. In the case of conserving the wild it was necessary to encompass 2,000 years of history since notions of conservation can be identified as part of the Judaeo-Christian ethic. But for the last of the 'issues', dealt within this chapter, it is important to give consideration first of all to the medieval village as means of building up an understanding of the present distribution and form of rural settlements. From such an early starting point, this perspective inevitably is synoptic. Because of this a number of key themes are discussed which offer some relevant insights to the dynamics of change in rural communities.

The Rural Community: Image and Diversity

The usual image of the rural community is that of cottages and farms, a manor house and church standing close together to form a village. Such distinct groups of dwellings typically are separated from other villages by several miles of open countryside containing only a light scattering of isolated farmsteads. This image is acceptable for many parts of lowland England, but in upland areas rural communities are characteristically scattered through hamlets (literally little villages) and many dispersed farmsteads and cottages. Settlement forms of this kind are also encountered in many of the woodland and heathland districts of south-east England, in some parts of East Anglia and in areas of reclaimed marsh and fen, around the Wash.

It is easy to fall into the trap of assuming that houses in old village streets occupy sites which have been in use even since the days of the Anglo-Saxon settlement. Perhaps nothing looks more stable and enduring than two parallel streets of stone or half-timbered dwellings with adjacent manor house and church, yet such double street villages are often the product of self-conscious medieval planning. On the other hand, Georgian and Victorian farmhouses standing in the fields are frequently the only houses to have stood on sites which were chosen when the enclosure of the open fields gave landowners the first chance to put farmsteads on the land worked from them. This dispersal of farmsteads is part of a long drawn out, and still continuing, process which has seen farmsteads in villages replaced by farmsteads in the fields.

In terms of people, as opposed to buildings, the usually accepted definition of the historical rural community is that of a group of families working the land, or servicing those working the land. Their sense of common purpose was sharpened, not only by the struggle for survival, but also by the fact that many families shared in both forms of activity.

Nucleated villages were usually associated with the medieval system of open-field farming (see Figure 5.1), a system which demanded highly organised communal effort and which was most prevalent in the twelfth cen-

Figure 5.1: Laxton in Nottinghamshire. A nucleated village surrounded by the remnants of the open-field system. This gives some impression of how a medieval settlement must have looked together with its unenclosed strips of cultivated land.

Source: Aerofilms.

tury. In those great fields of several hundred acres ploughing in particular required co-operation between different peasant families, since not many of them could afford enough oxen to make up a plough team on their own. The scattered nature of each man's holding of lands (selions, acres or strips), which gave him shares in soils of different qualities, meant that crop rotations had to be agreed communally, harvest times organised on a harmonious basis and with everyone sticking to the rules about grazing the stubble and fallow. Similarly, there was communal regulation of ditches, hedges, roads and bridges, of the mowing of hay in the meadows, the gathering of kindling in the woods, the grazing of the common waste, and so on.

Before the word 'village' came into the common use around 1800, each place with its own set of open fields and commons was known as a town (or a market town if it had a market charter). Townships were the basic administrative areas in the countryside and township meetings, often in the church vestry, elected constables, surveyors of the highways, overseers of the poor, and various officials to regulate farming, like pinders to deal with stray animals.

Manors were essentially legal entities of property. Some manors extended into more than one township, some townships contained several manors, while sometimes the two units coincided. Most medieval lords held several manors of the king, so they would only build or maintain manor houses where the produce of the manor was sufficiently great to make it worthwhile moving their household in order to eat or use up that produce. Not all manors, therefore, had manor houses. It was in the manorial courts, held in these houses, or in taverns if necessary, that transfers of rights in property were made between father and son, or between seller and buyer. The manorial courts were also used to solve communal disputes, to enforce the obligations of the peasantry to their lords, to try petty offenders, and, where convenient, to establish and maintain the rules of husbandry which concerned the whole of a township.

Sometimes townships were big enough to sustain a priest and a church of their own, that is, they were also parishes, but in the more thinly populated parts of England it frequently needed several townships to make up a single parish. For example, the West Riding parish of Birstall once contained 19 townships. In this vast area the tithes originally went to the mother church in Birstall for its upkeep and that of the priest. As the population grew, more townships acquired the status of parish, with their own churches, often passing through the intermediate status of chapelry, a place with a chapel-at-ease, served by the parish clergy and having an independent existence.

Most rural histories accept the model of a nucleated village where the territorial limits of manor, township and parish coincided, and this model, or something like it, is appropriate for many parts of lowland England. Here the medieval peasantry were closely controlled by manorial lords and their stewards within the disciplined framework of open-field farming. Before the period when tenants paid rent for their holdings, the peasants worked for many days each year on the land of their lords.

However, areas of the country which contained large stretches of moorland, fen, marsh, heath or forest experienced a different, freer regime. To begin with, the open-field system either never developed there, or common arable fields were restricted to such small areas that farmers were free to make many decisions without reference to the community at large. With a relative plenty of common grazings, there was much more scope for small farmers to make a good living than in the open-field villages with their scarcity of pasture.

There was more scope also for secondary occupations because raw materials, such as timber, minerals, rushes and tannin (raw bark) were available. The scattered settlement pattern, much of it the result of haphazard squatting on commons, made social control more difficult to exercise from above. Outlaws, brigands, cattle rustlers, seditious movements, smuggling and nonconformity all found a natural home in such surroundings where village constables, parsons, manorial stewards and, for Tudor times, the JPs, all had difficulty in coming to grips with irregularities.

Social Inequalities

It was in champian England, that is, the land of the open fields, that inequalities between men developed most noticeably from about the fourteenth century onwards. The plagues of that century, especially the Black Death of 1348, reduced village populations so much that many surviving families were able to bring together the tenancies of several holdings of about 30 acres with common rights, which had been a frequent norm of medieval agrarian society up to that period. In the fifteenth and sixteenth centuries many open-field villages were depopulated of their remaining peasant families by manorial lords who wished to make money out of large-scale sheep and cattle farming which required relatively little labour. This is the origin of the grassy shires of numerous farms of several hundred acres. A well known example is the estate in Northamptonshire and Warwickshire which belonged to the Spencers, the family of the Princess of Wales.

In corn farming areas also economies of scale began to favour the larger farmer. The problem of arable smallholdings was that such a large proportion of their corn harvest was needed for subsistence that the peasantry had none to sell in lean years when prices were high, and when they had a surplus, prices were low.

By the middle of the seventeenth century developments such as these, reinforced by rapid population growth, had deprived many men of a stake in the land. Some left the countryside and found jobs in expanding towns or became the beggars of Elizabethan folklore. In arable farming areas, especially East Anglia, corn farms steadily increased in size so that by the mid-nineteenth century many of them employed more than ten labourers each and the farmer rode around his extensive fields, never dirtying his hands. Contrary to popular

Figure 5.2: A Sixteenth-century Engraving of a Craftsman Smallholder.

Source: P. Isaac (1981), *The Farmyard Companion.*

belief, capitalism first developed in rural England and not in the dark satanic mills of Lancashire and Yorkshire, though both views of the modernisation of the economy leave out the important role of merchant capitalism, centred overwhelmingly on London and a few provincial centres such as Bristol, Norwich, Coventry and Southampton.

Village Trades and Crafts

In the days before well-developed transport could bring manufactured goods into any village, its near self-sufficiency was sustained by the existence of its own craftsmen and those of neighbouring villages. Traditionally, such men as the smiths, the carpenters, the millers, the wrights, the shoemakers and the weavers (see Figure 5.2) occupied smallholdings to assure themselves of at least some of their own food supply. Even a couple of cows and a flock of geese on the common, looked after by wives and children, could make a significant contribution to cottage economies.

Many craftsmen were further involved in the land by virtue of the fact that they needed to keep horses for their own means of transport. Additionally, they frequently worked full time for farmers in busy periods, particularly the corn harvest in areas which specialised in grain production, since this created the greatest of all seasonal fluctuations in farm work. All but the biggest towns were also caught up in the cycle of the agricultural year, since they had good reason to produce some food of their own in centuries when transport was poor and thus crop failures were a serious hazard to external food supplies.

In most villages and in most trades the peak period of activity was the first half of the nineteenth century. Over the centuries, crafts had become more specialised as technologies gradually developed. By the early nineteenth century blacksmiths were a distinct race from the farriers, who specialised in shoeing and treating horses and harness-makers were distinct from other workers in leather. The wrights were predominantly wheelwrights, but specialist millwrights could be found in most localities. The even more refined craft of ploughmaking was also identifiable. Yet these specialists would also turn their hand to a wide range of jobs. This point can be illustrated by reference to the account books of the Bealbys, a Collingham (Notts) family of ploughmakers in the 1870s and 1880s. They manufactured ploughs which were sold all over the East Midlands. They repaired and rebuilt ploughs for farmers within a radius of about ten miles. Within their own parish they were also general wheelwrights and did not turn down such work as the repairing of window frames, the sinking of a well or the turning of a quick penny on the sale of seed potatoes (probably collected from the station by a cart whose driver had dispatched a load of ploughs).

The 1850s saw both the peak of rural population growth and the establishment of a railway network which allowed mass products into many villages. By 1880 agriculture was also in a state of general depression which lasted until 1939, except for a brief break during the First World War. One example will demonstrate the irreparable damage done to the social fabric of the traditional village.

Thornborough, in north Buckinghamshire, had a population of 458 at the first census in 1801. By 1841 it had reached its peak of 762 and then sank slowly back to 440 in 1921, a level near which it stayed for 40 years. In 1853, Craven and Musson's *Directory of Buckinghamshire* listed the following trades and crafts in the village: four grocers, three each of stonemasons, boot and shoemakers, bakers and milliner/dressmakers; two each of maltsters, blacksmiths, butchers, sawyers and wheelwrights; and one each of tailor, builder/joiner, brick and tile maker, coal dealer, corn dealer, and corn miller. There were four pubs known as The Lone Tree, The Two Brewers, The Swan and The Case is Altered. Apart from those already quoted, there were ten dual occupationists, all but two combining a farm with a trade such as publican or maltster. Altogether, there were 34 such enterprises.

By 1929, Kelly's *Directory* shows that this figure had shrunk to only nine. The first three pubs had survived and had been joined by The New Inn, which was de-licensed after the Second World War along with The Swan. The water-mill and the bakehouse were still at work, but are now private residences, as is one of the two shops of 1929. The ninth enterprise on the list was the carrier who plied to Buckingham market and Padbury station, but not for much longer because of competition from buses.

Rural Industries

In many rural areas one particular craft developed into a local industry which provided materials or finished goods on a specialised basis for sale mainly outside the locality. The winning of minerals had always been a rural activity since the days of flint mining, but as demand expanded so did the scale of activities such as the production of lead in the Pennine dales, tin and copper in Devon and Cornwall, iron ore in the Weald, kaolin in the south-west of England, coal in many areas and building materials in almost every district. Again, miners and quarrymen were often also smallholders. Moreover, as minerals were generally found in forest and moorland areas, miners frequently had a share in common rights and their early settlements were often haphazard groups of squatters' cottages set up on the edges of these commons.

However, rural industry was by no means confined to minerals or even to the processing of local raw materials. The chief locational factor of many rural industries was the supply of labour, which in turn was dependent on a local food supply. Before canal and rail transport developed, there were severe limits to urban growth. London was the main exception, relying on river and coastwise shipping. The application of steam power to industrial processes from the late eighteenth century led to the gradual concentration of industry on coalfields or at points on the transport network where coal was available at

low rates of carriage (see Colour Plate 11). The traditional countryside, therefore, contained the bulk of the manufacturing industries (see Figure 5.3).

Figure 5.3: A Typical Village Factory, at Earl Shilton which Manufactured Hosiery.

Source: Open University.

The first of these to become more than locally significant was the woollen textile industry, which flourished in areas such as East Anglia and the Cotswolds, Wales and the Pennines. The adoption of water power favoured the hilly areas, but soon afterwards the introduction of steam engines gave the advantage to areas on the Pennine flanks where coal was available. Rural industries of these kinds were organised by merchants in market towns, who put out raw materials and acted as middlemen in the sale of the finished products. Thus Sheffield was the organising centre for nearby villages in which smiths mass produced items such as scythes, nails and cutlery.

Other examples of similar domestic industries include nail making in the Black Country, footwear in Northamptonshire, handknitted stockings in the northern Pennines, framework knitting of stockings and other knitwear in the East Midlands, lace making in Buckinghamshire and lesser known, but locally important specialities, such as besom making at Tadley (Hants) and basket making at Sutton-on-Trent (Notts).

Sustaining Rural Communities

In the period between 1700 and 1851 the population of the country quadrupled and since the urban population did not outnumber the rural population until the later date, much of this massive growth occurred in the countryside. In many rural areas it proved impossible for all the extra hands to find work. Where industry was rapidly expanding, surplus labour was drawn off the farms, but in vast areas of the south and east, now known as prosperous commuter belts, the story was very different. Domestic industries there were in decline and agriculture was in a depressed state from the end of the French Wars in 1815.

How, then, were these rural communities sustained? As far back as 1598 the Elizabethan Poor Law had formally confirmed the traditional responsibility of each township for its poor. So the village ratepayers of south and east England groaned under the weight of the poor rates which reached an unprecedented peak during the French Wars because of the astronomical prices of bread, and another peak in the 1820s when returning servicemen and agricultural depression were included in the underlying problems. Able-bodied poor were usually given outdoor relief — a dole received outside the workhouse. The 1834 Poor Law Amendment Act, in setting up Union work-

Figure 5.4: 'Home of the Rick-Burner'. This *Punch* cartoon (1830) suggests the temptation of the farmworker to take action against the increasing mechanisation of farming which was likely to put him out of work.

Source: *Punch*.

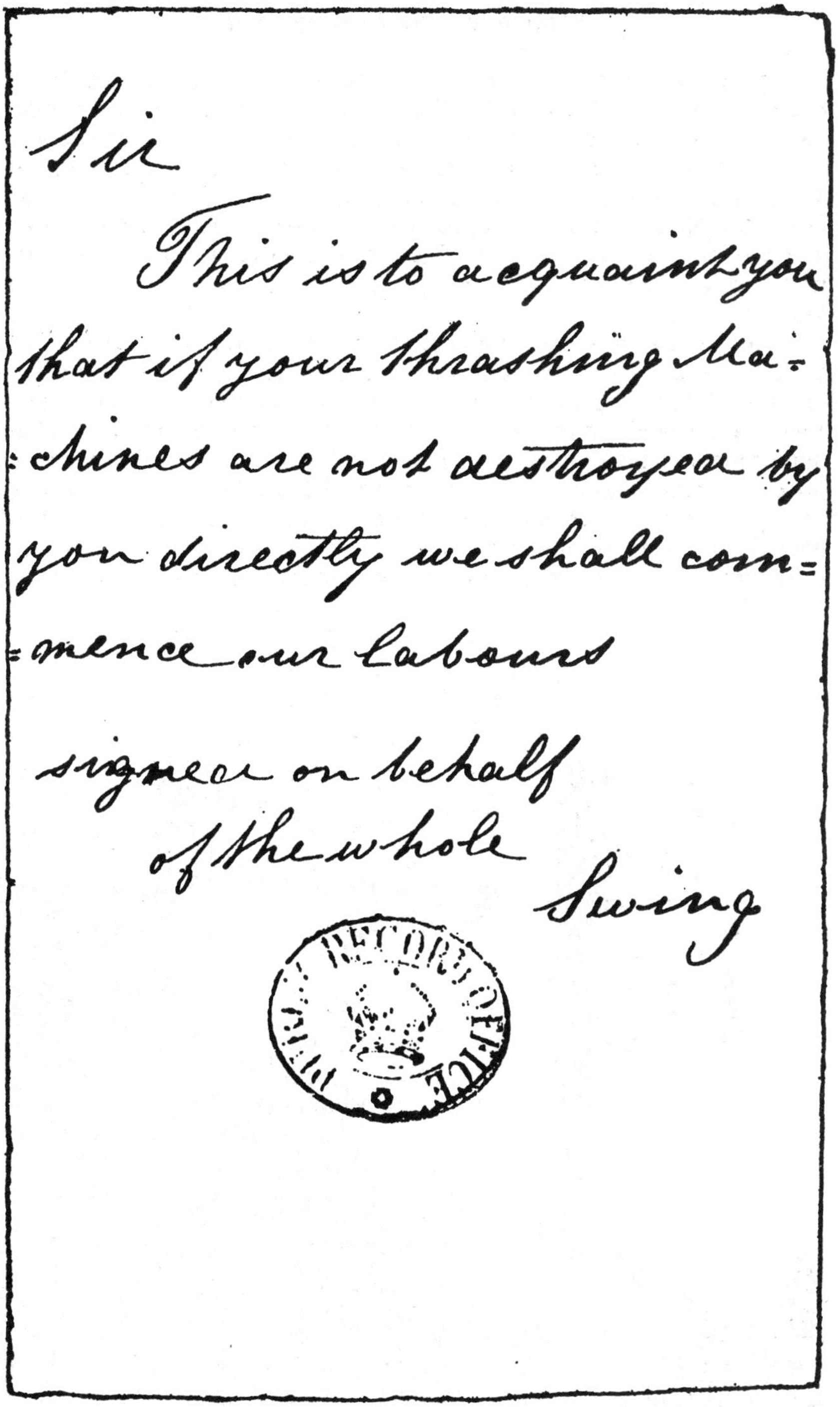

Sir

This is to acquaint you
that if your thrashing Ma=
=chines are not destroyed by
you directly we shall com=
=mence our labours

signed on behalf
of the whole
Swing

Figure 5.5: A 'Swing' Letter. This is typical of the threats made to farmers who had invested in labour saving capital equipment.

Source: Hobsbawm, E.J. and G. Rude (1970), *Captain Swing*, Lawrence and Wishart, London.

houses throughout the country reduced the chances of outdoor relief and took most decisions out of the hands of village overseers.

These were bitter days in the history of the countryside, when landowners, clergy and employing farmers, faced with a totally new situation, displayed less compassion as a class than they had done on many occasions before or were to do so again later. Rural crimes like poaching and sheep stealing, rick burning and threshing-machine breaking rocketed to new proportions and overt, organised protest swept the country in waves, the biggest of which were the 'Swing' riots of 1830-2 (see Figures 5.4 and 5.5).

From about 1840 the situation began to improve slowly. Growing urban populations provided an expanding market for food, and even the repeal of the Corn Laws in 1845, designed to protect home cereal production, did not lead to a flood of imports for another 30 years. More important, emigration to the colonies and the USA and migration to higher wage areas got into their strides, as the railway network, the postal system, the establishment of local newspapers and the growth of literacy all helped to open up ways and means and people's minds.

Social Divisions

The crisis of the early nineteenth century left scars on the rural community from which it never fully recovered in terms of social integration, though some of the factors leading to a 'loss of community' were more deep-seated and longer term. The gradual divergence between the two main groups in many villages — the employing farmers and the labourers — was further accentuated at this time (see Figure 5.6).

In the west of England the distinction between farmer and labourer remained very blurred down into recent decades, with small farmers inter-marrying with labourers' families. In the south and east, however, the social distinctions grew steadily until a point was reached around 1800 where, for example, most farmers' wives gave up boarding unmarried labourers, thus breaking the closest bonds between farmer and young servant and reducing the chances of intermarriage.

The decline of boarding was one of the factors which reinforced the trend towards a greater emphasis on the conjugal family and on income groups as the foci of social activity at the expense of the community at large. Another factor was religious change, which involved first of all a division between Roman Catholics and Anglicans and then between Anglicans and Dissenters of various denominations. It is an interesting coincidence that the Baptists and the Independents (Congregationalists), the two main denominations of the Old Dissent of the seventeenth century, were strongest in the south and east, where specialised corn farming was concurrently driving a wedge between employing farmers and others. Most Dissenters were small farmers and tradesmen, while few big farmers worshipped outside the parish church. In the eighteenth century Methodism produced a new schism in the Church and was especially strong in many areas of the north, as far south as Lincolnshire where Wesley was born. Even the distinction between Primitive Methodists and Wesleyans was socially significant, with labourers, miners and fishermen strong in the first movement and tradesmen in the second. Religion now divided rural communities, whereas before the Reformation it had helped to keep them together.

The history of leisure shows similar trends. While medieval and early modern accounts of pastimes, village feasts and festivals, of music and folk-song suggest widespread participation, as time went by leisure activities succumbed to social stratification. By the nineteenth century football had become an activity for young labourers, shooting for farmers, foxhunting for the gentry and gentlemen farmers.

Clergy and Justices actively suppressed village feasts because they regarded them as bawdy affairs during which too much drinking and fornication took place. Consequently many village feasts disintegrated into club feasts, run by a section of the community for its members.

A well-known example in the drive towards Victorian respectability is illustrated in Thomas Hardy's *Under the Greenwood Tree,* a piece of fiction true to life. This story centres round the way in which a reforming parson replaced

THE STABLE.

LANDLORD. "YES, MR. PUNCH. NICE, CLEAN, AIRY BOXES, PLENTY OF LIGHT, PERFECT DRAINAGE AND VENTILATION. THE BEST OF FOOD AND WATER, AND KIND TREATMENT. THAT'S MY PLAN!"

THE COTTAGE.

MR. PUNCH (TO LANDLORD). "YOUR STABLE ARRANGEMENTS ARE EXCELLENT! SUPPOSE YOU TRY SOMETHING OF THE SORT HERE! EH?"

Figure 5.6: 'The Stable and The Cottage'. Contemporaneous *Punch* cartoons satirising the differences in living conditions between the squire's horse and that of his workers.

Source: *Punch*; courtesy of MERL.

with a church organ the traditional village orchestra, whose association with the public house was too strong. In the later Victorian period, having suppressed most of the traditional boozy 'harvest homes', the clergy invented the synthetic, antiseptic version known still as the harvest festival.

'Loss of community' is particularly noticeable in administrative aspects of Victorian country life, since the New Poor Law of 1834 was only the first of many similar changes. Village constables were soon replaced by professional policemen, as counties adopted the County Police Act of 1839 at varying dates down to 1857.

From the 1830s to the 1870s rural education remained something of an administrative jungle, in which local charities and bigwigs worked in a variety of combinations with the British and Foreign School Society (nonconformist) and the National Society for the Education of the Poor in the Principles of the Established Church. From 1870 onwards many village schools came under the sway of School Boards, which usually incorporated several parishes, and in 1902 the County Councils took over, removing responsibility still further from the village body politic.

Likewise country roads gradually fell under the power of external agencies, main roads being transferred to turnpike trusts at various dates from about 1750. The 1862 Highway Act empowered Quarter Sessions of JPs to set up Highway Boards to administer the highways in combinations of parishes and they in turn were taken over by the County councils in 1894.

Declining Community Independence

External paternalism continued to weaken the independence of the village community with the provision of public amenities such as council housing, refuse collection, sanitation, water supply, gas and electricity. However, in the religious sphere it fell apart because of inward divisions. As nonconformists gained numerical strength in the early nineteenth century, they challenged the Established Church over the payment of tithes and church rates. In most parishes where enclosure had been carried out by private Act of Parliament at some date later than about 1725, the opportunity had been taken to abolish the tithes. This was done by allocating land to the tithe owners in compensation for the abolitions of tithe payments. In other places the tithes were dealt with under the Tithe Commutation Act of 1836 which, in the first instance, only converted payments in kind into a cash payment. These payments were finally abolished between the Wars. In the campaign against payments in kind the nonconformists had joined many Anglican farmers and even labouring men, who realised that tithes were a tax on farming which reduced their chances of a fair wage.

In the case of church rates, the battle was drawn up on much more strictly defined sectarian lines and was also of great significance in many towns. Church rates were those levied on the whole community for the upkeep of Anglican churches. Nonconformists objected, maintaining that only church members should be expected to pay. The two decades from about 1835 saw the struggle at its height. Characteristically, it took the form of nonconformists politicising the activities of the Vestry, forcing polls of all ratepayers on the unwilling churchwardens. In some parishes steadfast campaigners refused to pay their church rates and were taken to court by the churchwardens, egged on by the well-educated, resident Anglican clergy. To make matters worse, these cases could only go to ecclesiastical courts, thus inflaming nonconformist passions, since they felt they should have redress from the civil courts. By the late 1850s many parishes decided to avoid the hassle by relying on donations and in 1868 Gladstone, acting as a private member, succeeded in gaining a Parliamentary compromise which maintained the legality of church rates, but made them voluntary.

Rural Community Perspectives: The Nineteenth Century and Parish Divergence

Models of the Nineteenth-century Community: The Closed Parish

This chapter began by looking at different types of rural settlements in the medieval and early modern periods. The discussion then turned to different aspects of rural economy and social life. The threads can be drawn together by looking briefly at a model of nineteenth-century rural society which attempts to embrace all aspects of life and work and to relate them to control of the land, that vital theme of the countryside. This is known as the open-closed parish model, the terms 'open' and 'closed' deriving from the period when social writers were concerned about the sharply unequal poor rate burdens which often fell on neighbouring parishes.

Closed parishes were those in which one or a few powerful proprietors, controlling most of the land and cottages, were able to keep a tight rein on population in the period of rapid increase between 1780 and 1850. Typically, farms were large, modern, efficient and run by tenants carefully selected by the estate agent. Key workmen, especially those who looked after stock, were housed in convenient proximity. Day labourers and casual workmen were not encouraged to live in the parish, since it was they who were most likely to be out of work and, therefore, to become a burden on the poor rates. Many men commuted on a daily or weekly basis from open parishes, including towns. Similarly, independent tradesmen and craftsmen were thin on the ground, small freehold properties being scarce and estate owners careful not to create many suitable tenancies, since apprentices and journeymen were a threat to the maintenance of low poor-rates and, hence, to a good return on capital in the form of farm rents.

Closed parishes were essentially an expression of the estate system which had long roots in certain areas of English soil and concentration of ownership sometimes going as far back as records exist (for example, to the Domesday Book of 1086), though sometimes it was the result of quite recent accumulation. The accent on the control of poor rates was only part of the attitude of estate owners towards the lower classes. They were also seriously concerned about law and order (including the preservation of game), making a stand against enthusiasm in religion (nonconformity), and ensuring that education did not lead to too much free thinking and radical politics.

Nevertheless, the despotism of the English landed classes was much more benevolent than that of most of their counterparts on the Continent. Many of their model cottages were so soundly built to good standards that they still survive (see Figure 5.7) whereas most of those built by 'smock-frock' landlords in open parishes disappeared in the rural slum clearances of 1920 to 1960. The 'deserving poor' were better looked after by the rector's lady or the bailiff's wife than many in open parishes where the overseer could be a skinflint grocer overwhelmed by the number of cases on his hands. But one had to be deserving and that meant, among other things, accepting one's station in life. As a verse in the original of the hymn 'All things bright and beautiful' by Mrs C.F. Alexander maintains:

> The rich man in his castle,
> The poor man at his gate,
> God made them high or lowly,
> And ordered their estate.

(This verse does not appear in current editions.)

The power of the landed classes was in slow decline through much of the nineteenth century, because of the urbanisation of the country, extensions in the franchise and from about 1880 reductions in agricultural rent. Nevertheless, their influence on rural landscape and more indirectly on rural life has been pervasive during our own century. Estate villages have either become museums of themselves, visited by enthralled masses on Bank Holidays, or, when near enough to towns, the secluded haunts of prosperous middle class commuters, pleased to take on some of the status of the once-great house.

Figure 5.7: Model Cottages in the Village Street at Lockinge in Berkshire. Designed by Lord and Lady Wantage in 1860.

Source: MERL.

An example of this process is Blankney, a village ten miles south of Lincoln, with a big parish stretching west across the heath and east across the fen. In 1799, at the time of the Enclosure Award, the Chaplins owned 5,345 acres out of a total 5,828.

White's *Directory of Lincolnshire* of 1856 describes Blankney Hall as ' a large and handsome mansion, with a well-wooded lawn, ... the seat of Charles Chaplin, Esq. Lord of the manor, owner of most of the soil, and patron of the rectory'. The church, rebuilt in 1820, contained a vault of the Chaplin family. 'In the village is a National School, established thirty-five years ago by the Chaplin family' (a date in the 1820s was very early for a village day school). 'The present school is a neat building in the Elizabethan style.' This building is still there, along with equally neat pairs of cottages provided with big gardens so their occupants had control over some of their own subsistence. In this parish of 600 souls in 1851 (410 in 1801), only twelve trade and craft enterprises were listed in the 1856 directory, but employees of the estate who are mentioned include the coachman, two gamekeepers, the clerk of the works and the land agent. Later the village gave its name to the Blankney Hunt, which still covers the territory south of Lincoln between the rivers Trent and lower Witham.

Kelly's *Directory of Lincolnshire* for 1922 carries the story further, with the restoration of the church in 1879-80, the organ being presented by Lady Chaplin. The Earl of Londesborough was the owner of the estate in 1922 and ten of the farms were over 150 acres. The stud groom, the head gardener, the farm manager and the secretary to the earl are listed, as is the station master, although Blankney station was actually in Metheringham parish. Blankney Golf Club, situated in the park, was the only apparent concession to the twentieth century.

The Open Parish

Metheringham, the next parish to the north of Blankney, was of similar size to Blankney, but the enclosure award of 1779 listed 25 significant owners. White called it 'a large improving village', with a population which had increased from 536 in 1801 to 1,522 in 1851. Doubtless many of these worked in Blankney and other nearby closed parishes.

In the parish are three chapels belonging to the Wesleyans, the Primitive Methodists, and the Wesleyan Reformers, built in 1840, 1850 and 1853. The Wesleyan chapel has a large day school, aided by government grants. The Parish School was established by subscription in 1841. The Reformers' Chapel is called the People's Hall, from its being used for public meetings and the like. In the village is a flourishing Sick Club, and also a Cow Club.

(The latter's purpose was to insure farmers and cottagers against the loss of their cows.)

The directory listed no less than 57 trade and craft enterprises. In addition to the usual gamut, there were such specialists as a threshing-machine owner, toy dealer, straw hat maker, marble mason, ropemaker, watchmaker, plumber, basket-maker, hairdresser and two surgeons. Of the 24 farmers big enough to be listed, nine were owner-occupiers, whereas none were such at Blankney.

Kelly's *Directory* of 1922 reveals that the Wesleyans had gone to greater strengths and had erected a new chapel in 1908 at a cost of £2,000 with seating for 320 persons. This directory contains significant entries like: Frederick Chapman, town crier and billposter, three firms of coal merchants, two firms of motor engineers, Ernest Foster, waterproof cover maker, Metheringham Friendly Society, the Oddfellows (Manchester Unity), and the No. 6 branch of the Lincoln Equitable Co-operative Society.

While Blankney has seen next to no new building since far back in the nineteenth century, Metheringham expanded between the wars with council houses and the first individual private bungalows and was an obvious choice as a post-war 'key settlement', expanding with both council and private housing estates of considerable size. Feast day is still celebrated and Blankney station, reopened after a couple of decades of idleness, has been rightfully renamed Metheringham station, in recognition of where its principal custom comes from.

So Metheringham is a good example of an open parish where the wide distribution of property made population difficult to control. Indeed, some proprietors made money out of the construction of terraced cottages for labourers by charging an economic rent, whereas tied cottages on estates often came as part of a man's wage. For instance, at Melbourn (Cambs) in 1839, 46 of the 225 tenement cottages belonged to men in the building trades in the village and 54 to other small resident owners. The man with the largest number, 22, was Joseph Campkin, a farmer, grocer and draper, who served as overseer of the poor and, incidentally, refused to pay his church rate in 1848, unsuccessfully fighting a case which lasted three years.

Again, however, open parishes were not distinguishable from closed parishes merely because of differences in poor law administration, for they were also part of what can be regarded as the peasant system of traditional England. Here 'peasant' is used as an umbrella term for all small, independent, rural entrepreneurs, whether farmers, tradesmen, craftsmen, or dual occupationists (like Harry Hicks, farmer and farrier at Metheringham in 1856). Compared with the large tenant farms on estates and many town shops, these enterprises were small beer, but to escape or stay out of the labouring class was a constant ambition, which made the peasantry proud of their status. Some of them preferred to be 'their own boss' long after it made economic sense, due to the decline in rural population and prosperity and to competition from mass industrial products and imported food.

Nevertheless, many of the peasantry made common cause with the labour-

UNITED   DIVIDED

WE STAND   WE FALL

WE DEMAND SOCIAL LIBERTY,

POLITICAL & RELIGIOUS EQUALITY,

& THE COMPLETE RIGHTS OF MAN.

Figure 5.8: The Banner of the National Agricultural Labourers' Union. Founded in 1872 by Joseph Arch a hedgecutter and Methodist preacher from Warwickshire, the Union developed from one of a number of pioneering ventures at county level. It first pressed for higher wages but the banner expresses its broader ideals. These included an extension of the right to vote to rural workers. Although granted to townsmen in 1867, the Union's objective was not achieved until 1884.

Source: Nuffield College, Oxford.

ers in the fight against the rural establishment. They were prominent in the Swing Riots and other disturbances. In the latter part of the century, tradesmen and craftsmen gave moral and practical support to those who started agricultural unions (see Figure 5.8). One probable reason was that they found the farmers bad payers, traditionally having to wait until each New Year before they could get paid for any work in the previous year. And the Bealbys' account books show them taking farmers to court for the even then trifling sums of £2 or £3. Links between dissent and protest were as important as between beerhouses and protest and, ironically in view of the temperance Pledge, beerhouses and chapels were both concentrated in open parishes. Metheringham had four in 1856, in addition to the three named public houses. The beerhouses gave labourers somewhere to meet, discuss and organise, while their leaders gained confidence in speaking and giving leadership from their activities in chapel, especially Primitive Methodist chapels. It was in the open parishes, also, that there existed friendly societies which could be run free from the patronage of landlords and their minions.

The Models and Reality

Metheringham and Blankney, of course, are carefully chosen polar opposites, which conform to the black-and-white picture of the model. Reality was much nearer to an infinite number of shades of grey, but at either end of the continuum black and white did appear.

Qualifications to the model include the fact that only a minority of closed parishes contained mansions, since several parishes were needed to make up an estate of significant size. Most open parishes had one or two proprietors, sometimes institutions like Christ's Hospital or an Oxbridge college, who owned up to a quarter or a third of the parish. There were also the owners of substantial 'residential' farms. Sharp local contrasts between parishes were more commonplace in champion than they were in 'hamlet' England, because corn farming and large estates and large farms were less usual in the latter areas. In broad terms, open parishes, the peasant system and traditional life-styles went together, while closed parishes were where the estate system operated the cutting edge of rational modernisation to greatest effect.

Rural Community Perspectives: The Poor Relation?

Twentieth-century Trends

The review of the models of open and closed villages has provided a fleeting glimpse into the twentieth century and the forces at work in shaping the economic and social fabric of rural communities. The decline of agriculture from the late nineteenth century up to the First World War and then beyond into the 1920s and 1930s and the decreasing role of labour in the prosperous years after 1945, with farmers substituting capital investment in machines for manpower, has meant an increasing outflow of people directly involved in agriculture as well as their families to the nearby towns and villages. With them has gone all but the last vestiges of a one-time intricate system of service support which was sustained in all but the smallest villages. Yet if urban areas have been the recipients of such people they have also provided in recent decades the source of not only the retired seeking rural tranquillity, but an increasing mobile middle class. The affluence of this latter group and their ready access to personal transport has sent them in pursuit of a home in the country though the job of the breadwinner, certainly to the 1970s, invariably remained in the town (see Figure 5.9).

Attempts by the state to come to terms with what have been perceived to be the less desirable effects of these trends can be identified from the beginning of the century. As early as 1907 the need to arrest agricultural decline was recognised by the formation of a Development Commission. Although its remit was specifically to facilitate the reconstruction of agriculture this body was far from rural community orientated. Indeed the only real amelioration of one major problem, that of low agricultural wages compared with those obtaining in urban areas, came about as the result of the pressures created by the First World War and the need to ensure food supplies. Wages were at that time raised and regulatory wages boards established. But these wage levels were short lived and in the 1920s and 1930s, in a period of severe agricultural depression, little was done in any way to sustain the basic framework of rural life (see Figure 5.10).

After 1945, however, a number of important pieces of legislation were to have some impact on the rural scene. The passing of the 1947 Agriculture Act assured, for the first time, that agriculture would be maintained at the level of prosperity similar to that which it had enjoyed during the Second World War. The 1947 Town and Country Planning Act endorsed the wider aims of landscape conservation which were subsequently rather more strictly defined in rural terms in the 1949 National Parks and Access to the Countryside Act. Both pieces of legislation also played their part in ensuring agricultural prosperity. But whilst the 1950 Distribution of Industry Act was an attempt to promote the economic prosperity of selected areas of England and Wales, neither this nor any other legal enactment of the time properly recognised the real social and economic needs of rural communities. Indeed even the 1947 Town and Country Planning Act which it was believed would benefit those living in the country by preserving land for agriculture and protecting the environment really succeeded in blocking, certainly in the early years, the

(a) 1871

	Male	Female	Total
Agricultural labourer	236	—	236
Farmer	22	—	22
General servant	1	24	25
Other domestic servants	1	46	47
Gardener	16	—	16
Groom	11	—	11
Brickmaker	8	—	8
Bricklayer	11	—	11
Blacksmith	6	—	6
Carpenter	10	—	10
Miller	5	—	5
Wheelwright	5	—	5
Shoemaker	6	—	6
Dressmaker	—	7	7
Laundry worker	—	16	16
Schoolmistress	—	7	7
Bailiff	5	—	5
Grocer	7	—	7
Innkeeper	7	—	7
Butcher	3	—	3
Brewer	4	—	4
Other	46	3	49
Total	410	103	513

(b) 1971

1. Employers and managers in large establishments (over 25 employees)	2
2. Employers and managers in small establishments (under 25 employees)	32
3. Professional workers — self-employed	5
4. Professional workers — employees	2
5. Intermediate non-manual workers	44
6. Junior non-manual workers	69
7. Personal service workers	19
8. Foremen and supervisors — manual	25
9. Skilled manual workers	130
10. Semi-skilled manual workers	14
11. Unskilled manual workers	21
12. Own account workers (other than professional)	11
13. Farmers — employers and managers	10
14. Farmers — own account	6
15. Agricultural workers	32
16. Members of Armed Forces	—
17. Occupations inadequately described or retired	—
Total	422

Figure 5.9: The Contrasting Occupational Structure of Ringmer, Sussex (a) 1871; (b) 1971.

Source: P. Ambrose (1974), *The Quiet Revolution: Social Change in a Sussex Village 1871-1971*, Chatto and Windus.

movement of industry into rural areas. Had this occurred it might have helped to stem the flight from the countryside of those formerly employed in agriculture. In addition the Act also inhibited the provision of new rural housing required to replace the stock of old 'tied' agricultural dwellings. But it is perhaps the great paradox of this Act that although in its rural context, it was

primarily designed to stem landscape change, change was none the less most effectively achieved in the late 1960s and 1970s by that one industry to which, largely, it did not apply — agriculture.

Lest the Act should seem to have had an entirely negative impact, *some* building did take place in rural areas and agricultural related industries *were* allowed to be sited near their raw materials or their market. Indeed, food processing and agricultural engineering firms are not uncommon in villages and small rural towns. But these industries provided few alternative job opportunities for those lost from agriculture. Most employed low skilled, low paid and often female part-time labour. They did little to improve the economic prospects of rural communities (see Figure 5.11).

The further and more rapid growth in the importance of private transport and the generally greatly improved living standards brought new jobs to the countryside in tourism and its related services by the 1960s. Again low skilled and low paid work was the norm but with the added disadvantage of seasonal employment. Service industries concentrated mainly in centres of population. Their direct impact on rural communities was, therefore, limited. They provided a new range of job opportunities outside the village, but accessible only by private transport. For many villagers travel was essential to find work.

Publicity campaigns by local authorities brought other jobs to the countryside. Where branch factories could be located away from the parent plant or office headquarters, rural areas were popular locations when planning consent could be obtained. Despite the lack of natural economic advantage of some parts of the countryside, the attractions of a pool of labour which was not

Figure 5.10: The Village Pump at Eltisley, Cambridgeshire, near St. Neots. A mains water-supply to householders was just one of the basic services absent from many rural areas in the inter-war years. In this village, with a population of over 200, this pump was the only supply of potable water.

Source: MERL.

Figure 5.11: Relative Earnings of Agricultural Workers and Manual Workers in Manufacturing Industry, 1949 to 1972. Although no data are available comparing rural with urban based earnings, a comparison between agricultural weekly wages and hours and those in manufacturing industry, which is largely urban based, is instructive. There has been no significant *comparative* upward shift in farm workers' earnings since 1972.

Source: H. Newby (1977), *The Deferential Worker*, Allen Lane, Harmondsworth.

Year	Average weekly earnings (£ p)		Average hours	
	Agriculture	Industry	Agriculture	Industry
1949	5.49	7.25	51.1	46.5
1954	7.34	10.26	51.2	48.2
1959	9.99	14.21	52.1	48.2
1964	12.68	18.68	51.2	46.9
1969	16.96	25.54	49.2	45.7
1970	18.30	28.05	49.1	45.7
1971	19.18	31.10	47.7	44.4
1972	21.45	34.50	47.3	44.3

regarded as militant were not to be underestimated. That the rural workforce had, by the 1960s, been given the character of an acquiescent and law-abiding body can be related to the predominance, by this stage, of the middle-class ex-urbanites in village populations, an inversion of the nineteenth-century situation.

All the same the limited jobs available in the countryside and the attractions of other urban areas still encouraged and even forced many people to leave. Out-migration to the towns and centres of employment brought in its wake a further reduction in local opportunities. As people moved away so local demand for public and private services fell and many of the remaining shops, pubs and garages closed. Even the local schools were shut down in the interests of district rationalisation. These losses were not only significant in terms of the further attrition of local jobs, but in reducing local services the attractions of the town were enhanced. The increasing concentrations of populations and services in centres of population gave the young and old, families and individuals, every reason to leave the villages of England and Wales.

At the same time the counterflow of middle-class people moving out from the towns to the villages grew in strength. They reoccupied the now empty cottages converting and naming as houses the buildings which were once occupied by now defunct local services. Housenames like the 'old school', 'old bakery' and the 'smithy' depict what the village once supported. These rural in-migrants along with the natives who remained in the villages, relied largely on private transport and used urban services and facilities, whether for shopping or entertainment. They can either afford the journey between home and their place of work or can meet the costs of retirement to such an environment. All of these people in turn have encouraged and forced others to leave the village by increasing house prices and creating competition for now highly desirable cottages. They had been attracted by an image of the village as a pleasant place to live, not only because of its physical appearance, but because of the belief that friendliness, co-operation and community spirit are the characteristic attributes of all who live in such places. They in turn have reinforced the popular view of the village. Through their hanging baskets, cottages knocked together and renovated in picturesque fashion, their craft and antique shops, all in the place of small houses, a drab main street and village shops of the basic service kind, they have helped to promote and create a cosmetic rurality in the villages which has attracted yet more new residents.

'New' Villages, New Initiatives

Since the mid-1960s concern has been expressed that these 'new' villages are alien and that a traditional form of village life should be maintained. A fresh

Figure 5.12: 'Just ignore it, it's another local smart alec!'

Source: Thelwell, 1970.

perspective on village life which includes some of its problems — of few local jobs, difficult access to services, and competition for houses — has in recent years gained credence alongside the traditional view of happy rusticity. In this new perspective the need for action to still the changes occurring in villages and to maintain a balance of the social classes, local jobs, a full range of local services and above all, 'local people' are recognised. For the first time the need to sustain rural communities has gained considerable acceptance in academic and government circles.

This changed perspective is, in part, a reflection of government policies whose implications for rural areas have been all too apparent to observers of the rural scene, but not to policy makers. But more especially there has been a growing awareness that rural areas have not been given the same degree of attention by government as urban areas. In 1965 John Weller described rural planning as a 'Cinderella' compared with policies for urban areas and regional economic planning. Criticisms of the operation of the planning system in rural areas have been commonplace since then. In 1971, Ray Green concluded that the years since the 1947 Town and Country Planning Act had been a period of wasted opportunities for *positive* rural planning. Less than ten years later the lack of positive policies was still bemoaned and the argument put forward that rural needs had still not been fully assessed or understood.

Until the 1968 Town and Country Planning Act introduced a new system of strategic planning through structure and local plans, planning in rural areas was almost wholly articulated through the control of development. The introduction of these structure plans, explained in Chapter 3, called for the development of a strategic planning policy detailing the most desirable land uses throughout the area. The first structure plan to be developed incorporated the protection of rural landscapes. Indeed, it was not until the late

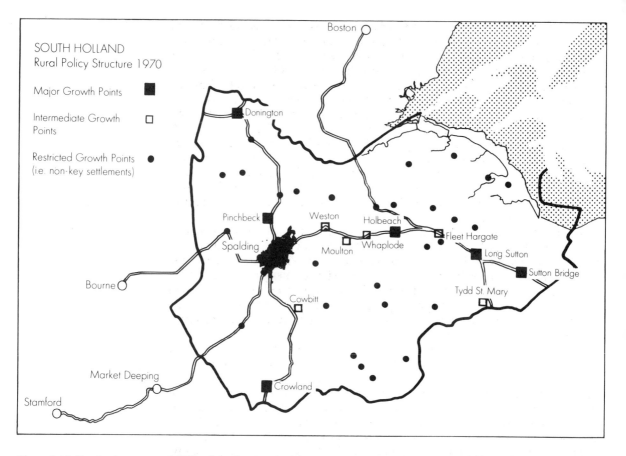

SOUTH HOLLAND
Rural Policy Structure 1970

Major Growth Points ■

Intermediate Growth □
Points

Restricted Growth Points ●
(i.e. non-key settlements)

Figure 5.13: Key Settlements
in the Planning Process. A
majority of counties, including
Lincolnshire, identified villages
in their structure plans within
which service facilities should
be concentrated.

Source: Martin and Voorhees
Associates (1982), *Review of
Rural Settlement Policy.*

1970s that these priorities were superseded in some plans by a recognition of the well-being of rural communities; for example, via economic development policies. This, of course, reflected a changing national climate. Over time rural structure plans for the shire counties also reflected a change affecting rural communities — notably the need to support rural services.

To provide the increasing number and range of services demanded by all communities in areas of limited and scattered population, the structure plans incorporated special policies to provide services as economically as possible and to co-ordinate them with development. Certain villages following their classification according to their size and the number of facilities they supported were thus designated as key settlements suited to specified levels of future development (see Figure 5.13).

Once established, key settlement policies characterised almost all rural structure plans. But before long they too were criticised for their lack of positive contribution to rural areas. Critics have pointed out that these policies sought economy of provision and economy of use. Thus they did not ease significantly the problems of service deprivation in country areas. Indeed, some studies have indicated that key settlement strategies exacerbated the problems of service provision for those communities which were not designated for growth and development. More recently, alternative policies have been sought which give priority to the needs of communities which do not house basic services. In this move, planning policies have to some extent fallen from the limelight as attention has been focused on the real providers of services such as the education or health authorities. Innovations in distributing services widely by making services mobile, or helping individuals to greater mobility so that they may reach services, have all been suggested.

Other government policies have been criticised too. The priority given to economic development in old industrial areas has been seen to be to the neglect of the needs and potential of rural areas. In some areas, positive steps have been taken to facilitate rural development. In Mid-Wales a special Industrial Development Association was formed in 1957 and was later replaced by a Development Board for Rural Wales (DBRW). This has responsibilities for social and community development. It has powers to acquire land and develop property; to encourage and sponsor industrial, commercial and special development; to build houses; and to give financial assistance to local authorities. In England the potential of rural development boards was investigated and a short-lived Board set up in the North Pennines. The Development Commission has promoted Special Investment and Rural Development Area strategies and set up the Council for Small Industries in Rural Areas (CoSIRA) as a special agency to facilitate the development of small industries in rural areas.

Whilst these initiatives have, however, been limited in their scope and effect in England, the DBRW has achieved a great deal in encouraging economic development in its area even though it has been based on specific selected centres. The main drawback is, in the view of many critics, that such measures have come too late and some 20 years after considerable attention and resources were given to improving the economic conditions of old, declining industrial areas and some 50 years after it was apparent that economic decline was clearly blighting rural life.

The Development Commission and the DBRW have promoted social development in the countryside alongside their economic objectives. In 1972, the Development Commision introduced a then experimental scheme to increase the resources of Rural Community Councils so that they might expand their work in bringing rural issues before local and central government and promoting self-help projects to ameliorate some of the effects of economic and social change in the village. As an example of the latter the development of unconventional services and local facilities for the elderly may be cited. Much has been achieved, but the resources allocated to these areas of work remain very small, especially when compared with those allocated to urban areas. It appears that even when rural needs have been recognised and solutions proposed the resources made available to achieve any improvements have been minimal. It may be concluded, therefore, that in the post-war years rural communities have been but a poor relation in the system for providing national help and assistance to particular areas of social and economic need.

The Early 1980s

Crisis Equals Opportunity

For rural communities the early 1980s may be seen as a paradox — as a period of crisis but also one of opportunity. Certainly this is a time of economic depression when jobs are scarce and wages low, in the countryside as in the town and of cuts in public spending which affect rural services. Yet underneath two trends are now apparent which may carry hope for the rural communities, *if* they can but be turned to good account.

First, many of the rural areas which were losing population in the 20 years which followed the war — indeed some of them since 1880 or earlier — have been gaining population during the 1970s (see Figure 5.14). This is part of a national process of movement out of the cities into the rural regions. It may be seen as an ebb tide, following the flow into the cities which accompanied the industrial revolution and the subsequent rural depression. It is based partly on the migration of people outwards from the cities and partly on a decrease in movement the other way, that is from country to town, a point considered further below.

Figure 5.14: Population Change in Norfolk. A comparison of the increasing population within this largely rural county (a) 1961-71, with (b) 1971-5. The two maps can be usefully compared to the changing population by district map produced from the 1981 census data (Figure 3.13).

Source: Norfolk County Council.

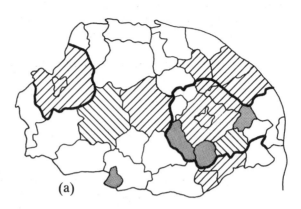

(a)

Percentage change per annum

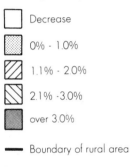

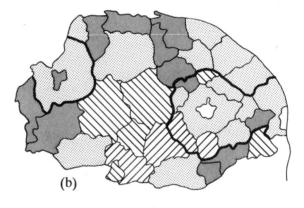

(b)

Second, there is in England and Wales — indeed in the world — a growing sense that centralised solutions may not be able to solve every problem. Small is seen as beautiful. Government alone cannot crack the problem of unemployment. Quality of life must be weighed alongside standards of living. Local resources must be harnessed to meet local needs. This line of thought plays into the hands of small communities whether urban or rural, who wish to tackle their own future in so far as they are able. The question is, can action by local communities make good the cuts in spending by local authorities, and in any sense ameliorate the problems of rural deprivation? In any attempt to answer this question, the two trends that have so far been identified require closer examination. Where population is concerned, movement out from the cities is the latest and most far-flung phase of a process which, as already noted, started when horse carriages, then railways made it possible for city workers to live in suburbs or further afield. With the arrival of the electric railways, followed by better roads, which were then taken full advantage of by the buses and private cars, commuters moved out yet further. From the 1940s, not only homes but jobs began to move out, into new towns, expanded towns and latterly into new cities like Milton Keynes and areas of economic growth like the Thames Valley and across south England following the M4 corridor into South Wales. More recently people have moved into more far-flung regions seeking retirement in the sun, moving their small firms out of the cities into the Assisted Areas, seeking the 'good life' of the smallholder in Pembrokeshire, or shifting their office into a cottage connected to London by teleprinter and computer.

At the same time the depression of the late 1970s and early 1980s, by creating massive unemployment in many cities as well as some redeployment out of them has switched off the magnet which used to attract many young and active people from the countryside into the towns. The rural economy in many areas may not offer high wages or varied jobs but for those who live there it may seem more secure than the dole queues of the city. As a result, some country people, who previously would have gone to the city, have tended to stay in their home areas.

This twin process — town people moving into and country people staying in the rural areas — has at last brought a halt to the long process of depopulation in many rural areas. The 1981 Census results show an increase in population from the previous census in virtually every rural district in England and in large parts of rural Wales. However, much of this population increase has been in the market towns and in the larger villages, those 'key settlements' where most of the new housing — whether public or private — has been concentrated. It is still true to say that many of the smaller villages, by contrast, have continued to lose population, not only in the more remote counties but also in prosperous ones. For example, 41 of the parishes in West Oxfordshire with less than 1,000 people in 1971 suffered further decline in the decade 1971 to 1981, many by 20 per cent or more. In West Kent, 9 of the 13 parishes with less than 2,000 residents also lost population.

Changing Social Structures

But the process of change is not just one of growth or decline whether consideration is given to the 1980s or the decades immediately before it. It is also one of change in *social* structure, and this can bring tension and conflict. In broad terms, the people who have been coming and continue to come into the rural communities tend to be town people, unfamiliar with agriculture or with the life of the countryside. A minority among them may both live and work in their newly-adopted communities. But most are there either as commuters, with homes in the countryside and jobs in the town; or as retired people; or as second-home owners, with their main homes back in the city.

The balance between these varies from region to region, from place to place. Howard Newby, for example, describes the impact of commuters moving in large numbers into villages in the Home Counties:

The outflow of labour from agriculture has denuded many villages of their working populations and replaced them by inhabitants who work in towns and who are not dependent upon farming for their living ... many of the controversies and conflicts which permeate contemporary rural life either stem from this fundamental change in the social composition of most villages or are exacerbated by it.

Elsewhere, as in many villages and small towns along the south coast and in Devon and Cornwall, the incomers have been mainly retired people. Their presence tilts the age-balance of the population and can cause concern about the calls which old people can make upon the social services and the loneliness and isolation which they themselves may suffer.

A third form of migrant into the countryside is the second-home owner. Though in national terms second homes are relatively few (involving 3 per

Figure 5.15: 'Pity really, I heard the English couple sold it to Gareth Edwards!'

Source: Jak; courtesy of The Open University.

cent of households, against 16 per cent in France and 22 per cent in Sweden), they are much more visible in those places, mainly rural and remote, where they are most found. These are mostly in villages where the decline in farming, quarrying, mining, fishing or other traditional activities has led to empty houses, which have been snapped up by city people for their holiday use. When the supply of empty houses is exhausted, continuing demand for second homes falls upon other houses in the area, thus competing directly with local people. Rural and coastal Wales, Norfolk, Cornwall, Devon and some other areas are particularly affected.

Growth of these sorts, by incursion of new population into rural settlements has, by paradox, one thing in common with *loss* of population in other rural areas — namely that it is seen to threaten the sense of stability or harmony in the rural communities. It is indeed a source of cultural conflict. Culture in the sense in which it is used here refers to the everyday circumstances of people — their value systems, attitudes, work, social institutions and all the other considerations interacting to create a distinctive way of life. It is apparent that a largely rural culture can be identified in many areas — for example in counties as far from major metropolitan influences as Somerset, the social activities such as those connected with the church, the chapel, clubs and societies are highly developed within the villages where, according to Margaret MacGregor, the social network shows a distinctive preference for rural as opposed to urban life. This contrasts strongly with the cultural conflicts developed in many parts of the Home Counties between the natives and the newcomers. Thus Howard Newby again observes:

There are now few villages without their complement of newcomers who work in towns. These new 'immigrants' have brought with them an urban, middle-class life-style which is largely alien to the remaining local agricultural population ... Their entertainment, their socialising, even their shopping, tend to take place outside the village ... A new social division arises in the village ... On the one hand there are the close-knit locals, who are the rump of the old occupational community, and on the other the ex-urbanite newcomers whose arrival in such relatively large numbers over the short space of time cannot help but be disruptive.

Often the newcomers fail ever to become integrated with these elements of the native community. Their work and their social activities continue to be focused on nearby towns, the villages being merely regarded as a pleasant place to live. Taken to extremes the local culture may become swamped and wither away. With the way of life totally changed the village becomes a mere dormitory for the town. However, in Wales, where a whole traditional rural way of life is vested in and articulated through the Welsh language, cultural conflict can be observed in a heightened form. Concern for the threat posed to such communities was expressed in emotional terms in the Manifesto of the Welsh Language Society:

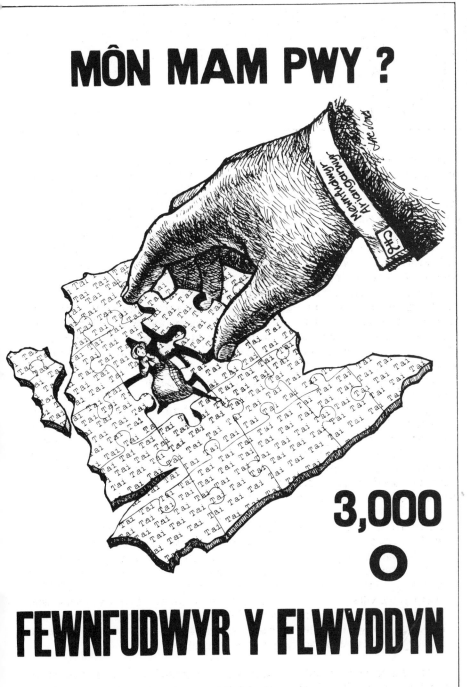

Figure 5.16: Protest Poster Used by Cymdeithas yr Iaith Cymraeg (The Welsh Language Society). This shows the Welsh people (depicted by the little old lady in traditional costume) being blotted out by plans to provide luxury housing (the nearly-completed jigsaw) for in-comers. The word *Tai* (house) is repeated across the map indicating that much of this development takes the form of new estates laid out in hitherto undeveloped countryside. The large bureaucratic-style hand together with the £ sign in the cuff-link completing the jigsaw represents collusion between the *mewnfudwyr* (in-migrants) and *ariangarwyr* ('lovers of money', that is, property exploiters). The upper caption *MÔN MAM PWY?* (ANGLESEY, WHOSE MOTHER?) is a pun on the well-known ancient motto *Môn Mam Cymru* (Anglesey, the mother of Wales) which has endeared the Island to many generations as the bastion of Welsh culture and this is now seen to be under threat. The lower caption *3,000 O FEWNFUDWYR Y FLWYDDYN* (3,000 IMMIGRANTS A YEAR) indicates something of the basic causes and perhaps the effects of housebuilding for commercial gain. This poster was pasted up during the night on the doors and windows of empty houses, old and new, throughout much of Anglesey in August 1983 — houses that already carried the 'for sale' signs erected by estate agents.

Source: Welsh Language Society.

189

It would be possible to maintain these villages as lively and satisfying social entities, and gradually to provide new work opportunities in them, were it not for that other misfortune, the plague of holiday homes. No one should underestimate the dangers of this threat to our most Welsh districts. House after house goes at an inflated price which puts it out of the reach of the ordinary buyer. Already in many villages an actual majority of the houses are summer residences for English visitors. This development is now accelerating to such an extent that ten to fifteen years could well suffice to eviscerate Welsh rural society completely, with all that would mean to our national heritage. [See Figure 5.16]

Concern about the impact of change upon rural communities is not confined to questions of cultural conflict. It strongly relates also to the perceived breaking of personal links, when people or families are for any reason unable to stay in an area. There is in many parts of the countryside a strong sense of continuity, of links from generation to generation, of the value of family and kinship ties as strong and socially precious as those whose destruction by post-war slum clearance in East London was deplored by Young and Willmott in their classic study in the late 1950s.

These ties not only enrich social life; they are a source of mutual support, in terms of employment, welfare and personal need of all kinds. Thus the easiest way for school-leavers in many rural communities to find jobs is through friends and relatives. Having a son or daughter nearby enables many an old person to continue to live at home rather than go into local authority care. In this sense, the sustaining of rural communities may have a direct financial pay-off. The Director of Social Services in Devon has estimated that a one per cent drop in the numbers of old people who are enabled (by the care of relatives and friends) to live at home would lead to a 20 per cent rise in the costs of local authority care for old people.

Thus the sustaining of rural communities is not simply a crude matter of keeping up population numbers, without regard to who that population may be. It is a more subtle matter than that, involving questions of continuity and the characteristics which enable people to stay in an area, alongside those who may migrate into it.

A Place to Live and A Place to Work

The nature of the challenge becomes apparent when specific issues are considered, such as housing. The outward movement of people from the towns into the countryside brings onto the rural housing market the demands of commuters, the retired, second-home seekers and others, whose income levels generally exceed those of the indigenous population. Thus, the price of houses in many rural areas has risen to way above that of equivalent houses in the towns and cities. More to the point, the sale prices now usually far exceed what rural people can afford. A recent survey by Avon Community Council of houses for sale in a number of villages showed no house at less than £35,000, whereas an agricultural worker in that area could not secure on his wages a mortgage above £15,000 at most.

The housing situation for lower-paid people is made worse by the fact that housing available for letting has been shrinking — or, at best, barely increasing — in many villages. Private landlords have been discouraged to let property because the tenants would gain security of tenure, and many district councils and housing associations have tended to concentrate their new house-building in the towns rather than in villages.

This lack of cheap housing has been one factor in driving young people of working age away from the villages, and thus weakening the ties of family and kinship which are significant in the vitality of communities. Even more significant, however, has been the urge to leave in the face of lack of jobs.

The decline in rural employment, described earlier in this chapter, has over the last 100 years and even up to the present day meant that many rural areas offer only a narrow range of jobs and low average wage rates. Jobs in farming are now in many areas confined to the farmer, his family and a few skilled contractors, with no paid hands. The other primary industries — forestry, mining, quarrying — have pushed up their productivity per man and reduced their labour force. Many rural areas, notably on the coast and in the national parks, have benefited from growth in tourism, which can bring a useful 'economic multiplier' through local purchase of labour and goods by the hoteliers and others who receive the visitors' money. But the last few years have seen decline in the total volume of tourism because of the recession and hence a drop in this benefit to the rural areas. There has been growth in other service industries and in manufacturing; but much of this has been located in the larger towns, while rural services themselves — shops, garages, post offices and others — have declined.

For these reasons, many young country people have in the past despaired of finding work near home and have gone into the city to seek it: their departure has in part disguised the problem. In the early 1980s with the urban economy depressed, there is less incentive to go, and more young people are staying in the villages. Unemployment levels are at or above the national average in many rural areas. There is also much under-employment — experienced, for example, by many women who do not register as unemployed but who would work if given the opportunity; and by many seasonal or part-time workers, as in the holiday trade, who would like more regular or full-time employment.

Declining Rural Services

A third key area of concern, related to the vitality of rural communities, is the decline in rural services. This decline — described earlier in the chapter — is continuing into the 1980s. For example, the number of village primary schools closed in England rose for a number of reasons from 26 in 1979 to 43 in 1980 and 79 in 1981. Programmes of school closure are still being pursued in many counties. Avon County Council alone may consider the closure of another 25 rural primary schools. At Carhampton in Somerset, the primary school is about to be shut down despite the fact that 20 new council houses are being built in the village. School transport services have, in many counties, been pared down to the minimum with sharply increased charges for the remaining discretionary services. Public transport services continue to decline both in length of routes and in frequency. Library and mobile library services have been reduced in many areas. Each year sees the closure of more village shops. The Department of Employment is in the process of closing Job Centres in many country towns.

These cuts in services are caused partly by falling demand, partly by the reaction of providers to the effects of inflation, and partly by the pressure on the funds of public authorities. For example, as car ownership levels (already high in many rural areas) continue to rise, the demand for public transport falls. Decline in population, or in the number of people in certain age groups, may mean that numbers who use a particular service — such as a school or a chiropodist — fall below what the providers of the service see as the threshold of its viability. Norfolk County Council, for example, has estimated that a village with a population between 300 and 500 can normally support a shop, a pub and a primary school with between 30 and 50 pupils — considered to be the minimum viable size for such a school. The Council estimates that a 'fairly economic' primary school of 100 pupils needs a 'support population' of about 1,000, that a regular village surgery needs about 1,800 people to support it, a butcher or baker between 1,500 and 3,000, a district nurse 3,000, a chemist 4,000 to 4,500, a three-doctor surgery about 6,000.

Inflation, plus the rising costs of wages and salaries as living standards and expectations rise, mean that services of these kinds — which tend to have heavy elements of labour and transport costs — become increasingly expensive to run as the years go by. The reaction of providing bodies to this is usually to search for economies, such as the use of larger buses and one-man crews in the field of transport. But the scope for such economies is limited, and the effect of inflation is to raise the thresholds of viability of services and thus to make it more difficult to run such services in a decentralised way. Moreover, there is continuing heavy pressure on local authority funds.

Rural areas have received, in past years, less than their share of public expenditure. For example, in 1981/2 local authorities in rural areas in England spent £364 per head of population, against a national average of £444. The tight constraints imposed by the Government are leading to further austerities which are bound to have direct impact on the level and quality of services. Government agencies and regional authorities such as those who run health and water services, are under similar financial pressure.

Thus rural communities in many counties are caught between the nether and the upper millstone — on the one hand, declining employment and services, and on the other competition on the housing market from incomers. Clearly, in due time, one of these trends may ameliorate the other, as incomers add to the rateable income of the local authorities and to the demands for services and employment. The severity of problems can vary greatly from one rural area to another, as is implicit in the quotations from the North of England which follow. But the prospect at present, for those who wish to sustain the vitality of rural communities, is not good.

Grassroots

The Clerk of a Parish Council on Dartmoor in Devon Comments on the Problems and Needs of that Upland Community

People here are concerned about these things:

- a continuing change towards a more elderly population;
- a lack of employment opportunities, particularly for young people;
- a reduction of rural services, and the increasing cost of transport;
- growing interference by outside authorities, officialdom and bureaucracy;
- a decline in the quality of the countryside environment because of its more intensive use;
- an apparently increasing emphasis on the needs of the visitor at the expense of those who live on the Moor.

What should be done about it is not so easy to say. I think most people here see the need for a broad 'balance' between the various conflicting demands of visitors, residents, agriculture, conservation, recreation, and access. Action is needed to check the apparent drift of younger people away from the upland, rural areas. Job creation for the younger age groups should have high priority. The continuation of some form of agricultural subsidy will be essential in maintaining a healthy level of farming activity. However, present systems tend to encourage inefficient farming methods. A subsidy system that provides incentives to good and productive *family* farming is badly needed.

The Parish Council recently opposed the conversion of a redundant farm building into a craft centre. Since the village already has a pub much used by visitors to the Moor, we felt that any new tourist development would make us into another Widecombe. There can be too much tourism: enough is enough. Rather than convert buildings into three-months-a-year holiday lettings, we'd like to see them used as year-round homes for local people.

As a Parish Council, we find it is very hard to get other authorities to take us seriously. We have been trying for years to get the District Council to make a small extension to the car parking space beside their houses in the village. It's been on their programmes, but it always gets pushed off by something 'more urgent'.

We know there are successful examples of Rural Development Boards elsewhere. But here there is widespread distrust of, and distaste for, more 'quangos' or their like. Similarly, any substantial increase in the role and powers of the Dartmoor National Park Authority would also be the cause of considerable concern. A more active and regionalised role for the Council for Small Industries in Rural Areas might be valuable, provided it had clear links to the Ministry of Agriculture.

The Director of a Community Council in a Remote Park of the North of England Reflects on Local Rural Problems

It's amazing how often the problem found and solutions applied elsewhere do not apply here. Either we don't have the problem, or we've been applying the solution for many years. This may be because we reached rock-bottom, in terms of population decline and a loss in rural services, a long time ago. Thus everyone, from the County Council downwards, woke up early to rural needs, and began to do something about them.

For example, we've had rural transport initiatives (which are quite new in some counties) for about thirty years. Similarly, with creation of rural jobs, there's never been any conflict here between the planners and the people who wanted to develop new rural industry or create jobs through, say, tourism. Or take post offices: elsewhere they've been closing rural sub-post offices and removing telephone kiosks. Here the Postmaster doesn't mention the criteria for closure of post offices, and agrees with us that they should be kept open. The regional manager of British Telecom seems to take the same view about telephone kiosks.

The people's attitude is also different from what it might be in areas near the big cities. Much of this county is remote, and is not affected by commuting or second homes or much tourism. These areas have not benefited from inward movement of population, and I don't think they're likely to do so. The people realise this, and they accept that they may have lower standards of service, or at least different conditions. For example, the closure of small village schools has been accepted without much fuss, and the research we've done suggests that this closure hasn't, in fact, done much harm, even where it means that very small children have to be bussed three or four miles to school.

I don't think we should count on any permanent reversal of population decline in these remote areas. Obviously, the depression of the late 1970s and early 1980s may mean that school-leavers, who ten years ago were leaving the rural areas in quite frightening numbers to find work in the towns, may now do so rather less, though we lack statistics to see whether this is so. Also, the informal economy is playing a bigger part, with people making a living from a bit of this and a bit of that. But I doubt if this change is permanent. If the national economy picks up, the rural areas won't be able to compete and will lose people again.

In a county like this, you can't in any case get new industries to locate out in the countryside. You have to put medium-sized firms into the market towns. That's why there was such an outcry when the Development Commission proposed to cut these towns out of the Special Investment Areas.

I'm glad the Development Commission is now talking about rural development programmes, with a social as well as economic component. The need is to galvanise people in the villages to realise the potential which they have for development. If every Parish Council or other village institution actually realised its potential, immense improvements could be made. To achieve this, we need community development on a much more intensive basis, with one field officer covering not (as now) a whole county but rather a district or even less. This means more field staff, backed up flexible system of capital grants and low-interest loans. We can always realise a few hundred pounds for a worth-while village initiative, but grants or loans would help tremendously.

A Doctor Comments on Working a Rural Group Practice in the North of England

The loss of population in this remote country area, and the official tendency to centralise services, mean that people now have to travel very long distances for some purposes and that causes hardship. For example, twenty years ago about three hundred babies would be born in our area each year; now, the number is about fifty. You can't maintain a midwife to do just one delivery a week. So mothers have to go to one of the big hospitals up to forty miles away, to have a baby now.

In the same way, those who are elderly and ill can't stay here. They have to go to sheltered accommodation or a hospital fourteen or more miles away. The result is that people hang on longer than they should before they agree to go; and relatives can have a rough time struggling in to see them in hospital.

So already you can't be born here, and you can't die here. The Area Health Authority would like to centralise services even more. We are resisting this. In particular, it would be devastating to close our cottage hospital. It's not very big, but it allows us to provide a far wider, more caring service than the general hospital alone can give.

For example, patients come in for tests and diagnosis, or for a period of convalescence after an operation or major illness at the general hospital; or for rehabilitation after a stroke; or for short periods of care to give a respite to relatives who normally look after them. These are all things which the general hospital wouldn't do. We run a twenty-four hour casualty service, and a day hospital where sick people come for a few hours of therapy and socialising, so their relatives can have a break.

We do a great deal of visiting patients' homes, which not all practices will do. Many people (particularly elderly) can't get to us for lack of transport, but they do have telephones, so they can ring us for help. We've got an ambulance nearby which can bring people in to the cottage hospital or take them to the general hospital in the nearest city. The district nurses, and the chiropodist come out to see people in their homes. The pharmacist based here also runs a mobile service, and has a daily delivery van running from the nearest city so that special prescriptions can be met very quickly.

Actions to Steer Change

Recognising Rural Needs

The last few years have seen a rapid growth in public and political awareness of the problems faced by rural areas and of the need for action to achieve what the Clerk of the parish council in Devon, cited above, calls 'balance' between different demands on the countryside, including the sustaining of communities. A report on the decline of rural services gained national attention in 1978. The Associations of County Councils, and of District Councils, both published reports recognising these needs and outlining policies to meet them. Eight national organisations representing rural communities set up in 1980 an alliance called *Rural Voice*. Its purpose is to ensure that the government, the media and the general public understand the problems of those who live in the countryside, and to encourage rural communities themselves to take action to improve the quality of rural life. Three major political parties produced policy documents which recognised the needs of rural communities. The Countryside Commission, when launching in early 1983 a national debate on the future of the uplands, placed strong emphasis on the social and economic (as well as the environmental) needs of these areas.

The climate of opinion may thus appear highly sympathetic to the pursuit of policies and actions which will secure the sustaining of communities in the countryside, hopefully in alliance with the other purposes outlined in earlier chapters of this book. But this growth of awareness needs has coincided, over the last five years, with economic depression and stringent control over public expenditure, particularly by local authorities. These factors have severely blunted the initiatives towards which the many reports and policy documents described above appeared to be pointing. What follows is thus a summary of the way that ideas appear to be moving, plus examples of action which is being taken in some areas in pursuing those ideas.

Encouraging Rural Development Initiatives

The ideas for the sustaining of rural communities, set out in several of the reports mentioned earlier, may be summarised as follows. Growth — in population, in economic activity, in physical development — should be encouraged in rural areas, but on an appropriate scale. Rural communities of whatever size, should be neither stunted by preventing new development nor bloated by excessive development. The particular needs of each community — such as for housing, jobs or services — should be studied by its own people as well as by officials; and official policies, which in the past have arguably been too standardised, should be 'flexed' to reflect these particular needs. There should be effective links between people and the jobs, housing or services which they need — by building or creating these things, at least partly, in the villages where the people are, not always in distant towns; by adequate public transport between villages and those services which have to be located in towns; by mobile services, such as mobile libraries or 'Meals on Wheels'; by involving the community in running its own services. More initiative should lie within communities to solve their own perceived problems. There should be closer integration between different agencies, and stronger links between the agencies and the people they serve (see Chapter 7).

Policies and actions which express these ideas are being pursued in some areas. Thus, in the field of housing, some local authorities are using both their planning and their housing powers to try to meet the needs of lower paid local people. In the planning field, some authorities — such as the West Wales and South Lakeland District Councils and the Lake District Planning Board — are seeking agreements with developers of new housing that the houses will be sold to people who work locally, though there is some doubt about whether such agreements will 'stick'.

As housing authorities, some District Councils are building new houses in villages; working with private developers on shared equity schemes; or providing land for house-building by housing associations or self-build housing groups (see Figure 5.17). West Derbyshire, East Hampshire and some other District Councils have policies to purchase houses which come up for sale, whether on the private-house market or from bodies like the Ministry of Defence, for use by people on the council housing lists. In some areas — such as North Wiltshire and Eden in Cumbria — they have worked out ways to bring private rented property into use for council tenants. Where council house tenants exercise their right to buy under recent legislation, the government has permitted some district councils — notably several in South West England — to impose conditions on re-sale so that they will continue to meet the needs of local people. Housing for local people is also being created in some areas by private and voluntary bodies, for example by housing associa-

Figure 5.17: Starter Homes at Lealholm in North Yorkshire. These houses were built by a housing association with funding from the Development Commission and the Housing Corporation.

Source: Development Commission.

tions with finance through the Housing Corporation. Sometimes the initiatives in such housing association schemes are taken by the parish council, such as those at Ringsfield in Suffolk and Chiddingstone in Kent. Elsewhere people who work locally and cannot afford houses on the open market are getting together in help-help groups to build their own homes: examples are at Slinfold in West Sussex and Winterley in Cheshire.

In the field of services, some public agencies and voluntary groups within the rural communities are finding resourceful ways to sustain and even extend services. Some local education authorities, anxious to keep village schools open, are forming 'clusters' of schools with one headmaster, some common services and peripatetic teachers. Others are accepting help from parents in order to keep up the quality of education at low cost. The Post Office is continuing its support to many small sub-post-offices and is encouraging their business by accepting agency work from other government departments. Some county councils, in their role as transport authorities, are subsidising not only conventional bus services but unconventional schemes like the minibus service run by Age Concern in Cornwall, and Devon County Council (see Figure 5.18). In some places, the school buses are being used by the general public as well as pupils.

Other authorities are seeking to reverse the past trend towards centralisation of services by dispersing them again, or running mobile services. For example, the Health Authorities in Oxford and in Exeter are considering the closure of large central hospitals (which are expensive to run) and reopening of cottage hospitals, local health centres and day-care facilities, or putting greater emphasis on domiciliary care. Some libraries and information centres are being put more on a mobile basis. Rural Community Councils, with the support of *Rural Voice* and of the Development Commission, organise in almost every English county, a programme called Village Venture. The object of this is to encourage communities to take the initiative in the creation or maintenance of their own services, such as community shops, pre-school playgroups, youth clubs, swimming-pools and community newspapers. These and other initiatives mean that in some areas the trend of decline in services is being slowed down; but it is too early to say that this decline can be halted, much less reversed.

Diversifying The Rural Economy

In the field of employment, also, initiatives are being taken to strengthen and diversify rural economies. In England, the Development Commission has, in recent years, increased the scale of its work in building advance factories in many rural areas (see Colour Plate 12). Also it has been given by legislation a more general, and more direct, concern for wider aspects of the rural economy and has reviewed the boundaries of the Rural Development Areas in which it focuses its main efforts in the economic field. It is working on proposals for the production of Rural Development Programmes, by which the work of different government and local authorities in each rural area may be better integrated. Its subsidiary, CoSIRA has had its brief extended beyond assistance to manufacturing and craft industries in rural areas to cover shops, garages, small transport companies and other service industries — although its staff resources are not yet adequate to fulfil this brief.

In Wales, as a similar agency, the Development Board for Rural Wales has recently stated what it sees as the overriding problem for the area:

A population of less than 200,000 is scattered over the Board's wide area — a bare 7% of the population of Wales ... The shadow over this area for a century has been the drift away of its population, mainly because of lack of work opportunities for young people. To reverse this drift and bring people back is at the heart of the Board's creation ... The essence of the task is to work at specific problems in particular places, recognising that the resources will not justify a general programme of development in the early days.

The prime focus of the Board's own action is on factory development. It aims to develop the building of warehouses and offices to encourage the growth of service industry; to grant aid social and community projects; and to encourage

Figure 5.18: Alternative Rural Transport. Mini-bus services such as this are increasingly replacing conventional services. A number are being run by co-operatives and the voluntary sector.

Source: NCVO.

action by local authorities and others in the fields of housing, communications, cultural activities, industrial training, farming, forestry and fishing.

Other agencies also contribute to the creation of jobs in the countryside. Many local authorities — County Councils, District Councils, even some Town and Parish Councils — are working with the Development Commission in the Rural Development Areas to lay out industrial estates, build advance factories and release land for private industrial development. Thus, many County and District Councils have taken advantage of the Commission's 50-50 scheme, under which the Commission and the local authority each pay half of the cost of small workshops (see Colour Plate 13). Outside the Rural Development Areas also, some local authorities are active. For example, the Isle of Wight County Council has built several small workshops in response to urgent demand. Somerset County Council has a revolving fund of £1 million which is used to buy land, develop it for factory use and sell it to industrialists.

Some local authorities are converting redundant buildings into factories and workshops: examples are a works depot at Ely in Cambridgeshire, an old police station in Shropshire, and a number of redundant primary schools in Gwynedd. Clwyd County Council had built a crafts centre — with a shop, cafe, workshops, and exhibition area — on the site of an old station yard at Ruthin; this development, with a capital cost of £600,000, is intended to provide a major tourist attraction on the main tourist route to North Wales and Anglesey and hence to provide jobs both within the centre and in the locality. Other local authority contributions to job creation are information services to small firms, seminars for those involved in business, marketing schemes, and grants to local enterprise trusts.

Local enterprise trusts, or small industry groups are being set up in many areas. Somerset, Devon and Cornwall (for example) have a total of six such groups, drawing their finance from local authorities, large industrial companies, banks, charitable foundations and the Development Commission. These informal bodies, staffed by experienced businessmen and able to draw on the voluntary help of local banks and entrepreneurs, are designed to help and support those who are seeking to set up new, or expand existing businesses. They do this mainly by skilled confidential advice, but also in some cases by organising trade exhibitions and securing premises for new small firms on a sale or lease basis. The Somerset Small Industries Group took a lease on a disused poultry farm, parts of which are now sub-leased to small firms who do the conversion work themselves and thus secure very cheap premises.

A major part of employment in rural areas lies within the private sector, and a big contribution to this has been made in the past by landowners. Although jobs on rural estates have dwindled in this century, there are places where new initiatives are creating more work. Some landowners and farmers are converting redundant farm buildings to house factories, craft workshops, self-catering tourist accommodation, and other tourist enterprises — often with grant-aid from CoSIRA or from the English or Welsh Tourist Boards. On the Lockinge estate in Oxfordshire, the conversion of buildings has provided space for 22 separate new businesses, thus creating 69 new jobs and bringing the owner a return in rents of about 26 per cent on the capital invested in conversion. The Lowther Estate in Cumbria runs a variety of enterprises — including a sawmill converting forest timber into industrial pallets and other products, a wildlife adventure park, and a large caravan and camping park — all of which provide significant employment in the area.

Keeping Pace With Recession

All these initiatives in the field of employment are, of course, barely able to keep pace with the continuing impact of economic depression in many areas. Unemployment figures are still high, both among school-leavers and among adults. This unemployment results in action on two further fronts — self-employment and the informal economy, and the activities of the Manpower Services Commission.

Many rural areas have traditionally had a quite high proportion of self-employed people, and a flourishing informal economy — that is, that part of the economic activity which does not involve formal full-time jobs or regular salaries and wages. People have gained income from several sources — say farming or smallholding, fishing, seasonal work in tourism — or have done jobbing work of various kinds. Scavenging, barter, cash transactions, the avoidance of tax have always been strong. Unemployment tends to provoke this kind of resourcefulness, and to encourage the sprouting of small firms of all kinds — vehicle repair, builders, window-cleaners, landscape contractors.

For example, the small town of Lynton on the north Devon coast, with a population of 1,600, has about 40 small building firms. Very few of them have a large turnover, some are very likely to fail, but meanwhile they provide a competitive service to the small hoteliers and householders of the town and help to keep the local economy going. Such small firms form the seedbed out of which large firms may grow, if and when the national and local economies pick up. A further example of creative response to unemployment is *Instant Muscle*, which describes itself as 'a network of professionally advised partnerships, owned and managed by young people and school-leavers who prefer work to the dole'. The first such partnership was set up in September 1981, at Farnham in Surrey, for four 19-year-olds who were fed up with being under-employed. They offer to do any jobs for house-builders or businesses that do not require a high level of craft skill or involve exceptional danger. They immediately attracted enough work to keep over 20 people employed. The network of partnerships now extends into five counties in southern England.

The Manpower Services Commission (MSC) supports a nationwide pattern of Youth Training Schemes (YTS) and community programmes (schemes for adult unemployed). These provide each relevant unemployed person with up to twelve months of work experience and training (for school-leavers) or of employment with some training (for adults). This temporary help itself may enable people to stay in a rural area. For some, it can also provide that stimulus, introduction or skill which enables them to find more long-lasting employment or to enter self-employment enterprise. The proportion who do find such activity after twelve months is lower than it was when the economy was more flourishing — currently about 30 per cent of YTS trainees find jobs when they finish their training. But the increase in self-respect, confidence and skill which the MSC schemes provide is bound to help a larger number.

The MSC schemes have another major benefit in many rural areas — they make possible the launching of schemes which bring benefits other than temporary employment to the rural communities and to wider purposes such as land use and conservation. For example, MSC teams have cleared and sign-posted footpaths in Dyfed, rebuilt a sea wall to protect a nature reserve at Leigh Marshes in Essex, cleared out ponds and built bridges in Epping Forest, helped to run community sports programmes in Hampshire, installed solar heating in school swimming-pools in Dorset, put insulation and draught-proofing in the homes of old people in Devon and restored derelict woodland in Cornwall.

At a time when the countryside is so beset by problems and conflicts, it is encouraging to see practical projects which simultaneously serve to encourage primary production, protect amenity and sustain the rural communities. For example, the upland management schemes — pioneered in the Lake District and now operated in all the National Parks — serve to protect the hill farmer from harassment by visitors, to maintain landscape features such as limestone walls, and to create jobs in the countryside. On Dartmoor in Devon, a joint initiative in wall-building and similar work by the National Park Authority and the Devon Rural Skills Trust is securing landscape improvements, training in traditional skills, and employment or apprenticeship for two-dozen men. Initiatives in woodland management in Cornwall and Cumbria are leading to the restoration of derelict woodlands, the production of timber and firewood, and the creation of rural jobs.

The Future Uncertain

What do all these initiatives offer towards the sustaining of rural communities in England and Wales in the second half of the 1980s? Do they provide the means to make opportunity out of crisis?

The answer must depend mainly on the three factors — the state of the national, and urban, economies; the policies of central government; and the amount of initiative shown by the rural communities themselves. If the national, and particularly the urban, economy picks up, the countryside may both lose and gain. Some of the young people who now stay in the countryside for lack of urban jobs may again start leaving. A rise in general wealth may impel further migration into the countryside, increasing the pressure on the housing market. Employment may start to grow again.

However, in considering the present state of rural communities, it cannot be pretended that the picture is a happy one. Whilst local initiatives may be applauded, the fact remains that there are in villages a disproportionate number of people living on incomes well below the national average and who exist in an environment of declining local government social services. And this means that the basic problem of rural deprivation is ever present. Indeed the latest evidence on this to come from research carried out for the Department of the Environment is hardly encouraging. Following detailed surveys in five areas in England and Wales, each chosen to represent a different form of rural economy, around 25 per cent of households sampled were found to be in or on the margins of poverty. The research also suggests that many of the households which exist in this state are elderly ones whilst in households where its members are active wage earners the fact that wages in rural areas are below those for national income groups must be significant. A strong contrast between male non-manual earning groups which are relatively affluent and largely employed in the larger towns to which they commute, and those who are employed locally is also very apparent. The wide difference between these two groups is also clear in terms of educational attainment.

Any idea that the income differential in rural areas might be reduced by environmental and other fringe benefits is seen to be largely mythical. The advantages of free medical insurance, company cars, payment of school fees, better working hours that accrue to the 'newcomer' are, as the report states, 'invariably more valuable than free wellington boots' which is likely to be the manual workers' lot.

The research report ends significantly:

> All the while the relative position of such groups and individuals continues to deteriorate as a series of interlocking public and private sector decisions interact to disadvantage them further relative to both 'new' rural residents and the rest of the country.

If this is so then it must be apparent that the continuation of present policies by central government over the next few years with their concomitant reduction in the activities of local authorities and in particular their spending in real terms on council housing, educational and social services can only greatly exacerbate the problem. In which case the degree to which the impact of such policies on rural communities can be ameliorated must depend on the degree of initiative shown by the private sector including voluntary organisations and community groups. The extent of this initiative in turn may depend on the effectiveness of those agencies and alliances — such as the

Development Commission, the Rural Community Councils, and *Rural Voice* — whose purpose is to encourage and help rural communities to take a lead in sustaining themselves.

Who Benefits, Who Loses?

Any assessment of which groups gain and which groups lose from living in rural communities is best undertaken through an examination of four separate viewpoints. The first involves addressing the issue from the perspective of those migrating from the urban areas; the second from the standpoint of the indigenous village population; and thirdly from that of the villager leaving to reside in the town or city. Finally, there is a national perspective concerning the sustaining of the community which should not be neglected.

Prevalent among those moving out of the towns to embrace country living are the young families who seek the benefits of fresh air, a larger living space than they might have afforded in the city and a chance to pursue rural leisure activities both in the village and the surrounding countryside. But more often than not this life-style — one of relative affluence compared with the indigenous population — will be supported by the head of the household commuting to his work. But there are also those who leave urban areas to *work* in the countryside. Where it has been possible to set up small industries, entrepreneurs in the business of producing small goods, with their value greatly enhanced by the manufacturing process, have tended to leave the congested, highly rated city sites to seek the benefits of a pleasant environment, lower outgoings on overheads and a docile, lower-wage labour force.

Other individualists have left the urban areas to pursue their life-long dream of earning a small country living from the land or to earn from their talents as writers or artists in a more congenial rural environment. However, the communications revolution is now offering to a wide range of others with business connections and similar country aspirations the opportunity to live and work at a distance from the head office in the city yet be in minute-to-minute contact with crucial decision-making.

Finally there are the retired who after a lifetime of work want to realise their ambition of returning permanently to their holiday haunts.

However desirable the fulfilment of the move to the country may appear to be, there are for each of these groups, disbenefits. Even to the retired the reality of the rural life (probably not truly experienced on holiday and in younger days) becomes all too apparent. There is the lack of shopping facilities that in towns may be just around the corner and the occasional absence of a doctor in close proximity. Even more likely, is the lack of a local optician, dentist or chiropodist. The hospital is often distant and the general lack of public transport facilities is more noticeable. As the retired find it increasingly more difficult to get about and make considerably greater demands on health facilities as they grow old, these services become even more important. Other social factors may also become significant — such as the fact that they will be living at a distance from their relatives, particularly their grown-up children who will have responsibilities to their own families. Moreover, some retired people, if the village is particularly favoured by others in a similar part of their life cycle, will be living in a very unbalanced community.

For other migrants to the village, the problems may be fewer. The family of the commuter or the businessman may find a lack of shops, medical services and even entertainments such as the theatre. However, this is a drawback which relative affluence and the ready availability of one or more private cars diminishes to the level of minor inconvenience. Even the teenage sons and daughters will have some form of transport of their own. For the businessman in his role as factory owner, his lines of communication for raw materials and to markets may become extended, but if his product is high value these may become insignificant cost factors. For the individual rural home worker, isolation from others pursuing a similar line may be a disadvantage. For the smallholder the cost of land may drive him or her to the most remote and marginal of agricultural areas though this can hardly be called a disbenefit since such activities really cannot be pursued in urban back gardens, except in television soap operas.

Where the indigenous inhabitant of a rural community is concerned the influx of newcomers from the city is a mixed blessing. They will spend money locally which will benefit the shops and the pub and other locally owned private concerns. They will help keep up numbers in the village and so assist in the maintaining of local public services, making it more difficult to reduce these in times of economic stringency. At the same time they can and do introduce an alien form of culture which strikes at the heart of traditional village pastimes. More important is the fact that in a situation where there are constraints upon the construction of new houses, the newcomers may compete with locals for the existing stock of property. This can drive up prices to way beyond the means of the local population who may find themselves driven out of the village and close contact with the rest of their family. The incidence of second-home owners may have a similar impact on property prices but at the same time may not necessarily have the same advantages in spending terms to the village as the newcomer who takes up permanent residence.

But of the indigenous villagers who do decide to leave for the city there is not only the breaking of family ties in the village but also the loss of those other close bonds of community which revolve around the church, the pub or some local sporting activity. However, the gains may be great to the migrant to the city and his family through a greatly enhanced variety of jobs on offer and a certain capacity to earn more money. Apart from a wider range of leisure activities and the much more accessible range of social services that urban areas provide, the migrant to the city can be assured of greater educational opportunities, if not for himself, for his children.

Moving finally to a consideration of benefits and losses at national level, it must be acknowledged that in the small heavily populated space that makes up England and Wales, there must be some virtue in the wide distribution of the people and not merely in their concentration in cities where overcrowding could give rise to a range of social ills. Moreover even the remoter agriculturally-less-favoured areas and their valued for those 'away from it all' qualities, as well as for recreation, demand a permanent residential population. Those in thinly scattered, small communities will require a minimum level of service provision though in such areas this will perforce be more expensive than in the towns and cities or even in the more urbanised countryside of South East England.

If it is ultimately deemed important that rural communities be properly sustained, this means, as the latest report to the Department of the Environment on rural deprivation makes clear, a more equitable provision of the necessary social infrastructure comparable with its urban counterpart. At the same time greater opportunities for new employment to come into the villages will be necessary, albeit in a carefully controlled way. So far the constraints imposed by development controls, especially outside key settlements, have benefited the farmers by allowing them to operate in a largely non-competitive labour market. Thus, the losers have inevitably been the comparatively badly paid farm-hands.

6
What Futures?

Introduction

'There is one thing of which all men are equally ignorant and that is the future.' Anon.

So far in this book a number of aspects of the countryside have been discussed in an inter-temporal context from a specific position in history through the present and into the immediate (and most likely) future. It is the purpose of this chapter to gain an impression of a slightly longer-term future for the countryside of England and Wales.

In doing so, this chapter breaks the mould of previous ones by deliberately drawing on more personal and polemical visions of the future countryside as seen from a number of disparate viewpoints. These viewpoints have been assembled either by direct invitation to the author or as edited versions of published work.

The art (or science?) of predicting futures, itself can be seen to fluctuate in relation to economic activity. During periods of growth, such as the late 1960s and early 1970s, impressions of the future were radical, imaginative and often of a global nature. During this period, much futurology was of a 'doomwatch' environmental and natural resource nature, best encapsulated, perhaps, in the now-notorious 'Limits to Growth' model published by the Club of Rome in 1973. At this time too, radical alternative life-styles came to prominence in visions of a future society.

In times of economic recession, however, futures scenarios are a little more cautious. Perhaps inevitably during these times, the future takes on a shorter-term, more problem-solving scale. Much writing about the future in the mid-1980s has this flavour. Ironically, therefore, it is often the case that more radical visions of the future predate more cautious ones — a characteristic that is evident to an extent in this chapter.

The contributions that make up this chapter fall into five discernible groups. They reflect a balance between shorter term and more radical futures, and concern themselves with the issues discussed in Chapters 2 to 5. The first five contributions consider the future of agricultural policy and policy for control over the rural environment. They all have their roots in current policy developments and provide contrasting views about the future directions that current policy might take.

The second four move from issues of policy, to future farming systems. Here, contrasting views are more stark in the consideration of alternatives for a longer-term future. From this more distant vision, the issue of urban containment is then considered in terms of the more immediate 'next steps' for both planners and the future of green belts. A fourth set of two short pieces again adopts a more distant visionary stance in considering the way new rural communities might be developed on lines quite different from those of today. Finally, a considered overview of all of these issues is presented, identifying priorities for the future development of the countryside as a whole.

Agriculture and Conservation: Towards the Year 2000

In this section, the Country Landowners Association see a new role for the private landowner as a rural custodian in the face of the inevitable demise of the Common Agricultural Policy. Charlie Clutterbuck and Tim Lang agree with the end of the CAP as it is known but envisage more radical shifts in agricultural policy. Marion Shoard feels strongly that the problem of agricultural impact on the countryside can be solved satisfactorily only with the imposition of planning controls, but John Bowers and Paul Cheshire disagree. They claim that the conservation of the countryside can be achieved only through substantial review of the economic basis of agricultural support. Chris Rose and Charlie Pye-Smith return to planning controls as one of a number of notions, drawn from disparate sources, in compiling an agenda for saving the rural heritage of England and Wales.

The Country Landowners Association
(This article was written specifically for this book.)

It will be clear from any study of our rural areas, that there is never a 'final solution' in the changing countryside. Straightforward prediction about the future is doomed to failure, if only because Nature herself sometimes takes a hand. Who, 30 years ago, looking at the likely development of the countryside by the mid-1980s, could have foreseen the desolation caused by Dutch Elm disease?

Certainly in the past 40 years, we have witnessed a genuine revolution in farming. The farming industry has responded in a remarkable way to the incentives provided first by the post-war drive for greater self-sufficiency in food production, and later by the EEC's Common Agricultural Policy.

There is, however, every sign that this era is at an end. Mounting European surpluses and the final unwillingness of the Community to support its rural electorates with virtually open-ended price guarantees point to a throttling-back of the drive to ever more intensive farming, with important implications for the future of the countryside.

These implications will have an impact on elements of the conservation and access lobbies — that is, to a large degree, those who want the privilege of enjoyment of the countryside without the responsibility of having to manage it — who will become even more vocal in blaming farmers and landowners in general for allegedly 'destroying the natural heritage' with an increasing tendency towards hostility and confrontation.

But this creates a distorted picture in the minds of the majority of the electorate, when every case of environmental vandalism by individuals becomes a *cause célèbre*, without a balancing acknowledgement of the positive efforts being made by a far greater number of those who hold land in private ownership to promote conservation and improved access to the countryside.

Mention of ownership of land raises, of course, the question to nationalise or not to nationalise? This is the hardest of all futures to take seriously — despite the Labour Party's 1983 election manifesto pledge to bring tenanted farm land into state ownership — a pledge recently renewed by a party spokesman in Parliament — and despite the absence of any official rebuttal of the statement by Lord Melchett that this would only be the prelude to nationalisation of all farm land.

The prospects of this ever becoming reality are too daunting to contemplate. The countryside we now enjoy is the result of countless thousands of individual decisions by generations of private owners. The prospect of a countryside suffering from the sort of apathy that comes with faceless bureaucratic ownership is appalling.

So what futures can we foresee for the changing countryside? Politically the broad choice seems to lie between an increasingly interventionist approach to countryside matters, with increased use of planning mechanisms, and management by policy directive in line with current political thinking; or the construction of a framework of incentives and disincentives within which individuals' decisions can be moulded in the general direction willed by the community, but which would remain free choices within those constraints.

The important difference between the two approaches is that the one tries to achieve its ends by bureaucracy, coercion and regulation; the other by offering freedom of choice and the right to make their own decisions to those who make their livelihood from the land.

The record of agricultural productivity over the last 40 years shows what a potent force the drive, enthusiasm and capacity for hard work of the rural fraternity can be. This surely is the way forward — to harness the dynamism to meet the nation's needs, rather than to cow it into sluggish submission to a draconian regime.

There are many encouraging signs. There is a consciousness among farmers and landowners of the environmental implications of their activities; a willingness to build conservation and landscape considerations into their management practices. Of course, there remains too a large body of countrymen who have always managed the land for themselves and their successors with a keen appreciation of its appearance and ecology.

Landowners have planted more deciduous trees in the past few years than for a long time. The careful oveseer will note many new plantings, as well as an increased number of hedgerow saplings being left to grow to maturity. They do not yet form a feature of any great significance in the landscape but 20 years and more ahead, the early 1980s will be seen to have been a period of regeneration of amenity broadleaved trees.

Such developments owe much to one of the most positive features of the last decade, the emergence of the Farming and Wildlife Advisory Groups — the 'FWAGS'. In a quiet, practical way, they have been doing a great deal to guide and advise farmers in managing their land with wildlife and landscape considerations in mind. Mainly voluntary, chronically short of money, the FWAGs have nevertheless achieved practical results at grassroots level — and, most importantly, with the goodwill of farmers.

The answers to the question 'Who pays for conservation?' will also be critical in determining the future of the countryside — the more so if agriculture is entering a relatively less prosperous period in the wake of the expected cut-backs in EEC support.

There is a need to sort out those activities of the landowner which bring him an economic return and those concerned with aesthetics and conservation from which the whole community also benefits. The provisions for compensation of landowners for non-exploitation of land is proving one of the most contentious features of the Wildlife and Countryside Act, and doubts are expressed as to whether the available funds can meet the needs.

There is, therefore, growing interest in the concept of tax reliefs for clearly defined conservation activities (or non-activities), by which the community could acknowledge the landowner's sacrifice of income in managing land for conservation rather than production.

The conclusion of this exercise in crystal ball-gazing is, therefore, an optimistic one. The circumstances and the means exist to develop the future countryside on an essentially voluntary basis, with a fair apportionment of cost and responsibility between individual landowners and the community.

There is also a great deal of good will, actual and potential, among all those who have the future well-being of the countryside at heart. A heavy responsibility rests with the leaders of the various interest groups to build on that goodwill, to give and take, to accept compromise in the time-honoured and immensely civilised British fashion, and to reject abuse, mudslinging and similar politically tempting but wholly negative pursuits.

The stakes are too high. There is far more to unite all who truly care for the countryside than to divide them, whatever their special interest. After all, it is disappearing while we argue — two million acres in this century, converted for ever into motorways, industrial estates, airports, new towns and urban sprawl. But it is not too late to get together to make the best of what remains.

Charlie Clutterbuck and Tim Lang
Condensed from *More than We Can Chew, the Crazy World of Food and Farming* (1982), Pluto Press, pp. 108-15.

The food system is characterised not by shortages, but by a tendency to over-produce. There is food for those who can pay. Much effort and ingenuity is, therefore, put by the food controllers into old and new ways of coping with surpluses and making a profit. Schemes vary in how they 'resolve' this problem: cheap or expensive food, where the subsidies go, and so on. National states and federations have made different choices, hence tensions between the USA, the UK and the EEC for instance. So what would we do?

*Buffer Stocks.*It would be nice to think that the food controllers would suddenly admit the error of their ways and pack up. We think this is unlikely. They are having too good a time. Surpluses there may be, under their system, but approximately one third of the world is malnourished, despite UN calculations that there is more than enough food to feed all people. Clearly, distribution could be improved overnight. Stockpiling is a financial mechanism in market wars. They come, they go. We would like to see genuine buffer stocks. These would lose their financial weight if local agricultures were allowed to release their potential. Whatever its faults, the Chinese post-revolutionary food system at least shows that once capitalist control is removed, feeding people can be made a priority. Stores help.

*Redirect State Expenditure.*Much of this depends upon some degree of public control over state food expenditure. The last century has shown the increasing control of the state in everyday lives. We are not in favour of taxes *per se*; accountants sidestep them all too easily. Direct investment is essential, not just in taking over wholesaling, for example, but also in redirecting where public money is invested in private hands. For instance, most state aid to farming goes to the best-endowed farms. A weighted rating system on farmland could help alter this — high on the best and almost nothing on the bleak hills. The Ministry already has a usable five-grade land evaluation, and this could easily be applied on holdings over, say, 50 acres or 20 hectares.

*Different Farming Methods.*There need to be different farming methods, that involve more organic methods and less reliance on petrochemical substitutes. For example, should Tanzanian natural fibre have been replaced by nylon bailing twine? There should be more mixed farming and greater variation of crops within any one enterprise. Smaller machines would be needed to cope with the more intensive cropping methods. Excess production should be re-cycled on the farm rather than going round the continent a couple of times.

*De-bug Research.*In the sciences, we want to see radically changed research criteria. Take another area dominated by multinationals — the seed industry. We want to see indigenous seed development. At present, for example, potato research is dominated by the food industry's needs: storeability, freezability, transportability, processability, broad-spectrum cookability (that is, usable for different markets), responsiveness to fertiliser use to increase water take-up, resistance to mechanical damage and resistance to diseases not dealt with by chemicals. Against these we want to stress variety, taste, nutrition, broad-based disease resistance and so on. Such research should be under community control, involving farmers, farmworkers and consumer groups, rather than a crude business logic, or green revolution thinking as in the International

Potato Centre, which sees new varieties as the solution to social problems. Often no new varieties are needed anyway, old ones are more varied, and locally suited.

Devolved Responsibility. To anyone who considers what we are suggesting either harsh or utopian, we can only say that past war-time experience teaches otherwise. In the Second World War there were the 'war-ag' policies and procedures. These were premised on maximising home production, a U-turn from pre-war years, so they took time. The County War Agricultural Executive Committees were, as the Ministry of Information said, 'perhaps the most successful example of decentralisation and the most democratic use of "control" this war has produced'. These were appointed but devolved responsibility down to local district committees. Each district committee member was a county resident, most were landworkers or employed in agriculture in one way or other. They set targets, allocated machinery and inputs, and generally oversaw land-use and management. They directed investment in drainage and improvements, as well as classifying land and judging whether best use was being made of it by farmers. What better democratic model could we initiate debate with?

This past albeit limited democracy contrasts sharply with the plans for the next war. The Home Office circulated to chief executives of all local authorities (reported in *Farmers Weekly*, 16 March 1979) a food and farming policy in the event of a nuclear attack. The government will put holdings into groups of about 800, controlled by an agricultural officer. Control will be passed down to farm wardens, each controlling 20 holdings. Everything will be 'controlled' from above.

Power to Buy Land. It would nevertheless be useful to have the power to buy land under certain circumstances. And we do not just mean the National Trust buying tracts of moorland, amenity conscious though they are. A leaf could be borrowed from Mrs Thatcher's book. One of Mr Heseltine's parliamentary bills was intended to get local authorities to state what urban land they own, what it is used for and, if not being used to central government's satisfaction, to be forced to sell it. Similarly, a socialist government could force private, rural landowners to assess what land they own. The land register is currently secret, so information on who owns what is hard to track down. Once this was known, owners could be required to say what the land is being used for and if unused or ill-used, be forced to sell.

Access to Countryside. As the old adage has it, whoever stole the goose from the common was dealt with as a thief, but whoever stole the common from the people got away with it. Ramblers have had to fight for the right even to walk on the land. Nationalising all land would be extremely difficult, but nationalising moorland would be feasible. Any difficulties with removing grazing from hill farmers (having been among them, we are aware of this) could be more than compensated by improved drainage of wet pastures. Most of the moorlands could then be released for a variety of purposes, whether to go wild, be ecologically 'frozen' or for forestry. Above all, access to the country must be on a different basis from either work, or ownership entitlements. In the district where we farmed there were many huge gentry houses unoccupied which should be taken over as holiday centres, or socialised in some other way. Life, as well as money, must be breathed back into the countryside, and into its whole social infrastructure.

Marion Shoard
Condensed from 'The Next Task for Planners', *The Planner*, Journal of the Royal Town Planning Institute, *68(1)*, Jan.-Feb. 1982, p.4.

At the heart of the now much discussed conflict between agriculture and conservation lies exactly the problem that planning was invented to solve. The pursuit of profit by those fortunate enough to own land is damaging an environment in which the whole community has an interest. Had development control not been introduced in the built environment, profit-induced change would have destroyed the character of our villages, towns and cities. Now, planning, extended to embrace landscape features, could rescue the country-side. At present, however, planners are not advancing their claim to this task as energetically as they might. They should.

Plenty of approaches to the problem of agriculture and the landscape which do not involve planning are now being canvassed. None of them would be at all likely to have a more than tangential impact on the problem, though this inconvenient reality is going largely unremarked. The Countryside Commission's favoured approach — exhorting farmers to heed the claims of conservation — serves as little more than a smokescreen for defeat. The education programmes now under way — including the Countryside Commission's ten demonstration farms and the five areas in which new agricultural landscapes project officers operate — are perfectly harmless. But it is plainly ridiculous to suggest that this kind of thing will in itself have more than a marginal impact. Few of the farmers who uproot landscape features are unaware of their landscape value; most do so because they stand to gain. 'Education' has already been tried to a considerable extent and, as Lord Melchett, the chief opposition spokesman on the Wildlife and Countryside Bill, said in February 1980 ... 'co-operation and persuasion have presided over massive, wholesale and accelerating destruction of the English country-side'.

Another popular suggestion, doomed to irrelevance, is fiscal reconstruction. Farmers receive an annual subsidy of £5,000 million from the taxpayer and consumer. It is argued that this support could be redeployed in such a way that farmers might be provided with an incentive to conserve rather than, as at present, to destroy. The largest part of the subsidy goes to supporting the artificially high price levels the EEC guarantees the community's farmers — stimulating both the overproduction of food and landscape destruction — and advocates of this approach see the radical reform of the Common Agricultural Policy as the one move to which conservationists should be striving. However, while it is certainly true that a radical reform of the CAP involving in particular a lowering of the guaranteed prices would be bound to benefit conservation in Britain, it is hard to see all the members of the Ten agreeing to such a move simply to promote conservation in Britain — or even to promote conservation in their own countries. For many countries in the Community, farm subsidies are supported by political forces much more powerful than the conservation interest is ever likely to be.

In theory, it should be far easier to reroute some of the subsidies to British farmers over which the British Government has total control. None the less, the impact of such moves on the environment is likely to be limited. Those farm capital grants that help finance potentially harmful activities like wetland drainage or reseeding old grassland with ryegrass monoculture could be abolished. But the impact of such a move would be likely to be small. It is certainly true that if these capital grants were abolished some fields would stay unploughed that would otherwise have been put to intensive cropland. But the overall number is likely to be insignificant.

As a recent Centre for Agricultural Strategy study confirmed, between 80 and 90 per cent of investment funds for agriculture are provided from the farmer's own resources — his profits, non-farm earnings and so on. Only between 10 and 20 per cent comes from borrowing or from Government capital grants. In other words, as in other sectors of the economy, capital investment usually takes place when a farmer has made a certain amount of money and sees the prospect of a healthy financial return from investing part of his profits in another piece of capital equipment or in a land 'reclamation' scheme. Withholding or abolishing Ministry of Agriculture capital grants would simply mean that a farmer would have to wait a little longer for a return on the capital he had invested — but not much longer.

The Wildlife and Countryside Act embodies in legislative form another approach to the issue which is positively pernicious rather than insufficiently effective. The requirement that a farmer can be compensated for income forgone if he agrees to enter into a management agreement to leave a tract of National Park moorland or a Site of Special Scientific Interest intact sets a highly unwelcome precedent.

It was the requirement for compensation that made nonsense of attempts by local planning authorities to control urban sprawl in the 1930s. Under the new Act, compensation may in some cases ensure that sites are conserved where otherwise they would not be. But the number of such sites is certain to be tiny, because the amount of money available is insignificant. This is an approach that can never be universalised for financial reasons. But creating the impression that farmers, unlike industrialists in the built environment, are entitled to compensation for profit forgone, creates an unwelcome precedent.

Only planning controls offer a means for giving the community as a whole, not just the 0.5 per cent of us who are farmers, a direct say over the shaping of the landscape. The Wildlife and Countryside Act has at least established the principle of modifying farmers' plans for landscape change in the interests of conservation. What is needed now is the extension of that principle so that it bears upon farmers as fully as planning controls bear on other industrialists in the built environment.

John Bowers and Paul Cheshire
Condensed from *Agriculture, the Countryside and Land Use: an Economic Critique* (1983), Methuen, pp. 135-6 and 142-3.

In the final chapter of *Conservation and Agriculture*, Joan Davidson writes:

> The idea of conserving those natural resources which have indirect economic value may seem inappropriate in periods of economic stress. The conservation of wildlife and landscape has always been most active at prosperous times and in prosperous places and among prosperous people. For Britain in the later 1970s it is not an auspicious time to be questioning the expansion of a major economic activity like agriculture: there is a continuing uncertainty about the costs and supply of food products from abroad and pressure to intensify the output at home. Farmers face rising costs for materials, energy and wages, as well as new taxes. In circumstances such as these suggestions for the modification of some established farming practices which do little or nothing to improve agricultural productivity even though they may limit the further loss of amenity values from the countryside, must seem to some frivolous and impracticable.

The whole tone of this argument is far too apologetic. Furthermore, because it fails to diagnose the basic economic cause of agricultural destruction of the countryside — subsidy-induced prosperity — it wholly misconstrues the problems. There is a hard-nosed economic argument in favour of conservation. Conservation policies, the most effective of which would be radical restructuring of farm support policies, would achieve a more efficient use of scarce resources. The beauty and natural fecundity of the countryside is a real resource, so too is the recreational use of it. This resource is intangible only in that it seldom commands a market price and so fails to ring up in landowners' cash registers. As any introduction to economics will explain, this constitutes a basic failure of market mechanisms to create an efficient use of resources. In the case of agriculture this problem has been made worse by policy rather than been reduced by it. We have chosen to subsidise precisely those activities

— the use of artificial fertilisers, hedgerow removal, land drainage, etc. — which cause the damage to a real resource; and these damage-causing activities are already financially rewarded by the market since they increase saleable output: food. But since we also have subsidised food production, by farm support policies, farmers have been subsidised twice over to despoil the rural environment. Common sense and hard-nosed economics suggest a completely contrary policy. Thus there is no single sentiment in the quotation from Davidson with which we agree.

A radical programme of reform would aim to change the basis of agricultural support. The starting point for this is the recognition of the fact that conservation and amenity are joint products with foodstuffs but, because amenity is unpriced it is under-provided. The problem then is one of what the economist would call market failure arising because the environment and the landscape are public goods, by which is meant that it is impossible or impractical to charge consumers of them for their use and that providing a good environment for one 'consumer' does not reduce the quantity available to others. This is not an altogether accurate portrayal of the problems since it is not that farmers have destroyed the environment and landscape because it yielded them no income. They have been subjected to a barrage of propaganda and advice, coupled with large financial incentives to destroy it. Any farmer resisting these strictures would have tended to be classified as inefficient and backward. Any policy of reform can only work if the arguments for 'scientific' farming are recognised for what they are, naïve and frequently spurious, and the powerful pressures for intensification are eliminated. Because this has not been done, the policy embodied in the Wildlife and Countryside Act, 1981 must inevitably fail.

If the problem is that of market failure as described above then the solution is either to tax the farmer for providing agricultural output by environmentally damaging techniques or to subsidise forms of production which conserve the environment. If this is done then community welfare will be improved since society will get a better, that is, preferred mix of agricultural output and amenity. If taxation or subsidy is not feasible then a second-best solution is given by imposing physical, that is, planning, controls on production techniques and cropping patterns.

The extension of planning controls to agriculture is the solution favoured by Marion Shoard. For areas of high environmental or landscape value she suggests that changes in agricultural practices, for example, grubbing out hedgerows, draining ponds or ploughing pasture, should require planning consent. Similar suggestions, for National Parks and SSSIs, were made during the debates on the Wildlife and Countryside Act. The persuasive argument for this approach lies in the analogy between valuable, historic landscape and environment and listed buildings, where planning consent is required for demolition or damaging alteration. The less-than-happy experience with the protection of buildings of historical and architectural value should make one view this approach with scepticism. Of itself planning control is a second-best solution. It never approaches 100 per cent efficiency and controls are costly and difficult to police. If market forces make it profitable to pull down a listed building and neither they nor the planning system provide an incentive for its upkeep then it, at best, falls down from neglect. Economic incentives, if properly designed, are to a greater or lesser degree self-policing and in the sort of context with which we are dealing, are in general superior to physical controls in influencing human behaviour. A degree of control may be necessary as a supplement to economic measures or as a means of making incentives workable, but not as a solution in itself. In the countryside there is a great danger of having one costly bureaucracy with massive financial resources, namely MAFF, paying farmers to do one thing and another, much weaker arm of government, the planning system, telling them not to.

Charlie Pye-Smith and Chris Rose
From *Crisis and Conservation*, Pelican, 1984, pp. 130-4.

The claim that Britain is one of the most efficient farming nations in the world is based largely on calculations of productivity per man. It is high time that we thought about replacing and modifying the present system to take account of employment needs, energy limitations and ecological constraints to the development of land. If we are to save the countryside from further devastation there are a number of courses open to us.

The first option open to conservation organisations is to continue buying land for Nature Reserves, as they have been doing for a long time. This, however, is becoming increasingly impracticable; the organisations have few resources and cannot usually compete on the open market with the big agriculturalists. Even the National Trust, with an income approaching £30 millions, is increasingly wary of taking on new properties without some guarantees of future financial help to manage them. The escalating price of land has, incidentally, also prevented many young people from setting up in farming.

Second, the government could introduce planning controls over agriculture and forestry operations. This is possibly the option which most conservationists would like to see. There is no reason why the small number of individuals who own and use land should not be subject to constraints which we all accept on towns and villages. There is no chance of the million acres of land identified by the NCC as being worthy of Nature Reserve status being protected unless such controls are introduced. We have pointed out that the present system whereby farmers and foresters are compensated for not altering or destroying SSSIs is ridiculous. As Chris Hall wrote in *Ecos* in 1981:

> The farmer takes on his land (whether he buys it or rents it) with the moorland, downland, hedges or whatever in position. By removing them he may be able to make the land *more* profitable, but it can hardly be claimed that, if he is not allowed to remove them, he *loses* anything for loss implies previous possession. If farmers are to be paid for these notional losses then by the same token the ordinary citizen refused planning permission to add a garage to his semi-detached ought to be able to claim compensation for the 'loss' of value to his property.

Hall also suggests that it is more than a question of equity; it is also a question of what society can afford.

However desirable planning controls (they may well be a precursor to the third option we discuss below), there is no reason to believe that they would help revive ailing communities in rural areas. They might protect our wildlife and landscape but they would not get people back onto the land. There is, however, a third option — land reform — which would go a long way towards saving our natural heritage and patching together the social fabric of the countryside.

There are few subjects guaranteed to cause greater disquiet than land reform, particularly when such reform entails the erosion of existing property rights of landowners. This is indeed curious. Looking back through the telescope of time to the days when the commons were appropriated from the community, we might shudder with disgust at the callousness of the acquisitors and the injustice of the theft. Yet we seem wary of undoing the process by introducing a system of ownership which would benefit the whole community rather than just those in whom land is presently vested.

Robert Waller, in his essay *Principles of Land Reform*, points out that there is an alternative to both private and state ownership of land. Those who oppose private ownership of land (including Waller, who claims that 'Title deeds to the ownership of land are records of theft from the community') do not necessarily believe, like the National Union of Agricultural Workers (now part of the Transport and General Workers' Union), that land should be nationalised. There is no reason to think that the state (whose policies, after all, are responsible for encouraging private landowners to act in the way they do) can be trusted with the ownership of land.

Waller's proposals for land reform, involving the introduction of a land tax, are based on those outlined by the American economist Henry George in his book *Progress and Poverty*. Both George's book and Waller's essay should be read in their original form, but here we can give a brief sketch of the reforms they envisaged. George wrote:

> The ownership of land is the great fundamental fact that ultimately determines the social, the political, and consequently the intellectual and moral condition of a people. Material progress cannot rid us of our dependence upon the land. Everywhere, in all times, among all peoples, the possession of land is the base of aristocracy, the foundation of great fortunes, the source of power.

Times, of course, have changed. Industrial depressions, which George attributed to the land monopoly, have little or nothing to do today with who owns and uses land. But much poverty, today as a century ago, stems from the unequal distribution of land and resources. (According to Susan George in her book *How the Other Half Dies*, 'a mere 2.5% of landowners with holdings of more than 100 hectares control nearly three-quarters of all the land in the world — with the top 0.3% controlling over half'.)

The land reform promoted by George involves the introduction of a land tax, or the nationalisation of ground rent. The use of the word 'rent' must be clarified here. To quote George:

> In the economic sense there is rent where the same person is both owner and user. Where the owner and user are thus the same person, whatever part of his income he might obtain by letting the land to another is rent, while the return for his labour and capital is that part of his income which they would yield him did he hire the land instead of owning it.

Private ownership, in its present form, would cease to exist, but the state would not be able to claim ownership. In Waller's own words:

> [The land tax] separates natural resources beneath and upon the surface of the land from wealth produced by labour and capital. Land is of no economic value until labour has been applied to it. If a site on which a land tax is paid were owned by the state, then it would have to be leased by the state and when the lease expired the product of all the labour and capital used could be claimed by the state ... But by separating what nature has created (land and natural resources) from what man has produced (houses, quarries, mines, factories, farms, etc.) we can lay the foundations for a new economic order that safeguards enterprises from being seized by the state without depriving the state of its just share in the communal wealth; for the wealth created on any site is partly the fruit of labour of those who work on it and partly the consequence of the prosperity of the community as a whole. Thus the community has of right a share in the wealth produced on its land. This is secured by a variable land tax related to the value of the site.

The introduction of a land tax has many attractions. Landowners could not be legally dispossessed; they would have to pay the tax or surrender their rights to the land. To quote George again:

Let the individuals who now hold [land] still retain, if they want to, possession of what they are pleased to call their land. Let them continue to call it
their land. Let them buy and sell, and bequeath and devise it. It is not
necessary to confiscate land; it is only necessary to confiscate rent.

Were a land tax to be introduced, land could no longer be subject to speculative hoarding and selling as it is today because, as Waller points out, 'all
benefits flowing from the rising value of land would be clearly reflected in the
site valuations and increased common wealth'. The occupier of a site could
not leave it idle as he would be unable to pay the rent (unless he was prepared
to offload wealth derived from other sources) and land would inevitably
become more equitably distributed. The 340 families and institutions which
own 65 per cent of the 10 million acres of the Highlands and Islands of Scotland would not be able to pay the land tax unless the land was used more
productively. Land would thus only be left idle, and people excluded from
working it, when the community wished to reserve it for other purposes: for
example, for conservation or amenity. In these situations the occupier could
be exempted from the land tax.

Before we leave the suggested reforms of George and Waller it must be
emphasised that statutory measures like those instituted by Lloyd George in
his 1908 budget may be counter-productive. In an attempt to break the land
monopoly Lloyd George introduced an Incremental Value Duty and Undeveloped Land Duty which had the effect of causing one-quarter of the surface of
England to change hands in the four-year period 1918-22. Henry George was
well aware of the dangers of such partial measures. By interesting a slightly
greater number in the continuance of the existing system, the lobby opposing
land reforms assume greater rather than less power.

Clearly, before any schemes for land reform can be fully implemented it
will be necessary to decide on a method of finding out what the community
wants with the land. In practical terms county and district councils might be
the best vehicles for administering the reforms, especially if they were given
the short-term responsibility of administering planning controls over farming
and forestry activities. Nevertheless, there will be real difficulties weighing
local priorities against national ones, for example over the use and development of National Parks.

The real attraction of the land tax is that once again it would be the community which really determines the fate of the land rather than either private
individuals or the state. As George puts it:

rent being taken by the state in taxes, land, no matter in whose name it
stood or in what parcels it was held, would be really common property, and
every member of the community would participate in the advantage of
ownership.

Of course, reform of landownership must be accompanied by reform in the
way we use the land. Michael Allaby has suggested that if we reduced the use
of chemicals and machines and turned to muscle power, we would have to
increase the farm labour force dramatically. If the labour force was increased
to the EEC average as a proportion of the total working population we would
create another 1.2 million jobs. Allaby suggests that such a shift would
account for a movement of four million people into the countryside when one
adds in the future workers' families. The final shift, he predicts, could be
around eight million when one adds the mechanics, doctors, shopkeepers, etc.
who will service the population.

To some, the ideas of Waller, George and Allaby may seem abhorrent; to
others, utopian. Others still will dismiss them as unworkable. However, the
only factor which is likely to thwart land reforms (and we already see this with

the opposition to planning controls over farming and forestry) is the power of landowners and vested interests. As Galbraith suggested in *The Affluent Society*:

> Few things have been more productive of controversy over the ages than the suggestion that the rich should, by one device or another, share their wealth with those who are not. With comparatively rare and normally eccentric exceptions, the rich have been opposed.

Radical Farming Systems and Conservation Impacts

In this section, futuristic approaches to farming systems and their impacts on the environment are discussed. Charles Secrett considers a farming future based on low-energy, high-labour lines with more public money going to environmentally sensitive activity. Konrad Smigelski echoes this type of approach in discussing the merits of organic horticulture as part of his vision of co-operative village development at Stanford Hall. The relative merits of commercial farming and subsistence agriculture are given in a balance sheet for Alternative England and Wales. Finally, a greatly contrasting vision is given by Roger Grimley who sees the future of farming being on a very large computer-based scale with hardly any use of labour at all.

Charles Secrett of Friends of the Earth
(This article was written specifically for this book.)

With our slowly growing population this country is well able to meet its food requirements into the next century without taking more marginal agricultural land, often prime wildlife habitat, into production. Instead we must balance the different regional capacities to produce food with the national need to preserve irreplaceable wildlife habitats, like ancient woodlands and un-improved hay meadows, and maintain rural communities.

If protecting the countryside in its wider sense is to mean anything, the Ministry of Agriculture must both interpret and implement European and national legislation in a manner which firmly supports the needs of conservation as well as agriculture *per se*. Given the current level of agricultural surpluses there is no reason to continue grant aid which either intensifies output in traditional landscapes or brings marginal land into production. These should be cut and a realistic proportion redirected towards countryside conservation, the maintenance of a minimum population and the support of tourism and craft industry. Coppicing woodland, building drystone walls, fencing to control stocking rates on sensitive moors, heath or woodland and maintaining healthy native woodlands are all obvious examples where environmentalism and sympathetic farming go hand-in-hand. If the Ministry is to serve farmers and society will in the future it must drastically change its attitudes towards organic and biological agriculture.

Between 97 and 99 per cent of all our vegetables and cereals are currently sprayed with one or more pesticides. Vegetables receive as many as 46 applications in a season, yet residues are hardly monitored and there are no legal limits. In 1981/2 there were 150 instances where the World Health Organisation's safe limits for nitrate content in ground drinking water supplies were exceeded. Eighty of these cases occurred in East Anglia. Other countries, notably the USA (2 per cent of the land organically farmed), France (1 per cent), Germany and China recognise the benefits of organic or low-input agriculture. Our Ministry of Agriculture does virtually no research into these systems, let alone encourage them on the farm. Yet their labour-intensive methods will be a positive social benefit.

The future growth of organic and biological systems are important: for the farmers, whose variable costs will inevitably diminish (and not necessarily be replaced by higher labour costs — why not have tax concessions on labour as well as machinery?), for the shopper able to buy safe and natural foods, and for wild species, who will no longer have to combat chemical hazards.

Energy efficient programmes will be an essential part of future agriculture. Energy consultant Gerald Leach has calculated that horse based rotation farming in the 1950s produced a probable ratio of food energy gained, to energy put in, of 200:1. By the 1970s this became 1000:1 — but if the hidden costs of fuel, electricity and petrochemicals were added a *loss* of 1:2 resulted. For the year 2000 the indirect use of solar energy through waste and residue utilisation (see Figure 6.1) should become common in anaerobic digestion and in the production of substitute liquid fuels from biomass projects. The direct use of solar energy will include water pumping, heating farm buildings, drying crops and glasshouse growing. And permaculture systems, the conscious use of ecological principles to design self-sustaining food, fibre and energy producing ecosystems, will probably be a familiar sight. Permaculture emphasises perennial rather than annual crops, high species diversity with close planting, and combines many varied activities — forestry, farming, aquaculture, grazing etc. — in close co-operation.

Inevitably agricultural and forestry activities will come under greater public control. While compensation payments for low income farmers, who have a high proportion of their land of special conservation interest, are a necessary incentive, so too is planning control over intensive developments. Such controls are needed particularly to regulate the activities of city-based institutional investors in farming (who have bought an average of 50,000 acres of land annually for the past five years) and agricultural and forestry development companies who specialise in improving marginal land. Both were unforeseen in 1947.

Development controls have successfully protected our most important urban heritage — Listed Buildings, Green Belts and Conservation areas. There is little reason why this familiar, practical system cannot help do the same for our natural heritage. Selective controls on major operations like felling ancient woodland, draining unspoilt wetlands or ploughing unimproved moorland will not freeze agricultural development. Rather it will give the wider community a democratic right to comment upon, suggest alternatives to, or deny if necessary, developments which demonstrably affect their environment.

Finally, we must ensure the highest protection for the most critical wildlife habitats — Sites of Special Scientific Interest. Like Listed Buildings they are irreplaceable cultural assets. Usually the result of hundreds of years of gentle evolution, once gone they cannot be recreated by planting a few trees or waving a packet of wildflower seeds like a magic wand.

Planning controls are not a panacea. If society wants to preserve living things it must also encourage their proper care. And grant aid is one way of doing that. So is education. For the future we must ask of our farmers and foresters new things. To look after the land and to care for its wild inhabitants as well as producing the food we want and need. If we can do that then conservation of rural wildlife communities will prosper at the turn of the century.

For the year 2000 it is no longer enough to rely on the platitudes and prejudices of many in the agricultural industries. Sentiments like 'the farms are our factory floors and we should be allowed to get on with production' or 'the countryside has always changed so it will be all right for the future' are not sufficient guarantees. The snakeshead fritillery was once so common along the flood plains of the Thames that it had a different nickname in every village. In the last 20 years it has been reduced to a handful of sites as a result of insensitive agricultural practices.

It is not just the loss of the species themselves that is important but also the larger cultural, social and economic losses for which they are indicators. People care about the countryside and their associations with its natural features. It is only right that in the coming years the countryside should be protected properly. Not as a living museum or as a food factory but rather as an environment supporting as wide a variety of occupations, habitats, wild species and people as possible.

Konrad Smigelski
Condensed from *Self-supporting Co-operative Village*, Building and Social Housing Foundation, 1978, pp. 19-20.

To quote John Seymour, 'The only alternative to capital-intensive, labour-free, large-scale farming is small-scale, labour-intensive farming.'

Another expert, Anthony Farmer, believes that in agriculture 'techniques of personal, small-scale multiculture could raise the food production of Britain by a factor many times greater than at present and at the same time promote the further evolution of the soil rather than detract from it as is the case under the present system of mechanical and chemical rape, fostered by the Ministry of Agriculture'.

Intensive market gardens can raise food production per acre to as much as four or five times the average level of industrial farming. Therefore, it is not surprising that in 1973 the net income of the 'growers' (market gardeners) was £3,500 while that of the farm workers was £1,400.

Even housing land, provided it has low density, is not completely lost to agriculture. Output per acre in gardens is so much higher than that under agricultural use, that the loss for building houses is more than compensated for.

The study of Hull School of Architecture revealed that a residential area with a density of 12 to 15 houses per acre contains vegetable gardens yielding 30 per cent of food and 60 per cent energy self-sufficiency. The study also pointed out that during the Second World War the number of allotment gardens

Figure 6.1: The Use of Waste Materials. Basic to the concept of organic farming is the ultimate return of animal and plant wastes to the soil. In this case, processing in a digester enables the methane gas given off by organic decomposition to be utilised before the organic residue is used on the land or forms the basis of fish farming.

Source: K. Smigelski.

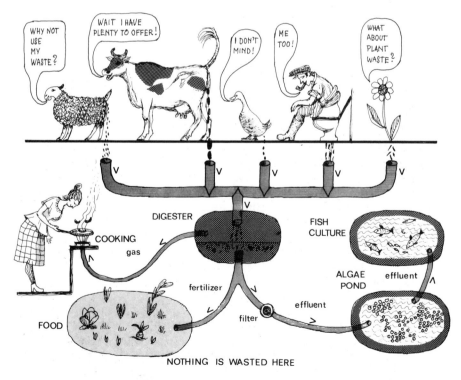

increased from 800,000 to 1,500,000, and that the 'dig for victory' trend made enormous contributions to the national food supply.

At the basis of 'organic farming' is concern about the soil. Soil is perhaps the most complex ecosystem in the biosphere. In many ways, less is known about it than about the surface of the moon. Soil consists of both the living and dead, the geological and biological. Microbes, animals, minerals, water, and gases all interact in a dynamic balance of life and death. The soil is not just a medium for holding plants upright; it is also a habitat for many living things, whose related activities feed the plants. And it is this biological energy in the soil that can be tapped to fertilise crops and give us food.

Chemical fertilisers and agricultural poisons disrupt that subtle balance of the soil, can permanently harm it and cause loss of soil fertility. But by adding organic matter in the form of natural fertilisers — compost, green manures, rock minerals, etc. — the balance of the soil is not disturbed (see Figure 6.1).

John Seymour, an advocate of organic farming, says:

> I farm three acres of my sixty-two acre farm very intensively. On that three acres, I suppose, I produce more calories, vitamins and all the rest of it, that the owner of an East Anglian barley-prairie does off any ten of his acres. And by drawing in produce from the rest of the farm, too, I keep a large family (generally eight of us) provided with bread, meat, all dairy produce, beer, vegetables in great variety, all soft fruit, increasingly more hard fruit. From hard experience, not from theory, I know that my sixty-two acres, once developed really intensively, would support thus completely at least six families the size of mine and also produce a large surplus for 'export' [see Figure 6.2] ... My own experience is that there is nothing like animal manure for making crops grow, nothing like pigs for clearing

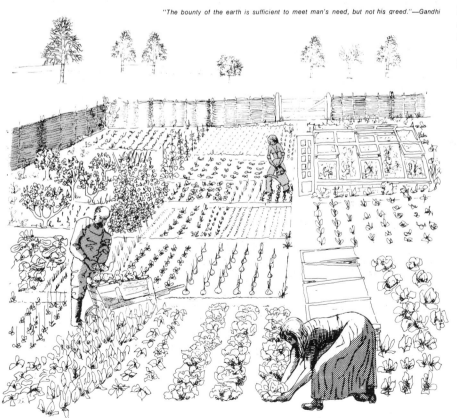

"The bounty of the earth is sufficient to meet man's need, but not his greed."—Gandhi

Figure 6.2: Smigelski's Vision of the Intensive Market Garden.

Source: K. Smigelski.

217

rough land, nothing like milk for making children grow up straight and strong (and you can't have milk without calves or kids — half of these will be male — what do you do with them if you don't eat them?), nothing like fresh eggs for putting me in a good temper in the morning.

The above quotation is most relevant to the design of the co-operative village at Stanford Hall.

Some farmers have investigated organic farming scientifically, and have shown that high yields and crops of excellent quality can be obtained with the use of only organic manures. Britain could go over to all organic farming and still feed itself, thus making itself free of imported fertilisers.

In conclusion, I would like to quote Kenneth Mellanby:

We need an efficient farming system, producing the foods that are needed to sustain the health of our population. I believe that with proper planning, a little self-sacrifice by the more carnivorous, and a joint effort by all sections of the community, we can build a better fed and more beautiful Britain in the future.

Nicholas Saunders
Subsistence Agriculture Roughly Compared to Commercial Farming
from *Alternative England and Wales*, 1975, p. 252.

A farmer has to produce eight times as much food as he can buy with the money he gets from selling his produce. And he has to work eight times as much land as he would need to grow his own food.

The same piece of land could supply food for:

One farmer like this:

He specialises in one product so as to earn as much as possible from his land. This needs expensive equipment, fuel and fertiliser or feedstuff. The high concentration of the same plants or animals opens up the risk of disease so he has to use insecticides and antibiotics. Non-standard products — like crooked carrots — are wasted, and so are some by-products like manure or straw.

Eight people like this:

They run a mixed smallholding where crops are fertilised by the animals' manure and the animals feed on some of the crops. With so much more manpower, expensive equipment is not needed and all their waste goes back to feed the animals or to fertilise their land.

Either way they end up with about the same amount of food.

This is just one kind of food and may be ready at one time of year only.

This is a variety of foods chosen so that there is always a supply all through the year.

So he sells it to buy other food to eat but some of it goes to pay off his equipment, fuel, fertiliser/feedstuff. And income tax!

So they all feed off it.

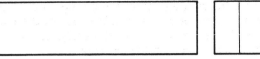

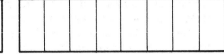

So he is left with only this to spend at the shops.

They get this much each.

But the shop's mark-up, processing, packaging, advertising, wastage, distribution and profits all along the line take three-quarters of what he spends.

They end up with fresh food — free-range, organically grown, and had the satisfaction of producing it. But they have to do more preparation. And eat what is ready rather than what takes their fancy that day.

So he gets only this much food.

It is attractively packaged; oven ready and his choice is enormous. But is it as good? Of course, he is not farming just to fill his belly — what he spends on food is only a small proportion of his income, like any other self-employed businessman. And so this piece of land is only a small proportion of what he has to farm to live off.

Simple methods take much more labour, but probably not eight times as much so they work no more for their food. Of course, they can't produce all their food (like tea or sugar) and need to buy other things too — so they can't live entirely off the land this way. But they could all earn less or two of the eight could produce their food.

Roger Grimley
(This article was written specifically for this book.)

Traditionally, farming has been seen as a way of life but economic pressures are bringing about a change in attitudes. It is becoming increasingly recognised that the farmer is a link in the food chain and if he is to survive and prosper he must change from a producer who is far removed from the market to a marketing-orientated food producing businessman.

At present the UK natural average yield of wheat is about six tonnes per hectare but this disguises a very wide range of performance by individual growers. Those at the top of the range are increasingly confident of their ability to achieve consistently 12 to 14 tonnes per hectare — more than double the average.

To achieve this productivity an intensive growing system is adopted with great attention paid to detail. There is an understanding of the soil and its structure and a realisation that it is a very sensitive medium. Seeds are planted with great precision and the plant is manipulated throughout its growing cycle. Chemical plant growth regulators allow the grower to maximise the use of nitrogen which is the fuel for production. Technical training has given growers a wider knowledge of the components of yield. It allows intelligent decisions to combat potential restraints on yields such as pests, diseases and weather. Machinery design reflects the desire to preserve soil structure with flotation tyres and wide-boom sprayers increasingly utilised.

What is the natural progression from this approach to food production and what effects would such a change have upon the use and shape of the country-side?

As the Common Agricultural Policy becomes increasingly difficult to finance pressure on growers will increase. Either costs will increase faster than returns or costs will continue to rise while returns actually decrease.

What can the farmer do to combat this? He has relatively high fixed costs and, therefore, the option to reduce inputs and restrict production is limited. Alternatively, he can take advantage of the technical advances to increase yield while at the same time, by intelligent use of seed, fertiliser and agri-chemicals, reduce his production costs per unit. Only those growers on land most suited to a particular type of food production and whose scale of business is large enough to allow economic costs of production will survive.

As the farmer becomes more attuned to his potential markets he will realise that the consumer wants adequate supplies of conveniently packaged food at reasonable prices. The present system is more likely to produce quantities in excess of demand at a total cost which is not perceived to be reasonable.

Therefore, a careful study of market opportunities and the economics of production will need to be undertaken. Let us take these trends and extend them into the possible 'ideal' farmer of the future.

Cropping. The farmer is able to produce protein, starch, fibre and oils and with advances in plant breeding a range of crops can be foreseen:

Cereals — High protein cereals with high yield potential used for processing into human foodstuffs or via animal feed and livestock into protein rich foodstuffs. The starch would also be converted to sugar, then fermented to alcohol. The straw would be suitable for industrial purposes or incorporation into feed for ruminants.

Legumes — Peas, beans, soyabeans for protein.

Oil Crops — Oilseed Rape for cooking oil and for industrial use.

Roots — High in sugar for human use and conversion to alcohol.

Grass — For conversion through livestock into meat and dairy products.

It would be possible to produce energy economically from cereals and then avoid the energy intensive processing by feeding grain on the farm to cold-water fish capable of converting the grain into meat efficiently.

Livestock would be housed with cattle, sheep, poultry and pigs being the 'processing unit' converting cereals or grass, etc. into meat, milk or other products.

Farming Operations. Day-to-day control of the business would be centred on an operations room. To this, information would be fed from a series of sensors placed evenly over the land area. With a computer link this would provide instant management information on micro-climate, plant growth stage, pests, diseases, weeds, etc.

The farm manager would be aware of the potential reduction in yield or quality as well as the cost of controls.

A series of computer controlled pipelines and gantries would be used to apply pesticides for control of fertilisers for growth and for irrigation. Initially fertiliser would all be in liquid form and agrochemicals would be applied singly, rather than in water, with electrostatically charged droplets to ensure that the chemicals adhere to the crop. Increasingly all fertiliser needs would be met by the management of bacteria in the soil to fix atmospheric nitrogen and sulphur. Nitrogen fixing molecules would also be bred into plants. Similarly biological methods would be extended to counter pests and diseases.

At harvest cereals would be cut, chopped and blown into containers. These would be taken to an industrial plant where the cut crop would be dried, separated and processed. The grain would be cleaned, weighed and cooled before storage. Straw would be separated into feed fraction, for chemical treatment and use as animal feed, or straight parts for industrial use. A 'total harvest' approach would be used for other crops.

The staff of a unit would consist of two people: one manager (an applied biologist) and one technician (computer expert).

Environment. A farm would consist of a regular pattern of 'fields' with no need for hedges for identification but advantages to be obtained from a series of (possibly moveable) wind-breaks. The unit would have to be of an economic size, probably large by today's standards. A 2,000-hectare block, three miles long and three miles wide could be envisaged.

It would not be possible to allow for a public access on such a unit but in view of the considerably higher production per hectare only about half the existing farming area would be required to produce the same quantity of crop.

In order to ensure that at no time were crops stressed by adverse climatic conditions either crops would be produced in glasshouses or removeable plastic bubbles utilised.

To optimise the climatic variations in the country, farms in the eastern half would predominantly produce cereals, legumes and roots while those in the west would treat grass as a crop using arable methods.

It would then be possible to devote marginal farm land, often in areas of scenic beauty, to leisure pursuits and the conservation of wildlife with enhanced facilities for public access and enjoyment while retaining prime farming land for food production.

Containment and Planning: A Critical Future

The next two pieces express views about the short-term future. The late Robin Best, undoubtedly one of the country's leading specialists on land-use, briefly summarises the state of play over agricultural land-loss to urban development before emphasising the critical role that town and country planners have in maintaining this land exchange balance into the future. John Daldry, in a letter to the Royal Town Planning Institute, calls for a more innovative and sensitive use of green belts.

Robin Best
Condensed from 'Are We Really Losing the Land?', *Town and Country Planning*, vol. 53, no. 1, January 1984, p. 11.

National rates of agriculture/urban transfer are not distributed equally over the whole of England and Wales. Far from it. Since 1945, there have been statistics to show farmland loss to urban growth by counties.

They demonstrate clearly that change has been concentrated in a wide corridor — the so-called axial belt — stretching from Merseyside in the north-west down through the Midlands, to London and the south-east coast. There are also two outliers in north-east England and south Wales/Avon.

The remainder of the country is relatively untouched by urban encroachment, and this includes our most valuable and productive agricultural areas down the east coast, and particularly in East Anglia. Large parts of good farmland in southern England are also little affected.

Another interesting feature of regional change is that its emphasis within the axial belt has altered considerably over time. Up to the mid-1950s, urban extension onto farmland was particularly concentrated in the London Region, especially to the north-west of the metropolis where new town development was going ahead strongly.

In marked contrast to the 1960s it was the north-west of the country (and, to some extent, the Midlands) which was showing the most vigorous change, while the London region faded away in its urban growing rates.

This reflected the redevelopment and the peripheral, greenfield relocation of people in and around many nineteenth-century northern cities. Conversely, in the south-east, development consisted increasingly of infilling without the take-up of a great deal of new farmland.

The latter half of the 1970s again saw a shift in locational emphasis. The former strength of urban development and farmland loss in the north-west has diminished relatively to the south-east so that the axial belt now shows no very marked variations throughout its length. The north-east and south Wales/Avon outliers still stand out as distinct entities.

These patterns of urban encroachment often bear little relationship to changes in population. The surge of urban expansion in the 1930s has already been mentioned, but this was at a period when population growth was experiencing one of its lowest rates of increase.

Similarly, in the 1960s, the highest rates of urban growth were in the north-west where some counties were showing an actual decline in population — and vice versa in the south-east. The spread of population away from the large towns towards more rural areas, as noted in the 1981 census, is also not noticeably reflected in shifts in agricultural/urban land-use at present.

Such discrepancies between rates of population and land-use change give a useful warning against too facile an approach to the interpretation of alterations in living space. Conventionally, urban growth has been closely associated with population growth in the minds of most people and indeed of many planners.

In modern times, however, this relationship is not nearly so close as it once was. The main reason is that, in the last 50 years at any rate, changes in standards of urban living space, or the increase or lowering of densities of development have frequently been substantial and persistent enough to override completely the demands on land made by population change alone. An important part of this process is the increasing formation of smaller households.

The containment and guidance of new urban growth over the last few decades into acceptable patterns of development has been largely brought about by careful planning control.

Such control could crucially assist in future years in keeping a desirable balance of land use between town and countryside; between urban use and rural use. But this presupposes that our system of town and country planning is allowed to continue in the same effective way as it has done since 1947.

Unfortunately, an increasing antipathy to planning — often ill-founded — is apparent as the years go by, and the present government is expressing this attitude very strongly in its actions.

For the first time ever, legislation has been introduced under the Local Government Planning and Land Act of 1980 which, in practice, weakens planning constraints. Several DoE circulars have shifted emphasis in this direction as well.

These events have also to be seen in relation to the new administrative structure of local government since 1974 in which many of the planning responsibilities of county authorities have been transferred to the district level. This has meant the removal of a valuable and more detached 'refereeing' element in the determination of planning decisions.

If nothing is done to arrest these trends, increased urban pressures, as and when the economy improves, and reduced planning constraints could combine to produce a new upsurge in urban development at the expense of agricultural and other rural land. Surely we do not have to learn the environmental lessons of the 1930s all over again?

John Daldry
Condensed from 'Reassessing Green Belt Boundaries', *Planner News*, February 1984, no. 4.

I believe the establishment of green belts is one of planning's greatest achievements. However, as a practising consultant operating very often in green belt areas, I am aware of many parcels of green belt land which do not make a positive contribution to the aims and objectives of the green belt policy and where some form of development would considerably improve the environmental quality of the area.

I am, therefore, in full agreement with the Royal Town Planning Institute that the detailed boundaries of the green belt should be drawn more carefully to exclude land parcels that do not make a contribution to the general mass of green and open landscape, which should be the character of the green belt.

I would like to see authorities adopting more positive attitudes towards planning applications which enhance rather than harm the green belt. Authorities should not rely solely upon the established strength of the green belt as a reason for refusal without considering whether or not the land which is the subject of the application is correctly zoned as part of the green belt. Often, in my experience, small sites are presented which make no meaningful contribution to the green belt but the Authority uses green belt policy to relieve themselves of the obligation to consider other material considerations which, without the green belt policy, they would be obliged to take into account.

One hears talk of the possibility of new villages being created in the green belt, which presumably would be constructed on open green belt land and such development will be of no real or economic benefit to existing small communities within the green belt. I believe that there is sufficient land to be found within existing green belt settlements which can be more readily developed without detriment to the general open nature of green belt land, and I sincerely hope that in some cases existing green belt boundaries will be reassessed.

Alternative Rural Life-styles

The two contributions to this section again move into a more distant and perhaps utopian future for village communities. Andrew Page outlines the main ideas behind the model for a high technology, ecologically sound village community of the future based on studies at the Dartington Institute.

The Greentown Group was formed with the intention of planning, building and living in a village community with some similar ideas to those expressed in the Dartington model. In extracts from its submission to Milton Keynes Development Corporation some of the Group's ideas, both in terms of the community and the environment, are outlined.

Finally, an annotated diagram from *Radical Technology* edited by Boyle and Harper gives some of these approaches visual expression (see Figure 6.4).

Andrew Page
Condensed from 'The Dartington Model of the Community for the Future' in *Future Communities*, Institute of Contemporary Arts, 1981.

The village community model attempts to draw together many strands of new and long established thought; to address directly some key present-day problems, notably: energy shortage, unemployment and environmental deterioration; and to reconcile two incipient revolutions — the 'green' or ecological movement and the microelectronics era.

The conceptual model, given visual expression in Figure 6.3 is based upon the following cardinal ideas:

A community of appropriate size — say 2000 people — large enough to embrace many skills and to justify a range of communal services; and small enough to be comprehended as a social unit by all who live there.

The re-integration of daily life, through the creation of a social and physical environment in which citizens of any age may within close proximity find home, work, school, leisure activity, shops, community government, caring schemes and much else.

A high degree of self-sufficiency, in that the community would contain many of its own services, produce much of its own food, provide more than its energy needs, make many goods and products for use and sale — without attempting to be an economic island.

Local action in that the community would be in significant degree self-governing, providing many of the social, education and welfare services normally provided by larger local authorities.

Co-operation, through which the residents would work together on many common tasks and services, thus gaining the 'synergetic' effect whereby the sum of local initiatives is greater than the parts.

A pooling of built space, whereby private dwellings are modest in size and communal spaces — such as library, school, crèche, village hall, health centre — are large and versatile, so placed in the centre of the community that they encourage participation and interpersonal contact.

A close link between people and the land, with labour-intensive farming, gardening and forestry and a chance for all to be involved in these production activities and in the processing of food and timber products.

The appropriate use of high and low technology — within a single communal life-style, high technology in information, education, control of energy flows and some production processes; low technology in the production, by the community, of food, clothes, utensils and many household goods.

One person, many jobs — by so doing (within or beyond the village) a mixture of jobs in the course of the week or year, each individual would develop varied skills, gain a balance of satisfactions (of kinds which many now secure only through leisure), and serve the needs (both simple and sophisticated) of the community.

Economy and self-sufficiency in energy — by means of energy conservation (building design, heat transfers, monitoring of energy flows, minimising of transport, recycling of materials) and local energy production from renewable resources (sun, wind, water, biogas, wood, waste materials).

Low-cost, non-intensive transport — a community free of cars; bicycle, electric or horse-drawn transport only within the community; a transport depot for breaking or forming loads, communal forms of transport further afield.

Respect for, and co-operation with, nature — use of organic fertilisers and natural pesticides; avoidance of all pollution; abundant landscaping, with native plants and high wildlife content; communal lake to act as reservoir, heat-store, fish pond, pleasure-ground and fire fighting source.

Life-long education, with nursery school (and constant crèche), primary school, skill training, library, links to schools and to Open University, adult education, work experience and learning through work.

User group first — the form and functioning of the community to be conceived by its potential residents; its creation and maintenance governed by those who live there.

Common ownership — the land, infrastructure, communal space and buildings to be owned by the community, all residents having shares in common property, all private property being built on lease with provision for the community to benefit from appreciation of values.

A village levy — paid by each individual in cash or in labour — this would secure the creation of some, and the maintenance of all communal services.

Greentown
Condensed from 'Draft Proposal for the Development of Crownhill Site', Document for submission to the Milton Keynes Development Corporation, July 1981, pp. 10, 12 and 19.

We view the environment, broadly separated into buildings and open space, as one interconnected and continually readjusting ecological unity. Therefore, not only are the buildings designed to make maximum use of natural energy resources (see below), but also open space is viewed primarily as a natural food producing zone.

The method of food production will not only be ecologically orientated but also geared to fit in with the educational views of the community. The relaxing influence of water will play an important role in the environment, as will the fruit-bearing, ornamental and buffering attributes of trees. We intend to live and work in as natural an environment as possible.

The housing and communal buildings will be grouped together, filling out the centre of the site, in order to create an intimate atmosphere. However, this built-up zone will be low and the streets will be virtually car-free. Vehicles will be left near the entry zone to the site in various car-parks and garages and only be allowed into most of the built-up area in exceptional circumstances. The streets will not be wide, will vary in width as need arises and will not require roadside landscaping. The network of lanes will not resemble any grid pattern but rather reflect the need of the inhabitants to get from one place to another. The irregularity of the junctions, road widths and patterns will not preclude emergency access by fire or ambulance services to all areas.

Trees and small open spaces will be interspersed among the concentration of buildings within the built-up zone. There will be a market square in the centre and a village green probably to the south and each cluster of buildings will have its garden or gardens. The residents within the housing clusters will decide how their gardens will be arranged and used. Beyond the built-up area the land will be cultivated primarily for vegetables and fruit, although a certain amount of animal husbandry will also be given space. It is felt that the educational and recreational aspects of the latter outweigh its commercial or purely food-producing benefits.

To the south and higher end of the site space has already been allocated for an uncultivated peace zone and meditation sanctuary, although orchards and grazing may still take place here. There will also be a small lake with a stream or streams to be run off and through the built-up area. If feasible a small fish farm will be established in order to make greater use of this facility. In the initial entry zone land will be largely given over to the visitors' hostel/storage building, entry road, car parks and garages, with gardens around the buildings and between the car spaces. It is envisaged that the houses at this end of the built-up area will have relatively immediate vehicle access. It is hoped that the community will have responsibility to maintain the boundary areas to the south and west of the site in conjunction with the local authority.

Thus the whole site will give the appearance of a cultivated parkland, interspersed and surrounded by trees, enclosing an intimate built-up area of clustered and ecologically designed buildings.

The importance of the community in its social context is that it will provide an open and non-threatening atmosphere in which the conventional barriers that alienate people can be dissolved. We hope to foster a community in which people can live and grow in a peaceful, joyous and caring interdependence. Learning is a life-process. It should never stop and we can all learn from each other, whatever our ages and abilities. Education, health and cultural activities will be geared to fulfil this aim.

The running of the community will be structured to incorporate this free exchange of skills, ideas and knowledge. A genuinely co-operative society

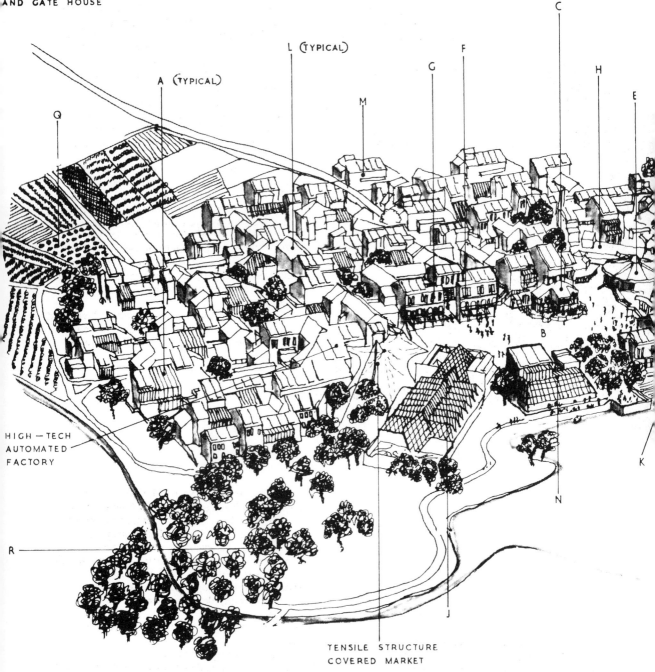

TO CAR PARK, VISITOR CENTRE,
AND GATE HOUSE

L (TYPICAL)

A (TYPICAL)

C

M

F

G

H

Q

E

HIGH — TECH
AUTOMATED
FACTORY

B

K

N

R

J

TENSILE STRUCTURE
COVERED MARKET

Key:

A HOUSING High density layout, maximum four-storey height, modular components with details designed by the occupier, the dwellings small but with adequate privacy. Designed for energy conservation with integral solar panels and conservatories, interspersed with gardens, workshops, offices, retail shops and other amenities.

B CENTRAL MARKET-PLACE As a focus of the community and of all routes within it. Setting of main public facilities, venue for open-air events. Free of motorised vehicles.

C CAFE-CUM-PUB Open 24 hours a day (self-service late at night) with outdoor terrace, open to all comers.

D MULTI-PURPOSE VILLAGE HALL For lectures, theatre, cinema, other cultural activities, sports, meetings, worship, peripatetic services.

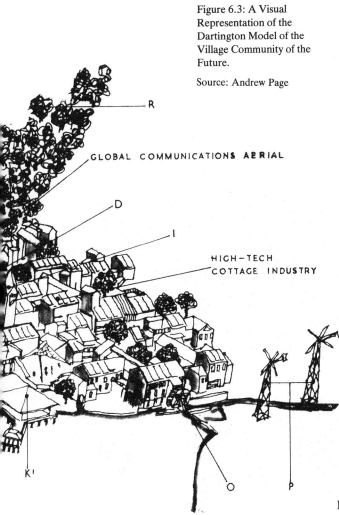

Figure 6.3: A Visual Representation of the Dartington Model of the Village Community of the Future.

Source: Andrew Page

R

GLOBAL COMMUNICATIONS AERIAL

D

I

HIGH-TECH COTTAGE INDUSTRY

K¹

O

P

LAKE

G LEARNING EXCHANGE Learning and skills sharing (secondary, university level and adult education) utilising television, Open University and Open School, and computers within personal tutorial programme. Tools Library and Mutual Aid Centre, including DIY repair and maintenance of domestic and workshop appliances. Arts laboratory.

H CRÈCHE, NURSERY SCHOOL & PRIMARY SCHOOL Operating constantly with a toy library.

I OUTLOOK TOWER Giving citizens and visitors a whole view of the settlement. Symbol of spiritual aspiration.

J SPA A health centre with swimming-baths (within solarium which is also a plant nursery and for cultivation of subtropical food), sauna, gymnasium, yoga room, rooms for the practice of alternative therapies; link to Motherhood House and Cottage Hospital. Village laundry using the Spa's heat.

K INN & HOSTEL Accommodating visitors and those attending courses; guest rooms for friends and relatives of villagers (compensating for resident's relatively small private dwellings). Restaurant adjoining (K¹).

L WORKSHOPS Of which there are others. Some used for food processing, some small-scale technology, many employment intensive, crafts, enterprises.

M TRANSPORT DEPOT With warehouse for breaking and forming loads and for storing bulk purchases or village produce. Base for communal transport (car-pool for outside travel, fleet of bicycle carts and horse-drawn wagon for transport within). Community garage (DIY maintenance and repair).

N AQUACULTURE CENTRE (Fish Farming) and waterworks adjoining lake. acting as reservoir, heat store, fish-pond, pleasure ground, fire-fighting water source.

O WATERWHEEL Rotational for hydro-electric generators.

P WINDMILLS Aerogenerators.

Q ALLOTMENTS Extending out from village perimeter into green belt.

R GREEN WEDGE Coming into centre of the community with fruit and nut bearing trees, fast growing copse, some allotments.

Not shown on scale model:

S VISITOR CENTRE Car parking and gatehouse.

T WASTE RECYCLING PLANT Methane and other biogas works.

U SANCTUARY Retreat for prayer and meditation.

V GREEN BELT For allotments, mixed crop agricultural land, small holdings and woodlands.

E COTTAGE OFFICE A 'resource centre' offering computer facilities, public telephones, message centre and answering service. Television with Teletext, Viewdata and other link-up, telex, Xerox machine, secretarial and accounting services, etc. Post Office, Village Bank, office and printing press for village newspaper and publishing. CB radio station. Centre for community energy monitoring, skills and needs matching and co-ordination of residents maintenance of public services. Centre for lateral network communications world-wide — global village concept.

F LIBRARY Books, periodicals, audio and video tapes. Records.

Figure 6.4: The Autonomous Housing Estate. A pictorial representation of what an ecologically planned and designed housing estate might look like. Some housing is independent of 'main' services. Waste treatment, some food space and water heating are provided at household level. Others — electricity, water, gas and some food — are provided at community level to enjoy economies of scale.

Key
1 Solar roof
2 Conservatory
3 Vegetables
4 Savonius rotor (pumping)
5 Windpump
6 Water tower
7 Wind generator
8 Methane digester
9 Power regulation, battery
  store

gives people more chance to realise their individual potential without the pressure of competition and fear of failure. We envisage a situation where such roles as teacher/pupil, doctor/patient may be interchangeable, with the emphasis being laid on personal awareness and responsibility.

The community will have a resource centre, or learning exchange, with certain basic facilities for people of all ages.

The building will be a mixture of hard and soft; some rigid classrooms, where formal teaching could take place; then in contrast, free areas where people can relax, lounging around and chatting; and intermediate zones where learning can be done informally. The design must be imaginative and flexible, with interesting but unlabelled areas — deliberately left incomplete in places, so that users can create their own environment and change it, daily or hourly if desired.

Equipment should include a computer, and all kinds of audio-visual materials, freely accessible, so that everyone gets used to handling these essential tools of modern society. Use would be made of TV programmes, films, slides, tapes, etc., and students would be encouraged to produce their own. There should be a good library, equipment and facilities for music, sports, art, science and mathematics, cooking, drama and reprographic centre. Several rooms will be made available for use as a health clinic. We believe that our health is our own responsibility and that it is directly affected by our life-style, including diet, activities, environment and thought. Through meetings and workshops we hope to exchange advice and information which will help each one of us to a better balanced and more harmonious way of life as we learn to be aware of our own particular needs.

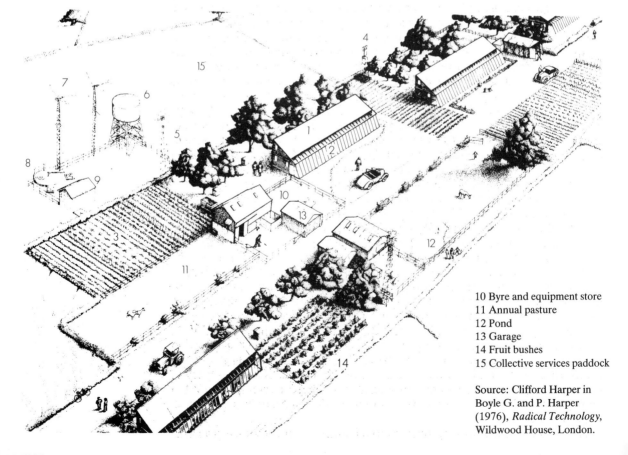

10 Byre and equipment store
11 Annual pasture
12 Pond
13 Garage
14 Fruit bushes
15 Collective services paddock

Source: Clifford Harper in Boyle G. and P. Harper (1976), *Radical Technology*, Wildwood House, London.

The building will be used by the whole community and should be open not only in normal working hours, but also on evenings, weekends and holidays. The users will be responsible for cleaning the building and minor maintenance. The centre will be democratically run, major decisions being made by consensus in weekly meetings, open to everyone, including, of course, children.

As the community grows, these facilities will be expanded and separate buildings added as required, for example, more sports facilities, a health centre, small theatre/concert hall, etc.

A Considered Overview

Finally, the leading pioneer in the development of countryside planning and land-use since the war, Emeritus Professor Gerald Wibberley, outlines his personal priorities for the development of our future countryside in all of the spheres discussed so far. This contribution was written on his retirement from Wye and University Colleges, both of the University of London.

Gerald Wibberley
Extracted from 'Countryside Planning. A Personal Evaluation',
Occasional Paper no. 7, Department of Environmental Studies and
Countryside Planning, Wye College, October, 1982, pp. 30-3.

The word 'concern' is a useful one. It is used especially by Quakers, to emphasise problems where personal and group involvement is thought to be worthwhile. Let me attempt to point out my areas of rural concern.

We should first consider those matters which have been with us for many decades. There remains the thorny issue of the allocation of open agricultural land to new land uses of a permanent character. Are the problems here the same today as before or have they significantly altered? The present position has, I believe, been admirably surveyed by my colleague Robin Best in his book *Land Use and Living Space*. I would certainly subscribe to his conclusion that knowledge of recent changes in the main uses of land in Britain should result in quiet confidence and not induce a state of alarm. Best shows by his evidence and argument that the alarmist statements expressed from time to time over the past 40 years are either completely false or grossly exaggerated. Nevertheless, a decentralised and weaker statutory planning system could throw us back towards a more scattered kind of urban growth, especially in the south of England, although high farmland prices would probably still act as a brake on loose housing densities. In any case the growth of 'science parks' and computer/microprocessor-type industry will take place in the more prosperous and attractive living areas of southern England at the expense of the wetter and colder west and north.

Over the years there has been the added fear that the quality of farmland being taken for urban development is well above average. Early research work given in my book *Agriculture and Urban Growth* showed this statement to be partly true. Ever since 1944 attempts have been made through the Ministry of Agriculture to shift urban development onto the poorer quality farmland. For five years I dealt with such matters on an *ad hoc* basis. Since then the methods used for evaluating farmland in relation to new uses have involved changing systems of physical land classification. Increasingly complicated techniques have been tried and tested with possibly the most sophisticated being used in the agricultural evidence provided to the Roskill Commission dealing with the choice of a third London airport. It is, however, a personal disappointment that very simplistic measures of agricultural land value are still being used in most planning decisions — little better in the 1980s than the ones being used in the 1940s.

As for the concept of long-term national land-use and resource planning, we have really made little progress over the past half-century. It could well be that this is because national plans of this nature are an unrealistic concept. How we use our land is a result of changes in people's circumstances, needs and desires, in their real wealth and in their attitudes, particularly as shown by the interaction of interest and political groups. Can anyone say, at this time, that we are all agreed as to what society needs with regard to agriculture and food, our policies for nature conservation and the size and nature of our afforestation programme? As a nation we have lost the simplified general agreement which seemed to be present in the decades following the Second World War. We know now, however, that the apparent national unity on land-use matters at that time was based on a precarious foundation, underneath which the pace of technical and economic change was increasing, especially in the agricultural industry.

An important current theme in rural affairs is the changing role of the agricultural industry in rural land-use in most developed industrialised nations. The agricultural land budget has for long been more favourable in this and other European countries than many people have thought. For many of these countries the situation is continuing to improve because of the fairly rapid advance towards the food self-sufficiency of many Western nations. This is markedly so in Britain, particularly in the temperate food products given guaranteed price support by the British Government since 1947. In these early years of the 1980s we are at, or close to, 100 per cent self-sufficiency in cereals with homegrown wheat at more than 85 per cent, illustrating the success of new milling varieties. Eggs, poultry, meat, main crop potatoes, liquid milk and pork are all now completely home produced, the only significant shortages being among the meats in lamb, bacon and ham. Even the British contributions to total home needs of sugar, butter and cheese are increasing fast.

The movement towards complete self-sufficiency in temperate foods was particularly marked in Britain during the 1970s. The implications of this for rural land-use and countryside planning in the future are tremendous. They include the suggestion that the physical size of British agriculture no longer needs to grow, unless we move into extensive farming systems for other reasons or the country becomes a permanent food exporter. It should also mean that intensive farming systems can be complemented by more extensive land uses in designated National Parks and Areas of Outstanding Natural Beauty and in areas thought to be important for outdoor recreation and large-scale nature conservation. It could also mean that afforestation and farming could become more, rather than less, complementary in the hills and uplands. Finally we could move agricultural policy into a combination of food production and conservation using mixed price signals to encourage new and necessary forms of multiple land-use. If there is not recognition of this improving situation by the Government, or by agricultural policy-makers or interest groups, there will be increasing conflict between continued agricultural intensification and other land-uses, especially in those upland and lowland areas where these other land-uses have a strong case. Agricultural policy, as it is now executed, will look increasingly idiotic for the nation as a whole and particularly in these areas of dispute.

What of problems elsewhere in the rural economy? These are primarily of a social and economic nature and involve a number of developments, which include the continual decline of agriculture as an employer, both directly on farms and in the provision of local services. Accordingly, there is still a concern to improve the amount and the mix of non-agricultural employment in rural areas. In addition, improvements in the housing supply and its conditions are also required, especially for local members of the rural population who are needed to underpin the local economy but who are less fortunate in their wealth, political power and private and family mobility. There are now moves to improve local physical and social services in rural areas through both statutory and voluntary agencies, but there is still a need for greater concern about the inequity of opportunity and treatment between the two sexes, and between different social groups, in the modern countryside.

The increase between 1971 and 1981 in the total population of rural areas masks a change in the character of rural residents. As young people continue to stream away from the more remote rural areas owing to lack of jobs and social contacts, older and retired people come back home or move into selected properties and settlements. Their needs and their contributions to local economies are real but are very different from those of young people. These changing migration patterns, linked with constant improvement in personal and general interactions with the outside world through micro-electronic inventions could mean some very changed attitudes to the physical marginality, and the reality of inaccessibility, in rural areas which are now thought to be remote in character. We may be seeing a strengthening counter-urbanisation trend in Britain, with rural areas increasing in population and activities, with rural problems taking a larger share of national concern and with new life-styles coming to the fore.

What of the politicisation of the countryside? There are several movements here. There has been the substantial increase in the membership of environmental groups from people who live in both rural and urban areas. New pressure groups have also arisen of which one of the more surprising is *Rural Voice*. This potentially powerful amalgam of rural interest groups has within it different and opposing views on some things (especially on land-use matters) but is united in its concern about living conditions and working possibilities in the countryside. The older political parties tend to have orthodox and 'conservative' views about rural policies. But there are changes of view occurring in the Labour Party, and the new alliance of Social Democrats and Liberals is producing policy statements which show an awareness both of the nature of environmental issues and of the conflicts of interest between different social groups. None the less, these slight changes in political awareness have to be set within a decision-making framework in rural districts which still contains a strong element of agricultural fundamentalism.

There is, then, an encouraging spread of knowledge of the complexity of rural matters, but is it adequate? The teaching of environmental matters in schools is now much better but, as it can sometimes be heavily ecological and conservationist, it might be said to induce and perpetuate hostility to established land users like farmers and foresters. We will need to change this. Knowledge and awareness of environmental matters are fighting still to gain a respectable place in the teaching of agriculturalists, agricultural scientists and agricultural economists, both at agricultural colleges and in University faculties of agriculture. It is still, sadly, an uphill battle. On the other hand, during the past decade the understanding of the complexity of the problems in the rural economy has increased in the training of young entrants to the planning profession. While this spread of knowledge is greatly helped by the increased numbers of books, monographs and articles on rural planning produced in the last decade, it is still true to say that the strong interest groups concerned tend only to read the books and journals which cater for their own particular point of view.

When I am lecturing on rural planning matters in Europe I am quite often asked what is the basic philosophy that should underlie countryside planning activities? (It is curious that this question is seldom raised by British audiences.) The reply I give is that the decision made and executed should increase and widen opportunities in rural areas — in activities, services and land uses. Each one of us is a partial prisoner of our personal backgrounds and my answer reflects my own feelings of deprivation of local opportunities when I was a youth. But I still commend the answer to the reader.

7
Who's to Change?

Introduction

'Will you tell me please, which way I ought to go from here?'
'That depends a great deal on where you want to get to,' said the Cat.
'I don't much care where,' said Alice.
'Then it doesn't matter which way you go,' said the Cat.
'— so long as I get somewhere,' Alice added.
Lewis Carroll, *Alice in Wonderland.*

Chapter 6 has been concerned with presenting a number of personal visions of the future of the countryside of England and Wales. These develop, and in places contrast with the suggested 'actions to steer change' proposed in each of the Chapters 2 to 5 which were offered as the most probable immediate future for each of the subjects discussed. This book so far then has given a number of perspectives on *what* the future of the changing countryside might be, and Chapter 6 has made a brief incursion into *how* these changes might take place. The purpose of this last chapter is to consider, more directly, the issue of *how* changes in the countryside might occur.

Considering how change might take place centres on an investigation of the policy framework and the use of policy instruments or tools that do or might shape the countryside. It is these policies and instruments that will determine the nature of change. Discussing policy also provides a common theme with which to draw together the disparate notions discussed in the book so far.

In discussing a policy framework for the changing countryside, this chapter provides, it is hoped, a catalyst for the reader in developing a personal approach to understanding, and speculating upon, this change. To this end, in this final chapter, related themes are pursued. The first of these draws upon all of the 'Who Benefits, Who Loses?' sections in Chapters 2 to 5 in speculating upon who might, in aggregate, be the relative beneficiaries and losers in the full spectrum of the changing countryside. Such a speculation is, of course, open to a number of interpretations and the reader is encouraged to develop these for his or her self.

From this discussion, elements of the policy basis that provide a prime influence on change in the countryside are considered. Here, the principal policy effects that usefully can be borne in mind when contemplating any changes in policy are looked at in terms of their efficiency and distributional fairness. It is important to be aware of these two types of effect since this will help in developing an understanding of the consequences of modifying existing policies for the countryside.

Next, the nature of rural policy as a totality in England and Wales is introduced and some of the problems associated with policy formulation are identified. Particular attention is given to the current policy context, where rural policies are sectoral and uncoordinated — characteristics that often lead to policy conflicts. The question of what policy tools actually are available to influence the changing countryside is then addressed. Examining this portfolio in a comprehensive way provides the reader with a 'bag of tools' that he or she may begin to use creatively in shaping the countryside.

Some worked examples of how existing policy instruments might be used in different ways or how policies might be modified in certain respects are then provided. This is done as a means of encouraging the reader to think about policy innovations. A number of instances of policy change that are the subject of current debate are cited, to give the reader an understanding of the degree of realism that other innovations might command.

The final section of the book summaries a notion of increasing currency in the countryside, which is the move towards programmes or plans of integrated rural development where the traditional sectoral policies and policy instruments are abandoned in favour of more comprehensive all-embracing approaches to steering the changing countryside.

Who Are the Beneficiaries and Who Are the Losers Overall?

From the 'Who benefits, Who loses?' sections of Chapters 2 to 5, it is clear that overall a great diversity of people and organisations suffer disadvantages and enjoy advantages in the changing countryside. Indeed, any one group of people may be disadvantaged by certain elements of change, but benefit from others. To be exhaustive in summarising this situation, therefore, would be to rewrite the book.

As a stimulus to the reader, however, it is useful here, rather than looking at the effects of change on various people, to consider examples of those people affected by change and (as a specific group) to assess their relative position vis à vis benefits and losses. These people affected by change have included farmers, landowners, rural in-migrants, indigenous rural dwellers, recreationists, conservationists, scientists and ecologists, agricultural support industries and even less directly, the whole of the British population and the rest of the trading world.

In considering two examples from this list, rural landowners are affected by changes discussed in each of the issues chapters of this book. In the context of agriculture, landowners have enjoyed increases in land values in agricultural use at a rate considerably in excess of the rate of inflation. Although they have faced the burden, usually, of the provision of fixed capital in the agricultural enterprise, particularly under the landlord-tenant system, they have enjoyed a high degree of eligibility for grant-aid through the structural support directives of the Common Agricultural Policy. Further advantages in an agricultural context include tax rollover provisions in selling and repurchasing agricultural land, and rate relief on agricultural holdings.

In the context of containing settlements, the landowner is constrained almost totally by the development control process in how he might dispose of his land to non-agricultural or forestry uses. Because of this, landowners in the 'shadow' of development may suffer a degree of 'blight' on their land with the attendant problems of land fragmentation and trespass. On the other hand, the conversion of land out of agricultural use will lead to planning gain, which may be in excess of 1,000 per cent in financial terms.

The landowner has a greater burden of responsibility in conserving the wild. The common ethos that the landowner is the custodian of the land places him increasingly in the public eye if 'improvements' to the land have detrimental conservation consequences. Because of this, the landowner and his representative body, the Country Landowners Association, must spend more time debating in the political arena which, it may be postulated, leaves less time available for developing good husbandry practices. The landowner, however, does have some incentives to conserve through, for example, management agreements and compensation payments in certain 'valued' landscapes.

In sustaining rural communities, landowners often have a traditional role of 'social' custodianship and may feel some responsibility, for example, for the release of land and buildings for industrial uses. Here again in areas of in-migration landowners may enjoy a degree of planning gain in releasing green-field sites for housing and industrial development.

In attempting to assess the impact of the changing countryside in terms of beneficiaries and losers, the future is very different for the traditional, rural population. In agricultural terms, the declining agricultural labour force has induced hardship among many rural families. The move towards agricultural efficiency has displaced labour with capital and has led to a decline in the 'informal' economy which often provided sustenance to the rural dweller. Even within agriculture the work force attracts lower wages than the national average due, in part at least, to a low level of competition for labour. Housing tenure has improved somewhat in rural areas but there is still difficulty in gaining access to the housing market for many people dependent upon rural wages.

The containment of settlements does provide advantages for this rural population. These are chiefly of an environmental nature where by and large human habitation and the open countryside remain distinct. On the other hand, this containment has been a prime cause of the lack of industry and thus job opportunities and better wages for the rural dweller. Containment has also had a strong influence on rising rural house prices through restricting housing supply.

The rural dweller again benefits from the conservation of the wild in terms of his or her living environment but it might be said that such effective conservation again restricts the opportunity for the development of a comprehensive industrial base for the rural population. Is conserving the wild anyway chiefly of more interest to the urban population than the rural dweller himself?

Rural populations suffer differential impacts in the context of sustaining rural communities. This depends to an extent on whether remoter rural areas or lowland England and Wales are considered. In remoter areas, service losses are common, with high levels of unemployment and few job opportunities. Out-migration frequently causes the break-up of the extended family and often the loss of a sense of cultural identity. Some of these characteristics are still evident in lowland England and Wales. Job opportunities, high un-employment and out-migration are still common. But here in-migration of the commuter and the retired presents an additional set of effects. Such in-comers do help to sustain certain types of rural services such as shops and garages and do introduce additional expenditure into the local economy. However, they often place a demand on rural housing that pushes the prices of housing stock beyond the reach of local people. Transport services, too, are often not enhanced by such an influx because of such a high incidence of car-ownership among in-comers.

These two examples of gainers and losers in the countryside, landowners and the traditional rural population, provide two threads in the complex web of differential impacts brought about by the changing countryside. Contem-plation of how other people and organisations are differentially affected will reinforce this multifaceted nature of the countryside, a characteristic which provides a starting point for this book.

Effects of Policy: Efficiency and Distribution

From speculations about who benefits and suffers most from the effects of change in the countryside it is now appropriate to consider how this change itself might be influenced. It is an understanding of these influences that offers the potential for some degree of control over the fate of those benefiting and losing from change. Rural policies provide a prime influence over this change. Before considering these policies themselves it will be useful, in this section, to summarise the two main impacts that policies are considered to have: the efficiency with which the resources are allocated and the fairness of their distribution. An understanding of these impacts, within the political process in which they are considered, will assist the reader in speculating about the effects of policy changes in the countryside.

The first of these impacts, allocative efficiency, relates to the way in which resources in the countryside are allocated by a policy. Is public policy wasteful of money or not? At what level, for example, do rural primary schools become too small to be worth keeping open? The notion of allocative efficiency is subject to various interpretations. Efficiency in its productive sense, for example, is discussed in some detail in Chapter 2. However, it will be useful to bear in mind that considering efficiency in general policy terms is concerned with the *allocation* of resources to different uses.

In practice, different people who have an influence on this allocation of resources in the countryside tend to view it with different degrees of precision. It tends to be used qualitatively by the planner who, in considering the relative merits or otherwise of, for example, key settlement policies, will consider the advantages in allocating services, employment and so on in village centres, rather than dispersing them more widely about the countryside. The economist, by contrast, has attempted to pursue more precise notions of allocative efficiency when considering rural resources. This has been done using a technique known as cost-benefit analysis, where all the advantages and disadvantages of any particular resource are assessed, as far as possible, in monetary terms. Thus the allocation of resources to the forestry sector was considered through a cost-benefit study of forestry carried out by the Treasury in 1972. The allocative effects of the Third London Airport on rural land were the subject of deliberations by the Roskill Commission in 1970, again using cost-benefit analysis. Recreation, conservation, amenity, service provision and rural employment have all been the subject of cost-benefit analyses aimed at determining the efficiency with which rural resources are allocated.

The varying degrees of precision with which allocative efficiency has been considered in rural policy formulation have been the subject of much criticism. Economists have accused others of being too vague in their understanding of the allocation of rural resources. Planners and policy makers have accused economists of being too specific in trying to quantify qualitative judgements — it is better to be vaguely right than precisely wrong.

It is important to note, however, that it is this consideration of the efficiency with which resources are allocated that has been the prime concern of all of those involved in the policy process. It is often claimed that policy makers and their advisors should restrict themselves to considering efficiency effects because they are relatively tangible and free from too many value judgements.

The other important effect of policies for the countryside, the equalities or inequalities in the *distribution* of resources as a result of the way in which they are allocated remains, therefore, relatively unconsidered. Indeed it is not infrequently the case that distributional consequences are overlooked altogether in policy decisions. Distributional issues might include, for example, assessing the effects on the community of the closure of primary schools. Do some people suffer more than others from such closures? As another example, should rural shops be subsidised directly (even though this might be wasteful of resources), for the social advantages they might provide? Indeed the whole issue of rural housing is concerned as much with the distribution of housing resources — should houses, for example, be built for local people, who often have relatively low incomes, poor job opportunities and so on, with restrictions on purchases by commuters or second-home owners? — as with building houses in as efficient a way as possible.

These distributional effects of policies for the countryside, therefore, invariably require a greater degree of value judgement in determining their magnitude. This, however, can never be an excuse for overlooking their significance to the changing countryside. Indeed from the assessment of the net gainers and losers in the countryside, are the gains and losses more a result of the way in which rural resources are distributed, than the 'efficiency' with which they are allocated?

The notion of the distributional consequences of policy is thus a fertile ground for personal thought and judgement about the changing countryside and this is very important to have in mind in the consideration of any policy options for the future. Because of this, a number of examples of distributional issues in the countryside are considered below.

In the context of policies both for containing settlements and sustaining rural communities, Paul Cloke, in his textbook on settlement planning provides two quotations from Walker and Neate emphasising the importance of distributional issues. Walker is analysing the problems of rural incomes and opportunities:

> These problems stem from the dual failure to distribute resources according to need and the failure to prevent or ameliorate the differential impact of policy decisions in different income groups. One important reason for the failure is that in the location and allocation of services, planners have apparently ignored the question of inequality in the distribution of income and other resources, concentrating instead on what they believe to be the value-free questions of *efficiency* and *optimal* location. By ignoring the former problem they are allowing the social costs of their decisions to fall unevenly on the population and are, therefore, reinforcing and in some cases exaggerating the existing structure of inequality in income, wealth and life chances.

Neate addresses the distribution consequences of political under-representation, stressing that it

> requires planners, as long as they are concerned with meeting needs, to put more effort into identifying the problems and aspirations of those much less able to express themselves than the well-educated and better off 'newcomers' moving into most rural settlements.

In fact, all rural policy has distributional consequences of one form or another. A further example is provided in the consideration of the Less Favoured Areas agricultural policy. A number of studies have been carried out in the early 1980s to assess the way in which this policy has been successful in promoting development. As part of this research, information was collected from Radnor in Wales and Eden in Cumbria concerning the amount of government expenditure allocated to each sector within these areas for promoting rural development. Estimates of those expenditures are shown in Figure 7.1.

Rather than pursuing the extent to which this allocation is efficient it is perhaps useful to consider, more subjectively, whether the distribution of such expenditure, shown most clearly in the pie segments in the figure, is likely to have any good or bad consequences for rural development in those areas.

From the analyses undertaken in Chapters 2 to 5, what are the likely consequences of 80 per cent public funds going to agriculture in Radnor? Does Eden have a better 'balance' of public support with 43 per cent being disposed to manufacturing? Obviously, answers to these questions will

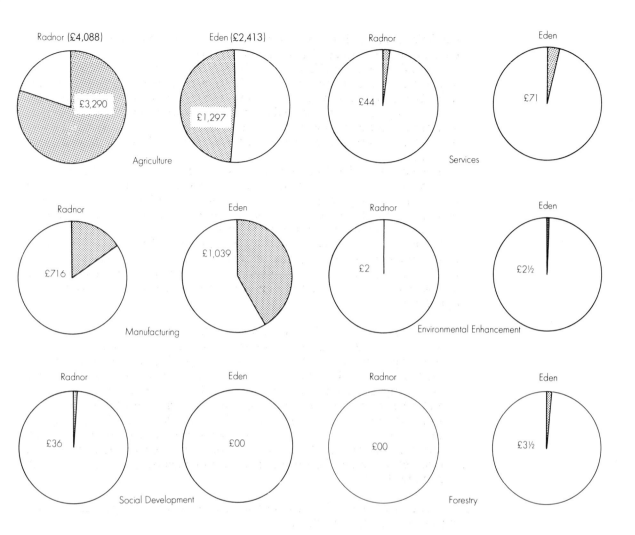

depend upon a number of factors which are not expressed in this figure. Nevertheless they are critical questions in the development of policies for a changing countryside.

A final example of the way in which distributional effects can be considered in the development of rural policy comes from the sphere of countryside recreation. This example provides a contrast to the previous two. It illustrates that policies for the countryside can have distributional impacts on urban as well as rural populations. Figure 7.2 below shows four different income distributions. Three are the income profiles of recreationists at different types of recreation site. The fourth is the income distribution of the United Kingdom as a whole. Clearly all of these distributions are different and although little can be inferred about a general case from these examples, they are useful for illustrative purposes.

For example, a smaller proportion of people in the lowest income category participated at any of these three sites than the proportion of people in that income group for the whole of the United Kingdom. Conversely, for the highest income groups the proportion of people at each site is higher than for the UK as a whole. Just comparing the three sites, the income distribution at the sailing club is skewed towards higher incomes, for the Country Park towards middle incomes, and for the casual recreation area towards lower incomes. If these site income distributions reflect a national pattern, are there any distributional consequences for national recreation sites policy? Would it

Figure 7.1: Public Expenditure in Radnor and Eden, 1981.
N.B. Actual figures are in '000's rounded to the nearest whole number.

Source: Alan Hearne, 'Integrated Rural Development in Less Favoured Areas', paper delivered to the Agricultural Economics Society Conference, Cambridge, April 1984.

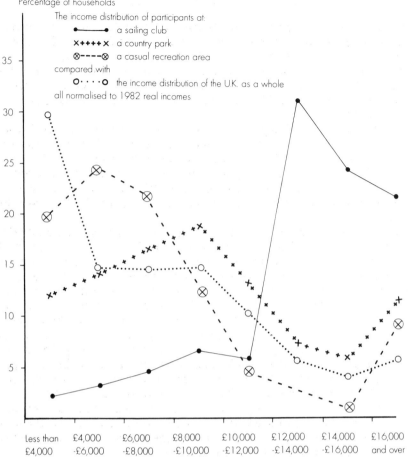

Percentage of households

The income distribution of participants at:
●———● a sailing club
×+++× a country park
⊗----⊗ a casual recreation area
compared with
○····○ the income distribution of the U.K. as a whole
all normalised to 1982 real incomes

| Less than £4,000 | £4,000 -£6,000 | £6,000 -£8,000 | £8,000 -£10,000 | £10,000 -£12,000 | £12,000 -£14,000 | £14,000 -£16,000 | £16,000 and over |

Figure 7.2: Income Distribution at Recreation Sites.

Note: These income estimates are gross income figures normalised to mid-year 1982 prices by changes in the retail price index from the time of data collection to mid-1982.

Sources: N. Curry, 'Equity Effects in the Estimation of Leisure Benefits', *Tourism Management*, vol. 3, no. 2, June 1982.
N. Curry, 'Crickley Hill Country Park 1982', *Main Report*, GlosCAT Planning Department, Research Report no. 4, October 1983.
J.A. Pinch, *Country Park Feasibility Study*, GlosCAT Planning Department, January 1984.

not be desirable, for example, to have a policy mechanism or instrument that encouraged lower income people to recreate in the countryside? Comparing these site distributions with that of the UK as a whole, does the existing policy of obliging local authorities to allow free access to recreation sites make sense in distributional terms? At a broader level, are the distributional consequences of policy for recreation sites really that important compared to these consequences in other policy areas?

Commonly, when change in the countryside is being discussed, proponents of certain types of policy call for more expenditure or more resources to be devoted to specific sectors or actions. Such proposals should be considered not only in terms of what the enhanced allocation of resources means in the countryside, but what its distributional effects are likely to be. For example, if the Development Board for Rural Wales is allocated an increased budget in real terms by the Welsh Office, the effects of the additional expenditure will be different depending on whether the DBRW uses it to further its existing policies of concentrating resource allocations into a few centres such as Newtown, or alternatively uses it to support smaller, more remote and more dissipated social and economic activity.

Thus, where policy options and instruments of change are considered, as, for example, in the remainder of this chapter, it is important to assess the distributional impacts as well as the efficiency of resource allocation in any new proposals.

Policy Instruments and The Policy Process

From considering the types of effects that are usefully taken into account when assessing policy change it is now useful to consider the policy instruments that may be used to bring about change in the countryside and the policy process within which they operate. It is clear from the flavour of this book so far that a unified and coherent policy for the countryside of England and Wales does not exist. Thus the future of rural policy is the subject of much conjecture.

Indeed, the history of public policy for the countryside since the Second World War has been the subject of much criticism. As has been noted in Chapter 5, commentators have defined the period from the 1947 Town and Country Planning Act as 'twenty years of wasted opportunity for rural policy'. Others have maintained that 'only since the 1970s has rural planning not proceeded by default'. There even have been calls for a new Scott Enquiry for the 1980s.

Emerging during the 1970s amidst these criticisms was the Countryside Review Committee, a Civil Service committee which, it has been said, had 'all the attendant problems of interdepartmental intrigues and a partiality for compromise'. This committee warned that developing a coherent rural policy was no easy task. Indeed, it was a prime generator of the rural policy 'buzz', word of the late 1970s — conflict. Figure 7.3 summarises part of their contribution to the rural policy debate. It is clear from this figure that the Countryside Review Committee, at least, considered that promoting any policy for the countryside would, through the actions taken to bring that policy about, generate a series of conflicts with other rural activities. Is this a helpful approach to considering the development of policies for the changing countryside? How can this circularity of policy and conflict be broken?

It is from this basis, a realisation that even in official circles there are perhaps more problems than solutions in policy formulation for the changing countryside, that the question of who will change in the future and how that change will come about, must be considered.

Figure 7.3: Policies and Potential Policy Conflicts.

Source: The Countryside Review Committee, *The Countryside: Problems and Policies*, HMSO 1976, Annex C.

Policy under promotion	Actions which may be taken in consequence (some with grant-aid from the Exchequer)	Policies in potential conflict
Increased food production and productivity	Ploughing, liming and fertilising	Conservation of scene, wildlife, remains; access to open country; pollution control
	Drainage work	Wildlife and water conservation
	Hedgerow clearance	Conservation of scene and wildlife
	Use of fertilisers, pesticides and herbicides	Conservation of wildlife: water quality: pollution control
	Farm and storage buildings	Conservation of scene
	Woodland clearance	Conservation of scene and wildlife
	Fencing	Conservation of scene: access to open country
	Bracken removal	Conservation of scene.
	Straw-burning	Conservation of scene and wildlife· pollution control
	Free running bulls	Access (along footpaths)
Increased timber production and productivity	Afforestation and fencing	Conservation of scene: access
	Block felling	Conservation of scene

Policy under promotion	Actions which may be taken in consequence (some with grant-aid from the Exchequer)	Policies in potential conflict
Increased piped water supply	Creation of reservoirs	Conservation of scene and productive land
Improved water quality	Groundwater schemes and estuarial storage bunds	Conservation of scene and wildlife
	Purification works	Conservation of scene
Prevention of damage by water	River training and flood protection	Conservation of scene; access
Increased mineral production	Excavation and spoil tips	Conservation of productive land; conservation of scene and wildlife; access; water quality; pollution control
	Transportation of materials	Conservation of amenity
National defence	Maintenance of training grounds	Food, mineral and timber production; conservation of scene; access
	Testing equipment and training	Conservation of amenity
Promotion of tourism	Erection of catering, accommodation and service facilities	Conservation of scene, amenity and productive land
	Holiday traffic (vehicles and people)	Conservation of amenity and wildlife
Improved accessibility	New roads; building; widening and straightening of roads	Conservation of scene, wildlife and amenity; production of food
Improved housing	Take-up of countryside for new development	Conservation of productive land; conservation of scene, wildlife and amenity
Promotion of industrial development	Take-up of countryside for new factories	Conservation of productive land; conservation of scene, wildlife and amenity; pollution control
Promotion of the recreational use of the countryside	Improving access to open country, conserving and protecting the footpaths system	Production of food and timber; conservation of wildlife and amenity (of country dwellers)
	Providing of more facilities (country parks, picnic sites, etc)	Production of food and timber; conservation of scene and wildlife
Clearing derelict land	Earth moving and creative landscaping	Conservation of wildlife
Conserving the amenity of the countryside	Designation of special areas, control of development and noise, dust and other nuisance	Improvement of accessibility; housing and industrial development; tourism, recreation; extraction of minerals
Conserving the scene	Designation of special areas, control of development and noise, dust and other nuisance	Hedgerow and woodland clearance; afforestation; development generally
Conserving wildlife	Designation of special areas, control of development and noise, dust and other nuisance	Hedgerow and woodland clearance; afforestation; development generally
Increasing energy supply	Extraction of oil, gas, coal	Conservation of productive land, scene, wildlife and amenity; pollution control
	Generation and transmission of electricity	Conservation of scene
Improved telecommunications	Erection of masts and aerials	Conservation of scene
Reducing rural depopulation	Promotion of industrial development	Conservation of scene and amenity

Policy Options

One approach to considering a policy framework for the future and how it might be applied is to take stock of the existing policy framework in some structured form. From this basis, changes to the framework can be considered, and the repercussions of these changes can be contemplated.

It is not the purpose of this final chapter to provide a policy panacea for the countryside of the future, but rather to set the reader thinking about ways in which policy improvements might be made. Indeed, what even constitutes an improvement will depend very much upon how the assessment of who benefits and who loses overall, discussed in the second part of this chapter, is interpreted.

In total, a large number of policies and policy instruments have been mentioned in Chapters 2 to 6. It is now pertinent to draw these together. Given that policies for the countryside are diverse and incremental, focus is placed in this section, on the instruments of policy. Figure 7.4 below provides a taxonomy of the diversity of policy instruments currently in use in the countryside, together with what they are used for. They have been grouped into five broad types: grant aid incentives, other types of incentive, tools of guidance, controls and agreements. Although a number of these policy instrments have not been discussed previously in this book they are included here to provide an indication of the complexity of instruments available. Policy instruments used, for example, in the context of recreation, forestry and minerals are included, even though they have not been given such close consideration as the themes of Chapters 2 to 5.

Figure 7.4: Countryside Planning Instruments and their Uses. This table is to provide an understanding of the complex web of instruments available for the shaping of change in the countryside. It is not intended to be exhaustive.

Source: Open University.

Policy Instruments	Available Types		Further Information	Uses
	General	Specific		
1. Incentives: Grants	Primary sector grants: Agriculture	Farm modernisation (all types) Farm management and improvement Farm amalgamation (Land purchase/early retirement) Less Favoured Areas (all types/headage payments)		Grant aid available for most structural change on farms through ADAS
	Primary sector grants: Forestry	Forestry grant scheme		For tree planting and adherence to management plan
	Primary sector grants: Water	Regional devt. grants (e.g. EEC regional fund)		Financial assistance often available in the construction of reservoirs
	Manufacturing grants	Grants from: CoSIRA MSC YTS Development Commission development boards etc.	Chiefly available in a number of 'priority areas': opportunity areas, rural development areas, special investment areas, intermediate areas, etc.	Depending on areas, grants are available for fixed and working capital, and/or labour
	Tertiary grants: Recreation and Tourism	Grants from Countryside Commission		To both public and private sector for capital and wardening services Grants for management through access agreements

241

Policy Instruments	Available Types		Further Information	Uses
	General	**Specific**		
		Grants from English and Welsh Tourist Boards		Tourism projects scheme. Hotel development incentives scheme
	Tertiary grants: Conservation	Grants from Countryside Commission		Amenity tree planting: general small grants
		Grants from the Nature Conservancy Council		Compensation payments: SSSI's general small grants
		Grants from National Parks		Compensation payments
	Grants for services	Grants from: EEC Social & Regional Funds Development Commission County Councils District Councils Parish Councils Voluntary Sector		To enhance service provision in a number of disparate ways (e.g. the development of integrated development programmes)

(N.B. In many instances where grant aid is available, loans may also be given.)

2. Incentives: Other	Tax concessions	Schedule D income for private forestry owners		Forestry losses can be offset against business profits elsewhere
		Capital Transfer Tax exemptions		For undertaking management practices for heritage landscapes
		Tax 'Roll Over' provisions		To the farmer in the sale & repurchase of agricultural land
	Price subsidies on commodity outputs	The CAP guarantee system		To support farm product prices differentially
	Import restrictions			To encourage agricultural production by keeping farm prices high

3. Guidance	Structure plans			Board policy at a county level
	Local plans	District, subject, action area		Policies for implementation
	Interpretation facilities	For: recreation conservation		Guidance on understanding the environment
	Demonstrations	Wardening, for farms		Education for specific purposes
	Experiments	Upland/urban fringe		To try out informal approaches to countryside management
	Management plans	Recreation sites	These are all elements of what has become known as 'countryside management'	A Countryside Commission requirement
		Forestry grant scheme		A Forestry Commission requirement
		Forestry conservancy recreation plans		Forestry Commission policy
		Farm plans		ADAS requirement
		Conservation plans		Nature Conservancy Council or Capital Taxes Office requirement

Policy Instruments	Available Types		Further Information	Uses
	General	Specific		
	Land use classifications	Agricultural Land Classification; Hill & Upland surveys		For grading agric. land (MAFF); For discerning improvable and unimprovable agric. land
		Section 43 maps	Under the Wildlife and Countryside Act 1981	For establishing by National Parks, moor & heath of conservation value
	National Park plans			Policies for the management of National Parks
	Advisory services	From e.g. ADAS Countryside Commission COSIRA Rural Community Councils		Advice to all sectors
4. Controls	Land use designations (statutory)	National Parks country parks picnic sites SSSI's LASDOs NNRs AONBs Local nature reserves		Protective status for recreation or conservation uses
	Land use designations (Non statutory or informal)	Landscape Improvement areas Special Landscape Areas Areas of high archaeological potential	Examples in Somerset Levels & Moors plan (Non-statutory)	For protective conservation status
		Areas of Great Landscape Value Areas of Great Scientific Value Tourism Restraint areas	Examples in Cornwall county's countryside local subject plan (Statutory)	For protective conservation status
	Tree Preservation Orders Felling licences			For the preservation of specific trees or coppices Permission from the Forestry Commission to fell trees
	Development control (Buildings etc)		Carried out by district councils usually	Permission required for most forms of development
	Development control (Minerals) Acts of Parliament		Carried out by county councils usually	Permission required minerals and after-use For very large developments in the countryside, including reservoirs
	Notifications	Made by NCC or National Park Authorities Made by counties and districts		If either wishes to object to a MAFF grant for farm improvement Notification of scheduled monuments & archaeological areas, for which compensation will be paid
	Land acquisition	Compulsory: public agencies		Possible for conservation when failure to make a management agreement
		Voluntary: public agencies		e.g. for forestry, agriculture or conservation purposes

243

Policy Instruments	General	Specific	Further Information	Uses
	Licences			May be taken out by a public authority to restrict development by an individual
	Orders	Access		Compulsory access to private land
		After-use management		For minerals sites
5. Agreements	Access	Under the 1968 Countryside Act		For access to private land
	Management	Under sections 39 & 41 of the Wildlife and Countryside Act		For conserving land in National Parks and SSSI's
	Section 52	Under the 1971 Town & Country Planning Act	Allows restrictive covenants to be placed on planning permissions	For controlling development
	Leases			Public authorities may negotiate leases for conservation purposes
	For Nature Reserves	Under the 1949 National Parks and Access to the Countryside Act		For the designation of Nature Reserves
	For field monuments	Under the 1972 Field Monuments Act		For designating field monuments
	For land near highways	Under the 1973 Land Compensations Act		Agreements for compensation for road schemes etc.

It will be instructive for the reader to relate his or her understanding of the instruments discussed in previous chapters to this table (Figure 7.4). Clearly, agricultural structural grants considered in Chapter 2 fall into the first category of policy instruments but price support, whilst still an incentive, falls outside of what may be considered grant-aid. The structure and local plan system, discussed in Chapter 3, provides mechanisms of guidance in controlling development, but development control itself has a degree of compulsion that takes it beyond guidance. A number of land-use designations, considered in Chapter 4, SSSIs, National Parks and so on are used as control mechanisms in conserving the wild, but agreements have a role to play in this sphere, as does grant-aid in the form of compensation payments. In one way or another, nearly all categories of policy instrument are used in sustaining rural communities.

Perhaps the most significant characteristic of these instruments considered together is their diversity. They range from economic incentives through fiscal concessions and measures of strict physical control, to agreement and advice. It would seem from this diversity that policy problems for the countryside do not stem from a lack of powers for shaping the rural environment. It is, rather, the way in which those powers are used that might offer the greatest potential for improvement. How existing policy instruments might be used in differing contexts and what sort of effects new uses for existing instruments might have on the changing countryside, is, therefore, the concern of the next section.

Policy Instruments: New Roles?

Using Figure 7.4 as a summary of the existing tools that are currently used to guide change in the countryside, it becomes possible to speculate on what might come about if these tools are used in different ways. Ultimately, this should be for the reader to ponder, but as an initial stimulus, this section provides a number of examples of ways in which existing policy instruments might be used in new ways. They are all uses that are the subject of current debate and thus provide a good indication of the scope for policy innovation that may be considered realistic for the short-term future. Together, these examples encompass every category of policy instrument defined in Figure 7.4 above.

Some examples of existing instruments in new uses will be obvious from Chapters 2 to 5. The debate concerning the relative merits of extending full planning control over all agricultural land has been widely discussed. But would planning control over agriculture be appropriate? Other proposals have been given less consideration in this volume. The use of farm management plans in a different way, for example, is of current interest to the Council for National Parks and the Landscape Institute. Although farm plans are required currently by ADAS before grant-aid for structural improvement will be given, these plans are orientated towards the economic feasibility (not even viability, it must be noted) of proposed improvements. The Council for National Parks and the Landscape Institute would like to see the use of such plans extended towards environmental rather than just economic criteria. Is this a viable proposition, given the current state of structural support outlined in Chapter 2?

Four further examples of new uses for existing policy instruments are outlined in more detail below. In considering each of these examples it is important to consider who is likely to benefit and lose from such policy proposals and what the efficiency and distributional effects might be.

Figure 7.5: Commercial Timber Production. Is planning control necessary to curb the monotonous nature and ecological narrowness of this type of monoculture?

Source: Geoffrey Berry/Ramblers Association.

245

Planning Control Over Forestry?

As well as for agriculture, there has been increasing criticism that the exemption of forestry from planning control has led to forestry developments that are detrimental to the environment. Chief among these are firstly, the extent of forestry lands and whether expanding forestry in 'high value' upland landscapes can be justified in economic terms. Secondly, the way in which trees are planted for productive timber — in monotonous regimented rows of coniferous monoculture — is widely considered to be visually detrimental as well as ecologically dubious (see Figure 7.5).

Does this then provide a case for planning control over forestry or would some other policy instrument be more effective? Criticisms of planning control over agriculture do not have an exact parallel for the forestry sector since the structure of the industry and its existing support are somewhat different. The private sector does have the opportunity for government assistance in timber production through the Forestry Grant Scheme of the 1981 Forestry Act. Here, fiscal concessions and management grants (higher for deciduous than coniferous trees) are available, but only for compliance with a management plan approved by the Forestry Commission acting in its role as a forestry authority.

Is not this policy instrument in itself sufficient to ensure an environmentally sensitive approach to forestry management? Certainly, removing management grants may not have the same impact as a reduction in economic support to agriculture would have on the agricultural sector since levels of support, generally, are not of the same magnitude as in agriculture. Some credence may be lent to this by the fact that the Forestry Commission, charged with selling publicly-owned land to the private sector under the 1981 Act, is having difficulty in doing so. Private forestry does not appear to be an overwhelmingly attractive economic proposition. It will be useful for the reader to consider the relative merits of selling publicly owned forestry land. Undoubtedly such sales will bring revenue into the Treasury but understandably, perhaps, the forestry unions fear job losses as a result (see Figure 7.6).

One of the complications in determining what would be the most appropriate policy instrument for controlling the environmental impact of forestry, however, is that it is not really the private sector that is the prime culprit in generating the above environmental impacts. The private sector contains a much higher degree of amenity planting and although the private sector and the Forestry Commission own roughly half the forestry lands each, the Forestry Commission's productive output as a forestry enterprise is much higher. This in itself has been achieved since 1919 when the Forestry Commission was formed through the use of a fairly radical policy instrument — that of purchasing land for forestry development, effectively land nationalisation.

Somewhat perversely the public sector itself is generating problems that the public sector must seek to solve. The Forestry Commission has made some concessions to amenity objectives, particularly since 1972, when forestry was shown to be economically not viable. Because of this the Commission has been keen to pursue wider objectives to justify itself, and amenity has been one of them. This, mainly, has taken the form of some cosmetic deciduous planting around the edges of linear coniferous plantations and some positive landscaping of new plantations. But would planning control 'guide' development more effectively? There is, of course, always the problem of assessing whether town and country planners are competent to make informed decisions about the control of the forestry sector. Since forestry lands are currently largely exempt from control, planners are by and large not very familiar with the operations of the forestry sector.

Perhaps, in considering the merits or otherwise of planning control over

Figure 7.6: Should Public Forestry be Privatised? The timber and forestry unions have introduced an active campaign of opposition to selling off the Forestry Commission estates, for fear of job losses.

Source: Agricultural and Allied Workers Group of the Transport and General Workers' Union.

forestry, it will be informative to consider the Countryside Commission's point of view. The Commission has had a long-standing aim of bringing afforestation under planning control. However, this policy was abandoned in 1982, when the Commission introduced a national debate on the uplands. In an opening statement to this debate, the Commission's chairman, Sir Derek Barber, maintained that planning control over forestry was simply 'out of tune with the mood of the times'.

A year later in the conclusions to the uplands debate one of the Countryside Commission's proposals *was* planning control for all bare land tree planting over 50 hectares in extent, to be vested in the counties and National Park authorities of the uplands. Is this a direct turn-about in the Commission's attitude to this particular policy instrument? In this context, of course, it is critical to understand exactly what bare land planting is and what exactly 'planting over 50 hectares in extent' means. Some quarters consider that this could be interpreted such that even with this proposal, very little forestry development would come under planning control. Are such compromises appropriate in the case of forestry's impact on the environment?

Land Classifications: A Need for Reform?

In considering how policy instruments might be adapted or changed in their use, it may be asked whether the way in which land is both registered and classified should be overhauled. The first land 'registration' took place in 1086, when William the Conqueror commissioned the Domesday Book as a means of restricting the Normans in their 'theft' of lands.

Today, documenting land ownership and land-use remains quite distinct. Untypical of the world at large, England and Wales do not have an open system for the registration of land ownership. The ownership of land is known by the Land Registry for most urban areas but details of ownership will not be released without prior permission of the owner! Ownership patterns in the countryside remain largely unknown even by the Land Registry. Would a comprehensive and accessible register of land ownership in the countryside be desirable?

Classifying land-uses and characteristics has, on the other hand, been undertaken a number of times and for a number of different purposes, as Figure 7.4 shows. Dudley Stamp undertook the first modern comprehensive land-utilisation survey in England and Wales in the 1930s. A second 'unofficial' survey was carried out in the 1960s by Alice Coleman. In addition to these general surveys, the Ministry of Agriculture introduced their Agricultural Land Classification in the 1960s to assist in determining the quality of agricultural land. An example of this is given in Colour Plate 14. The physical basis of this classification was criticised since it gave no indication of the land's economic value or the value of its output. The actual classifications also were considered to be rather too broad to be of much use in, for example, identifying land for development. Over half of all land in England fell into grade 3, for example.

Despite criticisms the Agricultural Land Classification has proceeded incrementally down this 'physical basis' path. Grade 3 has been divided into three sub-groups. And the Ministry's Hill and Upland Surveys have been used to define 'improvable' and 'unimprovable' land in the grades 4 and 5 categories more closely. Ironically, improvement grants may still be obtained on 'unimprovable land'. National Park land classifications, too (for moor and heath, at least) have now become a statutory responsibility under Section 43 of the 1981 Wildlife and Countryside Act. Is this incremental diversity of classifying land-uses and characteristics adequate, however, or would a more comprehensive land classification, newly developed, be of positive assistance in shaping the future of the countryside? The Department of the Environment think that a new system is necessary. The Secretary of State recently has approved a Domesday Book number two — a new register of land to resolve conflicts between local authorities and developers and to identify agricultural land loss. The survey is to be compiled by the Ordnance Survey at a cost of £500,000 a year with an open-ended commitment, using 19 separate land-use classifications. Already criticisms are being levelled at such a classification on the grounds of expense and lack of expertise. Will such a survey really represent money well spent at the interface between development and greenfield sites?

Section 52 Agreements: A Tool for Social Planning?

Section 52 of the 1971 Town and Country Planning Act allows agreement (known as Section 52 Agreements) to be made between planners and developers concerning a wide number of *physical* characteristics associated with development. Other types of agreements, such as access agreements, management agreements, field monument agreements, and so on are also concerned with physical controls, albeit through agreement rather than permission or coercion. Should it be possible, however, to use agreements to place *social* conditions on development? This has been quite a controversial question within the public sector, particularly in respect of Section 52 Agreements.

During the 1970s, the Lake District National Park Authority was concerned to do something about housing problems for local people in the Park. The demand for second homes and commuter homes was such that the price of housing was pushed up sufficiently to be beyond the reach of many people with local employment. The Draft National Park Plan of June 1977 consequently produced a statement of intent that new development should be restricted to that catering for local needs. The Development Control committee proposed that the policy instrument that should be used for this purpose should be a Section 52 Agreement. This was duly passed, adopted on the plan and became part of National Park policy. The Agreement basically defined a maximum area within which any future occupant of a new dwelling might be allowed to work. The use of this instrument in this context was both unusual and problematic. It was unusual in that National Park Plans normally restricted themselves to management policies for recreation and conservation whereas the Lake District Plan extended into the fields of social provision and housing. It was problematic, because nobody knew whether using Section 52 Agreements for social purposes was legal. The Department of the Environment advised that:

> local planning authorities should not concern themselves as a rule with the occupancy of the building and that such a condition in a planning permission would be regarded as an unreasonable one...the Department thought that development control was the wrong instrument for achieving the Board's social objectives...it must be doubtful that the Secretary of State would be able to approve such policies in a structure plan relating the provision of housing to local need.

The Department, however, stated that the legitimacy of using this policy in such a way would rest in the courts rather than (ultimately) with the Department of the Environment. Such a test case has yet to take place.

Interestingly, however, the Lake District National Park Authority which is one of the two National Parks in the country that also produces its own structure plan, has omitted any reference to Section 52 Agreements for local housing needs policy, in its Structure Plan. This has been done because the Structure Plan requires Secretary of State approval and any inclusion of Section 52 Agreements in it might well lead to a rejection of their use by the Secretary of State. National Park Plans, through which the Section 52 Agreement is operated, do not need Secretary of State approval.

Should Section 52 Agreements, then, be more widely used in this 'social planning' sphere, through the medium of development control? Ultimately, in general terms, this is a question for the reader to consider. In the Lake District, however, it is possible that such Agreements have made the housing problem worse. Since Agreements can only apply to new housing, the existing housing stock has no restrictions on who may purchase it. Since commuters and second-home buyers are now deprived of buying new housing, there is greater competition in the market for existing houses which accordingly pushes their price up further. It may well be that within this market, for example, for older terraced housing, the local prospective houseowner becomes relatively most deprived.

Since the existing housing stock provides the vast majority of total housing

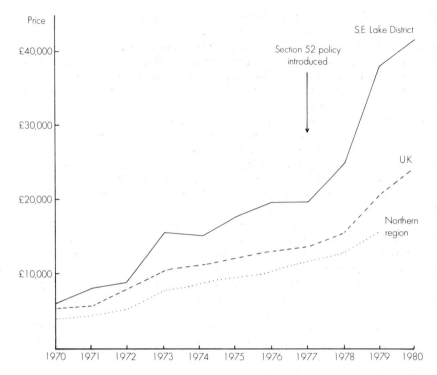

Figure 7.7: House Prices in The Lake District in Their Regional and National Context. Has the use of Section 52 Agreements been a prime influence in raising house prices in the Lake District?

Source: M. Shucksmith, *No Homes for Locals?*, Gower, 1981.

in the Lake District it may be postulated that in aggregate Section 52 Agreements have caused a greater rise in house prices than if they had not been introduced. This postulation is certainly not contradicted by Figure 7.7. Whatever future use planning agreements might have in general, care must be taken to look at their longer-term side-effects in social and economic terms.

Compensation Payments: a Bottomless Coffee-pot?

Other types of agreement that fall outside the development control process, such as management and access agreements have been commonly put forward as an alternative to influencing the primary resource sectors of the country-side, particularly in the development of recreation and conservation. Agreements, it has been argued, are a much more satisfactory way of bringing about environmentally sensitive rural custodianship, than any form of compulsion — willing hands are better than conscripts. It is often proposed, too, that the primary sectors are simply too important in the economy to be unduly fettered by external controls. The first of these notions may have a logic, but agreements of this nature, as they exist at present, are far from simply voluntary tools.

If authorities have difficulty negotiating Access Agreements with land-owners, for example, they can introduce a compulsory Access Order under the 1968 Countryside Act. Paradoxically, management agreements (for conservation purposes) under the 1981 Wildlife and Countryside Act are themselves compulsory once a notification has been issued. Land purchase also may be invoked, as a means of overcoming management agreement stalemates. Perhaps the salient difference between this type of recreation or conservation agreement and a Section 52 Agreement within the development control context, is that whereas the latter when it is made is simply compulsory, the former are compulsory but either compensation is paid for their introduction, in the case of management agreements, or grants are available for the management of access areas under access agreements. Referring back to the section 'Effects of Policy, Efficiency and Distribution' of this chapter, can the differences between these two types of agreement be justified on grounds of distributional fairness? Does the exemption of agriculture and forestry from planning control give these sectors unfair leverage in attracting some financial response for relinquishing development rights which other sectors, which may be subject to Section 52 Agreements without compensation, simply do not have?

If compensation payments under the 1981 Act are considered, their cost alone may inhibit their eventual comprehensive use. Few agreements and the costs associated with them are published, but Figure 7.8, drawn from a number of sources, does give an indication of how much it has cost for certain developments not to take place. Again, all of these developments relate to agriculture and forestry. As another example, Exmoor National Park spent £44,197 on some eight management agreements from April 1983 to March 1984. From these figures, it is difficult to visualise, on cost grounds alone, such a policy instrument being used that widely.

One problem with this type of agreement, of course, is that compensation payments are calculated in terms of the opportunity cost of output forgone. In the case of farming this output is calculated at inflated agricultural support prices and is, therefore, a misleading notion of the real or free market value of output. In forestry terms the fiscal concessions and grant-aid lost are also built into the calculations. It is quite possible, therefore, as in the case of Mr Phillip Merricks above, to make a landowner a millionaire for not doing something to the extent at least of grants and support prices no longer available to him. Is this a wise use of public resources?

As an alternative to these direct payments for conserving the changing countryside increasing attention is being given to the use of *tax* concessions to landowners for developing conservation strategies. The Landscape Institute, for example, has proposed the extension of Capital Transfer Tax exemptions (currently available under the 1976 Finance Act for 'outstanding' heritage landscapes) to more general exemptions from capital and revenue taxes for

Figure 7.8: Compensation Payments for Management Agreements Made Under The 1981 Wildlife and Countryside Act. This table has been derived from a number of newspaper sources. Because such information is confidential the accuracy of these figures cannot be confirmed. Nevertheless, the Nature Conservancy Council consider the figures illustrative of some of the larger payments made. Can such sums be afforded to ensure that developments do not take place?

Source: Open University.

Recipient	Awarding Body	Compensation	Purpose	State
Fountain Forestry	NCC	£75,000 (single sum) binding 20 yrs?	NOT TO plant Creag Maegaldh (Super SSSI) — golden eagles and rare plants — with sikta spruce and logpole pine	Under negotiation, May 1984
Lord Thurso	NCC	£278,000 (single sum) binding 20 yrs?	NOT TO plant conifers on 6,000 acres of Blarnam Faoileag, the biggest bog of its kind in Britain	complete
Sir John Musker	NCC	£10,000 per annum, over 10 years	NOT TO run free-range pigs on a National Nature Reserve at Bridgham and Brettenham heaths	complete
Mr Phillip Merricks	NCC	£100,000 per annum over 10 years	NOT TO drain 1,143 acres of grazing marsh on the Isle of Sheppey in North Kent	Under negotiation, Jan. 1984
Four Norfolk Farmers	Norfolk Broads Authority	£100,000 per annum, over 20 years	NOT TO drain and plough up 748 acres of Halvergate Marshes	Under negotiation, March 1984
Lord Cranbourne	NCC	£24,000 per annum, index linked for 65 years	NOT TO turn a Dorset deciduous wood over to cereals or to plant conifers	complete

specific conservation works. This, they propose, would be accompanied by a countryside register, the first half of which would be confidential, containing information about the financial implications and the associated management plan attached to such a tax exemption. The second, public, half of the register would provide a detailed data bank of countryside features, protected by membership of the register.

Is such an approach to tax concessions for conservation works more efficient or distributionally more fair than compensation payments? Or does revenue lost to the Treasury (in tax concessions) really amount to the same thing as expenditure (in compensation payments)? Do economic and fiscal tools generally appear to be an effective use of resources? Are they bureaucratically more efficient to administer?

Integrated Rural Development?

The previous section has presented a number of examples of ways in which policy instruments may be adapted and deployed in different contexts in the changing countryside. This approach to changing policy on a 'one policy at a time' basis has much currency within both government and the voluntary sector and has its attractions in that marginal changes to policy can be implemented without undue disturbance to the overall structure in which that policy operates.

Alongside these sorts of proposed changes, however, a more radical approach to total policy reformulation is emerging under the guise of 'integrated rural development'. This approach in essence, hinges on abandoning the traditional mould of developing policies in a sectoral way, in favour of considering the countryside in a more integrated and interdependent way. Frequently, too, such an approach to policy formulation involves a much higher degree of participation on the part of the affected population. Commonly such approaches have been termed 'community-led' or 'bottom-up' rural development.

This type of approach to the development of policy would, in principle at least, allow a single bureaucratic authority the power to make comprehensive resource allocations in rural areas in line with what the relative need was perceived to be. Essentially, within any given allocation of resources an integrated approach to development would consider how that allocation might be most appropriately distributed. In Figure 7.1, for example, public expenditure in Radnor and Eden was allocated by a large number of public agencies in an uncoordinated way. Thus the Ministry of Agriculture, the Forestry Commission, the Development Commission, the Development Board for Rural Wales and local authorities all have been spending money in pursuance of their own policy objectives without any necessary reference to the compatibility of these policies.

This can lead to a waste of resources in two main ways. Firstly, unco-ordinated agencies might end up spending money in pursuance of the *same* policy objectives (such as employment) leading to an unnecessary duplication of assistance. Secondly, and perhaps more perversely, agencies might end up spending money on *opposing* policy objectives with the effect that eventually such expenditures might annul one another. This has been observed in the context of the Less Favoured Areas policy with its subsidisation of capital through the Farm and Horticultural Development Scheme causing labour shedding and expenditure by regional development agencies and councils to encourage employment.

Surely then, policy integration for the countryside would provide an important advance for steering change in the countryside? Ironically, the greatest success in this direction, the ability to establish Rural Development Boards under the 1967 Agriculture Act, failed miserably. Boards were to be given relative autonomy over resource allocations for specific rural areas across sectors. Public opposition ensured that only one of these came into being, in the North Pennines, and this was wound up within two years.

The notion of integrated rural development may thus provide intuitive appeal but are the practical problems associated with its introduction insurmountable? Certainly few people speculating on the future of the countryside seem to see a vision of sectoral integration, as might be surmised from the contributions to Chapter 6. Nevertheless, proposals for this type of approach to rural policy, or at least elements of it, have come from a number of disparate sources — the European Regional Fund, for example, is experimenting with 'integrated' developments by introducing a quota-free section to the fund. One of the first of these programmes in Europe has been set up in the Western Isles of Scotland. County Councils in England and Wales, too, are increasingly moving away from the formal rigour of the statutory processes and introducing informal integrated self-help programmes that, through their informality, are more resource-efficient within the local authority budgets.

Government quangos and regional development agencies such as the Development Board for Rural Wales are also undertaking a shift in policy emphasis to look at the way individual policies interlock into a broader framework. The approach is also being investigated by institutions such as the Duchy of Cornwall, for the Scilly Isles, to counter problems generated by a structure plan that in many ways is of too large a scale for the islands. The Ministry of Agriculture, Fisheries and Food, too, has at least a remit for developing policies in this way, through the provision of socio-economic advice under Directive 71/161 of the EEC.

Additionally, the traditional work of the Rural Community Council officers funded by the Development Commission is having an increasing impact in providing a framework for community-based development. At the other extreme, and elsewhere in Europe, government ministries are funding community-led programmes on a large scale. In Belgium, for example, the Ministry of Walloon Affairs funds development plans in accordance with 'subject plans for rural regeneration', where the plans themselves have been drawn up by the local community.

These examples of a more integrated approach to rural development indicate an increasing commitment on the part of a number of organisations to breaking down the sectoral barriers that inevitably lead to inefficiencies in rural resource allocation. The success of such approaches, however, will remain limited as long as attempts are made to operate them within, rather than instead of, the existing policy context. Indeed, one of the principal criticisms of these community-led or integrated programmes has been that their superimposition on top of *existing* policies simply adds another layer of bureaucracy onto an already over-bureaucratic policy mechanism.

Integrated or community-led rural development, then, provides a more radical, and in the longer term more efficient and equatable, approach to policy formulation for the changing countryside, but is it a realistic proposition in terms of current policy entrenchment?

Epilogue

All of the different ideas about new policies considered in the last chapter and the modifications to policy instruments in this one, although representative of various interests, have been discussed somewhat in isolation from the political context within which they might have to gain acceptance and then, if successful, operate. Indeed, it is this political aspect which is perhaps a most critical factor in determining what actually *does* change in the countryside. Although in an epilogue of this kind it is not possible to do more than touch upon this matter, a little needs to be said in support of the contention that what has happened in the countryside, what is happening now and what will occur in the future is far from a direct outcome of social and economic forces alone. The fact that these forces have been able to take the *form* that they have and have operated in the particular *way* that they have is an obvious indication of a political dimension itself. It is a dimension that could not have been overlooked in each of the 'issue' chapters and it would be easy enough to return to these now in order to make a simple list of those points in the text where the political element is overtly stressed. For example, who could be unaware of the politics of the EEC and its impact on the theme of Chapter 2? Who could not comprehend the much-changed political atmosphere in which planning controls are now exercised in the countryside? Who could fail to appreciate the political differences in the passage of two not dissimilar Wildlife and Countryside Bills proposed in turn by the Labour government and then the Conservative administration.

But how governments choose to act in respect of the countryside, whatever their political complexion, is not the result of the machinations of some remote policy 'think tank'. These policies emerge as part of a process that not only involves internal policy cerebrations within the party in power, but more particularly as a result of pressures that are brought to bear from without. In terms of the countryside, what has therefore emerged as policy for it over the years speaks loudly of the comparative success of interest groups who would wish to use it as a resource for their own ends. That agricultural interests have, since the end of the Second World War, commanded a large slice of government financial and other support for their activities (even to the present day when the EEC has a substantial surplus in many foodstuffs), and that agriculture has never been substantially subjected to planning controls are not accidents but an indication, perhaps, of the adeptness of the organisations representing agriculture and indeed the landowners to impress upon successive governments their views.

At the end of 1945, when the first post-war Labour government was concerned not only about the future strategic role of the agricultural industry but was interested in using it to help minimise its balance-of-payments problems, the NFU immediately found itself able to negotiate a seat with government at the table at which farm prices and guarantees were to be settled each year. Since then its behind-the-scenes success in having the ear of the Minister of Agriculture, Fisheries and Food and his department has been remarkable to the extent that a relationship has evolved in which both sides need each other. The government department sees the NFU as a quick means of getting a more easily agreed deal than if it had to negotiate directly with a highly fractionalised industry, whilst for the NFU dealing with the Ministry provides a direct channel of influence into the highest government circles. More than this, the NFU has the organisational back-up and the finance to put its point of view over at all levels to politicians in local as well as national government. It employs full-time liaison officers in the Houses of Parliament and services an all-party committee on agriculture. Its public relations department is second to none and any analysis of its annual record shows evidence of its many hundreds of press releases effectively used in the national newspapers, a dozen or more major press conferences on important agricultural topics adequately covered by the news media and an impact on broadcasting which enables it to claim over 30 hours of time devoted to information provided by the NFU. It is not surprising that Howard Newby has concluded that 'in the post-war history of agriculture it is not only the government of the day, but the NFU which has been responsible for guiding and shaping the destiny of British farmers'. And he might have added that it has thereby also succeeded in controlling much of what has happened in the countryside of England and Wales over that period.

Also of no small importance as an interest lobby has been the Country

Landowners Association. Its claim that it has 'direct access to ministers and Head Office permanent staff have a close day-to-day working relationship with government departments' seems to be borne out by a number of political analysts. The work of the CLA has been, of course, directed to the more general interests of the landowner and much of its time is spent in lobbying for a more favourable tax regime with special attention being given to the amelioration of Capital Transfer Tax, the impact of which, it is claimed, could bring about the demise of the private landowner. However as Howard Newby has also said, 'If the private landowner has become adept at avoiding his long predicted oblivion this has been due in no small part to the CLA's political guile.'

Ranged against these two powerful independent pressure groups and promoting a largely opposing viewpoint are the smaller conservationist bodies, many of which are really effective only at local level and are divorced from that of directly influencing policy-makers. The 'Friends of the Lake District', now celebrating its 50th birthday, is one such example. However, the Royal Society for Nature Conservation, which is an umbrella group bringing together the 42 county Nationalists Trusts, operates nationally along with other organisations of a rather more specialist kind such as the Royal Society for the Protection of Birds. Whilst avoiding the temptation to list all these national bodies, it is probably true to say that hard evidence of their effectiveness in lobbying terms is difficult to find except on the one occasion when 20 of them came together under the chairmanship of Lord Melchett to oppose the passage of the 1981 Wildlife and Countryside Bill. It would certainly seem here that the strength of their campaign did force the government to modify and improve the legislation and was probably instrumental in persuading the Labour Party to its now avowed policy of extending planning controls to agriculture and forestry.

But even one of the most successful of the environmental groups, the Council for the Protection of Rural England, with a record of having fought for a number of important causes including the campaign for National Parks and AONBs, is only an *influencing* group. This, like other such organisations, depends for its success on convincing others of the rightness of its point of view. It differs from the NFU and CLA, which are in fact more than pressure groups because they represent clearly identifiable *sectors* of society. As Andrew Coleman has put it, 'they tend more often than not to be able to engage in genuine bargaining than do purely promotional or cause groups which do not speak for any specific interest other than society at large'. In this lies the strength of the NFU and CLA.

Under these circumstances it is perhaps indeed less than surprising that the legal framework of the countryside leaves the interests of agriculturalists and landowners predominant, and the two government guardians of the countryside, the NCC and CC, with so little real power, a fact reflected in their annual budgets. This, of course, is not to argue that these two organisations have not done what they should within the framework in which they are forced to work, but as the late director of the CC, Reg Hookway, concluded, 'everything we have achieved in protecting the environment has been by dint of fighting the combined opposition of vested interests'. But there is evidence even now, according to some observers, that their effectiveness could be further curtailed, certainly as far as the NCC is concerned. The chairman appointed in 1979 by the present government and the current incumbent who replaced him in 1983 have respectively represented landowning and business interests, leaving Christopher Hall, a former director of CPRE, in no doubt that these appointments 'owed much to the direct lobbying of the CLA and NFU'. The more recent change in the make-up of the governing body of the NCC has also alarmed conservationists since it formerly consisted largely of naturalists and ecologists. It is now allegedly dominated by landowning interests. As one not entirely disinterested commentator recently put it, 'We would not suggest that the Ministry of Agriculture and Department of Energy should be run by conservationists; by the same token we do not believe that farmers and foresters should be asked to run the NCC or CC.'

Having thus emphasised the importance of the political dimension, what may legitimately be asked is, what are the most likely legislative changes or policy adjustments for the countryside that are likely to occur in the future? Such a question inevitably involves looking again at the content of the earlier part of this chapter and Chapter 6. But even here it is possible only to engage in enlightened conjecture. Enlightened because there is evidence in the Wildlife and Countryside Act, for example, that the government which passed it through to the statute book is developing an ethos of reaching agreement in influencing the countryside environment rather than invoking control. Equally, it is known that the Labour Party has a commitment to extend planning controls to encompass agriculture and forestry. But even though there is evidence of a strong association between the Conservative Party and farming and landowning interests and the strength of the NFU and CLA as effective lobbies cannot be underestimated compared with conservation groups, the winds of policy change may well be beginning to blow inside the Cabinet. Undoubtedly, the costs of the present agricultural policy (some £400 millions in 1983) is proving so financially burdensome and consumptive of resources needed elsewhere that a Conservative Minister of Agriculture has already agreed to a modest withdrawal of support from the dairy industry. It will be evident enough that any fall in commodity production subsidies or other forms of agricultural assistance are bound to take the pressure off further plans to expand or intensify production. Also, the unprecedented step has just been taken (June 1984) by the Secretary of State for the Environment to extend planning powers to Needham Marsh of the albeit much larger Halvergate Marshes in Norfolk, a good deal of which is under threat from agricultural development. Yet against this countervailing forces are in evidence, of which changes in the personnel of the governing body of the NCC are just one. In addition, quite recently the government tried to oppose the establishment of the European Environment Fund by the EEC, but when it *was* set up it then tried to ensure its minimal funding. Policy directions are therefore difficult to read and predictions even more problematic. If any concluding remark may be made it is that the bases for concern about the countryside seem to be broadening. Even if, as the record would suggest, membership of most conservation groups may well be the prerogative of the middle classes, there is in evidence a rising tide of much more widespread awareness about what is happening to the countryside, other than that disseminated by the NFU. Radio and television have whole series of programmes related to ecology and conservation as well as living in the countryside. As was pointed out in Chapter 5, an average of nine millions watch 'Wildlife on One' each week, whilst audience research has indicated that among the programmes shown on both BBC channels, those concerning wildlife elicit the highest levels of satisfaction. Apart from regular series, special programmes on the impact of agribusiness on the rural environment have appeared with increasing regularity in the last two years. 'Harvest Gold' from ITV provoked such a furore because of its even-handed approach to agriculture and conservation that correspondence about it echoed through the pages of the farming press in the summer of 1983. The newspapers also provide ample coverage of rural matters and the *Observer* now has a regular 'Save our Countryside' series. Books from John Bowers and Paul Cheshire, from Marion Shoard, from Richard Mabey and Richard Body have all been influential, as was noted earlier, with their arguments explored in other journals and in broadcasting.

In effect, this book and its supplement *The Countryside Handbook* and the associated television programmes, broadcast on BBC 2, are further contributions to the debate but they are not of the polemic kind. The purpose of the authors of all these materials has been to explore the present nature of change in the countryside in all its manifestations and to relate these to the past and to possibilities for the future. It has been predicated on the desire to provide information coolly and objectively, ultimately leading the reader to make up his/her mind better about what is wanted for the countryside of England and Wales, now and in the future.

Figure 7.9: 'It was most enjoyable, but I think I've had enough of the rural environment for one day.'

Source: *The Dalesman.*

Further Reading

Expanding Agricultural Productivity

The only one-volume history of English agriculture is still Lord Ernle's book *English Farming: Past and Present* (Cass, London, 1961, 6th edn). It is very dated now, however. J.D. Chambers and G.E. Mingay's *The Agricultural Revolution 1750—1880* (Batsford, London, 1966) is also a little dated but remains the best book on the period.

Surprisingly little has been written on the great depression of English farming. P.J. Perry's book *British Farming in the Great Depression 1870—1914: an Historical Geography* (David and Charles, Newton Abbot, 1974) is a sound introduction. The inter-war period is perhaps too recent to attract much attention from historians but the eighth volume of *The Agrarian History of England and Wales* by E.H. Whetham, published in 1978 by Cambridge University Press, covers the events of the time in scrupulous detail.

Farming and rural life in nineteenth-century Britain are described in a fine series of essays beautifully illustrated in two volumes edited by G.E. Mingay, *The Victorian Countryside* (Routledge & Kegan Paul, London 1981).

There is an abundant literature on issues related to agricultural policy of the post-1945 period. The standard works by agricultural economists such as B.E. Hill and K. Ingersent, *An Economic Analysis of Agriculture*, 2nd edn (Heinemann, London, 1982) tend to be geared towards the student of agriculture. However, the most readable account of the development of agricultural policy is Tristram Beresford's *We Plough the Fields* (Penguin Books, Harmondsworth, 1975).

The background to European agricultural policy is explored simply by J. Marsh and P. Swanney in *Agriculture and the European Community* (George Allen & Unwin, London, 1980). S. Harris, A. Swindon and G. Wilkinson, *The Food and Farm Policies of the European Community* (Wiley, Chichester, 1983), gives a more detailed analysis.

There is much statistical information on agricultural change and the evidence up to 1966 is summarised by MAFF in *A Century of Agricultural Statistics* (HMSO, London, 1968). Agricultural statistics are published annually and post-1966 changes can be readily referred to in MAFF *et al., Agricultural Statistics* (HMSO, London, annually).

The theme of efficiency is explored by Colin Spedding in *An Introduction to Agricultural Systems* (Applied Science Publishers, Barking, Essex, 1979) from an agricultural scientist's perspective and by Dennis Britton and Berkley Hill in *Size and Efficiency in Farming* (Saxon House, Gower Publishing Co., Aldershot, 1975). The contribution of the Centre of Agricultural Strategy, *The Efficiency of British Agriculture* (Centre for Agricultural Strategy, Reading University, 1980) is demanding but worthy of scrutiny.

As with agricultral policy the student of agriculture has a wealth of information on the structure of the industry. Again, Hill and Ingersent's book covers this aspect well. But the most readable account of the problems posed both by the industry and to its participants is Howard Newby's *Green and Pleasant*

Land? (Penguin Books, Harmondsworth, 1979). Although subtitled 'Social Change in Rural England', Newby encompasses landownership, taxation, farming technical change, agricultural policy and environmentalism. The conflicts he identifies are very much those of the 1980s.

Two pieces of polemic writing have done much to focus attention on the harmful effects of current farming and the illogicalities of current policy. Marion Shoard in *The Theft of the Countryside* (Temple Smith, London, 1980) attacks farming in extravagant language for its practices and the Government system of agricultural support which, using public funds, encourages changes which are harmful to the environment. Richard Body's *Agriculture: The Triumph and the Shame* (Temple Smith, London, 1982) treats the failure to conserve the countryside as only one of the costs to the nation of maintaining present agricultural policies. The diversion of capital, labour, and other natural resources are alleged and the basic assumptions of what is in the 'national interest' are attacked.

Both Shoard and Body exaggerate their cases and use dubious statistics, but their arguments cannot be ignored. They are largely taken up in a more careful but still readable approach by J.K. Bowers and P. Cheshire in *Agriculture, the Countryside and Land Use* (Methuen, London, 1983).

Containing Settlements

A useful guide to the primary and secondary published works and to documentary evidence preserved in official and private archives pertaining to the campaign for the effective separation of town and country can be found in *The Evolution of British Town Planning* by G.E. Cherry (Leonard Hill, London, 1974) and in *Rural Conservation in Inter-War Britain* by J. Shaeil (Oxford University Press, Oxford, 1981). In terms of the changing attitudes towards town and country R. Williams uses the accounts of successive generations of writers to provide a perceptive and telling picture in *The Country and the City* (Chatto and Windus, London, 1975). This volume is also useful for an explanation of man's long-standing delight in nature and longing for past Utopias — a theme considered in the first part of Chapter 4.

For a broad view of economic and social changes in the nineteenth and twentieth centuries in so far as they account for the peripheral expansion of our major cities, F.M.L. Thompson's *The Rise of Suburbia* (University of Leicester, Leicester, 1982) is valuable, especially the introduction. However, the book also contains more detailed accounts of the suburban growth of London and Leeds. The outward spread of London is also described in a very comprehensive and readable book — A. Jackson's *Semi-Detached London: Suburban Development, Life and Transport 1900—1931* (George Allen & Unwin, 1973). A lively and refreshing account of suburban development around the metropolis but one which also looks at other towns and cities is *Dunroamin: the Suburban Semi and its Enemies* by P. Oliver, I. Davies and I. Bentley (Barrie and Jackson, London, 1981). In the more general area of housing, as seen in an historical perspective, J. Burnett's *A Social History of Housing 1915-1970* (David and Charles, Newton Abbot, 1978) offers a comprehensive review of such developments. For a review of the land use planning system and its operation in a more recent context J.B. Cullingworth's *Town and Country Planning in Britain* (George Allen & Unwin, London, 1982) is the standard work though that by Cherry (1974) is also of value here.

The debate about the losses from agricultural to urban development is most succinctly covered in *Land Use and Living Space* by R.H. Best (Methuen, London, 1981) though a contrasting view to his basic thesis is offered by R. Norton-Taylor in *Whose Land is it Anyway?* (Turnstone Press, Wellingborough, 1982). *Recreation and Resources: Leisure Patterns and Leisure Places*, by J.A. Patmore (Hutchinson, London, 1983) comprehensively reviews recreational planning and management.

The problems of agriculture and other open land-uses in the urban fringe are fully detailed in *The City's Countryside* by C.B. Bryant, L.W. Russwurm and A.E. McLellan (Longman, London, 1982) though the particular difficulties of these activities in the Green Belt are reviewed by R.J.C. Munton, *London's Green Belt: Containment in Practice* (George Allen & Unwin, London 1983). Finally, a concerned discussion about the post-1976 loosening of planning controls in the countryside appears in *Planning: Friend or Foe?*, from the Council for the Protection of Rural England (1981) London.

Conserving the Wild

In terms of the concepts of conservation, morality in relation to wildlife and the environment has been throughly explored, for example, by J. Black, *The Dominion of Man* (Edinburgh University Press, Edin., 1970), J. Passmore *Man's Responsibility for Nature* (Duckworth, London, 1974) and H. Montefiore (ed.), *Man and Nature* (Collins, London, 1975). Keith Thomas in his book *Man and the Natural World* (Allen Lane, London, 1983) has put forward an almost opposite view to the majority, namely that the growth of environmental sensibilities with civilisation shows that morals are not the rationalisation of the world as it is, but the attempt to reconcile the physical demands of civilisation with the new feelings it engenders.

The way in which the rapid changes of the parliamentary enclosures triggered the early conservation movement is described, *inter alia*, also in Keith Thomas, *Man and the Natural World*, op. cit., and B. Green *Countryside Conservation* (George Allen & Unwin, London, 1981).

The underlying motives of some key conservation figures can be found in their writings, see, for example, A. Leopold, *A Sand County Almanac*, (Oxford University Press, Oxford, 1949; rept. 1975); A.G. Tansley, *Our Heritage of Wild Nature* (Cambridge University Press, Cambridge, 1948); and D.A. Ratcliffe *Thoughts Towards A Philosophy of Nature Conservation, Biological Conservation* (1976), vol. 9, pp. 45—53. Few have managed to convey these feelings so effectively as Wordsworth. They form a fundamental theme running through nearly all his work. See also R. Jefferies *The Story of my Heart* (Longman Green, London, 1883) and Ralph Waldo Emerson's famous essay *Nature* (1836).

The White Paper, *Report of the Committee of Land Utilisation in Rural Areas* (Cmd 6378, Ministry of Works and Planning, HMSO London, 1912) prepared under the chairmanship of Lord Justice Scott, strongly influenced both ideas and practice in post-war planning and conservation. One of the members of the committee which produced it — Professor S.R. Dennison — disagreed so strongly with most of its major conclusions that he wrote a minority report putting his own views. It has proved to have been a much more perceptive and realistic appraisal of what has taken place.

The crucial role played by voluntary bodies in the evolution of conservation policy and action is well discussed by John Sheail in *Nature in Trust* (Blackie, Glasgow, 1976) and *Rural Conservation in Inter-war Britain* (Clarendon Press, Oxford, 1981). The idealism of the early advocates of National Parks and Nature Reserves comes through strongly in the visionary Hobhouse and Huxley Reports which provided the basis for post-war conservation legislation, *Report of the National Parks Committee (England and Wales)*, Cmd 7127, and *Report on the Conservation of Nature in England and Wales*, Cmd 7122 (both HMSO, London, 1947).

For the post-war period, Nan Fairbrother's *New Lives, New Landscapes* (Penguin Books, Harmondsworth, 1972) provides a thoughtful but lively polemical analysis of human impacts on the landscape. Bryn Green's *Countryside Conservation* mentioned above analyses and criticises British conservation concepts, policies and practices. Conflicts between different rural resource users are discussed and some challenging solutions are proposed — based around the idea that conservation and recreation have essentially *complementary* rather than conflicting land management objectives.

The science, the practice and the organisation of nature conservation are reviewed by various specialists in a book edited by Andrew Warren and F.B. Goldsmith entitled *Conservation in Perspective* (Wiley, Chichester, 1983). The achievements and difficulties of one particular type of conserved landscape are thoughtfully analysed in Ann and Malcolm MacEwen's *National Parks: Conservation or Cosmetics?* (George Allen & Unwin, London, 1982).

The annual reports and specialised publications of the Countryside Commission and the Nature Conservancy Council detail the progress of official conservation efforts, whereas the quarterly journal *Ecos* provides a critical review of current developments and coverage of topical issues in the field of conservation. (The survey of members of the British Association of Nature Conservation, referred to in 'The Early 1980s' section, is reported in *Ecos, 4 (2)* (1983).

A number of books have been published which describe the impact of the post-war agricultural revolution on the countryside. Any of the last four books presented in the Further Reading for 'Expanding Agricultural Productivity' are illuminating in this respect.

The politics of conservation are presented in *Cultivating Conflict* (Temple Smith, London, 1984) by Philip Lowe, Graham Cox, Malcolm MacEwen, Tim O'Riordan and Michael Winter, which analyses local and national conflicts between agriculture, forestry, land drainage and conservation, and reviews the various policy solutions which have been proposed. The activities, organisation and political relations of the conservation lobby are described by Philip Lowe and Jane Goyder in *Environmental Groups in Politics* (George Allen & Unwin, London, 1983). Richard Mabey's *The Common Ground* (Hutchinson, London, 1980) presents a stimulating exploration of the place of nature in contemporary society.

Sustaining Rural Communities

Two books which look generally at the village and are not specific to one period in time are *Man Made the Land: Essays in English Historical Geography* edited by A.R.H. Baker and J.B. Harley (David and Charles, Newton Abbot, 1973) and *Villages of Vision* by G. Darley (Architectural Press, London, 1975). The latter deals only with planned villages but is easy to read and well illustrated. The former goes well beyond considerations of the rural community but it does offer a useful, highly pictorial résumé of the function of the village from medieval times to the nineteenth century.

A general review of social conditions in rural areas in so far as they were articulated through discontent is to be found in *Rural Protest in Britain: 1548-1900* by A. Charlesworth (Croom Helm, Beckenham, 1982). This broad topic is well handled through an integrated series of maps and text. A more detailed interpretation of the life of the village labourer in the eighteenth and nineteenth centuries is to be found in *The Village Labourer* by B. and L. Hammond (Longman, London, 1978). If the book may be criticised for its preoccupation with the villages of lowland England with its contributed preface it still provides a fascinating and readable account of English village life during the period of major enclosures. An alternative view of the impact of enclosures on the rural community is *The English Village Community and The Enclosure Movements* by W.E. Tate (Gollancz, London, 1967). This is among the best of the very many books on this topic. Since the history of the Agricultural Workers' Union is essential to an understanding of village life, R. Groves, *Sharpen the Sickle: The History of the Farm Workers' Union* (Merlin Press, London, 1981) is useful in that it gives a clear description of the living and working conditions of the mass of rural residents and an understanding of the conditions which led to the agricultural strikes of the nineteenth century.

But an anatomy of protest at this period, setting it thoroughly in its socio-economic context is *Captain Swing*, by E.J. Hobsbawm and G. Rude (Lawrence and Wishart, London, 1969).

Three books usefully relate to the concept of the open and closed village: *Joseph Ashby of Tysoe 1859-1919: A Study of English Village Life* by M.K. Ashby (Cambridge University Press, Cambridge, 1961) looks at one of its leading 'peasant' figures; *Ashwell 1830-1914: The Decline of a Village Community* by B.J. Davey (Leicester University Press, Leicester, 1980) also concerns an open village, this time in north Hertfordshire. However, for a comprehensive discussion of both types which also shows how the estate system in the closed village and the peasant system in the open village influenced urban development, D.R. Mills *Lord and Peasant in Nineteenth Century Britain* (Croom Helm London, 1980) is definitive. The radical changes that affected the village community in the twentieth century, which were more far-reaching than anything experienced in the previous 100 years, are detailed for one settlement, Ringmer, by Peter Ambrose in *The Quiet Revolution: Social Change in a Sussex Village, 1871-1971* (Chatto and Windus, London, 1974). This uses both census data and oral historical material in the unfolding of its story. A more generalised but highly readable account of rural change from a social point of view after the Second World War again appears in Howard Newby's *Green and Pleasant Land?* (see 'Expanding Agricultural Productivity'). Whilst he underlines the many problems of rural communities over the last two decades in particular, a number of texts consider specific aspects of these and attempts at their solution. Of importance among these is *An Introduction to Rural Settlement Planning* by Paul Cloke (Methuen, London, 1983). As its title implies, this sets out the context for planning in rural areas and details the use of settlement planning policies and their achievements. On the rural housing front, *Rural Housing, Competition and Choice*, by Michael Dunn, Marilyn Rawson and Alan Rogers (George Allen & Unwin, London 1981) is a substantial work of research analysing different classes of housing need and outlining policy recommendations to cater for the diverse groups within the housing market. One highly specific problem in those parts of England and Wales which are important for their natural beauty has been the growth of second homes. Mark Shucksmith offers a formal analysis of the economics and planning relating to such homes and their local impact in *No Homes for Locals?* (Gower Publishing, Aldershot, 1981). But of rather broader significance is the review by Simon Neate entitled *Rural Deprivation: an Annotated Bibliography* (Geo Books, Norwich, 1980). Although this sounds hardly a promising volume except as a source of further reference, an excellent summary of the problems posed in rural areas is contained in the introduction. An alternative here, also from Geo Books, is a volume edited by Martin Shaw, entitled *Rural Deprivation and Planning* (1979) which takes a closer look at some of the processes which may put people at a disadvantage in rural areas.

Very recently a number of initiatives for rural problem-solving have emerged from the rural grassroots. Rural Voice offered its own *Rural Strategy* in 1981 and followed it with its *State of the Countryside*, 1982 publication from the National Council for Voluntary Organisations. This same body has also published *Rural Housing Initiatives* by David Clark (1981); *Alternative Rural Services: A Community Initiatives Manual* by Stephen Woollett (1982); and *Country Work: A Guide to Rural Employment Initiatives* (1982), being an account of the way in which a wide range of jobs in the countryside may be created.

Notes on Contributors

John Blunden is Reader in Geography at the Open University. A graduate in social studies from the University of Exeter, his doctoral thesis investigated spatial and temporal variations in the impact of agricultural support policies on farm enterprises. After working as a BBC producer, he returned to academic life through a fellowship at the University of Sussex. Since then his research interests in resource management have been reflected in a wide range of books and papers.

Sarah Buchanan studied geography at University College in the University of London before carrying out research into environmental pressure groups and their impact on rural planning, first at her old college and then in the Department of Town Planning, UWIST, Cardiff. She has made particularly detailed studies of the role of the National Trust in this context and the ways in which pressure groups have influenced the Suffolk County Structure Plan. She has been involved in the work of rural community councils and is presently employed by the Volunteers Centre as Development Officer for Countryside Volunteers. Her duties involve her in co-ordinating and advising volunteer groups working on environmental projects.

Nigel Curry is Senior Lecturer in Countryside Planning at Gloucestershire College of Arts and Technology. He holds degrees in economics and in agricultural economics and completed his PhD on recreation economics in the Land Economy Department at the University of Cambridge. He has published several articles on economic issues relating to the countryside.

Michael Dower has the countryside and country planning in his bones — his grandfather, father and mother were all involved in the same game. Based at the Dartington Institute in South Devon, scene of a sixty-year-old venture in rural revival where he is Director, he is concerned with rural research and initiative. He was founder-chairman of *Rural Voice.*

Martin Elson is Reader in Town Planning at Oxford Polytechnic. His research has focused on the land use problems of the urban-rural fringe and the changing attitudes and practices of a wide range of present and potential users of open land near towns. He is currently studying the implementation of land use policies in development plans for the Department of the Environment and is completing for publication a national study on green belts.

Bryn Green is Senior Lecturer in Ecology and Conservation at Wye College in the University of London. He has a doctorate but before joining the academic world he was the Nature Conservancy Council Regional Officer for South East England. A writer on rural conservation, he also founded the Kent Farming and Wildlife Advisory Group and is currently its Vice-Chairman. He is a member of the Nature Conservancy Council Advisory Committee for England and has recently been appointed a Countryside Commissioner.

David Grigg followed his studies in geography at the University of Cambridge with post-graduate research on the agricultural history of Lincolnshire, the county in which he was born and brought up. For the last 25 years he has lectured in geography at the University of Sheffield. His research interests remain in the field of agricultural history though his publications also reflect a wider concern, especially for agricultural geography.

Berkeley Hill is Lecturer in Agricultural Economics at Wye College in the University of London. He read agriculture at the University of Nottingham and completed a PhD thesis at Reading University on capital in agriculture. His more recent research reflects an interest in farm size and efficiency, tenure and farm incomes.

Philip Lowe has degrees in natural science, science policy and history. He is Lecturer in Countryside Planning at University College in the University of London and has written extensively in the fields of countryside planning, rural sociology, environmental politics and the history of ecology.

Dennis Mills has made the study of rural village life the subject of personal and research interest since he graduated from Nottingham University. After he completed his MA thesis there with a study of villages in Kesterven, Lincolnshire, he moved on to complete his PhD at Leicester University with research on villages in the county. Before joining the Open University where he is a staff tutor, he held a number of teaching posts including a university lectureship at Nottingham. He has published a number of works on English rural communities.

John Sheail is a Principal Scientific Officer in the NERC Institute of Terrestrial Ecology, Monks Wood Experimental Station, Cambridgeshire. Employed there as an historical geographer, he has now established himself as an authority on the history of conservation and has a number of publications to his name. He is a graduate of University College in the University of London where he also completed his doctoral thesis on the value of Tudor tax returns as a means of assessing the contemporary distribution of wealth and population.

Bill Slee studied geography at the University of Cambridge before undertaking research at Aberdeen University where he received his doctorate in agricultural economics. He is presently a lecturer at Seale Hayne College, Newton Abbot where his research interests are concerned with the interaction between agricultural and other rural policies. He has produced a number of publications in this field.

Alan Woods is a comparatively recent graduate from Wye College in the University of London, where he obtained a degree in rural environmental studies. Subsequently he worked for the Countryside Commission on a review of National Park plans before moving quickly on to a research post at the University of Birmingham. In his current work he is concerned with recent changes in land use management in the uplands of mid Wales.

Index

National Plan 33, 83-4
National Trust 79, 81, 102, 125, 137, 145,
   211; formation of 122, 124
nationalisation: of land 204-5, 207, 212;
   of landowners' rights 84
nature, reverence for 118-24
Nature Conservancy Council 54, 150,
   255-6; and agriculture 58-9, 117,
   137-8, 153, 158, 251; 'Biological
   Service' 128; grants 242-3, 251; and
   restoration of land 113; and wetlands
   151; and wildlife 143-5; see also
   National Nature Reserves, Sites of
   Special Scientific Interest
Nature Reserves see National Nature
   Reserves
Nature Reserves Investigation Committee
   (NRIC) 126
NCC see Nature Conservancy Council
Needham Marsh 256
needs, rural, recognising 194-5
Nettlefold, J.S. 76
New Agricultural Landscape projects 148
New Poor Law (1834) 173-4
new towns 88-90, 96, 106
new villages 100, 182-5
Newby, H. 182, 187-8, 254-5
Newcastle upon Tyne 95, 103
NFU see National Farmers Union
1980s, early: agricultural productivity
   45-59; communities, rural 185-92;
   conservation 139-47; containing
   settlements 96-104
NNRs see National Nature Reserves
Norfolk 59, 186, 191
North Kelsey, village 17
NPC see National Parks Commission
nucleated villages 164-6

open parish 176-8
open-field system 164-5
Operation Groundwork 111, 113
opportunity and crisis in rural
   communities 185-7
'organic' farming 217-19
Orwell, G. 13
Orwin, C.S. 23, 31-2
output, agricultural 26, 28-9
Oxford 95, 105-6

Page, A. 223
parishes 165-6, 174-9
parks 121-2; see also National Parks
part-time farming 49, 64
payments see compensation; support
permission, planning 84, 243
pigs and poultry 28, 38, 47, 53
Pinch, J.A. 238
planning: agriculture 157, 209-10, 215,
   229; conservation 157, 209-10;
   forestry 211, 246-8; industries 243;
   land use 107-10, 221-2; legislation
   109, 222, 239, 244, 248; see also
   Town and Country; permission 84,
   243; urban 79-80, 221-3; see also
   policy, settlements
Planning Act (1980) 109
Pliny the Elder 116
ploughing 25-6, 30

policy: agricultural 30-7, 44, 55-9, 63-4,
   204-14, see also support; conflicts
   57-9, 239-40; efficiency and
   distribution 234-9; future 204-14;
   instruments 239-40, 245-52; options
   241; and politics 254-6; recreation
   237-8; see also legislation, planning
politics 143-5, 231, 254-6
Poole, A.L. 162
Poor Laws 170
popular support for conservation 145-6,
   255
population changes and countryside
   pressures 96-8
Porchester, Lord 142
post-war: conflict and conservation
   131-5; control of urban expansion
   84-96; housing, rural 17-18
poverty 170-1, 181-2, 200, 236
power see energy
pressure groups 79-80
prices: houses 114, 190, 202, 250;
   intervention 35; land 46, 56, 91
Priestley, J.B. 72-3
project officers, countryside management
   103
public: expenditure see expenditure;
   sector response, urbanisation 98-102;
   support for conservation 145-6, 255
Pye-Smith, C. 117, 204, 211

radical systems of agriculture 214-21
Radnor 236-7, 252
railways see transport
Ramblers' Association 143
rape, oilseed 52, 220
Reading 92; Development Plan 86-7
Reagan, R. 117
reaper binder, horse-drawn 29
recession 198-200
recreation 18-19; and conservation 134,
   147, 240; and Countryside
   Commission 102, 110-11; and
   countryside management 102-4;
   grants 241; and income 237-8; policy
   237-8; and urban fringe 91-4, 102,
   110-14; in villages 172-3; see also
   tourism
reforms, conservation and agriculture
   153-9
refrigeration, invention of 27
religion in villages 172-4
Repton, H. 116, 121
research, food 206-7
restoration: of inner cities 94, 98; of land
   93, 111-13
Restriction of Ribbon Development Act
   (1935) 80
retirement to country 17, 163, 182, 187,
   201, 231; see also elderly
ribbon development 80-2
Rickmansworth 93
ridge and furrow farming 15
Ringmer, village 180
roads 80-2, 107, 186; see also transport
Rockham, O. 117
Rose, C. 117, 204, 211
Roskill Commission 152, 229, 235
rotation 25-6

Rother Valley Regional Plan 111
Rowse, A.L. 162
Royal Society for Nature Conservation
   255
Royal Society for Protection of Birds 136,
   145, 150, 153, 255
Rude, G. 171
Rufford Park 110
Rural Community Councils 185, 243, 253
Rural Development Area 185, 197-8
Rural Development Boards 33, 193, 252
Rural Voice 194, 231

St Bees, village 16
Sandford, Lord 159
Sandford Committee 137
Sandys, D. 70, 88
sanitation 74
scientific reasons for conservation 122,
   127; see also Sites of Special Scientific
   Interest
SCNP see Standing Committee on
   National Parks
Scott, Sir L. 31
Scott Report 31, 83, 117, 140
Seaith, Chief 119
second homes, rural 18, 187-8, 202
Secrett, C. 214
self-employed 199
self-sufficiency: co-operative 216-18;
   decline 28; growth of 39, 62, 230; in
   villages 167-8
separation of town and country 77-84
services in villages 183-5, 196; declining
   191-2
settlements, containing/urban expansion
   70-115, 221-3, 236; actions to steer
   change 107-13; and agriculture 85,
   91, 99-100, 221-2, 229;
   beneficiaries and losers 113-15;
   contradictory trends 75-6; grassroots
   104-7; in nineteenth century 72-5; in
   1980s, early 96-104; perspectives of
   town and country 72-7; post-war
   control 84-9; separation of town and
   country, campaigns for 77-84; urban
   fringe 91-4, 102, 110-13, see also
   green belts
Severn barrage 147
Seymour, J. 216-17
Shaw, G.B. 116
Sheail, J. 264
sheep 27-8, 36, 38, 53
Sheffield 72, 95, 169
Shoard, M. 22, 62-3, 133, 140, 204, 207,
   210, 256
shopping, superstores 107, 109
Shucksmith, M. 250
Sites of Special Scientific Interest 128,
   131, 134, 150, 215, 243-4; and
   agriculture 52, 58, 66, 143-4, 151,
   153, 158, 210-11; and compensation
   136, 211, 242; damaged 140, 143-4,
   153, 211, 215; and water supply 132
size of farms 24, 39, 46-7
Slee, B. 38-9, 43, 264
Smigelski, K. 214, 216-18
social: inequalities 166-7, 172-4; life,
   changes in 15-17; structures, changing

187-90; welfare and agriculture 57
Society for Promotion of Nature Reserves (SPNR) 124-6
Society for Protection of Birds 122, 124; *see also* Royal Society for Protection of Birds
Soissons, Louis De 78
Somerset 25, 191, 198, 243
South Holland, rural policy structure 184
Southampton 95, 167
Special Investment Strategy 185
Spencer family 166
SSSIs *see* Sites of Special Scientific Interest
Stamp, D. 248
Standing Committee on National Parks (SCNP) 125-6
Stanford Hall, co-operative village 218
state and agriculture *see* support system
Steers, J.A. 81
stock raising *see* livestock
Stoke-on-Trent 95, 103
structure plans 94, 242, 249
Strutt Committee 33
subsidies *see* support system
subsistence and commercial farming, compared 218-19
suburbs 76-7
sugar beet 30, 35, 37, 52
support system, agricultural 23, 26, 30-7, 55-6, 241; conflicts 58-9; England and Wales alone 30-4; England and Wales in EEC 34-7; farmer's opinion of 61; revision of 63-4, 156, 210; *see also* agriculture
surpluses, agricultural 23, 35, 57, 68, 204, 206
Surrey Amenity Council 104-5
sustaining rural communities *see* communities
'Swing' group 171-2, 178

Tansley, Sir A. 117
target price 34-5
taxation: and agriculture 59, 63, 67, 208, 210, 212-13; and conservation 205; land tax, suggested 212-13
technological innovation in agriculture 26-30, 38, 40, 49, 56, 171, 178; economics of 50-1; reduction of 213-14
Third World 57
Thomas, F.G. 163
Thompson, E.P. 162
Thompson, F. 16
Thornborough, village 168
Thurso, Lord 251
timber *see* forestry
Tithe Commutation Act (1836) 174
tourism 191, 198, 240-1; *see also* recreation
Tourist Boards 198, 241
Town and Country Planning Acts: *1932* 70, 77, 81, 125; *1947* 31, 84-5, 90, 113, 128, 179, 183, 239; *1968* 183; *1971* 244, 248
towns *see* settlements
townships 165-6
trades, village 167-8

transport: personal, growth of 75-6, 82, 90, 93-4, 102, 134, 139, 179, 186, 201; problems 16, 193
Trawsfynydd nuclear power station 132

unemployment 97-8, 163, 191, 198-9; *see also* employment, industries
Unwin, R. 75
uplands *see* hill
urban areas *see* settlements
Uthwatt Report 83
utilitarian reasons for conservation 122-3

Vaughan, R. 72
villages *see* communities
Volume Housebuilders Association 100-1

wages *see* income, personal
Wakeley, P. 127
Walker, A. 163, 236
Waller, R. 211-13
Wantage, Lord and Lady 176
wartime: agricultural growth 29-30, 37, 207; and conservation 126-31
waste materials, use of 216
Watendlath 137
water supplies and Water Authorities 17-18, 54, 74, 147, 151; conservation conflict 132-3, 240; grants 241; in villages 181
Weller, J. 183
Wells, H.G. 75
Welsh Language Society 189
Welwyn Garden City 78-9, 82
Wenham Grange, village 27
White Papers on agriculture 36
White's Directory 176
WHO 214
Wibberley, G. 71, 229
Wiggin, J. 118
wildlife 18, 143, 215
Wildlife and Countryside Act (1981) 142-3, 145, 149, 243-4, 248-51; and agriculture 58, 66, 117, 153, 154, 159, 205, 208-10; compensation 117, 149, 205
Williams, R. 72
Williams, W.M. 22
Williams-Ellis, C. 70
Winter, G. 27
Women's Institutes 16
Woods, A. 144, 264
Wordsworth, W. 120, 125
work *see* employment
World Conservation Strategy 123

Young G.M 22
Youth Training Scheme 199, 241

zones, land-use 80